Tourism Planning

Tourism Planning

Basics, Concepts, Cases

Third Edition

Clare A. Gunn

Taylor & Francis
Publishers since 1798

USA	Publishing Office:	Taylor & Francis 1101 Vermont Avenue, N.W., Suite 200 Washington, DC 20005-3521 Tel: (202) 289-2174 Fax: (202) 289-3665
	Distribution Center:	Taylor & Francis 1900 Frost Road, Suite 101 Bristol, PA 19007-1598 Tel: (215) 785-5800 Fax: (215) 785-5515
UK		Taylor & Francis Ltd. 4 John St. London WC1N 2ET Tel: 071 405 2237 Fax: 071 831 2035

TOURISM PLANNING: Basics, Concepts, Cases/Third Edition

1 2 3 4 5 6 7 8 9 0   E B E B   9 8 7 6 5 4 3

This book was set in Times Roman by Harlowe Typography. The editors were Diane Foose and Caroline V. Schweiter; the production supervisor was Peggy M. Rote. Cover design by Michelle Fleitz. Cover photo (beach) by Phil Brodatz. Printing and binding by Edwards Brothers, Inc.

A CIP catalog record for this book is available from the British Library.
⊚ The paper in this publication meets the requirements of the ANSI Standard Z39.48-1984 (Permanence of Paper)

Library of Congress Cataloging-in-Publication Data

Gunn, Clare A.
    Tourism planning: basics, concepts, cases / Clare A. Gunn—3rd ed.
        p.   cm.
    Includes bibliographical references.

1. Tourist trade.   I. Title.

  G155.A1G86   1993
380.1′4591—dc20   93-26160
                                                                          CIP

ISBN 0-8448-1742-2 (cloth)
ISBN 0-8448-1743-0 (paper)

Contents

List of Figures ix
List of Tables xiii
Foreword xv
Preface xix
Introduction xxiii

PART I: THE BASICS 1

CHAPTER 1 The Purpose of Tourism Planning 3
    Definition of Tourism 4
    Tourism Sectors 5
    Developer and Tourist Perspectives 9
    Goals for Development 11
    Planning's New Look 18
    Planning Scales 25
    Conclusions 29
    References 31

CHAPTER 2 Tourism as a System 33
    Market-Supply Match 34
    The Functioning System 41
    External Factors 43
    Conclusions 52
    References 55

CHAPTER 3 Components of Supply 57
    Attractions 57
    Services 62
    Transportation 69
    Information 70
    Promotion 74
    Conclusions 75
    References 77

CHAPTER 4 Growth and Sustainable Development 79
  Growth and Quality 79
  Environmental Issues and Tourism 82
  Sustainable Development 85
  Ecotourism 92
  Conclusions 99
  References 102

**PART II: CONCEPTS AND EXAMPLES
OF TOURISM PLANNING** 107

CHAPTER 5 Regional Planning Concepts 109
  Planning Antecedents 110
  Background 114
  Regional Development Hierarchy 128
  Planning Techniques 135
  Planning Processes 141
  Conclusions on Integrated Regional Planning 150
  References 157

CHAPTER 6 Regional Planning Cases 161
  Michigan's Upper Peninsula 161
  South Central Texas 171
  Oklahoma 177
  Upcountry South Carolina 186
  The Adirondacks 193
  Finger Lakes Region 200
  Japan 209
  Australia 216
  New South Wales 220
  Conclusions 223
  References 223

CHAPTER 7 Destination Planning Concepts 225
  The Imperative of Place 227
  Destination Planning Issues 231
  Destination Planning Guides 235
  Destination Planning Model 251
  Destination Zone Planning Process 252
  Special Destination Needs 261
  The Destination Zone Planners 272

Conclusions on Integrated Destination Planning 278
References 280

CHAPTER 8 Destination Planning Cases 285
Moorea, French Polynesia 285
Kosrae 288
Lower Rio Grande 294
The Mineral Wells Area 298
Gonzales 307
Chun-Cheon Resort Area 312
Allegheny Ridge Heritage Park 316
St. Maries, Idaho 322
Manchester, Salford, and Trafford 328
Conclusions 334
References 334

CHAPTER 9 Site Planning Concepts 337
Planning-Design Integration 337
Design Criteria 347
Sustainability 352
Processes 363
Conclusions on Integrated Planning/Design: Site Scale 371
References 373

CHAPTER 10 Site Planning Cases 377
San Antonio River Walk 378
Maho Bay Camps 387
Blue Ridge Parkway 389
Franconia Notch 393
Whiteman Park 397
Underground Atlanta 401
Great Lakes Crossroads Museum and Welcome Center 402
Orange Valley Resort 407
The Ironbridge Gorge Museum 412
Victoria & Alfred Waterfront 416
Wilpena Station Resort 419
Ausable Forks, Adirondack Park 422
Conclusions 424
References 425

CHAPTER 11 Conclusions and Principles 427
Basic Principles 427

Environment and Resources 431
Policies and Goals 434
Processes 436
Future Challenges 440

Index 447
About the Author 459

List of Figures

1-1   Decisionmaking and Tourist Use Compared, 10
1-2   Decisionmaking/Implementation Model, 22
2-1   Demand-Supply Balance, 39
2-2   Plant-Market Match Model, 40
2-3   Functioning Components of Supply Side, 41
2-4   External Influences on Tourism System, 44
4-1   Ecotourism Conceptual Framework, 94
4-2   National Park Tourism Model, 96
5-1   PASLOP Model, 116
5-2   Geographic Position, 122
5-3   Geographic Content, 123
5-4   Landscape Expression, 124
5-5   Regional Planning Concept, 1965, 125
5-6   Regional Planning Concept, 1972, 126
5-7   Geographic Pattern of Destinations, 127
5-8   Tourism Development Dependence Hierarchy, 129
5-9   Coastal Tourism Resource Inventory, I, 136
5-10 Coastal Tourism Inventory Process, II, 139
5-11 Process for a Regional Tourism Plan, 142
5-12 Continuous Planning Action, 150
6-1   Framework for Upper Peninsula Tourism Plan, 163
6-2   Market-Regional Relationship: Michigan's Upper Peninsula, 164
6-3   Summary Analysis of Foundation Factors, 165
6-4   Destination Zones, 167
6-5   Concept for Gateway at St. Ignace, 169
6-6   Concept for Gateway at Menominee, 170
6-7   Detail of Gateway Attractions, 171
6-8   Copper Country Attractions Complex, 172
6-9   Scenic Land-Water Concept, 173
6-10 A Texas Tourism Study Region, 174
6-11 Computer Composite—Touring Potential, 177
6-12 Computer Composite—Destination Potential, 178
6-13 Areas Best Suited to Touring Tourism Development, 179
6-14 Areas Best Suited to Long-Stay Development, 180

6-15   Oklahoma Tourism Plan Process, 181
6-16   Composite of Tourism Factors for Oklahoma, 182
6-17   Potential Development Zones, Oklahoma, 183
6-18   South Carolina Tourism Study Region, 187
6-19   Map Overlay Process, 188
6-20   Destination Zones Based on Natural Resources, 189
6-21   Destination Zones Based on Cultural Resources, 190
6-22   Combined Destination Zones, 190
6-23   Adirondack Park Destination Zones, 195
6-24   Map of Finger Lakes Region, 200
6-25   Agencies Involved in Tourism, 202
6-26   New Sites of Discovery, Japan, 215
7-1   Concept of Destination Zone, 226
7-2   Community Tourism Planning Steps, 237
7-3   Rural-Urban Destination Zones, 252
7-4   An Organic/Rational Planning Process, 256
7-5   The Scenic Roads Evaluation Form, 265
7-6   Flow Chart for Scenic Highway Designation, 267
7-7   Historic Inventory Process, 269
7-8   Model of Attraction, 271
8-1   Map of Moorea, 286
8-2   Map of Kosrae, 289
8-3   Lower Rio Grande Heritage Corridor, 295
8-4   Tourism Concept Plan, Mineral Wells, 300
8-5   Tourism Concepts for Palo Pinto County, 301
8-6   Potential Development, Mineral Wells, 302
8-7   Gonzales County Tourism Concept, 309
8-8   Potential Development, Gonzales, 310
8-9   Concept for Tower, Deck, Museum, 311
8-10   Tourism Plan for Chun-Cheon Lake Area, 314
8-11   Allegheny Ridge Plan, 319
8-12   Allegheny Ridge Corporation, 322
8-13   Plan for Manchester-Salford-Trafford Destination, 330
8-14   Irwell Redevelopment Plan, 331
8-15   River Irwell Promenade, 332
9-1   A Design/Management Hierarchy, 344
9-2   Proposed Park Visitor Sequence, 357
9-3   Site Design Planning Steps, 364
9-4   Relationship Diagrams, 369
10-1   San Antonio River Walk, 379
10-2   Subzones of San Antonio River Walk, 380
10-3   Maho Bay Camps Site Plan, 388

10-4   Franconia Notch Scenic Freeway, 394
10-5   Whiteman Park Related to Zone, 400
10-6   Bridging the Straits Site Plan, 404
10-7   Bridging Museum Site Plan, 405
10-8   Bridging the Straits Aerial View, 406
10-9   Orange Valley Project, Antigua, 408
10-10 Orange Valley Resource Analysis, 409
10-11 Plan for Orange Valley Resort, 410
10-12 Ironbridge Gorge Museum, 413
10-13 Plan of Ironbridge Gorge Complex, 414
10-14 Victoria & Alfred Waterfront, Cape Town, 418
10-15 Victoria & Alfred Waterfront, Cape Town, 419
10-16 Wilpena Station Resort Site Plan, 420
10-17 Wilpena Pound, Flinders Ranges National Park, 421
10-18 Hamlet of Ausable Forks, 423
10-19 Plan for Ausable Forks, 423

List of Tables

1-1   Economic Benefits of Travel and Tourism, 14
1-2   Interactive Planning vs. Conventional Planning, 21
2-1   Travel Market Segments, 38
2-2   Tourism Development Related to Natural Resources, 45
2-3   Tourism Development Related to Cultural Resources, 48
3-1   Classification of Attractions by Ownership, 59
3-2   Classification of Attractions by Resource, 59
3-3   Classification of Attractions by Touring/Long Stay, 59
3-4   Traveler Activities in Rural Areas, 61
4-1   Indicators of Tourism Condition, 87
5-1   Spatial Assumptions for GIS Maps, 140
5-2   Weighted Factors, Upcountry S.Carolina, 141
6-1   Weighted Factors for Touring Tourism, 175
6-2   Weighted Factors for Destination Tourism, 175
6-3   Weighted Factors for Oklahoma Plan, 182
6-4   Organizations Responsible for Action, 203
7-1   Tourism Development Opportunities in Alberta, Canada, 239
7-2   Taxonomy for Implementation of Community Tourism Action
      Plan, 260
8-1   Evaluation Matrix for St. Maries, Idaho, 326

Foreword

This completely rewritten third edition of *Tourism Planning* is a welcome addition to the growing library on tourism planning and development that has taken place in the last three decades of this century. The author, Dr. Clare A. Gunn, has been and continues to be one of the major contributors to this library. He has published several books, book chapters, and many journal articles on the subject since 1972. Perusal and analysis of these works will clearly demonstrate the change and growth of the subject matter, scope, and methodologies of tourism planning. His study and advocacy have occurred in a period when tourism itself has been under increasing pressure for change in the way that it functions.

Tourism is challenged by the rapidly changing economic and social environment in which it operates. These changes are presenting tourism with highly sophisticated and highly fragmented markets, in an economic situation that sees many of the old, heavy industrial regions in decline and new high-tech regions in ascendancy, and with an increasing sensitivity to the environment. Tourism developers must not only be aware of these changes and the impact they will have upon all aspects of tourism, but also be prepared to act on them. A completely changed tourism structure will be needed to meet the needs of the twenty-first century.

The often overlooked truth that tourists are seeking a satisfying experience must be at the center of any new tourism. In order to achieve their desired experiences, tourists select from a wide variety of options those that are most relevant to them. The absence of one or more of these elements at a destination, or the failure of one or more of them to deliver as anticipated, frustrates the tourist's search for satisfaction and, as a result, diminishes the quality and the reputation of the entire destination.

Thus the end product of tourism is a satisfied customer. All of the elements of the tourism destination are but the means to that goal. For too long the success of tourism has been measured in economic terms, and these measures have been related to the means rather than the end. It is undoubtedly true that tourism has critical economic benefits, but the success of tourism should not be measured by monetary value alone. Factors such as the image of the destination—has it improved or deteriorated; the satisfaction level of the visitor—was it high or low; the quality of the environment—is it improving, holding its own, or being damaged—must be included in any measure of success.

These factors must all be considered in the tourism decisionmaking process. Sound planning is the way all of the multi-faceted elements can be incorporated. Growth in the number of tourists and the amount of their expenditures cannot be the sole objective of tourism. A far better criterion would be the number of tourists the area can support, at a high level of satisfaction, at a profitable level of operation, and with improvement in the quality of the environment, over a set time period. Sound planning at all levels, from national to site, is the only way to ensure that all of the necessary elements are considered and given their proper importance at the time decisions are made.

Threaded through the entire book is the timely theme of balancing tourism with protection of the resources on which it depends. Perhaps now, as we approach the twenty-first century, with world attention focused on the ways people shepherd the fragile land upon which they live, there may be a chance that tourism's place in the resource spectrum will become clear. Both tourists and developers have an equal stake in the outcome. Both halves of this tourism equation, as well as those local residents impacted by tourism, must be in agreement with the objectives before tourism and sustainable development become possible. Each type of tourism—and there are many because of the diversity of reosurces and markets—requires examination, special policies, and certainly special planning if sustainable development is to be achieved. Merely throwing more promotion money at the issue, encouraging more tourists and more spending, is no longer an acceptable solution.

As Gunn points out, planning is too important to be left to planners. It must encompass a wide constituency, with the role of the planner being to bring all of the divergent parties together and to help them see how their particular interests are involved in the development of the tourism destination. When a plan is completed, the community should say "This is our plan," not "This is their plan." "Our plan" will be implemented; whereas "their plan" will all too likely join others of the same ilk collecting dust on a shelf. A great combination of training and skills is required to accomplish this new planning. *Tourism Planning* demonstrates how it can be done.

A highlight of this book is the number and diversity of case studies. Far too much of the good thinking that has been done in tourism is hidden away in the reports of consultants, government agencies, and academics, which rarely have a wide circulation. These examples demonstrate not only how essential and effective sound planning can be but also the diversity, complexity and time required for implementation. The final chapter should be thoroughly reviewed and understood by everyone involved in tourism. The principles set out will help ensure that tourism will gain a new luster and be able to provide satisfaction to the ever more demanding market of the next century.

Gordon D. Taylor

Preface

Readers deserve some comment on the origin and metamorphosis of this book. In a way, this book began in 1921 when, at the age of five, I was first exposed to travel. I was taken by my parents on my first trip in a brand new Model T Ford from Grandville, Michigan to the mining towns of the state's Upper Peninsula. However, most memorable was a six-week 7,000-mile camping trip across the United States in 1929 in a Model A Ford. Even today, over six decades later, impressions of landscapes, wildlife, cities, mountains, plains, missions, Indians, muddy roads, flat tires, and sociable campfires remain vivid. Perhaps this early exposure to the land of travel predestined a career in the field of planning for better tourism development.

But, most of the concepts and principles presented here had their origins within a two-decade period, beginning in 1945. These resulted from accepting the challenge of trying to balance tourism economics and social values with the environment.

First, as a technical consultant on buildings and grounds with the Tourist & Resort Extension Service in Michigan, I had the opportunity to work closely with several thousand businesses. A major observation was that they were influenced as much by external as internal factors. But the focus of all developers, public and private, was primarily internal. This was the way management was being taught and practiced in the field. Second, academic training and education in conservation and landscape architecture stimulated my concern over environmental abuse as well as my awareness of opportunities for creative resource use for tourism. Third, association with tourism leaders, organizations and chambers of commerce, with their preoccupation with promotion, revealed a void—the environmental, social, and planning aspects of tourism. Fourth, a pioneering experience with the creation of a regional tourism plan for Michigan's Upper Peninsula in the 1960s, alongside a doctoral dissertation, allowed me to identify some planning principles. These fostered the identification of the functioning tourism system and demonstrated that guidelines for future development could be created by applying planning and design processes and principles. Finally, it became a challenge to concentrate on the study of these issues, motivated partially by idealism but mostly by a desire to provide needed planning help for developers, managers, policy-makers, and especially students and educators.

And so, in 1970, after writing and illustrating some basic concepts of planning tourism development I was confronted by a publisher's dictum of the day: Books must either damn development or damn resource protection. My observations, concepts, and conclusions, intended for the improvement of tourism, appeared to run against the tide of contemporary publishing in spite of encouragement from the field. There appeared to be no room for addressing the combined issue of *planning tourism development as resources are protected.* Finally, in 1972, the Bureau of Business Research of The University of Texas, then involved in tourism research, took the chance of publishing my first edition of *Vacationscape: Designing Tourism Regions.* The positive response to this book, here and abroad, endorsed the need for more and better information in the field of avoiding pitfalls and improving tourism by planning and design.

As literature on tourism began to appear, as my professional experience broadened, and as teaching and research showed the need, the book *Tourism Planning* was the result, published by Crane Russak in 1979. After retirement from Texas A&M University at the end of 1984, I was free to explore in greater depth the realm of planning for tourism development. By this time, tourism journals had appeared, more scholars were writing about tourism, and I had many opportunities to visit, observe, make presentations, and perform consulting work in many locations in North America and around the world. From this experience, it became clear that both books needed updating and revising. The 1988 second editions of both were the result (*Vacationscape* by VanNostrand Reinhold, *Tourism Planning* by Taylor & Francis).

When the question arose of a third printing or new edition of *Tourism Planning,* reflection on changes in the field suggested the need for a rewrite. Feedback from professional colleagues, immersion in recent tourism literature, and some new field experiences revealed the need for major changes in content and organization of the book. Especially stimulating was the discovery of tourism planning examples and progress in tourism planning education that were not evident in past decades. For example, a major milestone in tourism planning education was reached in October, 1992, when the first conference on university curriculum development for tourism planning was held.

Readers familiar with past editions of this book will notice some major changes. Grouping the chapters into two parts sharpens the focus on tourism planning basics and principles, and case examples of planning. Organizing the principles and examples according to three scales—regional, destination, site—provides better guidance for planners and developers. Truncating the five chapters of description of the tourism system components from the Second Edition into one chapter allows greater space for discussion of examples and principles. Instead of placing examples in an appendix, they are given greater prominence in the body of the text. Finally, documentation of supporting works has been brought up to date.

It is my hope that this book is better organized, more direct, more applicable and even more challenging than earlier works. Even with these changes, many of the former concepts and principles that have proven useful have been retained in the manuscript.

Finally, a personal explanation may be in order. If readers observe reference to many of my own works, it is because I am most familiar with them. Intimate participation has given me the privilege of observing processes, issues, opportunities, and difficulties of planning for tourism development. Even so, the scholarly works, concepts, and opinions, and actual tourism development by many others are liberally reflected in this volume.

If these results of study, concepts and principles can stimulate planners, designers, developers, educators, students, and local citizens to create a better tourism world I shall feel that the effort is well rewarded.

Acknowledgments

Because so many people have assisted me with ideas, information, and examples of tourism planning, any listing of acknowledgment is done at great risk of omitting important contributors. Certainly, I have been helped greatly by the recent writings of researchers and observers, published in books and journals. I especially want to thank all those who have given me so many opportunities to learn: university administrators, who gave me freedom to study and teach; professional organizations, who invited me to be active and present papers; tourism businesses and agencies, who shared real-world experiences; teachers who taught me to appreciate the world's resources and challenged me to foster their perpetuation; and to my many students, who have taught me more than I have taught them.

Because of their special interest in and assistance for this work, I would like to acknowledge the helpful input from the following: Dr. John Ap, professor of tourism, Department of Hotel and Tourism Management, Hong Kong Polytechnic; Dr. Janice S.H. Auyong, Marine & Coastal Research & Education Services, Oregon; Pieter Bekker, director, sustainable development, Ministry of Tourism, British Columbia; Dr. Uel Blamk, tourism specialist, University of Missouri; E. Leroy Brady, chairman,

Parkways, Historic and Scenic Roads, Arizona Department of Transportation; Randall D. Cooley, director, Southwestern Pennsylvania Heritage Preservation Commission; Dr. David L. Edgell, Sr., director, Office of Policy and Planning, US Travel and Tourism Administration; Prof. Michael Fagence, Department of Geographical Sciences and Planning, University of Queensland; Donald F. Hilderbrandt, principal, LDR International; Dr. Jesus Hinojosa, associate dean for international programs, College of Architecture, Texas A&M University; John J. Reynolds, assistant director, design and construction, National Park Service; Richard A. Rigterink, principal, Johnson, Johnson & Roy, Inc.; Dr. J.R.Brent Ritchie, director, World Tourism Education and Research Centre, University of Calgary; Dr. Mario L. Sanchez, Texas Historic Commission; Stanley Selengut, president, Maho Bay Camps, U.S. Virgin Islands; Dr. E.L. Shafer, professor, School of Hotel, Restaurant & Recreation Management, Pennsylvania State University; Dr. Lawrence R. Simonson, tourism specialist, Grand Rapids, Minnesota; Valene Smith, professor of anthropology, California State University (Chico); Mark Sparrow, director of research, Western Australian Tourism Commission; Dr. Kobus Steyn, director, Cape Technikon, Cape Town, South Africa; Gordon Taylor, Travel & Tourism Research Association, Ottawa, Canada; Eva Thybo, Fyntour, Denmark; Conrad T. Tunney, executive director, Finger Lakes Association, New York; Pamela Wight, Tourism Business Development Division, Alberta Tourism; and Dr. Allan J. Worms, tourism specialist, University of Kentucky.

Finally, I want to express my deep gratitude for the patience and many hours of word processing for the entire manuscript as well as encouragement and constructive critique from a dedicated wife, Mary Alice.

Introduction

Once there was a time when travelers expected little more from host areas than freedom from highway bandits, minimum food and lodging, and their normal everyday hospitality (or hostility) toward strangers. Host areas did not develop tourism. That was several centuries before steamboats, trains, automobiles, and planes, and long before Thomas Cook's first promoted tour in 1855 to the Paris Exhibition (Bridges 1959, 35).

Today, as millions of people are in a travel mode every day, some form of planning for tourism is forced onto host areas the world over. Areas plan either to obtain the economic benefits from tourism or to keep from being inundated by visitors. "No longer can it be assumed that the residents of a tourism destination/region will automatically accept all (or any) forms of tourism development that the industry proposes or attempts to impose" (Ritchie 1992, 16).

After many decades of dominance by a philosophy of promotion, tourism leadership is beginning to take planning more seriously. In the past, public and private tourism organizations spent virtually all of their immense budgets on promotion, mostly advertising and publicity. This was done in the belief that promotion was the only way to develop tourism. The assumption was that the establishment of attractions, transportation, and services would take care of themselves.

New Planning Concern

Although promotion has its place and continues to dominate the role of most tourism organizations, more local communities and tourism leaders are beginning to show concern over what is to be promoted—where it is, how well it meets market needs, how well it fits the community, how it utililizes resources, and how it can be expanded or newly developed. This new concern is reaching beyond basic hospitality businesses once thought to be the core of tourism development. Planning for tourism development now is more than theory and is being seen by many as a practical necessity.

This change in tourism philosophy probably is due more to several converging factors than to persuasive zeal by planners. Economic decline, especially in many rural areas, is stimulating interest in planning for tourism as a new producer of jobs and incomes. Dramatic political changes throughout the world, especially toward democracies and market economies, are encouraging leaders to consider the export potential of tourism. Continuing improvement in air transport is opening up potential in nearly every part of the world. Certainly, the environmental movement is having worldwide influence on tourism development. Travelers are more aware of the quality of destinations and seek cleaner, safer, and more interesting locations. Host areas are increasingly aware of environmental issues of pollution, toxic waste, and destruction of resources.

Because of these and other important trends, the need for better planning is becoming more and more evident.

The Educational Need

Unfortunately, universities have not visualized this new demand for professionally trained planners with expertise in tourism. For example, of the 63 papers presented at a major international conference on tourism education (see Brandon, Gunn and Ritchie 1991), there was virtually no reference to planning. The focus by a majority of teachers and researchers around the world is upon travel service business training and education. Considering the general level of management and services in these businesses, this emphasis is commendable and may even need expansion. However, tourism as is stressed throughout this book, encompasses much more. Certainly more comprehensive planning principles and concepts need to be incorporated into research and teaching programs.

At least three new approaches to education for tourism planning are needed. First, existing curricula in architecture, urban and regional planning, landscape architecture, and environmental design need the addition of basic tourism planning principles and practices. Second, schools of hospitality management, such as for hotel and restaurant management, need curriculum modification to include tourism planning. Third, because many other disciplines have important bearing on tourism development, such as anthropology, archaeology, history, marketing, forestry, wildlife science, political science, and geography, they need additions to their curricula of tourism planning relationships. Gradually there is increased advocacy for multidisciplinary research and education in tourism (Ritchie 1991, 17; Gunn 1991, 3).

The Need for an Informed Public

Equally as important as the availability of more professionally trained tourism planners is providing developers and travel host areas with tourism planning knowledge and motivation. Experience is now demonstrating that the responsibility for tourism planning lies equally within two groups of people as well as with professional planners. Important groups are those who make tourism development decisions, and those who are affected by these decisions. No matter how many planning concepts, principles, and techniques are put forward by planners, they are of little consequence if there is no commitment by developers and host areas to agree on implementation. Unless the three developer sectors of tourism—governments, nonprofit organizations, and commercial enterprise—accept their planning roles, the future portends more business failures, less satisfaction by visitors, and greater social and environmental stress. Only now being recognized is the need for local people to be involved in all tourism decisions because their future way of life will be impacted by these decisions.

The Challenge

And so, the major purpose of this book is to describe state-of-the-art planning principles for tourism and some tourism planning accomplishments. Along with description is prescription—advocacy and concepts for improving the level of planning research, education, and implementation. Even though nations and communities the world over vary in economic development, traditions, values, and policies, all have some common tourism needs that planning can resolve. All need to understand the dynamics of travel markets and the extent to which they wish to meet these demands with supply side development. All have to be concerned over transportation, attractions, facilities, and services. All have special natural and cultural resource characteristics that may foster or inhibit tourism development. All need to decide how heavily they wish to develop tourism and yet protect resources and important lifestyles.

Scope of Book

Experience with tourism planning is demonstrating the value of approaching planning at three different scales. Actual land development, protection of resources, and building construction takes place only at the site scale. This scale requires project design processes that take ideas through stages of planning and design to building and managing. However, all such site scale development occurs within the context of destinations and regions.

For ease of understanding, the book is divided into two parts. Part I encompasses descriptions of fundamentals that are basic to tourism planning and development. For tourism areas more advanced in their development, these four chapters may serve as worthwhile review. For others, this information may be new and help greatly in their striving for tourism development.

Part II of the book is a synthesis of concepts, methods, approaches, and examples of tourism planning and design. This is organized along three scales—regions, destinations, and sites. This section is directed toward a fusion of meaning of the basics. The purpose is to provide the most meaningful fundamentals of value to those who intend to plan and develop tourism. The examples are very diverse in kind, approach, and fruition. Some represent only a first stage in planning and are quite recent. Others have been implemented in several stages over a period of many years. Even with this diversity, some common threads can be observed.

Chapter 11, Conclusions and Principles, is the culmination of the book's content. Within this chapter are concise summary statements of key conclusions and principles relating to the planning and design of tourism development. These are grouped under headings of Basic Principles, Environment and Resources, Policies and Goals, Processes, and Future Challenges. These conclusions and principles have been derived from the examples cited, research of other investigators, and a lifetime experience of study and observation of tourism.

Finally, an important purpose of the book is to stimulate decisionmakers, policymakers, and planners to go beyond the description and precepts presented here. Needed are new concepts, models, guidelines, and new practices. More and better information about tourism planning should be created and made available to developers and host areas. It is the intent of this book to provide planning guidance not just for scholars, educators, and planners but also for practitioners at all levels—national tourism offices, chambers of commerce, tourism organizations, investors, managers, host communities, environmentalists, and policymakers.

References

Brandon et al. (eds.) (1991). *New Horizons in Tourism and Hospitality Education, Training and Research,* conference proceedings, R. D. Brandon et al., eds. Calgary, Alberta: University of Calgary.

Bridges, J. G. (1959). "A Short History of Tourism." In *Travel and Tourism Encyclopedia*, pp. 28–42. Ed. H. Pearce Sales. London: Blandford Press.

Gunn, Clare A. (1991). "The Need for Multi-Disciplinary Tourism Education." In *New Horizons in Tourism and Hospitality Education, Training and Research*, conference proceedings, R. D. Brandon et al., eds., pp. 27–33. Calgary, Alberta: University of Calgary.

Ritchie, J. R. Brent (1991). "A Framework for Multi-Disciplinary and Multi-Level Tourism Education." In *New Horizons in Tourism and Hospitality Education, Training and Research,* conference proceedings, R. D. Brandon et al. eds., pp. 17–26. Calgary, Alberta: University of Calgary.

Ritchie, J. R. Brent (1992). "New Realities, New Horizons: Leisure, Tourism and Society in the Third Millenium." In *The Annual Review of Travel*, pp. 13–26. New York: American Express.

Part I

The Basics

Before one can understand and engage in tourism planning at any scale certain basic fundamentals need clarification. The purpose of this part of the book is to summarize some of the more important foundations. Designers, planners, and developers vary in their experience and understanding. For some, these chapters primarily will be review of their own knowledge. For others, these may provide new insight into better design and planning.

Chapter 1, The Purpose of Tourism Planning, is intended to establish the necessity of planning and also dispel past fears and misunderstandings of planning. If tourism is to reach toward better economic impact, it must be planned as well toward goals of enhanced visitor satisfactions, community integration, and above all, greater resource protection. Planning today has a new look, worthy of attention by all sectors involved in development.

Chapter 2, Tourism as a System, endorses the need for all developers, planners, and managers to understand the dynamic interrelation among all parts of tourism as a system. Essential is new understanding of the need for balancing development with demand even though market interests are constantly changing. Only by all sectors planning toward better integration of all parts will tourism avoid difficulties and meet desired objectives.

Chapter 3, Components of Supply, includes brief descriptions of the major components of the supply side of development. It presents important implications of planning for each of the supply side components: attractions, transportation, services, information, and promotion. Emphasis is placed on physical development.

Chapter 4, Growth and Sustainable Development, calls attention to today's need for greater environmental awareness and sensitivity in all tourism development. Instead of limiting opportunities, when properly planned tourism can even foster both positive objectives and strengthened conservation of resources. New market demand for travel to destinations and attractions of natural and cultural resource significance is giving rise to new ecotourism development.

These four chapters lay the base for the second part—concepts and examples of planning tourism at three scales (regional, destination, and site) and a final chapter of planning meanings valuable for future tourism development.

Chapter 1

The Purpose of Tourism Planning

Introduction

Massive development of resources is the consequence as millions more people travel to seek personal rewards from their experiences. This pervasive tourism growth is a significant part of the global expression of the new services economy. With the weakening of many other aspects of the economy, nations and areas see tourism as a quick and easy solution.

Closer examination of this trend shows mixed results. At the same time that improved technology of automobile and air transportation have given more people the opportunity to travel, destinations often have been glutted with congestion and overburdened facilities. As scenery and other natural resources are touted in promotion, the visitor often experiences more ugly commercialism than scenery. As coastal areas are promoted for clear water and pristine beaches, the visitor often discovers a concrete jungle of hotels and sometimes waterfront sewage pollution. As communities seek the economic benefits from foreign visitors, such rewards often come at the cost of cultural conflict and unfulfilled promises. Many scholars and observers have documented the negative as well as the positive impacts of tourism development.

Smith (1992, 306) has documented the typical evolution of unplanned tropical beach resorts. He cites eight stages:

1. Some local settlement; no significant tourism.
2. First tourism; second home strip development.
3. First hotel; high-budget visitors; new jobs.
4. More hotels; strip intensified; houses displaced.
5. More lodging; cultural disruptions; beach congestion/pollution.
6. More hotels; flood and erosion damage; tourism dominates.
7. Resort government fails; urbanized resort.
8. Serious pollution; lateral spread; fully urbanized.

But, too often, the wrong conclusion is reached—that tourism is inherently destructive. It is not. The truth is that tourism development is being

3

done by those who have too little understanding of what tourism really is and how to plan and design it. Tourism can enrich people's lives, can expand an economy, can be sensitive and protective of environments, and can be integrated into a community with minimum impact. Called for is a new mind set that demands better planning and design of all tourism development.

The need for planning may not be as blatantly conspicuous as other development concerns, but nevertheless it is real. Businesses today certainly realize travel is *more competitive* than ever before. In the past, growth of demand was so great that competition was not a worry. Now, throughout the world, thousands of investors are regularly developing new tourist businesses. At no time in history has the *proliferation of promotion* of travel places been so massive. Market specialists are discovering that traditional travel markets are not as simple as they once were. Now, they talk of market segments and the greater sophistication levels of travelers. New markets are burgeoning—adventure travel, cultural travel, ecotourism, and travel to spectacular events. Travel markets are extremely dynamic. Tourism, once considered the sole responsibility of hotels and travel promoters, is now being recognized as a very *complicated phenomenon*. The supply side of tourism involves nearly every citizen, every public agency, and every organization because the visitor is exposed to everything. How the voters support the development of streets, safe and attractive neighborhoods, educational museums, beautiful and well-kept parks, and even health services—all are as important to tourism as to local welfare of citizens. And, certainly not all is well with the many *environmental* foundations upon which tourism is built. Damage to natural and cultural resources is everywhere, and it is not improving. These and many other reasons can be cited for today's planning challenges. The older and easier paths toward development are no longer functioning. Planning by *everyone* involved in tourism today can no longer be escaped.

The intent of this chapter is to define tourism (as used here), identify the developer sectors, compare the perspectives of developers and tourists, describe key goals of tourism development, identify planning's new look, and provide planning implications at several important scales of development.

DEFINITION OF TOURISM

In this book, tourism is defined as encompassing *all travel* with the exception of commuting. This very broad definition seems necessary from a planning perspective even though it does not agree with many other views.

Some specialists restrict tourism to trip distances—over 50 or 100 miles from home. Some definitions require that a person stay overnight to be counted as a tourist. Other definitions, more traditional, include only vacation or pleasure travel. Whereas the negative image of pleasure travelers is no longer as prevalent, a pejorative element remains. For some, tourists are funny, stupid, unsure, ugly, philistine, rich, exploitive, and environmentally insensitive (Krippendorf 1986, 132).

Today the trend is toward the use of tourism and travel as synonymous terms (Hunt and Layne 1991). Some organizations and publications combine the terms "travel and tourism" to make clear that both business and pleasure travel are included. In both, all the support services for travelers are included. Perhaps the best working definition of tourism is that of Mathieson and Wall (1982, 1):

> Tourism is the temporary movement of people to destinations outside their normal places of work and residence, the activities undertaken during their stay in those destinations, and the facilities created to cater to their needs.

Such a simple definition dramatizes the complexity of the task of planning tourism. If one accepts this broad definition many facets become implicit parts of the overall responsibility of planning. The most conspicuous parts of course are hotels, restaurants, and airlines. For many regions, automobile travel is dominant, encompassing highways as well as automobiles, scheduled buses, rental cars, and motor coach tours. Some destinations are available only by water—cruise ship, ferry, or personal craft. The hundreds of things to see and do in cities and countrysides are also very important parts of tourism.

Parks, theme parks, beaches, resorts, camps, entertainment centers, convention centers, casinos, ski slopes, and homes of friends and relatives are among the many places important to travel destinations. Magazine advertising, travel guide books, and a variety of maps and schedules are also part of the tourism complex. Certainly, the traditions, customs, and policies of host communities are a part of tourism. Federal policy and political decisions are critical to tourism. Regulations, controls, and standards have much to do with the quality of what is offered to travelers and how satisfying the travel experiences really are. All these and more must come within the scope of tourism planning concern.

TOURISM SECTORS

There is a prevailing misconception that tourism is an industry. Instead, it is an agglomeration of land development and programs designed to meet the needs of travelers. This agglomeration has environmental and social as well as economic implications. It is made up of more than only a business sector. The better this is understood, the better tourism can be planned and the more successful it will be. Many of today's tourism problems can be attributed to a business-only scope of concern. It is true that the businesses of tourism, such as lodging, food service, and transportation represent the major economic inputs of tourism but they do not represent the cause nor whole of tourism. Organizations and agencies directed only to the businesses of tourism pursue an incomplete agenda. Those who make development and management decisions for tourism are grouped in three very important and interdependent sectors.

Business Sector

There are several reasons that the tourism business sector does not fit the definition of industry.

First of all, tourism does not produce a singular product such as the automobile industry. Tourism involves a tremendous diversity of products. Tourism products are in contrast to goods and services produced by industries.

Tourism products, loosely defined as visitor experiences, occur at destinations. The distribution system—transportation services—moves the markets to the products. This is the complete opposite of industries manufacturing products that are distributed to markets. The significance of destination places demands entirely different planning strategies for tourism as compared to manufacturing industries. Plant locations have very little importance to product markets whereas destination locations have everything to do with meeting the needs of tourism markets.

All destination places for travel may have some similar characteristics but it is because of each one's uniqueness that people travel to it. Places are different. They have different geographic positions, geographic settings, development patterns, histories, traditions, and societies. Planners have the obligation to discover the special qualities that make them different and to plan for the development of these special features that will appeal to markets.

Tourism products and their foundations are far more perishable than are manufactured products. If a manufacturer of children's clothing has discovered that a community has become primarily a place for retirees, the products may be redistributed to communities with a high birth rate. However, when a large capital investment is made in resort hotels, marinas, and theme parks and the travel market decides to go elsewhere, it is costly if not impossible to move the physical plant.

When an industrial committee of a community seeks new development, efforts are directed toward the chief executive officers of specific plants. Not so with tourism. Tourism development requires a large number and a diverse mix of decisionmakers. The task for tourism is far more complicated.

Finally, tourism development has much greater social and cultural scope than does industrial development. Travel has many enriching and educational dimensions. The expansion of tourism in a community and area has far more social and economic implications than does the addition of an industry.

There is value in organizations of the several tourism business sectors. Hotel and motel organizations have mutual concerns over internal operations, such as labor, taxes, insurance, and governmental regulations. Organizations oriented to food enterprises, attractions, travel agencies, and transportation companies also direct their activities toward internal affairs. But, to say these truly represent tourism is false. They may represent the business sector but there is much more to tourism.

Nonprofit Sector

Often omitted as a prime actor sector of tourism is the very important category of nonprofit organizations. In the United States and many other nations, there has been great growth of tourism development by voluntary organizations. Many health, religious, recreation, historic, ethnic, professional, archeological, and youth organizations plan, develop, and manage land for visitors.

Knechtel (1985) believes that this sector—voluntary, informal, and family—holds great promise for tourism expansion, especially in developing countries. Rather than inviting the large multinational firm to invest outside capital and labor, local talent can be harnessed for many indigenous and small-scale tourism developments. Because the goal is less for profit than for ideologies, many cultural benefits can accrue from nonprofit tourism development.

Although laws vary, the nonprofit sector generally is one in which charges can be made for products and services but all revenues must be expended for operational and capital costs, not as investments. Nonprofit tourist attractions typically receive revenues from gate receipts, admissions, and foundation grants.

In recent years, both cultural and natural resource attractions have increased in numbers due largely to nonprofit organizational support. Historical societies have recognized the value of mounting campaigns to preserve historic sites and buildings. But, in addition to protecting lands and structures, they have rebuilt and modified structures to adapt them to tourism. Retaining the historic patina of architecture, adaptations for visitors have been made—adding heat, air conditioning, special protection of floors and walks, exhibits, toilet facilities, descriptive materials, and guided tours. Important destination sites such as Williamsburg, the Alamo, and Mount Vernon, as well as festivals and events like the International Azalea Festival in Norfolk, the Calgary Stampede, the America's Cup Match, and New Orleans' Mardi Gras are sponsored by nonprofit organizations.

Without the accumulation of wealth as the primary motive, nonprofit tourist developments tend to support specific causes of the sponsor organizations. These often include health, fitness, historic preservation, performing arts, fine arts, ethnic custom perpetuation, environmental protection, and youth training.

Future planning and development of tourism must include nonprofit organizations because of their important functional roles, management plans, and strategies.

Governmental Sector

Contrary to tourism being an industry or dominated by the business sector, it is developed and managed by another very important group—government. Generally, the primary role of government is governance—enactment and implementation of laws and regulations. However for tourism, most countries have assumed many very important functions other than regulation.

In many countries, governments provide a great number of visitor attractions. National parks throughout the world not only protect valuable natural and cultural assets but also attract millions of visitors. In the United States alone in 1991, there were 267,840,999 visits to the national parks (1991 Annual Abstract, 2). Parks at state, provincial, county, and community levels also provide a great many outdoor recreation functions for travelers. A survey in Texas (Outdoor Recreation 1983, 1) showed that Texas travelers spent $9.3 billion on recreational trips that year. Many travel destination activities take place on publicly-owned and managed lands, such as:

Baseball or softball	Jogging or running	
Basketball	Motorcycling for pleasure	
Bicycling	Picnicking	
Boating	Sightseeing	
Camping	Snow skiing	
Fishing	Swimming	
Football and soccer	Tennis	
Golf	Using playgrounds	
Horseback riding	Walking or hiking	
Hunting	Water-skiing	(Outdoor Recreation 1983, 3)

In addition, the governmental sector owns and manages much of the infrastructure upon which tourism depends. From the community to the national level, this often includes water supply, sewage disposal, police and fire protection, streets and lighting, as well as electrical power and communications. Although the governing agencies may set policies and exercise practices primarily for residents, these utilities are of critical importance to travelers. For example, some destinations are not popular with travelers because water supplies and police protection are inadequate. Official city planning, building codes, and zoning have much to do with how tourism is developed.

In a great many countries, tourism promotion and marketing have been accepted as roles of government. Billions of dollars are spent by governments annually to promote visitors to their areas. For most of these agencies, advertising makes up the largest share of the budget. Only a few include moneys for research, planning, training, and information systems.

Certainly, understanding the many policies and practices of governmental agencies is essential to all tourism planning and development.

DEVELOPER AND TOURIST PERSPECTIVES

These three sectors of tourism developers—governments, nonprofit organizations, and commercial enterprise—are categories that encompass countless numbers of individuals, corporations, organizations, and agencies. Every developer makes decisions on development for its own specific role in tourism. Each development provides for one and only one item of use by the tourist at one point in time on the entire journey. Collectively, all these independent decisionmakers produce what we now call tourism development of the supply side. These are the action groups that facilitate travel by locating land, building structures, and managing places and programs. Without them, tourism would not function.

But, viewing tourism from the perspective of the traveler is entirely different from that of any developer. Figure 1-1 is a diagram that illustrates

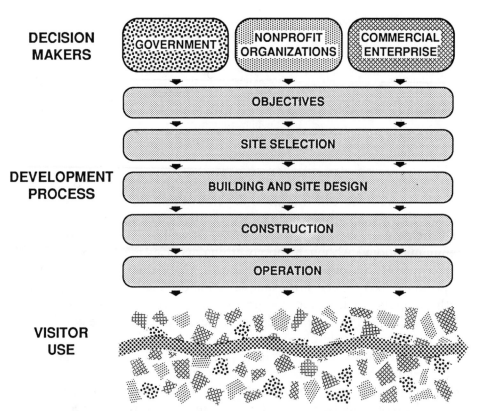

Figure 1-1. Decisionmaking and Tourist Use Compared. Individual decisionmaking for tourism development results in a mosaic of unrelated parts. Travelers, in contrast, are the only ones to view and use this mosaic as a whole. Needed is planning that integrates the many parts for visitor use.

this contrasting relationship. Every tourist trip cuts across hundreds, perhaps thousands, of developments resulting from independent decisions by the innumerable actors of all three sectors. The scope of the traveler's interest at each site is part of a sequence of experiences. Who built the object, who provides the service, who owns the land, what regulations apply, and what decisionmaking process was followed by the developer are of little interest to the traveler.

The sectoral approach to tourism development could be characterized as *static*. Decisions are for one function at one place. The tourist approach, on the other hand, could be characterized as *dynamic*. Theirs is a flow from place to place, engaging in a multiplicity of acts at places supplied by the three sectors. Even though these approaches are in balance some of the time, experience of tourism growth is revealing several deficiencies and challenges. Visitors often have difficulty in obtaining the satisfactions they seek; businesses often fall short of success or fail; many environments are being threatened; and many communities are upset with the consequences of tourism inundation.

The prime missing ingredient is *planning.* Those who make decisions for tourism development are not well versed in planning and design. Creating a hotel, hiring staff, and managing departments of housekeeping, engineering, food service, front desk, and sales are not planning tourism. The ownership decisionmaker looks only to its own success factors whereas the traveler is concerned not only about good service but also about many factors outside the facility—relationship to attractions (the reasons they came); price, ease, and comfort of access; and relationship to other needs (shopping, banking, and food diversity). The residents of the community are concerned about the traffic tourism generates, possible noise and disturbance, conflict with neighboring residential areas, and whether they really want masses of strangers congesting and littering their streets. Environmentalists may question the extra burden placed on the city's infrastructure, the blocking of traditional vistas, or possible damage to fragile resources. *These potential difficulties are not necessarily inherent to all tourism development—they are merely the result of poor planning or no planning at all.* Planning of the whole generally has not been accepted as a responsibility of decisionmakers.

GOALS FOR DEVELOPMENT

As an overall comprehensive activity, planning can provide betterment of tourism if directed toward several major goals. Here, goals are defined as different from objectives. Objectives are specific, real, and actual activities that can be accomplished within a given time. Goals are ideals or aims that one strives for but may never completely accomplish. Goals provide the framework for the identification of policies and accomplishment of specific objectives. For example, a nation may have the goal of economic improvement within which there may be objectives for specific roads, hotels, and attractions to be built by a certain date.

Experience has demonstrated that for betterment of tourism there are at least the following four planning goals.

Enhanced Visitor Satisfactions

Tourism begins with the desires of travelers to travel and ends with their satisfactions derived from such travel. But, as has been pointed out, the

complicated characteristics of modern tourism tend to reduce these satisfactions from the possible level desired. Mere volumes of mass participation, a popular method of evaluating success, do not necessarily translate
into satisfaction. Visitors often waste much time, money, and energy in
attempting to weave the myriad of development into a meaningful whole.
They are too often frustrated in finding their way about, seeking the
appropriate services and understanding the attractions when they do find
them. Furthermore, developers' lack of understanding of the tourist market results in less than satisfactory services, such as poor accommodations,
food services, and interpretive tours. Fragmentation of transportation services creates irritation and sometimes disappointments, especially when
packaged tours are aborted midstream.

> The amateur tourist needs help. He needs confidence that the strange world to
> which affluence admits him deals candidly with him and that there are standards of
> price, service and facility he can rely upon. He needs assurance that if somehow
> things do not turn out as expected, he has a recourse. (Destination USA 1973, Vol.
> I, 1).

Planning should not only eliminate the problems outlined above but
also provide the positive mechanism whereby land acquisition, design,
development, and management have the greatest chance of providing user
satisfactions. In this sense, planning is not only user problemsolving, it is
user problem avoiding. Planning should provide a check on interrelationships of development to make sure the participant's desires, habits, wishes,
and needs are satisfied insofar as physical development and management
can do so. The worth of the planned development is not to be judged
solely by the owner nor the planner but by the visitor. This standard
demands a user-oriented planning policy.

The importance of tourism to the individual and society was identified
in the Manila Declaration on World Tourism (Records 1981, 118) resulting
from the World Tourism Conference of 1980. The spiritual elements that
must be given high priority were cited.

> The total fulfillment of the human being.
> A constantly increasing contribution to education.
> Equality of destiny of nations.
> The liberation of man in a spirit of respect for identity and dignity.
> The affirmation of the originality of cultures and respect for the moral heritage of
> peoples.

This expression by 107 national delegations and 91 observer delegations
from international, governmental, and nongovernmental organizations
was evidence of the need for considering the human dimension in all
tourism planning.

All planners, developers, and managers of tourism must never lose sight of the major fundamental—the intrinsic value of travel for the individual and society. Although stakeholders cannot guarantee experiential satisfactions, they are bound to provide the best setting and programs most likely to make them happen.

The child's first thrill of paddling through foam and sand along a beach or observing the many wonders of nature, such as a colorful butterfly on a beautiful flower, are important outcomes of tourism. For families of all ages, seeing and photographing elk and moose in the north, the exotic animals and birdlife of the tropics, the snowcapped and glaciered mountain ranges, the brilliance of autumn foliage, or the full palette of sunsets over water, are the real substance of travel. At the same time that business proprietors must be concerned about airline schedules, hotel room maintenance, and labor payrolls, they must always maintain high sensitivity to visitor interests. The thrill rides of theme parks or whitewater rafting that push human endurance to the limit may be the most important of travel experiences for some. The fascination and revelation of scientific endeavor capture the interest of masses of tourists as they visit museums and science centers. New understandings of other cultures—their background, customs, crafts, philosophies, and human values—are the rewards for many who travel. For others, the change of venue for common local activities—socializing, games, and parties—is sufficient reason for travel to a distant location. Fantasizing the lifestyle, play, and battles of ancient peoples has no stimulus equal to actually being in the theaters and coliseums of the Greeks and Romans. These and hundreds of other experiences fill the rich and abundant cornucopia of travel values that must be considered in all tourism planning.

Therefore, one major goal of collaborative tourism planning is the *provision of user satisfactions*.

Improved Economy and Business Success

Most areas and nations place high priority on an improved economy as a tourism development goal. Too frequently this is interpreted to mean merely a search for new investment in facilities and advertising. Although both are important, questions of what should be developed and where are equally significant. For planning purposes, one must reach into many factors that influence tourism's success. Such factors as geographical relationship to markets, attractions and attractiveness, resources for development, and involvement of all sectors need to be examined for their potential in developing a tourist economy.

The measurement of a tourism economy is not simple nor universally agreed upon. Tourism does not lend itself to traditional industrial measurements of end-use activities (Frechtling 1987, 326). As a result many theoretical models of economic impact have been developed and applied around the world.

The positive impact of tourism, no matter how measured, shows that tourism does strengthen the economy of many areas. This economic benefit is best understood as a "gross increase in the wealth or income, measured in monetary terms, of people located in an area over and above the levels that would prevail in the absence of the activity under study" (Frechtling 1987, 328). Economic benefits can be expressed by both primary and secondary effects as shown in Table 1-1.

Just now being recognized in the United States (though well accepted in other countries) is the inducement of foreign tourism through expansion of domestic tourism. Evidence of the economic impact of tourism is so overwhelming that it is no wonder that undeveloped countries seek it and industrialized nations wish to protect it.

Frequently, in their desire to improve the tourism economy, governments constrain rather than assist in the process. Lack of communication and even antagonism between governmental agencies and private enter-

TABLE 1-1
ECONOMIC BENEFITS OF TRAVEL AND TOURISM

A. Primary or Direct Benefits
1. Business receipts
2. Income
    a. Labor and proprietor's income
    b. Corporate profits, dividends, interest, and rent
3. Employment
    a. Private employment
    b. Public employment
4. Government receipts
    a. Federal
    b. State
    c. Local
B. Secondary Benefits
1. Indirect benefits generated by primary business outlays, including investment
    a. Business receipts
    b. Income
    c. Employment
    d. Government receipts
2. Induced benefits generated by spending of primary income
    a. Business receipts
    b. Income
    c. Employment
    d. Goverment receipts

Source: Frechtling 1987, 330

prise frequently does not allow private investors adequate freedom to get an important commercial job done. When private development becomes "so involved in red tape and so expensive that it has no appeal to a potential investor," something is wrong (Brown 1975, 24). Successful private enterprise must make profits. Likewise, successful bureaucratic development, as in local, state, and federal parks and reserves, must meet those objectives of the common weal important to public goals. This kind of success is important for government agencies. Only adequate rewards of this nature can provide the incentive to develop. The desired economic impact then follows. Fragmentation and isolation of policies, regulations, and managerial practices tend to reduce greatly the potential of rewards.

Planning should not only address itself to the elimination of the problems above but also to the provision—the insistent provision—of positive rewards to those who identify, design, develop, and manage areas for tourism. In other words, cooperation, collaboration, and coordination must foster, not destroy, individual creativity and innovation in development to meet new needs. It must be self-serving at the same time that it is socially responsible. Private enterprise should be guided into locations and programs in which it can be *more*, not less, successful. Public agencies should be guided into locations and programs that meet their special governmental mandates and yet are compatible with commercial enterprise and nonprofit organizations.

Therefore, another goal of collaborative tourism planning is the provision of *increased rewards to ownership and development*.

Protected Resource Assets

The controversy between environmentalism and development continues. This stems mainly from kinds of development other than tourism but carries over into it as an ideological conflict. This paradox is difficult to explain because so much of tourism depends upon resource protection.

Traditionally, travelers have sought destinations with attractive scenery, recreational waters, esthetic landscapes, undeveloped mountain slopes and peaks, and protected wildlife. More recently, there has been a surge of interest in historic and archeological sites. All of these require environmental protection if they are to serve as foundations for development desired by visitors.

Yet, tourism business plans seldom, if ever, make any reference to environmentalism as a necessity of business. The obvious needs of market promotion and facility development capture the majority of time and money spent on plans. There is little discernable ground swell of interest among tourism leaders to support measures that protect wildlife from endangerment, reduce soil erosion, reduce runoff from pesticides and other agricultural additives, and prevent toxic wastes and other pollutants from destroying valuable water resources.

Both a tourism economy and visitor satisfactions depend upon the absolute necessity of stopping resource degradation so flagrant around the world. Tourism businesses, government agencies, and nonprofit organizations developing tourism—all will have little to promote in the future unless attitudes and policies change. For some areas, it may already be too late. In order to develop tourism, the resources may already have been so severely diminished that no one will wish to invest and no traveler will wish to come.

Essential then to all tourism planning is new commitment toward the goal of *resource protection*.

Community and Area Integration

Many communities and regions view tourism as a separate layer that is simply added to a community. Engaging in tourism from this viewpoint is always disappointing because it fails to integrate tourism into the social and economic life of the community.

A study in Cairns, Australia, by Ross (1992) found that residents perceived both positive and negative impacts from tourism development. Concerns centered on cost of buying land and houses, cost of renting a house, cost of living, and crime levels. Positive results included more job opportunities, more business opportunities, and greater entertainment, parks, shopping, and hotels and restaurants. As tourism developed, there appeared to be a lessening of friendliness and degradation of social life among residents.

Probably no other economic development of communities has so many far-reaching tentacles as does tourism. Tourism involves all the city's businesses, agencies, organizations, and segments of the public. It involves the local society and its ability to host masses of outsiders, often creating congestion, litter, and even competition for goods and services. It involves competition for land. It competes for amenities, such as parks, museums, and cultural events. And, tourism often demands extra utility infrastructure, such as water supply, waste disposal, police and fire protection, streets, lighting, and maintenance.

Integrating tourism planning into official community planning has been slow to take place. The majority of planning goals for legal planning agencies have been directed toward the citizenry, not visitors. Although this is logical, it ignores the role of all city departments to cooperate in satisfying the needs of citizens as they host travelers. As Branch (1985, 76) points out, the city planning department should be the catalyst (but often is not) to coordinate the actions of the many city operating units, commonly:

airport	fire protection	public works
animal regulation	harbor	purchasing
art	library	recreation
attorney	museum	sanitation
building	parks	social services
controller	pensions	transportation
data services	personnel	treasurer
engineering	police	water supply
health	power plant	

Certainly, the majority of these with their separate policies and practices, have much to do with how a community is able to provide all the supply side development so necessary for long-range tourism success.

However, the political and private organizational structure in most countries, such as in the United States, tends to mitigate against long range planning. Branch (1985) cites as one cause the reelection process whereby politicians hesitate to make commitments beyond their tenure in office. He states as another reason that, to politicians, long-range planning seems too difficult and demanding. These may be valid reasons why official urban planning tends to be short range. However, because of many social environmental and economic ills of cities, the populace may be more supportive of long-range and coordinated planning in the future—for all development including tourism.

An example of incorporating tourism development into official planning is the case of Viborg County, Denmark (Munk 1991). Both the physical comprehensive planning and business development program of the county include tourism as well as other development, such as agriculture, recreation, and extraction of raw material. The aims of the overall plan include increased work opportunities, high quality of life, and sufficient public and private services. The official plan is renewed every four years. All local authorities are involved in discussions of needed changes before revisions are made.

The aims of this county tourism plan follow those of the regional plan. The policy for tourism is to improve local conditions so inhabitants of the county, the trade, and institutions can receive Danish and foreign guests and give those guests an understanding of the county's qualities and characteristics. At the same time, this policy of tourism will promote those forms that, on one hand, can contribute to the economic and qualitative development of the region, and on the other, to thrive and develop together with local people as well as protect the county's natural, cultural, and environmental resources. This is to be accomplished through five strategies: product development, marketing and information, education, public planning and administration, organization, and economy.

Generally, tourism's positive economic impact is believed to be of great enough value to offset the costs of integrating tourism into a community. But, in order to make sure of this, tourism must be planned with the specific goal of fusing tourism with the social and economic life of a region and its communities.

Long ago, the rule of economic diversity was proved to be of value to communities. Diversity in the kinds of economic bases provides the best hedge against major drops in support from one kind. The same policy is true for tourism. Today, as many communities and nations look to tourism for economic strengthening, there is danger if tourism becomes the sole economic provider. This danger is especially exacerbated with tourism because travel markets are less secure than local markets. Travelers are located some distance away, making each area vulnerable to competition from other destinations.

In recent years, awareness of tourism's potential negative impacts—social, environmental, and economic—has increased. The tradeoffs in terms of employment, incomes, and tax revenues are often considered of greater value. But, in order to make sure of this, developers must analyze the potential threats *beforehand* and initiate plans and action programs to ameliorate them. An important goal of tourism planning is *integration into the social and economic life of communities and areas.*

These four goals—enhanced visitor satisfaction, better business, resource protection, and community integration—should be the motivating forces for all stakeholders in tourism to plan and develop the needed objectives and strategies to carry them out.

PLANNING'S NEW LOOK

Background

Physical planning as a concept and practice has taken place for centuries. As Branch (1985, 12) points out, cities in India as early as 3000 B.C. were divided into square blocks, oriented to the cardinal points, and laid out to allow circulation between. Medieval cities frequently were planned with encircling walls for fortification. Even building codes and zoning date back to ancient times. But, such order in city planning resulted from strong centralized authoritative control. Elsewhere, unregulated development had little order. Even in more recent times, socialistic and planned economy nations exacted strong land use controls from a central authority.

Town planning has been practiced in the United Kingdom for two centuries (Cherry 1984, 187) and physical layout planning reaches back to early Greek and Roman times. For England, interest in planning was stimulated by the physical and social ills resulting from industrialization. Visionaries and philanthropists dreamed of utopian cities. The bias for many years was on physical planning—the visual appearance of architecture and patterns of land use. This concept was followed by trends toward comprehensive planning set into law. In recent years two dimensions have been added to planning—social and economic.

> Planning is a multidimensional activity and seeks to be integrative. It embraces social, economic, political, psychological, anthropological, and technological factors. It is concerned with the past, present and future. (Rose 1984, 45)

Although such lofty goals are at the heart of the planning concept, carrying them out has not been simple or easy. For many reasons, including the complexity of thousands of decisions made by individuals, corporations, and governments all over the world, planning has not been as effective as planners might have wished. Professional planners have agreed upon some general directions—a better place to live and the like—but there is no neat body of theory for planning as can be found in other disciplines. In fact, planners generally agree that planning is not a distinct discipline but an amalgam of many.

In capitalistic market-economy countries, planning has become nebulously blurred in meaning, often even a pejorative term. Even though much planning is known to take place, several negative connotations have become strong enough in public opinion to block many planning efforts. A few of these are worth noting so that individuals, communities, and areas can take steps to cope with them.

Many people feel that the idea of planning places too much *power in a governmental bureaucracy.* Because urban planning departments have become a legally sanctioned institution of many city governments, many people resent bureaucratic control over what they believe to be their freedoms, especially for land use and development.

Much of this resentment is based on ascribing power and titles to *professional planners.* In the past, university programs of urban planning focused on professional elitism patterned after other professions of medicine and law. This was based on the educational criterion that there was a technical body of knowledge that was exclusive and essential to a profession.

Another negative public reaction has resulted from so many *plans being aborted.* It has happened so often that the phrase "plans collecting dust on the shelf," has become a popular planning cliché.

The New Planning

In spite of these beliefs, the entire philosophy and concept of planning has changed dramatically in recent years. Branch (1985, 73) has summarized this awareness succinctly:

> Even in the smallest and simplest communities planning involves many actions, participants, fields of knowledge, and levels of decision and implementation. It is impossible for any one person to comprehend analytically the network of major elements and interactions that are involved in comprehensive planning for a modern industrialized city.

This modern awareness of some of the foibles of earlier planning approaches and processes has led to a much broader and more effective planning philosophy by educators and practitioners. Frequently, terms such as public involvement, participatory planning, grass-roots planning, and integrative planning are being applied to modern planning. All of these reflect greater sensitivity to the interests of the decisionmakers and those impacted by planning directives. The emphasis is on planning *with* rather than only *for.*

Lang (1988, 93) emphasized that even though conventional planning of the past included some interaction, it usually was very limited. Often plans for public services, such as highways, were virtually fixed by the planners. Public involvement came later as a token. His comparison of interactive and conventional planning characteristics are illustrated in Table 1-2. This new approach emphasizes that better decisions can be reached by means of a participative process, even though it is far more difficult. This shift in emphasis does not mean that research and concepts by professional planners are abandoned. Rather, it means that many other constituencies, other than planners, have experiences, opinions and constructive recommendations. Final decisions have a much better chance of being implemented if publics have been involved. Lang (1988, 98) calls this a "learning adaptive mode of planning" and suggests it is capable of fulfilling two critical needs to:

TABLE 1-2
INTERACTIVE PLANNING VS. CONVENTIONAL PLANNING

Interactive Planning	*Conventional Planning*
Includes information-feedback, consultation, and negotiation	Mostly information-feedback; may be some consultation
Interaction occurs early on and throughout the planning process, with full range of stakeholders	Early interaction with implementors; affected interests not involved until late in the process
Assumes that open participation leads to better decisions	Assumes that better information leads to better decisions
Planner as value-committed advocate	Planner as value-neutral expert
Focuses on mobilization of support	Focuses on manipulation of data
Plan = what we agree to do	Plan = what we should do
Success measured by achievement of agreement on action, and by resulting change	Success measured by achievement of the plan's objectives

Source: Lang 1988, 92.

> Create a sense of commonality which may then motivate actors to seek new forms of collaborative action; and
>
> Build capability to respond effectively to changes as well as to generate change when that becomes necessary.

A similar process was recommended by landscape architect Marshall (1983, 96) in which citizen input is an integral element at every step. He states that even though planning may be coordinated by a governing body, it is "fueled by the energy and creative juices of the citizens of the community." (Marshall, 1983, 97) He diagrams his suggested planning/design process as shown in Figure 1-2.

Although nations vary greatly in their politics of planning it now appears that tourism planning responsibility lies equally with all the *constituencies affected* as well as with *professional planners* and *governmental agencies*. In other words, representatives of all tourism developer sectors—governments, nonprofit organizations, and free enterprise—have the most to gain by cooperating on their own tourism planning. Within a destination area, for example, a tourism development council could incorporate all three sectors in its planning. Within the free enterprise sector would be representatives of lodging, food service, transportation companies, retail shops, and commercial entertainment. Nonprofit sector representatives would include historical societies, church and youth groups (camps, assemblies), festival sponsors, conservation societies, and amateur sports groups. Within government, agencies should be represented governing highways, airports, parks, recreation, museums, preserves, health, secu-

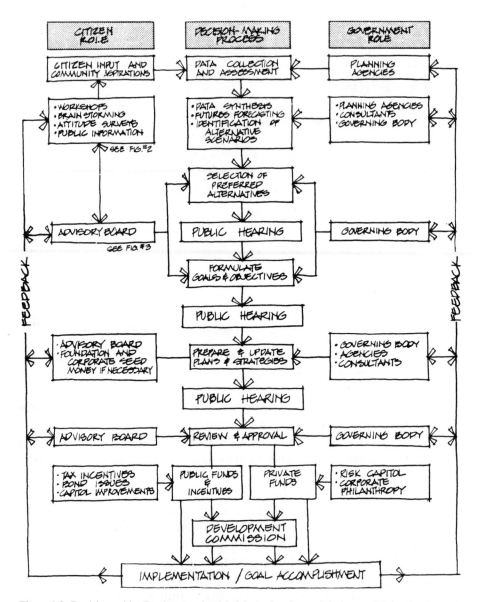

Figure 1-2. Decisionmaking/Implementation Model. A planning and design model that involves government, local citizens, and planners from the start. Constant feedback assures inplementation (Marshall 1983, 96).

rity, utilities, schools, planning, and tourism promoters. All have an equal stake in decisions that impact the future of all. Cumbersome and difficult as it may be to assemble such a council and to develop specific plans, this collectively is the most responsible group to do its own planning.

But, even though such an approach may be most logical, the great complexity of tourism also needs the input of professional planners. Such planners do not have a vested interest in a specific segment of tourism and can provide a coordinated and more objective view. Professional planners have planning as their major training and interest, and their time is not divided with other responsibilities.

In many countries there are two kinds of professional planners involved in tourism—governmental and private consultants. Canada and Australia are examples in which governmental tourist agencies contain planners. The advantages of this form include linkage with governmental policy, continuity of tourism responsibility, and concentrated application to tourism. Disadvantages may include an image of dictatorial control over tourism sectors, political rather than technical allegiance, and lack of integration with the tourism sectors. Private planning consultants have the advantages of unbiased and objective approach, use of unrestrained and creative processes, and input from a diverse team of specialists. Their disadvantages may be wasted startup time, sometimes greater overhead costs, and lack of follow-up ability because obligation ends at end of contract.

Again it must be emphasized that as yet, most official city and area planning agencies have no declared mandates, policies, or practices that explicitly define their role in tourism. This is unfortunate inasmuch as most of their planning decisions and regulations have a strong impact on tourism development. Probably the most ideal official and lay planning for tourism will result from collaboration among governmental agency planners, professional planning consultants, and lay constituency groups representing local citizenry as well as tourism interests.

An example of the development of a *tourism planning policy* can be found in Denmark. A Tourism Declaration of 1986 introduced a new national tourism policy for Denmark. (The following material is derived from correspondence, June 22, 1992, and the dissertation, "Guidelines for a Regional Tourism Planning Process for the Danish Region Flyn," by Eva Thybo, 1991.) The Danish Tourist Board, originally a promotional agency of government, was charged with a new Tourism Development Programme with two new objectives related to planning:

- to expand tourism, taking into consideration recreative planning, protection of the environment and conservation, and
- to integrate the use of tourism resources into physical planning in an acceptable way for Danish society.

The program included the following activities:

- a Domestic Tourism Grant Scheme
- a Grant Scheme for Profile Campaigns in selected countries
- Product Development Grant Scheme
- development of a booking information system
- development of a tourism education system
- establishment and operation of a secretariat for tourism education and training
- support of cultural mega-events
- pilot project for strategic planning (local)
- pilot project for museums and tourism
- market analyses

Important also is the Federation of the Tourist Industry (FTI), a private sector organization created in 1987, including the following eight sectors of member organizations:

travel agents	attractions
hotels and restaurants	retail trade
other accommodations	public transport, including airlines
tourist organizations	private transport

In Denmark, planning is divided into physical, economic, and sector planning, with most tourism planning taking place in the physical division. In practice, planning is almost entirely the responsibility of the counties (called "regions"), with a revised plan every four years. Each plan is a synthesis of national and local planning concerns.

In the first major tourism planning conference (1990), the following issues related to tourism were debated by those in attendance—750 politicians, planners, tourist operators, and representatives of the several tourist organizations.

1. The use of zoning for land-use planning. It was argued that concentration of tourist services in cities would be less harmful to the environment than allowing them to be dispersed in the countryside. Tourist business operators would be more successful in cities.

2. Expansion of areas designated for tourism. Although some advocated new areas, it was concluded that improvements in existing areas would be more desirable—increase summer homes, modernize marginal hotels, lengthen the season.

3. At what level should planning take place? At the same time that public agencies were accused of not being open and active enough, the private sector was criticized for its low inclination and competence. Local

planning was felt to be too narrow, suggesting that a broader destination scale, performed with public-private cooperation, was more desirable.

4. Green Tourism. The balance of environmental protection and tourist use seemed desirable. A symbiosis between hosts, guests and the environment was cited as an important goal.

A result of this conference was the formation of a Tourism Planning Coordination Group, made up of representatives from the National Agency for Physical Planning, the National Agency for Woodland and Nature, the Danish Tourist Board, and the Federation of the Tourist Industry. The agenda of this group includes the preparation of guidelines for tourism planning throughout the nation. This is a precedent inasmuch as there is no tradition of tourism planning in Denmark.

As tourism matures throughout the world, the need for formalizing tourism planning policy will become more evident. Already, emerging policies are including emphasis upon public-private cooperation and collaboration for best planning toward all goals and objectives.

PLANNING SCALES

Experience with tourism planning demonstrates that it needs to be approached at three different scales. The most popular planning today is at the *site* scale—individual property development. However, when tourism functions are better understood, it becomes clear that there are opportunities for better tourism success by planning at the *destination zone* scale. In order to determine greatest potential for a region or nation, a *regional scale* of planning is needed. Integrating tourism development at all scales holds great promise for guiding development toward the desired goals.

Site Scale

All three sectors—businesses, nonprofit organizations, and government agencies—have increasingly employed professionals to plan and design their properties. Gradually, professional firms of architecture, landscape architecture, engineering, and planning have found opportunities in the tourism field. Owners of lands have increasingly engaged their services to plan a wide range of facilities, services, and attractions. Perhaps the most popular approach is by the larger firms bringing together several specialists depending upon the need of the project. For example, some projects require design and planning teams that include historians, golf course specialists, and exhibit experts, as well as the traditional design specialists.

At the lower end of the economic development scale, many entrepreneurs do not avail themselves of professional designers. Sometimes this results in unusually creative tourism developments, such as for bed-and-breakfast, craft stores, gift shops, farm vacations, and outdoor sports guiding (e.g., for hunting, fishing, and trekking). These are especially successful when the owner-planner understands all factors of market demand as well as location.

However, this individuality often produces esthetically ugly and noneconomic tourism development. Just because an owner holds a piece of property is an insufficient factor for locating a tourist business. It may not meet the needs of travelers nor gain from related businesses and attractions nearby. If built in an unattractive and shoddy fashion, it may be within the owner's budget but fail to meet the needs and desires of the traveler.

Too frequently, a series of such individual developments strung along a highway can be damaging on many counts. They can destroy attractive roadside scenery, create marginal business operations, and often leave derelict monuments to business failure because they are improperly located for most favorable site and market factors. In a sense, nonprofit and public sector developments can create similar problems.

Governments, however, pose another issue. Park agencies, for example, generally follow one of two policy directions for site planning and design. Some maintain full-time staff with these responsibilities so that they can respond more quickly to planning needs and are familiar with the agency's policies. Delays in letting out design and planning proposals to consultants are avoided. Some claim that this also saves public moneys by using staff rather than paying consultants with their overhead costs. Critics, however, believe that this in-house policy tends to prevent innovation and creativity. Furthermore, they remind the agency that there is wasted overhead when staff are not busy on projects. Some believe that public agency policies, such as the U.S. National Park Service agreements with concessions, place excessive constraints on what can be built as well as how it is to be designed, priced, and managed. Furthermore, their policy of a concession monopoly for each park prevents competition, thus inhibiting the diversity of services and products desired by the travel markets. Although it may be desirable to have esthetic and management controls over businesses within the park, nearby communities should be free to develop services for the complete diversity of travel markets.

There is little question that there is need for new cooperation and new guidelines between the decisionmakers and the designers-planners at the site scale for tourism development. The individual's freedom to develop tourism properties can be protected at the same time such owners can become enlightened on their greater opportunities for success when exercising many worthwhile principles of planning. Perhaps the most important principle is that of balancing internal with external influences on success. For example, a hotelier may be implementing state-of-the-art in-house management practices and still fail because external factors were not considered. Equally significant are plans and developments for traveler attractors and attractions, transportation, and information systems. Planning for every tourism facility and service must encompass many relationships if they are to be most successful. (Site scale tourism examples are described in Chapter 10.)

Destination Scale

If tourism development is to reach toward improved social, economic,and environmental goals, the *destination zone* is as important to plan as the site unit. The term is popularly defined in many ways, sometimes referring to an administrative or marketing area. For planning purposes, *destination zone* is defined here as *a geographic area containing a critical mass of development that satisfies traveler objectives.*

A *critical mass* of tourism development implies a large enough and diverse enough amount of attractions and services to meet the needs and desires of several travel market segments. Attractions are developed and managed sites that form the basis for travelers' interests in things to see and do. The reason for a large number and diversity of attractions is to increase the demand for services—lodging, food, retail sales, and transportation. These services are the economic generators for tourism but require volumes of visitors to make them feasible. When only a few attractions directed to only a small number of travel markets are in place, the tourism economy is subject to great fluctuations. This is demonstrated by resort destination zones that offer only seasonal attractions. The support businesses have difficulty maintaining staffs and meeting year-round fixed costs of operation. A destination that contains attractions for both business and pleasure markets is most successful.

The basic elements of a destination zone are:

- Transportation and access to one or more communities.
- One or more communities with adequate public utilities and travel services.
- Attraction complexes (clusters) that meet market needs.

- Efficient and attractive transportation linkages between cities and attractions.

Destination zones must be planned with sensitivity to social, environmental, and economic impacts. When sites are properly designed and the entire zone is properly planned, masses of visitors will create minimum negative impacts, socially or environmentally.

Because a destination zone is a collection of a great many sites and encompasses numerous jurisdictions, considerable cooperation is needed. This may represent the major obstacle and challenge for the planning and development of destination zones. The area included in a zone may reach 50 or 100 miles around a community depending on the location of attractions and how they can be reached. When a zone has been planned for attractions, access, services, and facilities, it can stimulate and guide developers into projects that provide the best relationships between all parts at the same time it fosters individual project success. (Destination scale tourism examples are described in Chapter 8.)

Regional Scale

Today, many states, provinces, and nations seek better tourism development for the entire region. Too often, however, this is approached with the naive belief that simply attracting new hotel investors will create the desired tourism. Planning at the regional scale is even more comprehensive than at the site and destination zone scales. Many more resource areas are involved, a greater number of political jurisdictions are included, and the time periods of accomplishment are much longer. Nevertheless, the main reason for planning at this macro scale is better integration of the whole. The better that each site and destination zone relate to one another the better it will be for individual tourism success and for the region as a whole.

For example, today it is increasingly difficult for the isolated resort to succeed. It cannot benefit from related developments and programs. It has great difficulty in meeting market needs for the diversity of activities required at all seasons. Infrastucture costs may reduce feasibility because they are not shared with other developments.

Other regional planning efforts can benefit from the creation of a regional tourism plan. For example, overall regional transportation plans by both private and public sectors can benefit by knowing the needs of tourism. All purposes for personal movement to and within the region can be planned together. Too often, tourism objectives are omitted from such plans. The planning of industrial development, agriculture, forestry, and settlement can be integrated with tourism only when a tourism plan is known.

When a nation seeks investors, public and private, for tourism development, it is difficult to attract them with only generalizations about the attractiveness of the region. When regional plans identify the zones where opportunities are well founded on study of tourism development factors, investment feasibility is more appealing to investors and developers. (Regional scale tourism examples are described in Chapter 6.)

CONCLUSIONS

This chapter focused on six basic fundamentals essential to planning tourism. First, tourism was defined as all travel not just pleasure travel—so that all aspects related to planning could be included. Second, the pluralistic nature of decisionmakers was described, emphasizing that tourism is run by more than business. Third, all sectors need to understand the difference between their perspective of development and that of travelers. Fourth, experience has demonstrated that planning can and should be directed toward goals of visitor satisfactions, protected resource assets, and community and area integration as well as the more commonly accepted goals of improved economy and business success. Then, the very important changes in philosophies and processes of planning itself are described, emphasizing today's greater public involvement in planning. Finally, when planning for tourism development, differences must be considered in scope and content for regional, destination zone, or site scales. It is from these principles that the following conclusions were derived.

Planning should encompass all travel.

In the past, the term tourism has often been applied to only pleasure travel. When tourism is viewed from the perspective of the individual firm, this definition is too limited. Hotels, transportation, food services, and shops are interested in sales to all travelers, no matter their purpose. Furthermore, if planning is to be comprehensive, it should include all the elements that need to be integrated for best success of all involved.

Planning must predict a better future.

Planning tourism is not merely a perfunctory or bureaucratic exercise. Its main purpose must be the long-term betterment of all involved. This means not only greater individual success but overall betterment through greater team action. Tourism involves so many individuals and organizations that it must be planned with greater unity of purpose. Unless planning can predict a better future it will be ineffective.

Both planning and plans are needed for tourism today.

It is valuable for a nation, state, or area to make specific plans for tourism development from time to time. These plans give focus and direct action to specific project and program development. However, to be most effective, these plans should be coupled with a system of ongoing planning. Too often plans have been seen only as documents and not integrated with action on a regular basis.

Economic development must not be an exclusive goal of planning.

Tourism planning efforts are most popularly directed toward improving the economy—more jobs, income, and taxes generated. Although this continues to be an important goal it will not be achieved unless planning for the economy is accompanied by three other goals—enhanced visitor satisfaction, protected resource assets, and integration with community social and economic life.

Planning must incorporate all three sectors of tourism.

The business sector of tourism is well known. Generally, it produces the greatest economic impact. However, tourism cannot function without the equally important sectors of nonprofit organizations and governments (as developers), especially for attractions, infrastructure, and transportation. Planning that includes only business will not succeed in reaching desired tourism development objectives.

Planning processes today are becoming much more interactive.

The new planning processes require involvement of decisionmakers and other influences at each step in the process. The experience, training, and conceptual ideas of professional planners are as essential as ever. But, the older perception of top-down planning is being replaced by bottom-up planning under coordinated professional leadership. The role of the planner/designer is becoming more strongly one of a catalyst or facilitator.

Three scales of planning need integration.

Site planning for tourism development, no matter how well done, falls short if it is not related to more macro-scale planning. How sites fit into community, destination, and regional development is critical to individual as well as collective nationwide success of tourism. Today, all three levels of tourism planning are in great need.

REFERENCES

1991 Annual Abstract (1991). Washington, DC: U.S. National Park Service.

Branch, Melville C. (1985). *Comprehensive City Planning; Introduction & Explanation,* Washington, DC: American Planning Association, Planners Press.

Brown, D. R. C. (1975). "The Developer's View of Ski Area Development." *Man, Leisure, and Wildlands,* proceedings, Eisenhower Consortium, September 14–19, Vail, CO. Springfield, VA: National Technical Information Service.

Cherry, Gordon E. (1984). "Town Planning: An Overview." In *The Spirit and Purpose of Planning,* 2nd ed., M.J. Burton (ed.), pp. 170–188. London: Hutchinson.

Destination U.S.A. (1973). Report of the National Tourism Resources Review Commission, Vols. 1–6. Washington, DC: U.S. Government Printing Office.

Frechtling, Douglas C. (1987). "Assessing the Impact of Travel and Tourism— Introduction to Travel Impact Estimation," Chap. 17. In *Travel, Tourism and Hospitality Research,* Ritchie and Goeldner (eds.), pp. 325–332. New York: John Wiley & Sons.

Hunt, John D., and Donlynne Layne (1991). "Evaluation of Travel and Tourism Terminology and Definitions." *Journal of Travel Research,* 29(4), 7–11.

Knechtel, Karl (1985). "The Role of the 'Third Sector' in Tourism Development," unpublished paper, Ottawa, Canada.

Krippendorf, Jost (1986). "The New Tourist—Turning Point for Leisure Travel." *Tourism Management,* 7(2), 131–135.

Lang, Reg (1988). "Planning for Integrated Development." In *Integrated Rural Planning and Development,* F. W. Dykeman (ed.), pp. 81–104. Sackville, New Brunswick: Rural and Small Town Research and Studies Programme, Mount Allison University.

Marshall, Lane L. (1983). *Action by Design—Facilitating Design Decisions into the 21st Century.* Washington, DC: The American Society of Landscape Architects.

Matheison, Alister and Geoffrey Wall (1982). *Tourism—Economic Physical, and Social Impacts.* London: Longman.

Munk, Inger (1991). "Quality of Life—Planning Processes and Models of Cooperation." (Viborg County) presentation, IVLA meeting, Paros, Denmark.

Outdoor Recreation 1983 (1984). "1983 Outdoor Recreation Trips Expenditures in Texas." Austin, TX: Texas Parks and Wildlife Department.

Records of the World Tourism Conference (1981). Madrid: World Tourism Organization.

Rose, Edgar A. (1984). "Philosophy and Purpose in Planning." In *The Spirit and Purpose of Planning,* 2nd ed., M.J. Burton (ed.), pp. 31–65. London: Hutchinson.

Ross, Glenn F. (1992). "Resident Perceptions of the Impact of Tourism on an Australian City." *Journal of Travel Research,* 30(3), 13–17.

Smith, Russell A. (1992). "Beach Resort Evolution." *Annals of Tourism Research,* 19, 304–322.

Thybo, Eva (1991). "Guidelines for a Regional Tourism Planning Process for the Danish Region Flyn." Dissertation, University of Surrey, England.

Chapter 2

Tourism as a System

Introduction

A major purpose of planning is to increase success, especially in the business sector. Most countries seek successful tourism businesses to enhance employment, incomes, and tax revenues that in turn help support public services. Most businesses believe success is derived primarily from superior management. Hotel schools, for example, stress subjects of accounting, housekeeping, sales, front desk, food service, and engineering as keys to success.

Certainly, well-managed businesses are essential to success. But, for the field of tourism, businesses (and the other sectors) are equally dependent upon others for their success. This is due to the simple tourism truth that the tourism product is not captured by a single business, nonprofit organization, or governmental agency. The *tourism product* has often been defined as a satisfying visitor experience. If accepted, this definition encompasses every activity and experience on the entire trip away from home. For example, a hotelier's product includes convenient access and the attractions that induced the traveler to come as well as an enjoyable room and food service. Every development for tourism is dependent upon many other developments for its success. This functional truth complicates planning but helps to explain why it is so necessary to view and plan tourism as an overall system.

The purpose of this chapter is to demonstrate that every part of tourism is related to every other part. No owner or manager has complete control of his own destiny. But, the more each one learns about the others, the more successful he can be in his own enterprise no matter whether it is run by commercial business, nonprofit organization, or government. Tourism cannot be planned without understanding the interrelationships among the several parts of the supply side, especially as they relate to market demand.

33

MARKET-SUPPLY MATCH

Travel Markets

As any manufacturer knows, the best product to manufacture is one preferred by the market. This is equally true with tourism. People in the
travel market are those who have the *interest* and *ability* to travel. Because
the majority of travel markets live in areas of population concentration in
industrialized nations, the cities become primary sources of travelers. But,
such populations have a great diversity of ability and interest in travel.
Some segments cannot afford even the minimal costs and some prefer to
spend discretionary incomes on purchases other than travel. Even more
complicated are the divergent preferences of those who are able to travel.
Therefore, a major topic of planning concern is the understanding of travel
markets—their location, preferences, purposes, and ability to travel.

   In recent years many studies and models have been put forth to identify
travel market characteristics. Sources, such as *Travel, Tourism and Hospitality Research—A Handbook for Managers and Researchers*, and journals, such as *Annals of Tourism Research*, *Journal of Travel Research*, and
Tourism Management, should be reviewed for current information on markets. In the United States, a Travel Outlook Forum is held annually to
provide information and forecasts on all travel trends including markets.

   Chadwick (1987, 52) classifies travel market studies into three groups.
Household surveys are made at places of travel origin and often cover
nontravelers as well as travelers. A statistically random sampling process
can reveal information about the entire population within reasonable limits
of accuracy. Data on frequency of travel volume, such as personal trips, party
trips, and vacation trips are popularly obtained. Travel expenditures, on or
before trips, are important economic data obtained by household surveys.

   Location surveys are made at sites on trips, such as in-flight surveys,
exit surveys, entry surveys, and highway counts. These surveys cover one
visit and may relate to the entire trip or only to the site experience. Data
may be obtained on expenditures, activity participation, opinions and
attitudes, as well as socioeconomic status of travelers.

   Business surveys approach travel from the other side—the supply side.
Surveys of travelers in hotels and at theme parks can reveal many important facts about such visitors. Sources of travelers, extent of visits, size of
parties, place of residence, socioeconomic characteristics, and modes of
travel are often measured.

   One of the most popular forms of traveler research has been measures
of economics (Frechtling 1987, 325). Nations, states, and communities
often wish to distinguish between expenditures of foreign and domestic

travelers. This is based on the concept of tourism as an export, creating economic impact only from new dollars coming from outside. *Direct observation* of expenditures is often used as a method but it is cumbersome and costly. Secondary effects are difficult to measure in this way. Estimation by a *simulation* model of key relationships is set up in equations and data are collected for basic impact. An elaborate equation has been established by the U.S. Travel Data Center for measuring economic importance of tourism in all states of the country. Frechtling identifies the following criteria for evaluating economic studies—relevance, coverage, efficiency, accuracy, and applicability.

As yet, economists have not agreed upon a standardized methodology for tourism research. Therefore, a reader of reports must be alert to definitions and scope, especially when comparing study results.

Forecasting of travel demand is desired by the planner but is one of the most difficult to accomplish. *Forecasting* is defined as the art of predicting the occurrence of events before they actually take place (Archer 1980, 5). As the uncertainties of travel increase—taste, policies, international currency exchange, and diversity of destinations—projections become less reliable. Because planners, developers, and promoters are in constant need for forecasting, the concept continues to occupy an important place in market evaluation. Although scientific research methods are used increasingly, forecasting as defined remains an art based on experience and judgment.

Uysal and Crompton (1985, 7) have provided helpful descriptions of qualitative and quantitative approaches to tourism forecasting of demand. Under qualitative approaches, three methods used by experts are described. *Traditional approaches* include review of survey reports to observe consistent trends and changes. Sometimes surveys within originating market sources are made to obtain the past history of travel as well as opinions of future trends. The *Delphi method* is an iterative type of research inquiry using opinion of knowledgeable experts. It consists of several iterations by a panel that responds to specific questions about trends. Each panel member is anonymous to one another. Of course this method relies heavily on the extent of expertise of the panel members and the influence of the director. But, it is a useful tool, especially when used alongside other measures of prediction. A *judgment-aided model* (JAM) uses a panel in face-to-face contact and debate to gain consensus on several scenarios of the future. Each scenario is based on a different set of assumptions, such as political factors, economic tourism development, promotion, and transportation.

Among quantitative approaches, Uysal and Crompton describe three kinds. *Time series* studies are often statistical measures repeated year after year. Here it is assumed that all variables are working equally over time. In order to reflect changes in influential variables, transfer function models have been developed but involve complex mathematical and statistical techniques. *Gravity and trip generation models* assume that the number of visits from each origin is influenced by factors impinging upon those origins. The primary factors are distance and population. Some researchers criticize gravity models on the basis of not reflecting price, not accounting for shrinking of distance perception by new modes of transportation, and other difficult variables. *Multivariate regression models* allow the use of many variables in predicting travel. Income, population, travel cost, international context, and other variables can be introduced.

This brief discussion is offered only to suggest that much experimentation of methods for forecasting demand is taking place. Some quantitative and statistical approaches can provide clues to future tourist flows. Although professional market analysis may be required for major planning projects, less complicated study by local people can be productive. As a guide, the Western Australian Tourism Commission has issued an excellent self-help publication, *Tourism Research for Non-Researchers* (1985). In any case, understanding travel markets is essential to all planning for tourism development.

Market Segmentation

Until recently any tourist was considered like all other tourists and all planning and management strategies treated tourists as a homogeneous whole. As has been found in marketing other products, there is much merit to dividing the totality of tourists into groups with similarities.

Market segmentation has been defined by Pride (1983, 40) as "the process of dividing a total clientele into groups consisting of people who have relatively similar service needs." Generally, marketers suggest three basic conditions which should be met for segmentation. First, there must be great enough numbers in each segment to warrant special attention. Second, there must be sufficient similarity of characteristics within each group to give them distinction. Third, the subsets must be viable—worthy of attention. When planning for physical development, as well as assessing social, economic, and environmental impact, it should be very helpful to have segmented refinements of potential tourist groups who might travel to the area.

Earlier segmentation was directed toward grouping tourists by demographic characteristics—age, sex, income, ethnicity, stage in life cycle, and occupation. Generally, it has been found that grouping according to these characteristics has not been as useful as anticipated. While some extensive foreign vacations are relatively costly and require higher income markets, income is more of a limitation than a determinant. Many people with a wide diversity of incomes are found at tourism destinations. Even though ethnicity has not been widely researched, there seem to be similar traveler characteristics across several racial and national groups.

Ages of travelers have a bearing on what is developed. Ryan (1992, 135) points out that children constitute a significant segment of travelers. They influence the design of exhibits and educational programs and play an important role in adult satisfactions. One bracket that has increased in importance in the United States is the 50-plus traveler. Norvell (1986, 126) found that convention travel is just as popular with 50-plus travelers as with others. The 50-plus travelers are more likely to travel for entertainment, sightseeing, theater, historical sites, and shopping than for outdoor recreation. Regarding regional destination preference, there was little difference from other travelers. Older travelers tended to spend more time on trips but stay less frequently with friends and relatives than younger travelers. Athough the use of recreational vehicles (RVs) was greater among the 50-plus group, this use declined in favor of package tours over the age of 65. In 1984, the 50-plus traveler accounted for 30 percent of all domestic travel, 30 percent of all air trips, 32 percent of all hotel/motel nights, and 72 percent of all RV trips. Continuing research on age segmentation will be of value in planning destination and site development.

One of the best summaries of tourist market segmentation is that prepared for use in Canada. Seven categories of travel market segments are described and brief comments are offered regarding their effectiveness in tourism planning and promotion (Table 2-1) (*Marketing* 1986)

Another approach that may have value to planners of tourism development is segmenting markets by expenditures (Spotts and Mahoney 1991). A study of 2,732 travelers in Michigan's Upper Peninsula revealed a strong correlation between expenditures and choice of lodging, information sources used, length of stay, recreational activities in natural resource areas, and comparative volume of visitors (much greater volume among higher spenders).

Anthropologist V. L. Smith (1992) has put forth a possible distinction between the *pilgrim* and the *tourist*. Pilgrimages, travel with primary religious motivations, have become especially significant worldwide in recent years. Nolan and Nolan (1989) described pilgrimages in three categories: centers of interest for religious tourism; shrines; and events related to religion, folklore or ethnicity. Other scholars have documented the many

TABLE 2-1
TRAVEL MARKET SEGMENTS

1. Purpose of Trip/Use Segmentation
   Pleasure travel
   Personal business
   Other business
   Conventions/meetings
   Tournaments/sports groups

   ● This is usually the most effective segmentation approach because the target market is actively seeking a specific kind of product.

2. Channel of Distribution Segmentation
   Direct customer sales
   Travel agents
   Tour operators
   Tour wholesalers
   Airlines
   Government marketing
   Regional/local tourism associations

   ● This approach is effective in further afield markets that cannot be reached directly at reasonable cost or where travel trade companies have a market that is closely matched.

3. Socioeconomic or Demographic Segmentation
   Age   Family life cycle
   Sex   Social class
   Education   Home ownership
   Income   Second home ownership
   Family size   Race or ethnic group
   Occupation

   ● This is a commonly used segmentation approach, since these segments are often easy to reach and information on them is usually available.

4. Product-related Segmentation
   Recreation activity
   Equipment
   Brand loyalty
   Benefit expectations
   Length of stay
   Transportation mode
   Experience preference
   Participation patterns

   ● These are difficult segments to reach, but they are well matched to the use of specific products

5. Psychographic Segmentation
   Personality traits
   Lifestyle
   Attitudes, interests, and opinions
   Motivations

   ● In tourism, this can be an effective segmentation approach, since tourism product use is extensive among certain psychographic groups. Also, many advertising media are segmented this way.

6. Geographic Segmentation
   Country
   State, province, and county
   Region
   Urban, suburban, and rural
   City size
   Population density

   ● This is the most common segmentation approach because these markets are clearly defined and accessible. It is often not an efficient approach, however, unless it is used in combination with other approaches.

7. Use Frequency/Seasonality Segmentation
   Heavy users
   Moderate users
   Infrequent users

   ● Data should be readily available on these customers, so this method is likely to be cost-effective.

Source: Marketing Management, 1986, 60

forms of travel pilgrimages today and throughout history. However, Smith (1992, 4) points out that secular tourist travel has become increasingly diffused with pilgrimage travel.

A generalized market segmentation, especially important to physical tourism planning, is by activities dependent upon development using *natural* or *cultural* resources. It has been the foundation for geographic assessment of destinations with tourism potential, as described in Chapter 5. Forbes and Forbes (1992, 141) emphasize special interest travel, such as adventure travel and ecotravel, as a growing segment. They characterize these travelers as interactive, highly involved, and interested in quality experiences, focusing on in-depth activities within destinations.

Planners and developers—public and private—must have current information on travel market characteristics in order to understand why, where, and what development is most appropriate.

Matching Supply with the Market

In order to satisfy this market demand, a nation, region, or community must be able to provide a variety of development and services—the supply side. How well this supply side matches the market is the key to reaching the ultimate in correct tourism development (Figure 2-1). Taylor (1980, 56) called this the market-plant match and his model is illustrated in Figure 2-2. He based the model on his observations in Canada that "the characteristics of tourism demand are changing rapidly and these changes outstrip the present ability of the plant to adjust and that a measurement system can be devised that will permit the plant to adapt to changing demands in a rational manner." Although the search for such a measurement system continues, there is fundamental logic in always striving for a balance between demand and supply. An Australian tourism research guide recommends steps for a gap analysis, determining the difference between what travel markets seek and what is provided for them in the region (Tourism Research 1985, 14).

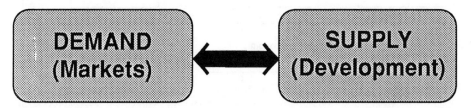

Figure 2-1. Demand-Supply Balance. The planning of tourism should strive for a balance between demand (market) and supply (development). This requires an understanding of market characteristics and trends as well as the process of planning development to meet market needs.

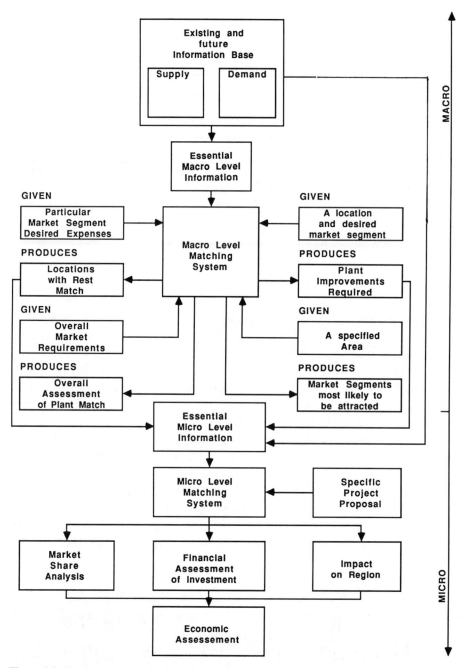

Figure 2-2. Plant-Market Match Model. This macro-micro systems model of planning is directed toward matching appropriate supply development with market segment demand. Such a process can reveal needed development projects (Taylor 1980, 58).

THE FUNCTIONING SYSTEM

One can take this demand-supply balance one step further by identifying components of the *supply side* and their relationship to demand as illustrated Figure 2-3. Although others may use different terms, this relationship is now described much the same as identified in Gunn (1972, 21). Leiper (1979) described the system in a similar manner with "tourist generating regions" connected to "tourist destination regions" by means of "transit routes." Boniface and Cooper (1987) called this a system of generating areas connected to destinations by routes traveled between these two sets of locations. No matter how it is labeled or described, tourism is not only made up of hotels, airlines, or the so-called tourist industry but rather a system of major components linked together in an intimate and interdependent relationship. This model is one way of describing the *functioning tourism system.*

The Supply Side

The supply side includes all those programs and land uses that are designed and managed to provide for receiving visitors. Again, these are under the control of all three sectors—private enterprise, nonprofit orga-

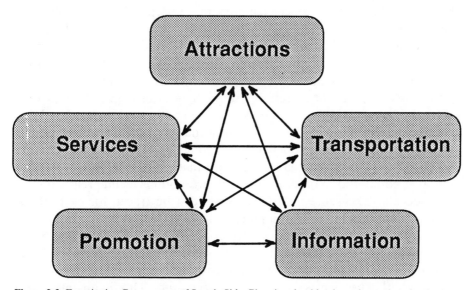

Figure 2-3. Functioning Components of Supply Side. Planning should strive to interrelate development of all components of the supply side of tourism. Developers and managers within each component include all three sectors—commercial enterprise, nonprofit organizations, and governments. This model emphasizes the dynamic relationship requiring regular monitoring. Change in any component influences all the others.

nizations, and governments. For purposes of planning, the supply side could be described as including five major components, as shown in Figure 2-3. Although others have described these with different labels, it is generally agreed that these represent the supply side of tourism. Jafari (1982, 2) refers to these as the "market basket of goods and services, including accommodations, food service, transportation, travel agencies, recreation and entertainment, and other travel trade services." Murphy (1985, 10) also includes similar components of the supply side. Mill and Morrison (1985, 2) combine attractions and services into a destination component. Focusing on community tourism, Blank (1989, 6) combines transportation, communications, attractors, services, and other community components for the supply side. But, no matter how they are labeled, these are the components that *together* make up tourism supply. (A more detailed description of these components is contained in Chapter 3.

Implications

For all three decisionmaking sectors, there are several important implications when these supply components are understood as operating in a system. First, all components are *interdependent*. For example, a hotelier—a member of the services component—is dependent upon planning decisions made in all other components. Transportation is critical. Airline price changes or bankruptcy, highway rerouting, and changes in fuel price can dramatically influence hotel success. Equally influential is the addition or demise of a major attraction. A river impoundment that creates new opportunity for outdoor recreation, a major new museum, or a new convention center could greatly increase the volume of visitors needing lodging. The accessibility and quality of informational literature—attraction location, admission fees, open hours—could greatly influence whether visitors come to the area near the hotel. Finally, the effectiveness of promotion as compared to other destination promotions could greatly impact hotel success. The same interdependency can be traced for each of the other components and all development within each. Promotion, for example, cannot be productive if the attractions or services are inadequate. Each individual within each component is critically influenced by individual plans, development, and operation within the other components.

Second, the tourism system is very *dynamic*. This is an important dimension of interdependency. Changes are continually taking place not only within each component but also between supply and demand. Perhaps this is the greatest factor making tourism planning so difficult. Few planners, developers, or managers today are monitoring changes in each component or maintaining data on trends.

Third, the system is *difficult to manage*. It is owned, developed, and managed by thousands of separate actors within the three developer sectors. In the United States, over 50 federal agencies and hundreds of state agencies own and manage parks, reserves, and cultural areas of significance in attracting tourists. Hundreds of nonprofit organizations own and develop land important to tourism. Add to this the great number of businesses involved in tourism and it becomes clear that the tourism system is not under single management control. It should not be implied here that such a control would be desirable; quite the contrary. But, it is a basic principle—the complexity of ownership and control—that demands special cooperation on planning and processes.

Fourth, each component, and every actor within it, is dependent upon the characteristics of the *market*. Tourism markets are much more capricious than local retail markets. Tourists are much more mobile and have a much greater diversity of destination opportunities. For example, for a traveler located in New York, a small price differential could cause a switch in travel plans from the western United States to Europe. Conversely, internal conflict or war in a destination could remove it from consideration, bringing another one at an entirely different part of the world into equal competition.

These and other implications of the tourism system must be taken into consideration when tourism plans are laid.

EXTERNAL FACTORS

Such a core of functioning components is greatly influenced by many external factors (Figure 2-4). Planning cannot be concerned solely with the core only because all sectors may be as subject to outside influences as those inside their own control. Several factors can have great influence on how tourism is developed. A brief examination of these may help in understanding the complicated reality of tourism, critical to planning the proper functioning of the tourism system.

Natural Resources

The popular emphasis on tourism economics and businesses tends to divert attention from very important foundations for tourism development. Again, the *causes* of travel to a destination are grounded in the destina-

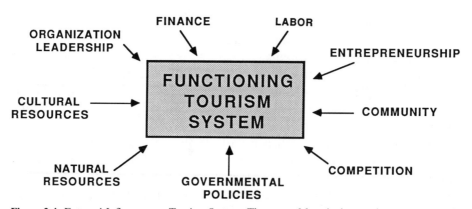

Figure 2-4. External Influences on Tourism System. The core of functioning tourism components is influenced greatly by several external factors: organization, leadership, finance, labor, entrepreneurship, community, competition, governmental policies, natural resources, and cultural resources.

tion's resources, natural and cultural, and the attractions that relate to them. Even destinations such as Walt Disney World that seemingly are contrived and unrelated to the resource base, in fact benefit greatly from it. Nearby Orlando and its surrounding area have many complementing attractions—art museums, a science center, a 72-building historic district, Lake Eola, wildfowl (ducks, geese, herons, anhingas, cormorants, and moorhens), Leu Botanical Gardens, Florida Audubon Society Center for Birds of Prey, Bok Tower Gardens, and Wekiwa Springs State Park (Whitman 1992). Natural and cultural resources identify the uniqueness of place, very important to travelers and their objectives. Even a cursory review of publicity and advertising of travel today demonstrates the high value that promoters place on attractions related to natural resources. Generally, the term *natural resources* refers to five basic natural features: water, topographic changes, vegetation, wildlife, and climate. Table 2-2 summarizes the relationships between these factors and tourism development.

Outdoor recreation has been a major travel purpose for many years. Although promoted primarily for its health and social values, outdoor recreation is very important to tourism economics. For example, a study in Texas (Texas Parks and Wildlife 1984, 6) revealed that Texas travelers spend approximately $9 billion annually on only 20 outdoor recreation activities. Critical, then, for future tourism development is the location and quality of the natural resources that support these activities sought by travel markets.

Probably the most popularly developed natural resource for tourism is *water*. Surface water is magnetic and has appealed to travelers for many years, stimulating many kinds of waterfront development. Ancient fresco paintings of the Egyptian dynasties include generous illustrations of

TABLE 2-2
TOURISM DEVELOPMENT RELATED TO NATURAL RESOURCES

Resource	*Typical Development*
Water	Resorts, campgrounds, parks, fishing sites, marinas, boat cruises, river float trips, picnic areas, water scenic areas, shell collecting areas, water festival sites, waterfront areas, scuba diving sites, water photographic sites
Topography	Mountain resorts, winter sports areas, mountain climbing, hang gliding areas, parks, scenic sites, glacier sites, plains, ranch resorts, scenic drives, vista photography
Vegetation	Parks, campgrounds, wildflower sites, autumn foliage areas, scenic overlooks, scenic drives, vacation homes, scenic photography sites, habitat for wildlife
Wildlife	Nature centers, nature interpretive centers, hunting, wildlife observation, wildlife photographic sites, hunting resorts
Climate	Sites suited to sunbathing, beach use, summer and winter resorts, sites with temperature and precipitation suited to specific activity development

water's attractiveness. Brittain (1958, 124) has aptly stated that in addition to commerce and defense, historically, water

> . . . drew men together in common pleasures, strengthening, no doubt, a sense of individual participation in a larger life that enhances neighbors and strangers, and even foreigners from distant lands wearing their exotic clothes and clacking away in incomprehensible languages.

Reflection pools, ponds, fountains, rivers, lakes, waterfalls, and the seas continue to provide appeals that have no substitute. The appeal of water to both residents and visitors is bound up in cultures throughout the world. "We still like to go beachcombing, returning to primitive act and mood. When all the lands will be filled with people and machines, perhaps the last need and observance of man will be, as it was at the beginning, to come down and experience the sea" (Sauer 1967, 310–311). It is for its great value to tourism that water quality and its protection must be seen by all sectors as absolutely essential to tourism's success—economically as well as socially and environmentally.

Historically, and even today, *topography*—hills, mountains, and valleys—provides the physical setting for much of tourism. Land relief is an essential ingredient in contemporary culture's assessment of landscape scenery, now heightened by the boundless popularity of photography. Hillsides and mountaintops offer spectacular vistas, near and far. Mountain resorts, winter and summer, retain their appeal for contemporary travel market segments. Related to topography soils are of significance to tourism development—construction stability, landscape modification, and erodability. Because some mountainsides and slopes are highly erodible, resource protection must be part of the catechism of tourism development. Also related is the geological foundation, often influencing the stability of land and lakes, the absorptive capacity of sewage, and the reliability of water supply.

For many kinds of tourism development, from the tundra of the north to the rainforests of the tropics, *vegetative cover* is an important natural resource for tourism development. While deserts may have some appeal to tourists, much more popular are verdant landscapes. Forests create appealing scenic vistas, support wildlife, offer dramatic panoramas of color in autumn, and aid greatly in preventing soil erosion. Often special plant areas (redwoods, the Big Thicket, silverswords in Hawaii, Michigan jack pine for Kirtland warbler) are singularly important in travel destinations for some market segments. Wildflowers are spectacularly attractive in forests in the North and over open fields in the South in springtime. But, forested and vegetated regions are extensive and are subject to varying policies by owners and managers. Some timber harvest practices, such as clear-cutting, destroy landscape scenery and stimulate soil erosion. Vegetation is dynamic; trees sprout, grow, and die, and may be damaged by disease and fire. Management for tourism requires special policies and practices if vegetative resources are to maintain their value to tourism.

Once primarily of interest only to travel segments interested in game hunting, *wildlife* today is even of greater importance for nonconsumptive tourist markets. Viewing and photographing wildlife have grown significantly in recent years. It is estimated that about $18 billion was spent by travelers on wildlife watching in the United States in 1991 (USFWS 1992, 7). Photo safaris are far more important today in Africa than hunting ever was. Color slides and videos are becoming important tourist trophies. Animal habitat management is necessary if the resource is to continue for tourism. Some wildlife is extremely sensitive to human intrusions, requiring special design and management techniques if visitors are to be enriched by this resource. Tourism developers are dependent upon environmental protection of wildlife.

Climate and weather are qualities of place that greatly influence the planning and development of tourism. Travelers generally prefer sunny weather even in winter sports areas and certainly for beach activities. For example, for many of the national parks of the United States, peak visitation occurs during sunniest weather. Some northern countries, such as Canada, do not try to promote travelers seeking sunny and warm beaches but other attractions more appropriate to their climate. Without doubt, climate plays an important role for the popularity of the Hawaiian and Caribbean islands. There is little evidence to suggest that storm hazards—

lightning, tornadoes, and hurricanes—have more than a temporary impact on travel. In fact, some fishing in the Gulf of Mexico is stimulated during periods of hurricanes. Related to climate are conditions of air quality. Although air quality controls are lessening air pollution in some parts of the world, travelers object to areas where odor, manufacturing gases, and automobile pollution are prevalent.

This brief review should be sufficient to endorse the need for vigorous natural resource protection advocacy for all tourism sponsors and developers in order for the tourism system to function at its best.

Cultural Resources

In recent years, several travel market segments have increasingly sought destinations with abundant cultural resources. This category of resource base includes prehistoric sites; historic sites; places of ethnicity, lore, and education; industries, trade centers, and professional centers; places for performing arts, museums, and galleries; and sites important for entertainment, health, sports, and religion. Examples of development related to cultural resources are shown in Table 2-3.

Peterson's research (1990, 209) categorized cultural travelers as aficionados (sophisticated, professional), casual visitors (urban backyard visitors), event visitors (activities at sites), and travel tourists (historic site visitors). She cited three reasons for visiting cultural sites: experiencing a different time or place, learning, and sharing knowledge with others. A major international conference on cultural and heritage tourism (Hall and Zeppel 1990, 55) concluded that in spite of the surge of interest within the travel market, there are major gaps in planning and operation of such attractions. Also stressed was the need for greater public-private cooperation. (Twenty papers presented at the ICOMOS conference are contained in "Cultural Heritage and Tourism," (1990) *Historic Environment*, (7): 3–4.) The field of cultural resources spans virtually all resources except those that can be called natural.

The travel market interest in *prehistory*, such as archeology, has stimulated development of these resources for visitors. Locations where scientists are discovering structures and artifacts of ancient peoples are of increasing interest among travelers. Nautical archeology (discovery and analysis of ancient ship transport and ways of life) is becoming as important as terrestrial archeological digs. But, because of their rarity, these sites must be under rigid control to prevent their destruction by visitors. Archeologists emphasize the fact that the context (relationship to setting and other artifacts) is more important than the artifact. Documentation

TABLE 2-3
TOURISM DEVELOPMENT RELATED TO CULTURAL RESOURCES

Resource	Typical Development
Prehistory, Archeology	Visitor interpretive centers, archeological digs, prehistory parks and preserves, nautical archeological sites, festival sites related to prehistory, exhibits and customs related to prehistory
History	Historic sites, historic architecture, historic shrines, museums depicting eras of human history, cultural centers, historic pageants, festivals, landmarks, historic parks
Ethnicity, Lore, Education	Places important to legends and lore, places of ethnic importance (customs, art, foods, dress, beliefs), ethnic and national cultural centers, pageants, festivals, dude ranches, gardens, elderhostels, universities
Industry, Trade, Professionalism	Manufacturing and processing plants, retail and wholesale businesses, conference centers, educational and research institutions, convention centers, performing arts, museums, galleries
Entertainment, Health, Religion, Sports	Spas, health centers, fitness resorts, health specialty restaurants, religious meccas, shrines, sports arenas, night clubs, gaming casinos, theaters, museums (history, art, natural history, applied science, children's, folk), art galleries

of what these clues suggest for ancient peoples—dates, foods, and customs—is more important than collecting. Special design and management, such as interpretive visitor centers and museums, are needed to handle volumes of visitors to prehistoric sites.

Popular literature and films have heightened traveler interest in *historic* areas. Even though every place has a history, places of local significance are of less interest to visitors than those of state, provincial, national, or world importance. Generally governmental agencies and nonprofit organizations have been the leaders in preserving, restoring, and developing sites important to history. The topic of history deals with the documented past. For tourism, sites, structures, and events related to places are the foundations for historic attractions. As with archaeological sites, historic sites require very special control, design, and management so that the resource is protected at the same time visitors gain historic appreciation and enriching experiences. It is important for tourist businesses to support the development and maintenance of historic sites because they stimulate the market for services.

For discussion purposes, places important for *ethnicity*, *lore*, and *education* have been grouped together as a category of cultural resource foundations for tourism development. Travel interest in the exotic and special customs, foods, costumes, arts, and entertainment of ethnic groups continues to rise. As an example, 42 percent of the visitors to South Dakota want to see Indians (Mills 1991). Because native resources are rooted in the past, they are prone to disappear because of the social and economic desire of localities to progress and modernize. Many cultural organizations have established programs to protect early cultural elements, and special design and management is required to develop such places for tourism. For example, Barry Parker, executive director, First Nations Tourism Association of Canada has identified goals and objectives for organization (Parker 1991, 11):

Goals:
  To position native tourism business as a major player in the Canadian tourism industry.
  To preserve, protect and promote cultural uniqueness in the tourism industry.
  To facilitate growth in the Canadian native tourism industry.
Objectives:
  Communications—to enhance image/perception by establishing a data base and networking system.
  Human resource development—to coordinate national level training to ensure cultural integrity through standards, quality, certification.
  Advocacy—to influence policy development at the federal, provincial and territorial levels.
  Marketing—to develop a national marketing strategy.

Close cooperation with ethnic groups is essential in order to avoid misinterpretation that may demean a past society. Often legends and lore are as important to visitors as true ethnic culture. Universities, colleges, technical institutions, and research centers are of interest to many travelers but require special access, exhibits, and tour guidance for tourism.

Travel objectives of *industry*, *trade*, and *professionalism* continue to be very important for several travel segments, and are often combined with pleasure. Manufacturing and processing plants are not only of interest to business travelers but also to pleasure travelers if the sites provide tours, facilities, and services for visitors. Trade and business centers are important cultural sites for many travelers. Places that establish meeting services and convention centers are attracting many travelers for professional and technical seminars, meetings, and conventions. Many areas are major tourist objectives because of the diversity of shops. Shopping is a very important activity for many travelers.

Places for *performing arts, museums, and galleries* are very important for many travelers. Tighe (1988) cites many examples of the significance of cultural tourism. Aspen, Colorado, known primarily for its skiing, also hosts over 55,000 people annually for a music festival and other performing arts activities. The Spoleto Festival of Charleston, South Carolina, holds 125 performances a year with over 90,000 in attendance. The Port Authority of New York-New Jersey reports arts institutions contribute $5.6 billion annually to the economy. In all instances, a high percentage of attenders are tourists. United States Travel and Tourism Administration's in-flight surveys have indicated that about 27 percent of all overseas visitors to the United States went to an art gallery or museum and some 21 percent went to a concert, play, or musical. In 1984 the Los Angeles Olympic Arts Festival drew 1,276,000 people.

Finally cultural resources also include places that provide for *entertainment*, *health*, *sports*, and *religion*. Health spas, centers for physical fitness, weight reduction, and special medical treatment become travel objectives for many travelers. Sports arenas throughout the world attract millions of visitors to special events such as the Olympic Games. Some communities are known as centers for certain religious groups. Others attract many visitors because of their cultural resources such as gaming casinos, music halls, opera houses, and night clubs.

Entrepreneurship

Because tourism is dynamic, entrepreneurs are needed who visualize opportunities for new developments and creative ways of managing existing developments. The ability to see an opportunity, to obtain needed financing, to obtain the proper location and sites, to engage designers to create physical settings, and to gather the human resources needed to manage the physical plant and services is important for travel development. For industrialized nations, entrepreneurship is a part of the culture. It is known that the lack of this factor in many underdeveloped countries is a major handicap that increases the difficulty of creating and expanding tourism.

Finance

Certainly, capital is required for the development of tourism. But, the ease of obtaining the financial backing for tourism varies greatly. Public and private lenders are often skeptical and have a negative image of the financial stability of tourism. Because so much of the tourism physical plant is small business and has attracted many inexperienced developers, some of this reputation is justified. However, recent trends have demanded much greater business sophistication and higher capital investment. Tourism takes considerably more capital than is popularly believed. Investors are more likely to support projects that demonstrate sound feasibility. Financial backing is an important factor for both public and private tourism development.

Labor

The availability of adequately trained workers in an area can have considerable influence on tourism development. As markets demand higher levels of service, well-trained and competent people are in greater need. The popular view that the untrained can perform all tasks needed in the diversity of tourism development is false. When the economic base of any area shifts, those taken out of employment may be retrainable but are not truly available for tourism jobs unless such training is provided. Remote locations become more costly for development because employees must be housed on site. The labor capacity of an area has much to do with tourism development.

Competition

The freedom to compete is a postulate of the free enterprise system. If a business can develop and offer a better product, it should be allowed to do so in order to satisfy market demand. However, before an area begins tourism expansion it must research the competition—what other areas can provide the same opportunities with less cost and with greater ease? Is there evidence that tourism plant has already saturated a market segment? Certainly, competition is an important influence upon the tourism system.

Community

A much more important factor influencing tourism development than has been considered in the past is the attitude toward tourism by the several community sectors. While the business sector may favor greater growth of tourism, other groups of the local citizenry may oppose it on the grounds of increased social, environmental, and economic competition for resources and other negative impacts. Political, environmental, religious, cultural, ethnic, and other groups in an area can make or break the proper functioning of the tourism system.

Governmental Policies

From federal to local governing levels, statutory requirements may foster or hinder tourism development. How the laws and regulations are administered—loosely or rigidly—can influence the amount and quality of tourism development. Policies on infrastructure by public agencies may favor one area over another. The policies of the many departments and bureaus can have a great bearing on how human, physical, and cultural resources are utilized. Smooth or erratic functioning of the tourism system is greatly influenced by governmental policies.

Organization and Leadership

Only recently being recognized is the great need for leadership and organization in tourism development. All planning is subject to implementation by many sectors. Many areas have hired consultants to plan for tourism opportunities but frequently such plans for development have not materialized for lack of organization and leadership.

Without doubt, as tourism development research and experience broadens, more influential factors will be found. Any planning for tourism in the future must take into account the core of the tourism functional system and the many factors influencing it.

CONCLUSIONS

Every stakeholder of tourism will *gain*, not lose, by making plans in the context of tourism as a system. Governmental agencies can gain because their plans and decisions on parks, highways, infrastructure, and promotion will be more supportive of development by the other sectors. As capitalistic and market economies grow, privatization can be integrated to a higher degree with public agency activities. Nonprofit organization development of tourism can fulfill goals and objectives more successfully if it is designed and managed in the context of the overall tourism system. Certainly, the business sector of tourism will benefit greatly when it takes advantage of the complementary action by the other two sectors. And, finally, the tourist and the travel experience, the true product and purpose of all tourism development, will gain because the system is working in greater harmony. Travelers benefit when all parts of all supply side components make their travels easier, more comfortable, and more rewarding. Difficult and challenging as system planning for tourism may be, it holds promise of the greatest rewards for everyone. All parts depend upon one another for smoothest functioning. By considering tourism functions as a system, several conclusions can be drawn.

Markets, as well as supply, drive tourism development.

Critical to all tourism development and its planning are the many characteristics of travelers' tourism demands. All physical development and programs must meet the interests and needs of travelers. If not, economic rewards may not be obtained, the environment may be eroded, and local conflict may ensue. Planning for visitor interests can ameliorate or prevent these negative impacts. All sectors seeking improved tourism must be fully cognizant of market characteristics and trends.

Supply development must balance demand.

All sectors involved in the development of the supply side of tourism should strive toward meeting the desires and needs of the travel market. Whenever demand and supply are out of balance, planning and development should be directed toward improving the supply-demand match. Only through analysis of both demand and supply can a region, destination, or site know how to plan. All supply side components—attractions, transportation, services, information, and promotion—must be planned and developed to meet the needs of markets.

Supply side components are owned and managed by all three sectors.

Supply side development is not exclusively under control of the business sector. All five major components of supply—attractions, transportation, services, information, and promotion—are created and managed by governments and nonprofit organizations as well as business. This means that for tourism to function properly, planning should integrate policies and actions by all three sectors.

Supply side components are interdependent and dynamic.

Successful development within any component is dependent on action within all other components. Because changes in demand and supply continue to take place, the system is dynamic, not static. Therefore, constant monitoring of demand and all five components of supply is essential to planning successful tourism. Every developer must be aware of this dynamic relationship.

The tourism system requires integrated planning.

Even though private and independent decisionmaking are cherished by most enterprises in all tourism sectors, each will gain by better understanding the trends and plans by others. The public sector can plan for better highways, water supply, waste disposal, parks, and other amenities when private sector plans for attractions and services are known. Conversely, the private sector can plan and develop more effectively when public sector plans are known.

External factors impinge on the functioning of the tourism system.

The tourism system does not operate in an isolated manner. Several factors need to be analyzed and worked into plans for best future operation of the system. These external factors include: natural resources, cultural resources, entrepreneurship, finance, labor, competition, community, governmental policies, and organization and leadership.

Business success depends on resources and their protection.

Tourist business enterprises are as dependent upon natural and cultural resources as internal management. Good business practice is not the only cause of travel. Equally important are the attractions nearby that, in turn, depend primarily on basic natural and cultural assets. Without protection, restoration, and visitor development of these assets, business cannot thrive.

Tourist business location depends upon two markets.

All tourist businesses gain revenues from sales of products and services to local as well as travel markets. Therefore, their business operations, and especially site locations, must be planned to serve both markets. It is important for all community planning to recognize this fundamental for best economic input.

REFERENCES

Archer, Brian H. (1980). "Forecasting Demand: Quantitative and Intuitive Techniques." *Tourism Management,* 1(1), 5–12.

Blank, Uel (1989). *The Community Tourism Industry Imperative: The Necessity, The Opportunities, Its Potential.* State College, PA: Venture.

Boniface, Brian G., and Christopher P. Cooper (1987). *The Geography of Travel and Tourism.* London: Heinemann.

Brittain, Robert (1958). *Rivers, Man and Myths.* Garden City: Doubleday.

Chadwick, R. A. (1987). "Concepts, Definitions and Measures Used in Travel and Tourism Research." In *Travel, Tourism and Hospitality Research,* Chapter 5, pp. 47–66. New York: John Wiley & Sons.

Department of Environment and Planning, Adelaide, South Australia. (1990). "Cultural Heritage and Tourism." *Historic Environment,* (7), 3–4.

Forbes, Robert J., and Maree S. Forbes (1992). "Special Interest Travel." *World Travel and Tourism Review,* pp. 141–144. Oxon, UK: C.A.B. International.

Frechtling, Douglas C. (1987). "Assessing the Impacts of Travel and Tourism— Introduction to Travel Impact Estimation." In *Travel, Tourism, and Hospitality Research,* Chapter 27, pp. 325–332. New York: John Wiley & Sons.

Gunn, Clare A. (1972). *Vacationscape: Designing Tourist Regions.* Austin: Bureau of Business Research, University of Texas.

Hall, C. M., and Heather Zeppel (1990). "History, Architecture, Environment: Cultural Heritage and Tourism." *Journal of Travel Research,* 29(2) Fall, 54–55.

Jafari, Jafar (1982). "The Tourism Market Basket of Goods and Services." In *Studies in Tourism, Wildlife, Parks, Conservation,* Tej Vir Singh et al. (eds.). New Delhi: Metropolitan.

Leiper, N. (1979). "The Framework of Tourism." *Annals of Tourism Research,* 6(1), 390–407.

Marketing, Management (1986). (Marketing management program, Maclean Hunter Ltd.) Toronto: Canadian Hotel and Restaurant.

Mill, Robert Christie, and Alastair Morrison (1985). *The Tourism System.* Englewood Cliffs, NJ: Prentice-Hall.

Mills, R. (1991). "The U.S.A. Experience," presentation, National Native Tourism Conference, Winnipeg, Manitoba, May 22–23.

Murphy, Peter (1985). *Tourism: A Community Approach*. New York: Methuen.

Nolan, Mary Lee, and Sidney Nolan (1989). *Christian Pilgrimage in Modern Western Europe*. Chapel Hill: University of North Carolina Press.

Norvell, H. "Outlook for Retired/Older Traveler Market Segments." *1985–1986 Outlook for Travel and Tourism*, (1986) proceedings of the 11th Annual Travel Outlook Forum. Washington, DC: U.S. Travel Data Center.

Parker, Barry (1991). Proceedings of the National Native Tourism Conference, Winnipeg, Manitoba, May 22–23.

Peterson, K. I. (1990) "The Heritage Resource as Seen by the Tourist: The Heritage Connection," proceedings of the 21st Annual Conference, Travel and Tourism Research Association, pp. 209–215. Salt Lake City: Bureau of Business and Economic Research.

Pride, W. M. and O. C. Ferrell (1983). *Marketing: Basic Concepts and Decisions*. Boston: Houghton Mifflin.

Ryan, Chris (1992). "The Child as a Visitor." *World Travel and Tourism Review*, pp. 135–139. Oxon, UK: C.A.B. International.

Sauer, Carl O. (1967). "Seashore—Primitive Home of Man. In *Land and Life*, John Leighly (ed.). Berkeley: University of California Press.

Smith, V. L. (1992). "Introduction: The Quest in Guest." *Annals of Tourism Research*, 19, 1–17.

Spotts, D. M., and Edward M. Mahoney (1991). "Segmenting Visitors to a Destination Region Based on the Volume of Their Expenditures." *Journal of Travel Research*, 29 (4) Spring, 24–31.

Taylor, G. D. (1980). "How to Match Plant with Demand: A Matrix for Marketing." *Tourism Management*, 1 (1) March, 56–60.

Texas Parks and Wildlife Department (1984). *1983 Outdoor Recreation Trips Expenditures in Texas*. Austin: Texas Parks and Wildlife Department.

Tighe, A. J. (1988). "The Arts and Tourism: A Growing Partnership." In *1988 Outlook Forum for Travel and Tourism*, pp. 247–252. Washington, DC: U.S. Travel Data Center.

Tourism Research for Non-Researchers (1985). Perth: Western Australian Tourism Commission.

U.S. Fish and Wildlife Service (1992). *1991 National Survey of Fishing, Hunting & Wildlife Associated Recreation*. Washington, DC: USFWS.

Uysal, M., and J. L. Crompton (1985). "An Overview of Approaches Used to Forecast Tourism Demand." *Journal of Travel Research*, 23 (4) Spring, 7–14.

Whitman, S. (1992). "Discovering the Real Orlando." *Rotarian*, 160 (3) March, 28+.

Chapter 3

Components of Supply

Introduction

When nations speak of wanting to increase investment in tourism, they are making a sincere but an ambiguous request. Such obscurity usually does not result in the desired development because it is not clear to investors and developers what is being requested. Plans should identify opportunities in all five components of supply. All sectors need to know how these components function and the main considerations involved in creating a more viable tourism system. Even though nations vary in their development levels, traditions, and political systems, all must deal with these components of supply if they seek to improve tourism.

Because planning tourism involves all the components in concert with each other, it is incumbent upon stakeholders to have current knowledge of these components. Hoteliers should be aware of trends in attractions, transportation, information, and promotion. Attraction developers must be aware of market trends as well as activity taking place in the other components of supply. So the following discussion is not meant to be exhaustive but rather to stimulate awareness of the major components of the supply side of tourism and their interdependence.

ATTRACTIONS

The attractions of a destination constitute the most powerful component of the supply side of tourism. They make up the energizing power unit of the tourism system. If the market provides the "push" of traveler movement, attractions provide the major "pull." Service businesses are facilitators, not major causes of travel. Without attractions, these services may not be needed except for local trade. Attractions provide two major functions. First, they *entice, lure, and stimulate* interest in travel. As people in their residential locations learn about attractions of destinations, they make decisions on those that appeal the most. Or, for business travel, the trade center, convention center, or industrial complex may provide the pulling power. Second, attractions *provide visitor satisfaction*, the rewards from travel—the true travel product.

Scope

Attractions are those developed locations that are planned and managed for visitor interest, activity, and enjoyment. Even though a destination may have an abundance of resources that are attractors, they are not functioning as true attractions until they are ready to receive visitors. Attractors and attractions have stimulated travel throughout the world for centuries.

Attractions are numerous and extremely diverse. One issue of a contemporary travel publication (Tours & Resorts 1992) includes: European universities for travel-study, beach resorts, casinos, marine parks, historic landmarks, tours of primitive tribes, Daytona beaches, Kennedy Space Center, Colonial Williamsburg, Chincoteague National Wildlife Refuge, Piazza San Marco (Venice), Camelback Mountain resort, the harp seal area in the Gulf of St. Lawrence, and many others. Another (European Travel & Life 1992) features: Victoria and Albert Museum (London), Côte des Blancs (France), Floriade (Netherlands), Finlandia Hall (Helsinki), Abruzzo (Italy), Parisian pastry shops, Rotes Rathaus (Berlin), British mazes, and Denali National Park (Alaska). Yet another publication (Travel Holiday 1992) highlights: Parc Guell (Barcelona), Stewart Island, Antarctica, Great Smoky Mountains National Park, Haleakala Crater (Hawaii), and many advertisements of tours, cruises, and historic sites.

Classifications

Although this potpourri of current attractions seemingly lacks any similarity or definition of help in planning, attractions could be classified in several ways. Such classification may be of assistance to individual enterprises and other stakeholders in tourism when they plan for the future. Offered here are three classifications.

Ownership. Attractions are owned and managed by all three sectors—government agencies, nonprofit organizations, and commercial enterprise. Table 3-1 lists examples of attractions classified by ownership.

Resource foundation. Attractions can be grouped according to the basic resource foundation, natural or cultural, as listed in Table 3-2.

TABLE 3-1
CLASSIFICATION OF ATTRACTIONS BY OWNERSHIP

Governments	Nonprofit Organizations	Business Sector
National parks	Historic sites	Theme parks
State parks	Festivals	Cruises
Wildlife reserves	Organization camps	Shopping centers
Scenic/historic roads	Elderhostels	Specialty food
Recreation areas	Historic architecture	Resorts
National monuments	Theaters	Golf courses
Wildlife sanctuaries	Gardens	Theaters
Zoos	Museums	Craft shops
Bike/hike trails	Parades	Plant tours
Sports arenas	Nature reserves	Race tracks

Touring/long stay. Although recent market trends have shown a striking reduction of time devoted to each trip, attractions could be classified by whether they are best adapted to touring circuit travel or long-stay in-place travel. Some examples are listed in Table 3-3.

Other classifications might be made, such as outdoor versus indoor, primary versus secondary, and market preference of activities.

TABLE 3-2
CLASSIFICATION OF ATTRACTIONS BY RESOURCE

Natural Resource Foundation	Cultural Resource Foundation
Beach resorts	Historic sites
Campgrounds	Archeological sites
Parks	Museums
Ski resorts	Ethnic areas
Cruises	Festivals
Golf courses	Medical centers
Nature reserves	Trade centers
Organization camps	Theaters
Bike/hike trails	Plant tours
Scenic roads	Convention centers

TABLE 3-3
CLASSIFICATION OF ATTRACTIONS BY TOURING/LONG STAY

Touring	Long Stay
Roadside scenic areas	Resorts
Natural areas	Organization campsites
Historic buildings, sites	Vacation home complexes
Specialty food places	Gaming centers
Shrines	Dude ranches
Zoos	Convention centers

Planning Considerations

Experience is demonstrating several planning considerations related to attractions. These are conceptual as well as based on research.

Attractions are created and managed. A popular error practiced by promoters of travel is listing attractive features prematurely. Until a site has been identified, designed, built, and managed for visitors, it cannot function as an attraction and should not be promoted. Historic homes as well as natural resource sites can be damaged greatly if hordes of visitors come too soon, needing parking, tours, and interpretation. Without proper design and management valuable assets may be eroded.

Attractions are places in which the entire array of physical features and services are provided for an assumed capacity of visitors. Again, market and supply are the two sides of tourism that require close examination for attraction planning. For whom are plans being made and what are their interests? What are the features most critical for the site and how can visitors gain an experience without undermining the resource? What design and operational techniques are appropriate for solving these questions? An estimate of peak visitor volume is essential to the planning of every feature of the attraction—parking, trails, walks, exhibits, lectures, toilet facilities, tour guidance, spectator seating, and possibly, food service and souvenir sales. The attractor may be the ecosystem, rare plant, landmark, or animal, but the attraction is a developed and managed entity.

Attractions gain by clustering. In today's mass tourism, the minor and isolated attraction requires too much time and effort by the visitor to reach that it is seldom worth it. Mass travel systems, such as fast trains, expressways, and air routes, necessitate stopping and walking before attractions can be enjoyed. Such a transportation factor supports the planning principle of having several attraction features in close proximity.

Attraction themes are best carried out when attractions are grouped together, physically or by tour (garden tours, historic tours, architectural tours, and cruises). National parks are examples of attraction clusters, offering many complementary nature attractions, such as beautiful scenery, hiking trails, wildlife conservation parks, challenging topographic features, and outdoor recreation sites. Winter sports resorts frequently contain a combination of attractions: snow and ice sports areas, cross-country ski trails, competitions, indoor entertainment, and sometimes summer attractions for greater revenue production.

Clustered attractions have greater promotional impact and are more efficiently serviced with infrastructure of water, waste disposal, police, fire protection, and power.

Attraction-services linkage is important. Attractions, although fulfilling a major portion of the travel experience, need support by travel services. Park plans, for example, are incomplete if the nonattraction needs of travelers are ignored. Food service, lodging, and supplementary services (purchases of film, drugs, and souvenirs) must be within reasonable time and distance reach of travelers. This fact has posed a policy and planning dilemma for park planners for quite some time. It suggests that many attractions need to be planned for day-use only, providing the majority of services in nearby communities where they can be serviced more efficiently and gain from local trade as well as travelers. More remote attraction features, however, may require minimum services within the attraction, such as food service, toilets, and visitor centers.

Attraction locations are both rural and urban. Rural areas and small towns have their own assets to support attraction development. Some market segments prefer the homeyness and less congestion of these areas. Table 3-4 lists some of the more popular tourist activities in rural areas and small towns (Gunn 1986, 2). Vernacular landscapes, such as farmsteads and rural scenic roads, demand special planning and control to assure scenic appeal in the future.

Urban locations are equally viable for tourism development of both cultural and natural resource attractions. Urban rivers, parks, and nature centers as well as museums, theaters, arenas, auditoriums, universities, convention centers, and industries are foundations for attractions. Often, urban and rural attractions can be planned with complementary themes and linked together with tours.

TABLE 3-4
TRAVELER ACTIVITIES IN RURAL AREAS

Picnicking	Canoeing
Camping	Cross-country skiing
Hiking	Swimming
Horseback riding	Resorting
Bicycling	Historic touring
Hunting	Rural festivals
Fishing	Scenic touring
Boating	Visiting friends/relatives
Waterskiing	Nature appreciation

SERVICES

Scope

Greatest economic impact from travel occurs through the travel service businesses. Accommodations, food service, transportation, travel agencies, and other travel businesses provide the greatest amount of employment, income, and taxes generated. This category is most frequently called the hospitality service industry. Economists point to not only the direct impact but the multiplier effect. For example, hotels, restaurants, and retail shops offer specific products and services. But, revenues received, in turn, provide economic support for contract food services, contract laundries, and indirect services such as housing, food, medical service, and transportation of employees.

Service Sponsorship

Fundamentally, commercial tourist services and facilities operate with the same purpose of all other business—to make a profit. However, there seems to be continuing misunderstanding of the term profits, some believing that in the tourism, recreation, and resource development field, profit making is evil. Many, especially those sponsoring government recreation and park areas, seek a more altruistic and expansive social responsibility from business. But first and foremost is the responsibility for private enterprise to remain economically viable. Such economic viability comes from profits, which in reality are costs of doing business. According to Drucker (1975),

> There is no conflict between "profit" and "social responsibility." To earn enough to cover the genuine costs which only the so-called "profit" can cover, is economic and social responsibility—indeed it is the specific social and economic responsibility of business. It is not the business that earns a profit adequate to its genuine costs of capital, to the risks of tomorrow and the needs of tomorrow's worker and pensioner, that "rips off" society. It is the business that fails to do so.

In a sense, all owner-managers of tourist services and facilities (governments as well as businesses) have similar ultimate goals: the satisfaction of needs of tourists. Crudely stated, a motel owner would not sell rooms if travelers did not arrive at that location seeking overnight accommodation. The businessperson has to be creative enough to develop the facility and service and offer it at a price acceptable to the public.

> It is the customer who determines what a business is. It is the customer alone whose
> willingness to pay for a good or a service converts economic resources into wealth,
> things into goods. . . . What the customer thinks he is buying, what he considers
> value is decisive—it determines what a business is, what it produces, and whether
> it will prosper. (Drucker 1973, 61)

For the planning of tourist services and facilities, it may be helpful to recognize differences among four types of ownership-management.

First, the *independent ownership* and managership, typical of the "mom-pop" category of business, operates on its own forms of personal enterprise policies—market segmentation, pricing, and range of services and facilities. One researcher (Bevins 1971, 3) found that the economics of operation among the small outdoor recreation owner-managers varied greatly according to their goals. He grouped them into three categories: (1) those who do not wish to maximize financial returns but are in business because of beliefs in conservation, recreational values for family members, or for retirees to keep busy; (2) those who seek supplementary incomes for unemployed or underemployed family labor and (3) those who seek the more typical economic goals of all business—revenues that will return on the investment. The trend of small tourist business continues to dominate in spite of the more conspicuous large and multinational firms.

Second, the *franchise, chain*, and other multiple establishment organizations have grown greatly in recent years. The advantages cited are greater marketing through single image and toll-free reservations, increased buying power, and uniform standards. Arrangements vary from those in which the properties (land and buildings) are owned and managed by company employees to those that are independent ownerships but agree to certain operational standards and advertising logos for promotional advantages. Best Western in 1975 became the largest organization of travel lodging in the world (Best Western 1976, 1). A popular mode is one like the Holiday Inns, that use similar design of buildings, central purchasing, uniform signs and logos, and uniform operational standards. Most of the inns are owned by local people who have a franchise arrangement with Holiday Inn.

Franchising, born in the United States, has promise for tourist service development elsewhere. It provides for local control but has the advantages of a larger organization. Experience has shown that there may be some difficulties in adapting franchising to other countries. Ashman (1986, 41) identified the difficulties of lack of understanding of the function of franchising, arbitrary governmental restrictions against it, labor requirements, property ownership laws, and quality control.

Franchising demands the proper balance between centralized control and unit management. Kaplan (1984, 20) cautioned the application of centralized manufacturing techniques to food service organizations. Too much decisionmaking at the top with few rewards to unit managers can divorce a company from the realities of consumers and service. Production speed, product quality, freshness, speed of service, and sales promotion, as well as administration and training of personnel, operations, and quality control are best handled at the unit level. The more successful franchise operations recognize the importance of unit level decisionmaking with adequate rewards at the same time efficiencies of large scale are obtained.

Third, *quasi-government* commercial operations, usually called concessions, are of increasing importance. In the United States many federal and state resource and land agencies have concession agreements with private businesses to provide services to the public on government land. Such services include hotels, motels, trailer and other camping facilities, restaurants, stores, service stations, and marinas. Reasons cited for a concession arrangement—private profit-making operation on government land—are:

1. Private investment and arrangement reduces the need for public financing.
2. Revenues can accrue to public agencies from concession operations.
3. Innovation and economy may result from management responsibility shared with the private sector.
4. Local economies may be strengthened through profit opportunities for the private sector.
5. Greater recreation opportunity for the public may result from the provision of facilities or services which the managing agencies could not provide.

At the same time, several barriers exist to limit greater use of concession arrangements on public lands:

1. Concession interests may conflict with the management purposes for the public lands.
2. Such businesses are highly seasonal and profits are affected substantially by weather conditions.
3. Concessioners do not hold title to the land, making loans difficult to secure and tenure uncertain.
4. Federal and state civil service regulations may create difficulties in contracting for personal service.
5. Inconsistent or shifting public policies create uncertainty for entrepreneurs.

6. A high degree of on-site supervision by the public agency is generally needed in order to ensure acceptable standards of public service. (Bureau of Outdoor Recreation 1973, 82)

Because each concession usually holds a monopoly as a business, it is not subject to the same competition as other businesses outside the control of the agency. Sometimes the political and managerial constraints can perpetuate bad service.

Fourth, *non-profit organizations,* such as youth clubs and churches, often own mess halls, lodging, and campground facilities with extremely varying policies. Some are of poor quality due to poor financing and incompetent management and depend solely on donations for support. Others are virtually palatial resorts that are profitable in the sense that the revenues far exceed their immediate operating expenses. Some are oriented to conservation-resource protection whereas others are strongly program oriented. Each depends upon the policies of its parent institution.

One area of contention between private enterprise and government is the problem of control. Participants of the public and private sector hearings of the U.S. National Tourism Policy Study (Senate Committee 1977, 30) cited several problems including time-consuming bureaucratic procedures, inadequate and unimaginative strategies for implementing programs, and a lack of continuity in implementing programs. The study found that:

> Participants felt that ineffective implementation of federal programs had exacerbated inadequacies in tourism development activities, (created) difficulties for small business survival, conflicts between environmental and developmental goals, energy constraints on development, and inadequacies in promotion of travel opportunities in the United States, both domestically and internationally. (p. 30)

Fundamentals of Free Enterprise

Throughout the world private businesses dominate the tourist services. The degree to which these are free enterprise depends upon the extent to which the free market system is not interrupted. It was the Scotsman Adam Smith who in 1776 in his *The Wealth of Nations* identified the basic principle of free enterprise as dependent on a *voluntary* exchange between buyer and seller. While pure free enterprise business may not exist, even in market-economy countries, the more it strives toward certain fundamentals, the more successful it is.

Allen et al. (1979) has identified the following five fundamentals as essential to a free enterprise economy.

1. Private Property. In a free enterprise system all property is owned by private individuals. This is based on several premises. First is the premise that individuals know best how to manage their property. The individual is believed to have a strong interest in not littering his property and conserving its resources because he is responsible for the consequences. The property owner has certain rights.

- The owner's right to determine how his property is used.
- The owner's right to transfer ownership to someone else.
- The owner's right to enjoy income and other benefits that come his way as a result of his ownership of the property.

2. Economic Freedom. By voluntarily cooperating with each other at the same time, individual interests are pursued and the freedom of individual choice is protected. No outside force, such as government, dictates this choice. The following rights are important but do not guarantee business success.

- The right to start or discontinue businesses.
- The right to purchase any resource they can pay for.
- The right to use any technology.
- The right to produce any product and to offer for sale at any price.
- The right to invest in any way.

The seller and buyer make a voluntary exchange. The market, by its own selection, tells the producer what to produce and at what price. Of course, total economic freedom must be conditioned by the rights of society as a whole.

3. Economic Incentives. When there are incentives to work efficiently and productively, business becomes more efficient and productive. Workers receive incentives through wages and other rewards for doing good work. Businesses receive their incentives through profits. The more productive and better a business meets market needs, the more profitable it usually becomes. However, punishments, in the form of business loss or failure, can come when the questions of what to produce and how to produce are not answered properly. For this system to function properly there must be a minimum of outside interference. Economic incentives serve to direct scarce resources to the production of goods and services that the market values the most.

4. Competitive Markets. In a free enterprise system, the individual can choose and people vary in their preferences. Preferences of markets are expressed to producers by means of what is purchased. This means that there must be competitive businesses rather than monopolies. Each business can then strive for its market share. If it becomes very profitable, it invites competitors who seek their market share through even better products or services. This competition stimulates greater efficiency and lower prices. Competition spreads the decision of what to produce over many producers rather than by governmental decree.

5. Limited Role of Government. The greatest role of government in a free enterprise system is to stimulate business freedom and provide only basic rules and regulations for the good of society. Governmental intervention in day-to-day economic decisionmaking is not part of a free enterprise system. It does not interfere with what or how to produce. Its role is to keep the system free and competitive.

At the same time that tourism has provided the opportunity for many entrepreneurs to create new travel-oriented service businesses, the field has been plagued with a high percentage of business failures. Some would argue that too many amateurs are attracted to these businesses. The business appears simple and glamorous to amateurs who soon become disillusioned by long hours, greater responsibilities, and less profits than anticipated (Lundberg 1979).

In order to remedy the tendency for excessive failures and poor service in many tourist businesses, educational programs at all levels have been provided worldwide. Governments and business associations provide guidelines for successful operations, such as *The Inn Business* (Minister 1982) produced by the Minister of Supply and Services Canada. The guide provides constructive information on pertinent topics, such as entering the business, planning and development, operation (staff, repairs, maintenance, marketing, and other sources of help). In the United States business advice and guidance is offered by agencies such as the Small Business Administration and U.S. Department of Agriculture's Cooperative Extension Service.

Planning Considerations

Service businesses for tourism have both traditional and special planning needs.

Location is influenced by two markets. All the businesses providing basic and supportive services for travelers also serve local resident markets. Because restaurants, shops, entertainment, and local transportation businesses receive much of their trade and revenues from residents as well as travelers, this fundamental influences location. Remote locations generally are much less successful compared to city and even small town locations.

Balanced economic base is more stable. When tourism and travel businesses provide the major economic input, the economy can fluctuate greatly with changes in travel markets. Industry and trade, combined with tourist businesses, provide the best balance of diversity.

Tourist businesses need urban infrastructure. Isolated locations require greater investment to provide for water supply, waste disposal, police, fire protection, and sometimes electrical power as compared to urban settings. This factor tends to encourage the location of lodging, food service, and other travel services in communities.

Service businesses gain from clustering. At one time, entrepreneurs believed that they should locate away from their competition. Today the prevailing belief is that food services or lodging accommodations are best adapted to traveler demand when grouped together. When the traveler begins to think of needing food service, it seems best to be located near other kinds of food services.

Fragile environments should be avoided. Care in location is essential to avoid damaging the very reason for providing a service. Too often, tourist businesses have been located too close to the water's edge or on sites that have important value for attractions—natural and cultural resource sites.

Services depend on attractions. Service business function is intimately related to attractions. Therefore, the business sector should cooperate on plans for increased development of attractions. Because so many attractions are based on natural and cultural resources, these businesses should exercise strong environmental protection advocacy.

Entrepreneurship is critical to tourism planning. Because of the dynamics of tourism, opportunities for innovative service businesses continue to appear. But, if a culture does not have a tradition of entrepreneurship, it may have difficulty in creating new businesses. There needs to be a volume of business people interested in and able to see opportunity, obtain a site, gather the financial support, plan, build, and operate a new business.

Small business continues to offer the greatest opportunities in spite of the many risks and obstacles.

TRANSPORTATION

Scope

Passenger transportation is a vital component of the tourism system. It provides the very critical linkage between market source and destination. Transportation between cities and attractions within urban areas and within attraction complexes requires special planning consideration. Except when touring is used as an attraction, transportation is not usually a goal; it is a necessary evil of tourist travel. Therefore, in the planning for tourism development, it is essential to consider all travel modes for movement of people throughout the circuit in order to reduce friction as much as possible.

In contrast to a person's work transportation, which usually employs only one mode, it is not unusual for a modern tourist to utilize several modes on one trip. Planning increasingly requires intermodal considerations. It is not unusual for a tourist to utilize air, automobile, taxi, cable car, and horse carriage (in a historic district) on one trip. Because the several modes are designed, built, and managed by many different owners, a great amount of confusion and uncertainty can upset the traveler. Probably the increased use of motorcoach and cruise ship tours is due to their handling of all transportation arrangements, thereby reducing confusion. Poorly understood is the role of pedestrian movement in tourism. Increased traffic management has solved mass movement of vehicles but often destroyed personal amenities in the process. Attractions and tourist service businesses do need access but the final, and most important, mode is on foot.

Planning Considerations

All owners and managers of tourist attractions and services have a critical stake in all transportation development policies and practices. Changes in routes, pricing, schedules, convenience, and interfacing between modes can foster or spell disaster for tourism. This issue is further complicated by the different needs of local as compared to long distance travelers. Some highway planners design routes and capacities for business commuting only. A few key planning considerations for the very important component of transportation follow.

The transportation sector must involve tourism implications in plans.
Because tourism has grown to major significance internationally, the transportation role must be strengthened. Modern engineering and technology
have greatly increased the quality of construction of highways, bridges,
airports, railways, and harbors. But, needed is closer input from tourist
service businesses and attraction leaders into the transportation decisionmaking process. Both can gain from greater integration.

Intermodal travel requires new planning cooperation. Tourist demand is
seldom directed toward a single transportation mode as created by business and government. Increased availability (price, scheduling, and airline
options) of air travel has introduced many more destination choices to the
prospective traveler. But access to the specific attractions and circulation
within a destination frequently put several other modes into play.
Increased popularity of package tours forces greater integration of travel
modes. If any one travel link fails to provide the quality of service desired,
the entire trip may be spoiled. The planning of intermodal transportation
centers is needed for domestic local, as well as outside, visitor markets.

Transportation is more than engineering planning. Greater sensitivity to
the human dimensions of travelers is required for transportation planning.
Finding one's way is increasingly complicated with freeways which tend to
disorient and isolate travelers from their objectives. Better signage and traveler information continues to present a planning challenge. The experience
of travel, especially on byways and rural routes, is often a part of the tourism
product. Scenic routes require special controls on adjacent land use.

New highway routing requires greater sensitivity to the environment.
Although highway design and planning techniques have advanced in
recent years, special care to protect natural and cultural resources is
needed. Although traveler access is very important, the building of a major
highway into virgin territory can drastically upset the local social and
physical environment. National park planners have experienced excessive
road kills of wildlife along improperly placed highways.

INFORMATION

Scope

An increasingly important component of the tourism system is traveler
information. Many public tourism agencies still confuse information with

promotion. Advertising is intended to attract whereas information is description—maps, guidebooks, videos, magazine articles, tour guide narratives, brochures, and traveler anecdotes.

Although much of the provision of information is outside the realm of physical planning, one form of traveler information linkage—the visitor center—is growing rapidly. As ecotourism evolves and as visiting historic sites increases, there is danger of environmental damage. A popular solution is the creation of major visitor centers where masses of tourists can be managed and where they can gain a great experience without destruction of the environment.

Increasingly, zoos, aquariums, nature centers, museums, interpretive centers, and visitor centers are designing and managing facilities and programs to provide a surrogate attraction. For example, the Canadian Museum of Civilization, Hull, Quebec, stimulates, educates, and entertains the visitor with a variety of exhibits, live presentations, a children's museum, and Cineplus (a dramatic video experience). Over 900 years of history and cultural development are depicted in ways impossible by any other technique (Lancashire 1990). The Leid Jungle, the largest of its kind, at the Henry Doorly Zoo, Omaha, provides 61,000 square feet of exhibit space and contains 3,000 species of plants and 125 species of animals. Visitors gain an enriching experience without damage to fragile environments in their native settings (Cunningham 1992, 41). Several major aquariums give millions of visitors close exposure to marine life and capsuled environmental information with no impact upon real water resource settings. These and many other large attractions are beginning to respond to the plea of the Smithsonian Institution's secretary (Adams 1992, 13) for greater responsiveness of museum specialists to the diversity and dynamics of social change:

> Museums need to see themselves, increasingly, and to be publicly recognized, as important institutional means by which every group in our pluralistic society can define itself and represent its place within the complex, dynamic circumstances of contemporary life.

Simonelli (1992) has been working toward improved interpretive programs in the Canyon de Chelly, a Navajo area designated as a national monument in northeastern Arizona. She emphasizes the need to balance the interests of residents, preservation managers, and visitors. This is not an easy task in an area occupied by the Anasazi for 2,000 years and by the Navajo in the last 250 years. She states, "The chief aim of interpretation is provocation, not instruction; it is revelation based on information" (Simonelli 1992, 20). Potential conflict arises between archeologists who wish to designate important prehistoric sites and the Indians now using these lands for agriculture and homes. Plans for limiting visitor use, both spatially and quantitatively, are being considered in order to protect the Indian culture—in other words, sustainable tourism.

Directly related to land planning and development for tourism are the behavior and attitudes of visitors. Social and environmental conflicts often result from lack of destination understanding on the part of visitors. Needed are educational programs that help prepare travelers for their travel. Such education should include information on all topics that might cause conflict or reduce the likelihood of gaining anticipated experiential satisfactions. These topics could include:

- Weather conditions—needed clothing
- Physical demands—travel rigor
- Customs—host mores on dress, language, and gestures
- Social contact—host-guest taboos
- Host privacy—trespass rules and regulations
- Foods—differences between cultures
- Etiquette—behavioral mannerisms
- Religious beliefs—avoidance of conflict
- History—understanding backgrounds
- Politics—avoidance of conflict
- Communication—how to approach natives
- Facilities, services—different features and standards
- Health—avoidance of medical problems

Seminars, videos, books, and tour guidance on these topics need not diminish the traveler's ability to obtain adventure.

Planning Considerations

Special information needed for travel segments. In the past, some informational literature and guidance has been so generalized that no one has really benefitted. Instead, special places require special descriptive information and guidance. Historic sites, for example, may require several options related to the sophistication and interest of the visitor. Busloads of schoolchildren require planning different from the casual visitor arriving by personal automobile.

Travel information systems are different from promotion. Much of promotion is directed toward the market before travel decisions are made, but information is needed both before and during travel. Generally, road-side billboards are of greater scenic destructive value than either inform-ative or promotional value for travelers. A mix of maps, guide books, well marked highways, and visitor centers can assist the traveler in finding his way and understanding what he is seeing and doing. Interactive comput-erized information devices, when properly located at travel stops, may solve many travel information needs.

Planned visitor centers offer many opportunities. A well designed visitor center complex adjacent to resource-based attractions promises to solve many issues. First, it can be designed to accommodate personal cars as well as tour buses. It can handle masses of visitors without environmental damage to the primary resources of importance to the attraction. It can provide a vicarious resource experience for the visitor as a surrogate for direct contact and its accompanying noise, litter, and physical wear and tear. Cooperative planning between public agencies, nonprofit organiza-tions, and commercial businesses can take much of the financial burden away from public agencies. A visitor center complex could provide food service, retail sales (crafts and souvenirs), pageantry, museum, exhibits, and demonstrations as well as lectures, videos, and publications.

A national and regional information system is needed. Some nations, such as Australia and Great Britain, have planned and established net-works of information centers of great value to the traveler. Tourist maps and roadside signs identify with a uniform symbol, such as an "I", where such centers are located. Here the traveler can obtain additional literature, maps, and personal counseling. In order to reduce costs, these may be incorporated into local businesses, such as restaurants and shops. This system is more effective, better liked by visitors, and creates less visual clutter than excessive roadside signs.

An informed host area. Planning for improved tourism information for visitors requires an adequately informed local citizenry. Too often travelers are given no information or even misguidance when asking a local citizen for aid. Local hospitality training programs can be effective for improving knowledge of services and attractions as well as the ability to properly greet visitors.

An enlightened visitor population. Equally important is a body of trav-elers who understand that they are strangers and have responsibility for their own behavior in a destination. Needed are informational programs that help train prospective travelers *before* they travel. Such informed travelers are less likely to get sick, be robbed, or offend hosts at the same time that they learn more, have more fun, and are more enriched by the travel experience.

PROMOTION

Although promotion is dominantly programs rather than physical development, it is an important component with strong linkage to all other components. Tourism promotion is a major policy and program activity of many nations, provinces, states, governmental developments, and businesses. Promotion for tourism usually encompasses four activities: advertising (paid), publicity (unpaid), public relations, and incentives (gifts and discounts).

Because so much money is spent on promotion the important planning linkage is the matter of *what* is promoted. All promotional planning must be closely integrated with all other supply side planning and development.

For example, Baker (1992, 1) found that the marketing program of the U.S. National Park Service to promote off-season use did accomplish that objective but exacerbated the overall use problem. Whereas over 95 percent of the park use was in June, July, and August previous to their campaign, the percentage dropped to 78 in 1990, after the program began. However, the program resulted in a significant *increase* in total visitors. The effort increased burdens on national park staff, already overextended because of budget reductions.

While promotion is an important tool for increasing economic impact, it must be used with great sensitivity to the goal of user satisfaction, closely related to land development. For example, the planning and management of attractions within destinations may not allow the visitor to experience the view or the objective illustrated in promotional literature. A professional photographer, hired by the promoters, may have required special access permission and many days of waiting for ideal weather to obtain the beautiful and enticing image of a scenic or historic attraction—all of which were unavailable to the visitor. Understanding visitor use and site management are especially important for all tourism promotion.

Closely related to land planning for tourism is the use of billboards and signs along highways. Although *informative* signs at exits of freeways and at highway intersections may be needed, promotional signs have questionable value. In most instances today, promotional signs are less effective for luring visitors than other media—tour guidebooks, radio and TV spots, publicity (magazine articles), and word of mouth from friends and relatives. Furthermore, scenic appreciation of roadsides is such a strong desire among travel markets that defacing the landscape by billboards hardly seems desirable. Many regions, such as Hawaii, a very successful travel destination, have banned billboards and severely limited the use of signs.

CONCLUSIONS

Those wishing to improve tourism at any scale, region to site, must evaluate how well the tourism system is functioning. Although some influence may be made to alter market trends, change will occur primarily by alterations in the supply side of tourism. The supply side components are under the control of three action sectors—governments, nonprofit organizations, and commercial enterprise. Progress will be measured by how well they manipulate the five basic components of the supply side. In addition to the several planning considerations presented in this chapter, some important overall conclusions also can be drawn.

Planning for tourism depends on physical development and programs in five supply side components.

All three sectors of tourism development and management control their destiny by how well they plan attractions, services, transportation, information, and promotion. Equal to individual planning and development is integration of all the components. In order to accomplish this it may be necessary to initiate new mechanisms of cooperation and collaboration.

Attractions provide the energizing power.

Attractions—developed areas and programs—provide the stimulating force for the tourism system to function. They serve two purposes—to lure travelers and provide satisfaction. They depend greatly upon natural and cultural resources. Therefore, the distribution and quality of these resources are strong determinants of tourism development. Planning for tourism development must place emphasis on those areas best suited to the establishment of attractions.

Services are key facilitators.

The planning of primary services—lodging, food, and transportation—must be integrated with attraction planning. Because these services depend on two markets—travel and local—their locations must reflect the needs of both. New cooperative, collaborative, and even financial relationships between service businesses and other components of the tourism system may be needed as planning takes place. Even though the service businesses are the focus of economic impact from tourism, their success depends as much on relationships with other components as internal management.

All components depend on transportation.

For regions, destinations, and sites, tourism development must have access. Simple and direct as this statement may be, frequently there is little planning and managerial linkage between transportation decision-makers and tourism developers. An essential part of the success of hotels, food services, entertainment, shops, and attractions is an ongoing understanding of the changes and trends in transportation.

Information is critical to the tourist's experience.

Travelers today seek greater understanding of places and activities that they visit. Planning policies and practices must include frequent information centers, clear directions for wayfinding, and techniques that assure the fulfillment of experiences. There is a growing need for well designed and conveniently located visitor interpretive centers that not only provide information and guidance but entertainment and enrichment. Pretravel information is as important as en route and on-site information.

Promotion follows development.

Only after attractions, services, transportation, and information have been developed are they ready to be promoted. Promotion that is too generalized, obtuse, or even misleading is readily recognized by today's sophisticated traveling public and should be avoided. An essential part of the tourism planning process is to assure that promotion will contain the right content at the right time and for the right travel segment of the market.

Planning at all levels can integrate components of the supply side with each other and with market demand.

Because of the complexity of the entire tourism system, it does not always run smoothly. Planning at the regional, destination, and site levels can monitor how well the system is working and what policies, practices, and development are needed to improve its functions.

REFERENCES

Adams, R. McC. (1992). "Smithsonian Horizons." *Smithsonian*, 23(1) April, 13–14.

Allen, J. W. et al. (1979). *The Foundations of Free Enterprise*. Center for Education and Research in Free Enterprise. College Station: Texas A&M University.

Ashman, R. (1986). "Born in the U.S.A." *Nation's Business*, 74(11) November, 41 + .

Baker, P. (1991–1992). "The National Park's Unique Marketing Phenomenon." *Arizona Hospitality Trends*, 6(1) Winter, 1 + .

Best Western 1975 Annual Report (1976). Phoenix: Best Western.

Bevins, M. I. (1971). *Private Recreation Enterprise Economics*. Proceedings of the Forest Recreation Symposium, Pinchot Institute Consortium for Environmental Research.

Bureau of Outdoor Recreation (1973). *Outdoor Recreation for America: A Legacy for America*. Washington, DC: U.S. Government Printing Office.

Cunningham, D. (1992). "The Lied Jungle." *Nebraskaland*, 70(2) March, 40 + .

Drucker, Peter F. (1973). *Management*. New York: Harper & Row.

Drucker, Peter F. (1975). "The Delusion of Profits." *Wall Street Journal*, February.

European Travel & Life (1992). 8(1) March.

Gunn, Clare A. (1986). "Small Town and Rural Tourism Planning." In *Integrated Rural Planning and Development*, Floyd W. Dykeman (ed.), pp. 237–254. Sackville, New Brunswick: Mount Allison University.

Kaplan, A. (1984). "Overworked and Undertrained; Unit Managers Need Attention." *Nation's Restaurant News*, November 5.

Lancashire, D. (1990). "Canada's Cultural Dynamo Enlightens While it Entertains." *Smithsonian*, 20(12) March, 114 + .

Lundberg, Donald E. (1979). *The Hotel and Restaurant Business*, 3rd ed. Boston: CBI.

Minister of Supply and Services Canada (1982). *The Inn Business*. Ottawa: Canadian Government Publishing Centre.

Senate Committee on Commerce, Science, and Transportation (1977). *National Tourism Policy Study: Ascertainment Phase.* Washington DC: U.S. Government Printing Office.

Simonelli, J. M. (1992). "Tradition and Tourism at Canyon de Chelly." *Practicing Anthropology*, 14(2) Spring, 18–22.

Tours & Resorts (1992). 7(4) February/March.

Travel Holiday (1992). March.

Chapter 4

Growth and Sustainable Development

Introduction

Environmental awareness has been raised to new heights worldwide. For tourism, this new wave has been met with a range of reactions—from apathy to enlightenment and conflict. Some tourism leaders preoccupied with promotion have shown no interest in environmental matters, believing these issues are outside the realm of tourism. Others, especially some hoteliers and restaurateurs, have begun recycling waste for promotional as well as environmental advantage. Advocates of environmental protection are maligned as emotional "greenies" and obstructionists to progress by some tourism developers. Some even have been known to criticize health departments for closing polluted beaches at the peak of the tourism season.

Confused understanding of tourism's relevance to environmental matters endorses the need for greater enlightenment. Because of the new awareness of many environmental issues, the subject has not been given exhaustive research study, especially for tourism. Even so, observation and some scholarly writing are demonstrating basic relevance to tourism. The purpose of this chapter is to highlight some of the environmental responsibilities and opportunities facing all tourism developers as they plan for a better future.

GROWTH AND QUALITY

No discussion of tourism planning would be complete without including the topic of growth. For many individuals, the term of planning implies growth. For most underdeveloped regions of the world today, tourism growth is seen as necessary to economic salvation. Governments and businesses invest heavily in promotion to increase visitor volumes.

But, in all these generalizations about growth, it is not clear what kind of growth is most desirable. For example, equal economic growth requires a relatively small number of the hotel-staying visitors to equal the impact of large numbers of campers or visitors staying with friends and relatives. However, if an area pushes only for one travel market segment, it will not enjoy a diversity of trade that is necessary for greater stability. When its resources are studied, there may be opportunities for growth in a variety of attractions that will stimulate a better balance of visitor markets.

Perceptions of tourism growth vary. Murphy (1983, 10), in his study of some communities in England, found that local perspectives on tourism growth varied among three groups. The administrative group—political, professional, planning, and official—was most positive, believing that greater development would enhance employment and improve local facilities. While the business sector was positively inclined, it was somewhat skeptical that all the benefits from tourism would materialize as promised. Perhaps this was influenced by their concern over new competition and allegiance to local resident markets. Opinions of the third sector, the residents, ranged widely from very favorably inclined to negative. The author concludes that if leaders favoring tourism wish support from all three sectors, greater accountability and better understanding of tourism are required at the earliest stage of planning and development.

Many localities make remarkable adaptation to invasions of tourists even though these outsiders are known to disrupt usual community life. Rothman (1978) found resort cities realized that residents required extra effort to cope during the peak season: church schedules were changed, residents tended to avoid popular visitor places, and the pace of activity and congestion increased. But for them, the tradeoff was worth it.

Throughout the world, many destinations have adapted to great volumes of visitors. Mega-attractions, such as Walt Disney World, were specifically designed to handle masses of visitors that have produced great economic growth throughout Orlando and the entire state of Florida. These experiences support the belief that growth is desirable and workable. But, not all agree that growth is always positive. Molotch (1976, 328) questioned land development growth as a prime political goal. Growth in numbers and land development can exact costs of environmental degradation, social problems, expanded infrastructure, and public taxes, and may be perceived as benefitting only a few.

Many wonder that "left to our own devices, are we destined to overdevelop all of our principal tourism attractions in a frenetic effort to maximize the influx of tourist dollars?" (Okrant 1991, 32). A single policy of growth may not be compatible with the realities of capacity limits—social, environmental, and economic. Nelson (1991, 40) advocates the creation of codes of practice and other local agreements to monitor tourism on the ground. Such was accomplished by a consensus of tour operators of the Queen Charlotte Islands and southwest Alaska (Falconer 1991, 21). All of the 40 tour operators agreed to a code of conduct "primarily to regulate our own activities in Gwaii Hannas/South Moresley, British Columbia" (p. 21). Content of agreements is extensive and includes the following key issues: etiquette; wildlife; archeological, cultural, and historical sites; food gathering; garbage; camping; and local cooperation. Taylor (1991, 29) observes that some destinations may not be able to accept more visitors no matter how well designed and managed. He states that "a concept of demarketing may have to be developed as it becomes necessary to reduce rather than increase the number of visitors to an area."

Another approach to economic growth is to regenerate existing physical development rather than developing new land. Many destinations contain sites with obsolete uses that, with creative design and planning, could be converted to tourism. The wave of growth in bed-and-breakfast facilities in the United States is evidence of this opportunity. If the emphasis is more upon improved *quality* than *quantity*, there may be fewer negative impacts.

The Main Street programs in the United States and Canada (Holdsworth 1985) are directed toward rejuvenation of existing development rather than creating more. For example, to date in Texas, more than $200 million of private sector reinvestment has taken place in neglected downtown buildings in 68 small towns (population under 50,000) (Read 1988). The Texas Historical Commission designates five cities a year, not for public funding but rather for a technical and self-help program. The three-year program includes help in locating and training a local Main Street director, providing help from a resource assistance team, design assistance, and visual merchandising help. With this program, the city of Brenham has reversed downtown decay so that over 40 new businesses have been established, 81 buildings have been rehabilitated, and new apartments have been developed in previously vacant historic buildings. Areas once believed unsafe are now filled with tourists and local shoppers who enjoy and are enriched in a rejuvenated historic setting. Although not all cities may have such opportunities, there is value in considering a policy of reuse rather than new land development growth.

Even though there is often criticism of tourism growth as being too much, there are no standards upon which to make such judgment. Attempts to create capacity rules on optimum numbers of visitors have failed. Instead the solution to capacity seems to lie within a case by case planning situation where the many social, environmental, and economic factors are monitored in order to guide further development.

ENVIRONMENTAL ISSUES AND TOURISM

In spite of the fact that tourism sometimes exacts environmental disturbance, it needs to be put into proper perspective. The overwhelming volume of resource threats comes from other sources. At the present time, greater overall recognition of the role of mankind is needed to initiate environmental improvement—for tourism as well as all other development.

Sargent (1974) explains that even though all animal life is shaped by the environment and organisms also shape the environment, mankind is dramatically different from other organisms. People have taken over control not only of their own destiny but also that of all other organisms. In organisms other than man, "the natural ecosystem's organismic detritus is fed back into the environment and recycled" (Sargent 1974, 16). But, this is not so with mankind.

Environmental Degradation

The Worldwatch Institute identified the magnitude of environmental issues globally in its 1991 *Report of Progress Toward a Sustainable Society*. These are cited here because they impact the future of tourism development.

Since the first Earth Day in 1970, as many as 200 million hectares of tree cover have been lost (Brown 1991, 3). Deserts have expanded some 120 million hectares, utilizing more land than is currently planted to crops in China. Water pollution continues to threaten all animal life. Industrial and municipal wastewater with acids, arsenic, oil, grease, and other toxic wastes as well as sewage discharged into Galveston Bay caused a seafood and tourism loss of 2.5 million dollars a day (Bryan 1991a, 58). Also in Texas, it was reported that in one county alone, 80,000 cattle produce about 7.9 million pounds of manure a day resulting in odor and water contamination threats to the vicinity (Bryan 1991b, 2A).

Farmers have lost an estimated 480 billion tons of topsoil (Brown 1991, 3). Carbon dioxide, the main greenhouse gas in the atmosphere, is now rising 0.4 percent a year. Air pollution is at health-threatening levels in hundreds of cities. The stratospheric ozone layer continues to thin, the number of plant and animal species is diminishing, and damage from acid rain is seen on every continent. Throughout the world, governmental policies on pesticide subsidies have greatly increased the threats from toxic chemicals (Postel and Flavin 1991, 178).

These environmental issues are dominantly caused by development *other* than tourism. They are cited because they are vital to tourism's success or failure. Tourism planning must address not only its own environmental impact but also those critical worldwide environment issues.

Tourism and Environment

When examining environmental damage related to tourism, a planner must distinguish between true causes. Whereas some erosion and pollution of resources is caused by great numbers of visitors, most environmental damage is caused by *lack of plans, policies, and action to prepare for any economic growth.* Most of the ills cited by environmentalists are the result of the failure by governments and private sector leaders to cope with *any* economic growth, not just tourism. With growth comes need for decisions concerning natural areas to be protected and designed for park usage; location and design of water supply and waste disposal systems; land use locations that are compatible; and on protection of cultural resources, such as historic and archeological sites. Tourism cannot be blamed for environmental deterioration caused by bad decisions rather than real visitor impacts. Examples follow to illustrate this essential point.

For many years Santa Catalina, a small island off the California coast, has maintained a reasonable balance between environmental protection and tourism development. Most of the island has been under a resource preserve policy with the exception of the little town of Avon, the harbor tourist village. A major limitation on development that kept tourism in balance with the environment was water supply, dependent wholly on rainfall catchment. However, this balance has been broken by the installation of a desalinization plant allowing a major new resort condominium development to deface some of the natural landscape. It is not tourism per se that is now destroying some of the natural environment but rather the political and private decision to allow further development based on a new water plant.

Henry David Thoreau is known and revered worldwide for his insightful writings about man and nature. Many of these writings were inspired while living alongside a small lake near Concord, Massachusetts. Until recently, the lake and forested setting were much the same as Thoreau saw them in 1845. Today there is recreational congestion on the lake and destruction of shoreline vegetation by visitor overuse that appear to be caused by tourism. But, the true cause of environmental deterioration was state agency planning policy that fostered the design and management of the area not as a historic shrine but as a recreational area.

The island of Moorea, near Tahiti, was studied in 1990 by a task force sponsored by the Pacific Asia Travel Association and French Polynesia

Government (PATA 1991). Market surveys had documented visitors' rewards as the scenery, unspoiled settings, and the sea—outstanding resource assets of the island. However, the findings of the task force showed that the comparatively low occupancy of resort hotels was due largely to lack of planning and management of the very resources cited as important to visitors. There was evidence of mountainside erosion, water-front sewage pollution, reduction of wildlife habitat, and threats to rare archeological sites. Virtually no planned visitor access and interpretation had been developed to meet market needs of enjoying the rich and abundant natural and cultural resources. It was not excessive tourism but rather governmental and private sector lack of planning and policy that caused environmental problems. The failure to build central sewage treatment; to place the mountain and several beach areas under public park control and planned uses; to establish new attractions and visitor centers; and the failure of the resort owner-managers to utilize off-site resources for enrichment and enjoyment were the causes of poor business and resource threat. If public and private planning were to be improved, the environment could be enhanced and the tourism economy increased.

Excessive visitor use of national parks is often cited as threatening the resources for which the parks were identified and established. But, closer examination reveals again that it is not tourism per se but rather inadequate design and management that threaten the resources. Machlis and Tichnell, in their study of national parks worldwide (1985, 24) showed that the major threats were not visitors but rather poaching, pollution, and erosion. A 1980 study (Becker 1986, 243) indicated that about one-half of the environmental threats to national parks come from outside the parks, such as acid rain, toxic chemicals, timber harvesting, and exploration for oil, gas, and minerals. Threats inside national parks include soil erosion, air and water pollution, nonnative plants and animals—all issues that could be controlled with proper design and management.

The U.S. national park director of tourism (Baker 1986, 51) states:

> Problems that have arisen over tourism-related issues such as the location of an airport or the routing of a highway pales in comparison to the effects of acid mine drainage on an entire watershed, subsistence in residential areas, and the destruction of inland waterways by acid rain, for example.

Threats to the natural park resources in Canada have been identified as not caused by tourism but by disease in buffalo, past mismanagement of forests (overprotecting pine), commercial fishing, pollution from outside the parks, and poaching. Recommended is "cooperative action and integrated planning between parks and sites and their neighbors" (State of the Parks 1991, 26)

It is becoming clear that many visitors can be accommodated without environmental damage provided that areas and regions accepted greater responsibility to plan and manage for all economic growth including tourism. A scholar and designer of resource-based development has stated that the major problem worldwide is not tourism but rather "the inadequacy of the existing agencies to deal with the challenges of growth" (Hamed 1990, 18).

SUSTAINABLE DEVELOPMENT

Sustainable Development and Capacities

The issues described above are now being addressed by the newly coined term, *sustainable development*. This is merely one step beyond what has traditionally been termed conservation—wise use of resources. Sustainable development has been defined many ways but the following, developed in British Columbia, Canada (Rees 1989, 13), may be most applicable to tourism planning.

> Sustainable development is positive socioeconomic change that does not undermine the ecological and social systems upon which communities and society are dependent. Its successful implementation requires integrated policy, planning, and social learning processes; its political viability depends on the full support of the people it affects through their governments, their social institutions, and their private activities.

Examination of this definition reveals key applications to tourism. The basic premise of "positive socioeconomic change" allows growth but requires that it be positive. This implies that such change must provide social and economic good.

Second, it then qualifies change by stating that it "does not undermine the ecological and social systems." This again is human ecology, avoiding wanton—useless, reckless, and undisciplined—use of resources. It states further that these social and ecological systems are the foundation upon which communities and societies depend.

Then, the definition states that successful implementation requires several public and private policies and actions, such as "integrated policy, planning, and social learning processes." This is the heart of tourism planning, principles and practices.

The province of New Brunswick, Canada, is involved in a Sustainable Communities Project (Dykeman 1992). Six pilot communities will be selected on the basis of their approaches to the concept of sustainable development. It is a three-stage project with the following objectives:

Demonstrate the abilities of smaller communities to design and implement a sustainable development strategy.

Test different leadership and strategic planning approaches and evaluate them within the context of a framework for action.

Develop the best way to introduce and implement a community-based, self-help project of this nature.

Create self-directed support material which will assist communities to employ existing, under-utilized, and unrealized personal and physical resources in a Sustainable Community Development Strategy.

Leadership approaches will pursue the following five steps:

1. Orient. By changing attitudes and approaches, many things can be done to improve the local quality of life. Leaders must orient themselves to these new attitudes and approaches.

2. Evaluate. The internal and external influences must be evaluated. This includes the community's economic, social, and environmental characteristics.

3. Facilitate. Based on these steps, a strategy of sustainable development is created.

4. Innovate. A search is made for new and superior methods for meeting everyone's needs in the best possible way.

5. Create. The final step is to actually create a more sustainable future.

Williams and Gill (1991, 3) have stated that much of the concern over limits, ceilings, and thresholds in order to control visitor impact on the environment has come from the outdoor recreation field. This topic became known as carrying capacity. Attempts have been made to scientifically quantify optimum numbers of visitors in order to assist designers, planners, and managers of outdoor recreation areas. Of main concern were sociological, physical, and ecological carrying capacities. Williams concludes that it is difficult to generalize such standards from site to site, that there are just too many variables to organize into a planning and management context (Williams and Gill 1991, 20). Instead, he recommends a systems approach to the goal of planning and developing tourism within the concept of sustainable development. This approach involves:

- Developing tourism goals and objectives linked to the broader comprehensive plan for a region and /or local community.
- Formulating a set of performance indicators reflecting the objectives of tourism development (Table 4-1).
- Implementing management strategies designed to direct tourism toward the achievement of the stated objectives.
- Monitoring the performance of tourism with respect to these indicators.

TABLE 4-1
INDICATORS OF TOURISM CONDITION

Indicator Types	Measures	Possible Indicators
Physical	Infrastructure Superstructure Land/space Transportation	Crowding Danger Supply
Economic	Capital Operation costs Opportunity costs Labour Inflation Market	Funding Labour shortages Tourism competition Other sector competition Rampant inflation
Ecological	Process changes Fire risk Pollution levels Erosion levels Wildlife viability Vegetation viability	Disaster expectation Irrevocable change Threatened uniqueness
Perceptual	Visual amenity User preference/motivations Activity satisfaction Resident satisfaction	Dissatisfaction Loss of visitors Landscape quality change
Socio/Cultural	Population stability Standard of living Services/amenities Community viability Social problems Traditions/language	Lost traditions Inequitable benefits distribution Crime/disruption Tourist resentment Visitor/resident mix
Political/Administrative	Policy/program priorities Receptiveness to change Assistance levels	Inability to achieve objectives Failure to cope with pressures

Sources: Getz 1982; Williams and Gill 1991

- Evaluating the effectiveness of selected management strategies in influencing the performance of tourism with respect to these indicators.
- Developing strategic policies for tourism management based upon the monitored effectiveness of these techniques.

Because of the finite quantity of some critical resource areas, a policy decision to manage visitor capacities may be necessary. Many now believe that the number of visitors to the Galapagos Islands has reached maximum capacity to be supportable without environmental damage. In response to increased scuba-diving tourism in the Cayman Islands, the government has passed a marine conservation law and established a marine park system (Long 1990, 49) and Bermuda has reduced the number of cruise ship visitors. Perhaps the most fragile of all sites demanding controls on numbers of visitors are historic buildings. Mass use must be restricted to walkways and view points that are designed for certain maximum capacities. Frequently, this planning issue can be resolved by establishing museums and visitor centers nearby that are designed for mass tourist use, providing an acceptable vicarious experience without damage to the resource.

Achieving Sustainability

Stanley (1991, 116), in his summary of a conference on sustainable development and tourism, concluded that no one should expect rigid standards for its achievement. Instead he identified seven different threads of importance in research and policy if sustainable development is to be achieved. (1) Sustainable development is determined largely by *what the stakeholders want it to be*—a wilderness or a developed resort. (2) It can be accomplished only when people have found mechanisms for *working together.* (3) Environmental impacts result from *many forms of tourism* other than only visiting natural resources. Visiting friends and relatives, business travel, and visiting urban historic sites require special planning if sustainable development is to be achieved. (4) Because most tourist establishments are small businesses, unable to obtain research and professional studies, *much education is needed.* Guidelines and computer models may assist. (5) Research can demonstrate that *sustainable development pays.* (6) *Economic measures*, such as willingness to pay and contingent value, can demonstrate the real value of sustainable development. (7) *A review of cases* where sustainable development of tourism is being achieved can help communities and rural areas plan to reach their own sustainable objectives.

The best solution to sustainable development is likely to occur not from advocacy of environmentalists or governments but from developers of tourism. When the fundamental of the dependency of all tourism upon the resource base becomes more apparent to developers, they will see that it is in their best interests to sustain the quality of the natural and cultural resources. The process by which this is to be achieved is through codes of practice and agreements locally—"information, monitoring, communication, and adaptation among an array of groups and individuals with different and similar interest" (Nelson 1991, 40).

Increasingly, examples of sustainable tourism development are appearing. An excellent case is the tourism adaptation on the island of Yap, 870 kilometers southwest of Guam (Mansperger 1992). Instead of typical enclave, large scale, and externally owned development that often creates shock and conflict to a local society, tourism here has been slow, small scale, and mainly locally owned, resulting in strong resource protection. Hotels employ mostly Yapese and the foreign exchange from over 3,000 tourists annually is adding to the economy. Controlled tours of historically important Bechyal give tourists insight into a native community house, a chief's house, shell money, a sailing canoe, and fish traps. The new locally owned Manta Ray Bay Hotel caters to divers who enjoy the unusually close contact with manta rays and pristine coral formations. Every Saturday, a cultural show is held in the village of Maaq on Tamil-Gagil Island. This features native Yapese dances portraying the traditional search for stone that in ancient times was quarried and used for money. Actually, in this location, tourism is fostering the preservation of a culture. The Yapese have been very selective in accepting only those forms of tourism they feel are most appropriate. They want the benefits of tourism but are unwilling to sacrifice their culture to obtain them.

There continue to be many locations where good design and good management can accept a great volume of travelers while at the same time protecting the environment, thus accomplishing sustainable development objectives. National parks have increasingly demonstrated this principle. When visitors are guided only into areas where they do no damage to the environment, design has been successful. When management gives visitors descriptive information by means of literature, guidance, lectures, exhibits, and demonstrations, travelers gain rich experiences without deteriorating the setting.

An example is the planning for an interpretive resort complex, Wilpena Station, within Flinders Range National Park, Australia (Williams and Brake 1990, 62). This is planned with two major objectives: (1) a satisfied park visitor and (2) a managed outcome of the consequences of park visitation. The basic principle underlying all development here is "Well planned and thoughtfully implemented site modification to accommodate an increase in the number and range of visitor groups to a particular site does not work against the conservation goals of a park." (More detailed description of this case can be found in Chapter 10.)

A strong land ethic is traditional for Canada. In 1992, the Tourism Stream of the Globe '92 Conference was held in Vancouver. Resulting from the presentations and discussions were the following elements of a Challenge Statement pertaining to sustainable development of tourism (Manning 1992).

1. Policy, Legislation and Regulation
   • Building the institutions and the foundations for sustainable tourism.
   • Protecting the resources base.
   • Mobilizing industry action for sustainable tourism.

2. Technology and Research
   • Understanding the natural resource base.
   • Understanding cultural values.
   • Measuring tourist demands and expectations.
   • Measuring tourism impact.
   • Information for better decisions.
   • Mobilizing appropriate technology.
   • Visitor management techniques and practices.

3. Economics and Finance
   • Incorporating environmental costs.
   • Modifying reporting procedures.
   • Using market influences at home and abroad.
   • Benefitting from the environmental market.

4. Communication and Outreach
   • Mobilizing the firms and employees.
   • Self-regulation.
   • Modifying decreased tourist expectations and actions.
   • Becoming proactive.

Low versus High Impact Tourism Development

Experience is increasingly demonstrating that there are differences between low-impact and high-impact development. Low-impact is tourism development that is characterized as small scale and slow in progress whereas high-impact development refers to large scale and rapid development.

There are arguments for high-impact development. In areas that are not yet known as destinations, some large-scale attractions and accommodations may be appropriate. High-impact development may be needed to attract support services such as airline access and promotion and provide the noticeable change to attract local support for other tourism development. However, feasibility needs to be carefully examined to make sure that environmental, social, and economic change will not be detrimental.

Low-impact development, however, may be integrated more readily into the existing social and economic life of a community. Because developers are residents, they are more likely to be well acquainted with resource limitations. Low-impact development has a greater opportunity for feedback from each increment of growth. However, this type of development requires long-range planning so that each new development is a logical part of the whole of tourism and not dispersed so widely that it is inefficient to service and confusing for visitors. Many regions are finding that both kinds of development may be needed, provided that they are kept in balance.

Appropriateness

Much of the criticism of tourism development by environmentalists stems from the *quality of fit*. How well will this new development fit into the dominant qualities of the land and existing development? Sometimes it may be in conflict with the setting. Wight (1988) described tourism as sometimes extrinsic or alien to the existing environment and cited the proposal of a monorail from Ayers Rock to the remote Olga Mountains in Australia or a waterslide just outside Waterton National Park, Canada, as inappropriate tourism development.

The issue of appropriateness is founded upon two major factors influencing all tourism development. First is the factor of market segment preference. Esthetically, it may be quite distasteful to visitors to see some development that just does not fit. For example, a garish food service structure beside a prominent historic site may actually reduce the quality of the visitor's appreciation of history. A more appropriate location for restaurants may be some distance away from the historic site and in a cluster of other commercial development. Or, an alternative, as is being done by McDonald's in many historic areas, is to break from the standard architectural style and adapt the facade to the site and architectural character of the surrounding historic district.

The second factor relates to the resource base. If the area has qualities that contribute to the attractiveness and user activity interests, it should be protected rather than eroded by inappropriate development. This suggests that major tourist services are most appropriate when located in communities rather than dispersed throughout natural areas. Tourists are able to select from a greater diversity of services and the criticism of ugly commercialism is avoided in natural areas.

ECOTOURISM

A Renewed Concept

In order to identify the market trend of travel to natural areas, the term *ecotourism* has been coined. The universally increased awareness of natural resources has stimulated a surge in development to meet an expanding travel market segment. This contradictory combination of meanings— resource protection and mass travel—is a paradox and a planning challenge. Although the market segment that seeks man-made attractions, such as Walt Disney World, has also increased in size, it has not been at the expense of ecotourists. The U.S. National Park Service reported that visits to national parks have increased by one-third in the last decade and that there were 96.5 million visits to the National Park Service cultural areas in 1989 (Statistical Abstract 1989).

Although the term ecotourism appears to be recent, the concept of balancing tourist use with resource protection was put forward many years ago. The original National Park Act of the United States in 1916 mandated a dual policy of resource protection and public use. Smardon (1991, 704) pointed out that Dickert and Sorensen (1974) and Gunn (1978) called for application of ecological principles of tourism planning several years ago.

Ecotourism has captured the interest of conservationists, biologists, and wildlife specialists as well as developers. Packard et al. (1991) identified over 200 references relating to ecotourism. In the U.S., the National Parks and Conservation Association, a nonprofit advocate organization, has developed with the National Park Service cooperative public educational workshop meetings on ecotourism corridor issues. Van Hyning (1991, 15) cited nonprofit interests in ecotourism in Pennsylvania, such as the Lackawana River Corridor Association (LRCA) and the Rails-to-Trails Conservancy (RTC). The LRCA has worked jointly with communities to deal with local environmental damage as an initial planning tool for initiating ecotourism. The RTC has stimulated local interest in environmental enhancement along the Allegheny River.

Even though there is no universally accepted definition of ecotourism, it has some common interpretations. Some define it as low-volume visitor use of natural areas by well-trained and sophisticated visitors seeking a new learning experience. Others view it as mass adventure tour tourism in natural areas. In any case, it again emphasizes the need for integrated planning to balance resource protection with visitor use.

Colvin (1991, 578) described one type of ecotourist as "scientific," having the following characteristics:

Wants an in-depth, "authentic" experience.
Considers the experience worthwhile, personally and socially.
Abhors large tour groups on strict itinerary.
Seeks physical and mental challenge.
Wishes interaction with locals, cultural learning.
Adaptable, often prefers rustic accommodations.
Tolerates discomfort.
Seeks involvement, not passive behavior.
Prefers to pay for experience rather than for comfort.

Managing such tourists is being accomplished through the University of California Research Expeditions Program (UREP). Follow-up of presentations and exchanges of information are important byproducts.

One form of ecotourism that has expanded greatly, especially in Hawaii, has been tourist interaction with dolphins. Because scientists fear some negative impacts on natural life activities of these interesting creatures of the sea, recommendations for planning and management have been prepared (Simonds 1991, 675):

Sponsor workshops by experienced specialists to determine impacts.
Develop measures for standardized recording of interaction.
Study influence of humans on dolphin behavior.
Develop tourist "etiquette" guidelines.
Monitor visitor reactions to dolphin-human experiences.

Sectoral Cooperation

Fennell and Eagles (1990) have modeled conservation visitor use with the conceptual framework shown in Figure 4-1. They identify the resource tour as the central focus of ecotourism. The visitor not only searches for his own experience but seeks help and guidance from a tour operator as interpreter. The supporting management activity is here labeled service industry and includes tour operation, resource management, and com-

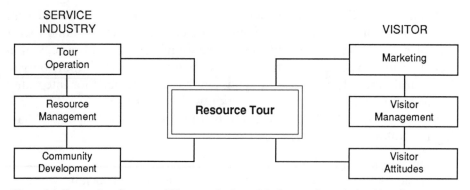

Figure 4-1. Ecotourism Conceptual Framework. A model of ecotourism relationships. Central is the resource tour. The ecotour operator must address issues of tour operation, resource management, and community development. Planning must also address issues of visitor marketing, management, and attitudes. (Fennell and Eagles 1990, 27).

munity development. The diagram again dramatizes the intimate relationship between resource protection and community development of tourist facilities and services. The visitor component encompasses marketing, visitor management, and visitor attitudes. Fennell and Eagles conclude that ecotourism success depends greatly upon integrated planning between the public and private sectors if the objective of sustainable development is to be achieved.

Stewart et al. (1990, 146) summarizes it thus: "comprehensive ecosystem management implies some degree of mutual understanding and reciprocity across multiple sociopolitical systems." He states further that ecotourism planning and development requires: "(1) integration of non-financial objectives; and (2) a planning process which encourages participatory decision-making encompassing entrepreneurs, land managers, host community, and interested tourists or visitors."

Perhaps the greatest premise of ecotourism for better planning is the concept of stronger linkage between the public and private sectors. The public sector role for managers of national parks and wildlife reserves in Costa Rica (11.2 percent of the land) is protecting the assets of interest to ecotourists: deciduous forests, mangrove swamps, rainforests, marshes, paramos, cloud forests, Raphia swamps, oak forests, coral reefs, riparian forests, and a great diversity of bird and animal life (Fennell and Eagles 1990). Private sector entrepreneurs are developing the tours, tour guidance interpretation, lodging, food service, and transportation. There is a strong local understanding that these two forces are working together to a high degree, producing not only economic betterment but also increased public support for resource protection.

A combination of new planning and management of the Manu Bio-sphere Reserve, Peru, has effectively proved a balance between resource protection and visitor use (Groom 1991). The area encompasses 2 million hectares including prime nesting and tourist viewing areas for black skim-mer, large- and yellow-billed terns, pied lapwing, collared plover, and sand-colored nighthawk. Unplanned and uncontrolled bird-watching tours were exacting severe disturbance upon this important wildlife. In 1987, several planning and management practices were implemented. Beaches used by birds were marked with red flags, and blue flags identified beaches suitable for tourists. Tourists are still able to observe the birds but nesting areas have been protected. Total visitor use has been limited to 500 per-sons per year. The success of this program has resulted from close coop-eration among tour company managers, local and national governments, and park and reserve administrators as well as the Ministry of Tourism. Further planning and management concepts have been applied to visitors arriving by boat: motors equipped with silencers, prevention of animal harassment by tour groups, restricting some areas, and regular monitoring of visitor impacts.

Ecotourism Stimulates Conservation

Many observers and researchers today are finding evidence contrary to many beliefs that tourism is always destructive of resource foundations. There are numerous examples demonstrating *increased resource protection* because of tourism—ecotourism practiced in a responsible manner. Boo (1991, 518) defines this very simply as "nature tourism that contributes to conservation." She identified key elements of planning, design, and man-agement needed in natural resource areas such as national parks:

Entrance fee collection system
Tourism training for park personnel
Trail systems with interpretation
Visitor center with interpretation
System of monitoring environmental impacts
Services: snack bar, lodging

Although park managers and policymakers have accepted visitors in varying degrees for many years, their role in tourism has not been well understood nor incorporated into policy. Parks and conservation areas have been established, planned, and managed as isolated oases of special natural and cultural resources. Commendable as has been their protection of these resources, handling visitors has been treated mostly as nonconforming and only to be tolerated. Needed is new understanding of the role of parks and conservation areas in tourism. The new concept of ecotourism is finally forcing the issue of providing a new awareness of the linkage between resource protection and tourism values—economic, personal, and community enhancement.

The diagram in Figure 4-2 is a concept of how tourism functions could be planned and integrated into conservation areas and parks. A similar concept of park zoning was advocated by landscape architect Richard Forster (1973) and endorsed by the International Union for Conservation of Nature and Natural Resources. He described patterns of concentric use zones. The three-zone configuration includes a protected wild land core surrounded by an outdoor recreation buffer zone. An outer zone includes

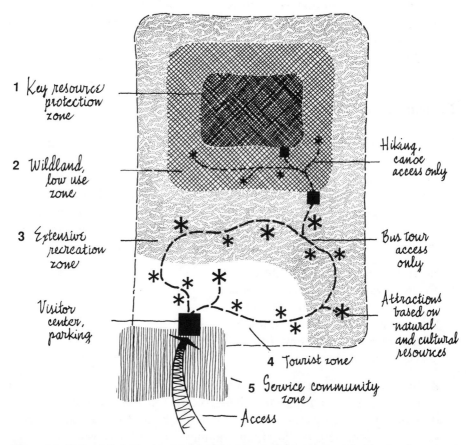

Figure 4-2. National Park Tourism Model. This diagram illustrates a sustainable planning concept that identifies relationships among five zones: resource protection, wildland and low use, extensive recreation, tourist zone, and service community zone (Gunn 1988, 85).

intensive use and visitor services, such as lodging and food. A five-zone pattern was used by the Canadian National and Historic Parks Branch and included:

1. *Special areas*—protected natural and cultural resource areas.
2. *Wilderness recreation areas*—protected resources but minor and controlled access.
3. *Natural environment areas*—protected, but greater visitor use.
4. *General outdoor recreation areas*—planned use, such as campgrounds, trails.
5. *Intensive use areas*—major visitor services. (Forster 1973, 63)

Fundamentally, these require not only a broader geographical context but a more comprehensive administrative action. By allowing nearby communities to function in their normal ways, parks can be relieved of providing these visitor services internally. For example, most travelers seek communities for the majority of their services—food, lodging, entertainment, car service, and shopping. Communities also serve residents in many ways. Communities are able to provide basic infrastructure that is more costly to install and operate within remote areas of parks. Park planners could relieve themselves of developing these services by cooperating and supporting the establishment of these services in nearby communities. Through reciprocal agreements, technical park assistance could be provided to communities, and communities could return portions of tourism revenues to support conservation measures in the parks. This is sustainable tourism development.

A corollary to concentrating services at communities is planned and controlled visitor use of the resource area. Analysis of plant, animal, and cultural artifacts can provide a basis for zoning the area. It can be divided into several zones, scaled from those where human intervention should be prohibited to those where concentrations of visitors can be handled with good planning and management.

Increasingly, ecotourism is being defined as nature-oriented travel that promotes and finances conservation and resource protection (Ziffer 1989, 24). Visitor revenues in protected areas can be derived from entrance fees, donations, ancillary services, or products and private investment. Even though these offer potential support, each local situation must be evaluated on its own merits. Sometimes entrance fees, though substantial, are not earmarked for protection of the areas visited and go directly into the nation's coffers. Because local people feel they already support protected areas with their taxes, a policy of variable entrance fees (larger for foreign visitors) may be initiated. Some tour operators make direct donations to conservation areas out of their profits. Gift shops, food services, and hotels may be able to donate funds to the protected areas nearby that bring them volumes of customers.

Wight (1993) cited several cases in which ecotourism is stimulating greater collaborative interaction. For example, the Association of Independent Tour Operators (AITD) has taken a joint initiative with Green Flag International to promote sustainable development. Wight described the case of Sobek Expeditions as providing a remarkably high amount of its proceeds (6.7–10%) to local conservation groups for their use in protecting resources, especially those related to Sobek's Environmental Adventures. Green Flag is a nonprofit organization dedicated to working in partnership with tourism decisionmakers to improve the environment.

Wight identified principles that should underlie the concept of ecotourism:

- It should not degrade the resource and should be developed in an environmentally sensitive manner.
- It should provide first-hand, participatory and enlightening experience.
- It should involve education among all parties—local communities, government, nongovernmental organizations, industry, and tourists (before, during and after the trip).
- It should incorporate all party recognition of core values related to the intrinsic values of the resource.
- It should involve acceptance of the resource on its own terms, and in recognition of its limits, which involves supply-oriented management.
- It should promote understanding and involve partnerships between many players, which could include government, nongovernment organizations, industry scientists, and locals (both before development and during operation).
- It should promote moral and ethical responsibilities and behavior by all players.
- It should provide long term benefits: to the resource, the local community and industry (benefits may be conservation, scientific, social, cultural, or economic).

If ecotourism is to be planned and developed, consideration must be given to several issues in the earliest planning stages if they are to be avoided or overcome. Those identified by Collins (1991, 106) are paraphrased as follows:

- Displacement of local people

- Direct and indirect erosion of resources
- Loss of access to resources by local residents
- Misleading promotion
- Adequate funding for planning
- Costs of establishing basic infrastructure
- Cultural conflict with natives
- Better road access that may exacerbate resource destruction

Although everyone, developers and visitors alike, would prefer to avoid controls, society and the environment cannot live together without them. For sustainable tourism development, certain controls are being accepted by both developers and visitors as necessary, even for their own welfare. For example Charles Wendt of the U.S. National Park Service (1991, 537) listed several workable controls that have met with success in balancing tourist use with resource protection:

Entrance Stations. These imply authority of management and provide information to visitors.

Visitor Centers. Such centers reduce violations because the public is better informed. Environmental education begins here.

Effective and Courteous Law Enforcement. Volumes of visitors require the same exercise of police protection as in other locations, perhaps even more so because tourists are in a more vulnerable attitude.

Resource Management. The flora and fauna and land resources cannot be left to "nature" in order to sustain these valuable reserves.

Environmental Interpretation and Education. Guided trails, evening programs, environmental education, extension programs in surrounding communities, living history interpretation, self-guided automobile tours, rock climbing school, and exhibits can provide rich visitor experiences without environmental damage.

CONCLUSIONS

Because the environmental dimensions are so important to tourism and its growth, this chapter has highlighted some of their fundamental relationships and issues. The issues are not idealistic nor motivated only by altruism; they are essential to business success and tourism economics.

First, the dominant economic force of growth needs further examination in its relationship to quality; enhanced quality may be the better objective. Second, tourism may exact some environmental impact but greater degradation is created by many other sources. Most environmental damage is related not to volumes of tourists but to inadequate policies and practices to cope with any growth. The concept of sustainable development is examined and its implications for tourism are discussed. Related are low- and high-impact tourism development. Appropriateness is a value measure that concerns the environment and tourism planning. Finally, ecotourism as a new thrust of tourism development offers new challenges for the planner. From this examination of growth and sustainable development of tourism, the following conclusions have been reached.

Policies should be directed toward quality as well as quantity.

Although growth is universally desired for economic expansion, it needs to be put in proper context. Social and environmental impacts resulting from tourism growth are important elements of planning. Not all segments of society view tourism growth with equal enthusiasm. In many instances, improved quality—design, functional relationships, and service—can be as strong a driver of tourism enhancement as sheer growth of numbers.

Global environmental deterioration demands tourism's attention.

Because natural and cultural resource quality forms the foundation for tourism, degradation is critical to future success. Yet, tourism leaders, especially the private sector, have not seen environmentalism as an important mission until recently. Water and air pollution, toxic waste, erosion of soils, loss of animal habitat, acid rain, and most other environmental damages are not caused by tourism but by inadequate policies by other kinds of developers. Tourism and its economic gains cannot be developed where this environmental damage has occurred or is threatened.

Park protection and tourism development can be compatible.

The ideological premise that park protection of resources is incompatible with tourism development is false. With proper planning and management these two forces can be mutually supportive. Such planning requires that activities of mass tourists be concentrated where they do not disturb fragile and rare resources, and that advocates of resource protection and tourism development enter into new cooperative planning with developers.

Sustainable development is a planning principle for tourism.

In order to achieve the goal of sustainable development, tourism planning must be comprehensive enough not to undermine ecological and social systems. This requires that the existing piece-by-piece tourism expansion be replaced by larger scale cooperation and integration and much greater awareness of tourism's dependency upon natural and cultural resources.

Capacities cannot be determined mathematically.

Top limits to visitor uses of environmental settings have not succeeded in the past. Instead, planning and management processes need to be put in place that monitor incremental changes and impacts. With this approach, decisions can be made for design, planning, and management changes to cope with growth as it occurs. The capacity of the environment to withstand great tourism growth is quite elastic, provided that the growth is properly planned and managed.

Low-impact tourism offers great potential.

Massive, and often externally driven tourism development has proved to produce the greatest environmental, economic, and social shock to an area. Instead, slow growth with lower scale development has a much better chance of adapting to existing conditions. It also has the advantage of greater public involvement locally, providing better integration and greater returns to the local society.

Tourism development should be appropriate to the setting.

Much of the conflict between environmentalists and tourism developers stems from esthetics. Although this is heavily value laden, there are some observable relationships that can be resolved through better building and site design. Especially critical are new developments adjacent to historic architecture and natural resource settings.

Ecotourism requires special site, area, and regional planning.

Market demand for visitor use of natural and cultural resource settings has increased dramatically. New planning, design, and management principles are required. Serious damage to the environment can result unless developers implement integrative action involving professionals and local community citizens. Ecotourism as a concept must be accompanied by resource management controls.

Ecotourism can foster conservation.

Increasingly, ecotourism businesses are returning a portion of their revenues to support management of resource areas that attract visitors. This symbiotic relationship fosters resource protection as well as good business. But, this ideal requires care in planning, development, and management.

REFERENCES

Baker, P. (1986). "Tourism and the National Parks." *Parks and Recreation,* October, 50+

Becker, R. H. et al. (1986). "Threats to Coastal National Parks: A Technique for Establishing Management Priorities." *Leisure Sciences,* 8(3), 241–256.

Boo, Liz (1991). "Ecotourism: A Tool for Conservation." In *Ecotourism and Resources Conservation,* J. A. Keesler (ed.), pp. 517–519. Berne, NY: Association of Wetland Managers.

Brown, Lester R. (1991). "The New World Order." In *State of the World,* Chapter 1, pp. 3–20. New York: W.W. Norton & Company.

Bryan-College Station Eagle (1991a). "Galveston Bay Seafood Threatened by Pollution." (AP) 117 (September 9).

Bryan-College Station Eagle (1991b). "State to Analyze Impact of Dairy Cattle's Manure." (AP) (October 21).

Collins, Michael (1991). "Ecotourism in the Yucatan Peninsula of Mexico." Dissertation. No. 91-1, Faculty of Landscape Architecture. Syracuse: State University of New York.

Colvin, Jean (1991). "The Scientist and Ecotourism: Bridging the Gap." In *Ecotourism and*

Resource Conservation, J. A. Keesler (ed.), pp. 575–581. Berne, NY: Association of Wetland Managers.

Dickert, T., and J. Sorenson (1974). "Social Equity in Coastal Zone Planning." *Coastal Zone Management Journal,* 1, 141–150.

Dykeman, Floyd (1992). "Pilot Communities for Sustainable Development." *Community Horizons,* (3): Rural and Small Town Research and Studies Programme, Mount Allison University, Sackville, New Brunswick.

Falconer, Brian (1991). "Tourism and Sustainability: The Dream Realized." *Tourism-Environment-Sustainable Development: An Agenda for Research, proceedings of the Travel and Tourism Research Association Canada,* Hull, Quebec, pp. 21–26.

Fennell, D. A., and P. F. J. Eagles (1990). "Ecotourism in Costa Rica: A Conceptual Framework." *Journal of Park and Recreation Administration,* 8(1), Spring.

Forster, Richard R. (1973). *Planning for Man and Nature in National Parks.* Morges, Switzerland: International Union of Conservation of Nature and Natural Resources.

Getz, D. (1982). "A Rationale and Methodology for Assessing Capacity to Absorb Tourism." *Ontario Geography,* 19, 92–102.

Groom, Martha J. (1991). "Management of Ecotourism in Manu Biosphere Reserve, Peru." In *Ecotourism and Resource Conservation,* J. A. Keesler (ed.), pp. 532–540. Berne, NY: Association of Wetland Managers.

Gunn, Clare A. (1978). "Needed: An International Alliance for Tourism, Recreation, Conservation." *Travel Research Journal,* 2, 3–10.

Gunn, Clare A. (1988). *Vacationscape: Designing Tourist Regions,* 2nd ed. New York: Van Nostrand Reinhold.

Hamed, Safei El-Deen (1990). "Integrating Elements of Natural and Cultural Resources into the Development of Tourism in South Sinai and the West Coast of the Red Sea: A Strategic Management Plan." Paper presented at Council of Education of Landscape Architecture Annual Meeting, Denver, Colorado.

Holdsworth, Deryck, ed. (1985). *Reviving Main Street.* Toronto: University of Toronto Press.

Long, D. (1990). "Resource Management: A Global Perspective." *Tour & Travel News,* 179 (May 7), 1+.

Machlis, Gary E., and David L. Tichnell (1985). *The State of the World's Parks.* Boulder, CO: Westview Press.

Manning, Edward W. (ed.) (1992). "Challenges to the Tourism Sector for the Coming Decade." Based on presentations, Tourism Stream of the Globe '92 Conference, Vancouver, Canada, March.

Mansperger, M. C. (1992). "Yap: A Case of Benevolent Tourism." *Practicing Anthropology,* 14(2) (Spring), 10–13.

Molotch, H. (1976). "The City as a Growth Machine: Toward a Political Economy of Place." *American Journal of Sociology,* 82(2) (September).

Murphy, P. E. (1983). "Perceptions and Attitudes of Decisionmaking Groups in Tourism Centers." *Journal of Travel Research,* 21(3) (Winter), 8–12.

Nelson, J. G. (1991). "Are Tourism Growth and Sustainability Objectives Compatible? Civics, Assessment, Informed Choice." In *Tourism-Environment-Sustainable Development: An Agenda for Research,* proceedings of the Travel and Tourism Research Association Canada Conference, October 17–19, Hull, Quebec, pp. 38–42.

Okrant, M. J. (1991). "A Skeptics View of Sustainability and Tourism." *Tourism-Environment-Sustainable Development: An Agenda for Research*, proceedings of the Travel and Tourism Research Association Canada Conference. October 17–19, Hull, Quebec, pp. 31–33.

Packard, Jane M., et al. (1991). *Ecotourism: A Bibliography*. College Station, TX: Institute of Renewable Natural Resources, Texas A&M University.

PATA (1991). *Moorea Tourism*, Report of Task Force sponsored by Pacific Asia Travel Association and French Polynesia Government. Sydney, Australia.

Postel, Sandra, and Christopher Flavin (1991). "Reshaping the Global Economy." In *State of the World,* Chapter 1, pp. 170–188. New York: W.W. Norton & Company.

Read, A. (1988). "Success on Main Street: The Texas Connection." *Main Street,* 37 (July), 1–5.

Rees, W. E. (1989). "Defining Sustainable Development." *CHS Research Bulletin*, University of British Columbia, (May), 3.

Rothman, R. A. (1978). "Residents and Transients: Community Reaction to Seasonal Visitors." *Journal of Travel Research,* 16(3), 8–13.

Sargent, Frederick (1974). *Human Ecology*. New York: American Elsevier.

Simonds, Mary Ann (1991). "Dolphins and Ecotourism: Determining Impacts. In *Ecotourism and Resource Conservation,* J. A. Keesler (ed.), pp. 662–675. Berne, NY: Association of Wetland Managers.

Smardon, Richard (1991). "Ecotourism and Landscape Planning, Design and Management." In *Ecotourism and Resource Conservation,* J. S. Keesler (ed.), pp. 517–519. Berne, NY: Association of Wetland Managers.

Stanley, D. (1991). "Synthesis of Workshop Sessions." *Tourism-Environment-Sustainable Development: An Agenda for Research,* proceedings of the Travel and Tourism Research Association Canada Conference, October 17–19. Hull, Quebec, pp. 116–118.

State of the Parks: 1990 Report (1991). Ottawa, Canada: Minister of Supply and Services.

Statistical Abstract (1989). Washington, DC: U.S. National Park Service.

Stewart, W. P. et al. (1990). "Sustainable Tourism Development: A Conceptual Framework," pp. 145–146. Presentation, Third Symposium on Social Sciences in Resource Management, Texas A&M University.

Taylor, G. (1991). "Tourism and Sustainability: Impossible Dream or Essential Objective." *Tourism-Environment-Sustainable Development: An Agenda for Research,* proceedings of the Travel and Tourism Research Association Canada Conference, October 17–19, Hull, Quebec, pp. 27–29.

Van Hyning, Thomas E. (1991). "Ecotourism: A Key Survival Link," *Pennsylvania Recreation and Parks,* (Summer), 14–15.

Wendt, Charles W. (1991) "Providing the Human and Physical Infrastructure for Regulation Ecotourism Use of Protected Areas." In *Ecotourism and Resource Conservation,* J. S. Keesler (ed.), pp. 520–528. Berne, NY: Association of Wetland Managers.

Wight, Pamela (1988). *Tourism in Alberta*. Edmonton, Canada: Environment Council of Alberta.

Wight, Pamela (1993). "Ecotourism: Ethics or Eco-Sell?" *Journal of Travel Research*, 31(3), 3–9.

Williams, M., and Lynn Brake (1990). "Wilpena Station, Flinders Ranges National Park: Planning for Cultural Tourism," *Historic Environment*, (7), 3–4, 61–71.

Williams, P. W., and Alison Gill (1991). *Carrying Capacity Management in Tourism Settings: A Tourism Growth Management Process*. British Columbia, Canada: Centre for Tourism Policy and Research, Simon Fraser University.

Ziffer, Karen A. (1989). *Ecotourism: The Uneasy Alliance*. Washington, DC: Conservation International.

Part II

Concepts and Examples of Tourism Planning

After many decades of apathy and even distrust, the reality of tourism planning can be documented, albeit erratic and inconsistent. Finally, it is being recognized that the many complexities and great growth of tourism cannot be left to muddling along. Too much is at stake—in terms of the economy, society, and the environment—for this to be the dominant mode of development. The chapters in this part include concepts, processes, and examples of several approaches and degrees of planning accomplishment at three scales—regional, destination, and site.

Chapter 5, Regional Planning Concepts, traces some origins of models and approaches toward better planning at the larger scale, such as for nations, provinces and states. Planners and researchers have developed techniques for identifying zones of potential, policies, and guidelines that integrate overall tourism and provide valuable assistance to developers at the destination and site scales.

Chapter 6, Regional Planning Cases, is a random collection of examples at the larger scale. The great diversity of processes and achievement reflect the present state of the art. These are not held up as ideal models in their entirety but are presented for the lessons that can be read into them.

Chapter 7, Destination Planning Concepts, focuses on the way leaders, planners, and developers can guide better development of the travel market areas—destinations. New planning methods are available to assist destinations in their discovery of potential and the need to protect indigenous qualities of communities and their surrounding areas.

Chapter 8, Destination Planning Cases, includes examples at the community and its surrounding scale. These demonstrate planning opportunities and principles that have been implemented in a variety of situations. They show the need for considering resources, access, and potential for creating satisfying attractions—the foundation for service business.

Chapter 9, Site Planning Concepts, provides new insights into planning and design paradigms so critically important to the site scale of tourism development. It is at this level that all goals and objectives are finally played out. New design collaboration, ethics, and recognition of externalities are required for success today.

Chapter 10, Site Planning Cases, demonstrates how specific supply side development by the several sectors is being designed. These cases illustrate the new planning that integrates concerns of several public constituencies with the owner's and designer's creativity.

Chapter 11, Conclusions and Principles, is a summary of the more important meanings derived from the entire study for the book's purpose—better planning for more successful and more satisfying tourism development.

Chapter 5

Regional Planning Concepts

Introduction

Even after gaining new understandings about the many characteristics of tourism—its functioning system and components—the question remains How can tourism plans and planning be made and implemented? Are there techniques and processes that nations, provinces, and states can follow that will assist them in reaching their tourism development objectives?

Experience is demonstrating that planning is taking place and producing results. Worldwide there is an increasing awareness that tourism can no longer rely only on heavy doses of hucksterism. Greater planning and care must be exercised to avoid negative social, environmental, and economic impacts and reach the positive objectives desired.

It must be emphasized that the ideas put forward here are more conceptual than proven processes. Experience well demonstrates that planning for tourism is more art than science. Certainly the results from scientific inquiry should be utilized. Logical sequences—the *discursive* aspects should be incorporated into planning whenever possible. However, equally important, and perhaps in greater need, is *intuition*. Conscious reasoning needs to be tempered by intuitive perception. Leaders of tourism planning and development as well as local constituencies must allow feelings of rightness as well as facts and logic to influence plans and decisions.

However, experience is also showing that there is no *right* way to plan especially at so large a scale. And, probably no one should look for such an ideal model. Rather, any process that can respond to needs should be applied. The purpose of this chapter is to suggest some planning antecedents, some planning models, and ways of discovering zones of potential and processes for regions in their desire to create and implement tourism plans. Planning concepts for destinations and sites follow in Chapters 7 and 9.

PLANNING ANTECEDENTS

For most areas today, tourism development means encouraging an investor to make a study of economic feasibility of a project. Such projects are focused on sites. Too frequently there is no guidance at the regional scale on whether the site and project are suited to regionwide resource foundations, the social and economic milieu of the area, public policy, and transportation and access as related to market sources. As a consequence, even if well built and managed, the business is likely to be less successful than anticipated and to result in environmental, social, and economic stress on the area. Planners would respond to such situations by advocating better planning. But merely creating a plan in the traditional sense may not have solved these issues. Before initiating specific planning processes, there are several issues that should be addressed. Actually, these antecedents may be considered a first step in a revised planning process. The following are put forward for consideration by tourism leaders and stakeholders of regions.

Early Implementation Considerations

Because planning is often considered the process of creating plans and then implementing them, too often they are aborted. This two-step process—plan, implement—assumes that there are implementing agents ready, willing, and able to follow through with completion. Although this process functions well at the site scale with one owner, it encounters many obstacles at larger scales with a multiplicity of owners and developers. The reason is that the greater the number of implementing agents involved, the more difficult it is to cooperate, reach consensus, and activate a plan. At the destination and regional scales, plan concepts are often initiated by only one agency, organization, or individual. Many action and affected constituencies are omitted in this process, inviting opposition or apathy and resulting in inaction.

Instead of thinking of plan implementation as a two-step process, there is value in *integrating implementation at the outset.* Unless the several involved parties see the need for planning, there is little likelihood of action taking place only because a study and report were prepared. Conversely, premature plans that appear to be too costly, grandiose, and complicated may even stimulate polarization of conflict. This may set back many years the opportunity for planning new development.

The motivation for planning tourism development can come from many sources. Each community and region has a different history, tradition, politics, leadership, and aspirations. No kind of development is any more complicated socially, economically, and environmentally than tourism. These fundamentals make it difficult to generalize the initiating principles that can be applied universally. Improved tourism planning may be sparked by a national tourism office or nationwide tourism organization.

Impact Considerations

Plans will bear little fruit unless *those most affected are involved from the start*. All three implementing categories—commercial enterprise, non-profit organizations, and governments—must be committed to a regional plan. Representatives of public and private tourism organizations must be given a voice in the preparation of regional plans if there is to be any hope of implementation. Today, environmental organizations must be brought into the planning process at an early stage. In a large nation such as the United States composed of hundreds of public and private organizations, the task of involving many publics is difficult. But, there are political and organizational mechanisms by which cooperation can be obtained. No matter the method, it is important that it take place early in the process.

Communication/Education

A very important element of planning antecedents is *communication* and *education*. Although tourism has been a reality worldwide for many years, it still is not well understood. Good understanding of internal hotel operation, travel agency management, and food production and service does not mean that tourism as a system is understood. Before tourism plans are created, the several fundamentals of tourism need to be communicated to the diverse constituencies involved. This public education may involve specially prepared public meetings, seminars, and workshops. For example, few business people and public agencies are aware of the tourism research literature that has appeared in only the last two decades. New tourism research findings, concepts, and observations have been documented in books, reports, and journals and should be required reading for all national organizations and agencies anticipating tourism planning and development.

Promotional Ethics

Another important planning antecedent is the *avoidance of exaggerated claims*. Proponents of tourism must be held accountable. Frequently, only half-truths are presented in early stages of tourism development, promising only increased jobs, incomes, and tax revenues. These benefits have proved to be true rewards from tourism development but they represent only one side of tourism growth. It is equally vital to recognize the other side—the costs of tourism development. These costs can be dealt with better at the outset than coming as surprises later on. Cultural and social costs—possible conflict or erosion of cultural values—can be reduced by means of planning physical development and programs so that host-guest relations are fostered. Economic costs—expanded infrastructure of water supply, waste disposal, police, and fire protection—can be accommodated only when facts about existing capacities are known. Environmental costs—degradation of natural and cultural resources—can be ameliorated or entirely avoided by anticipating tourist needs and interests as well as potential threats to the environment. Proper design, planning, and programming can prevent most environmental stress from tourism development. There can be considerable public backlash if only a biased representation of tourism development is presented in the beginning.

Policy

An important antecedent to planning is *policy*. Nations are increasingly identifying policies for tourism development and management. Edgell (1990) cites many policies—political, economic, and social—exercised by governments that have implications for planning.

For example, because of war, disease, or improper protection of travelers, travel bans are sometimes imposed by nations. The Citizens Emergency Center of the U.S. State Department issues travel advisories regarding travel abroad. Other travel bans have been implemented wherever threats to traveler safety have appeared.

The very fact of allowing foreigners to enter a country is an act of policy. Thus, immigration policy may be detailed so carefully as to restrict the opportunity for pleasure or business travel. Because nations vary in their political ideologies, some travelers are not admitted if conflict is likely.

Many political efforts have been initiated to lessen tension of travel between countries of contrasting ideologies. The Shanghai Communique of 1972 between the United States and the Peoples Republic of China specified strategies necessary to avoid accident, misunderstanding, and poor experiences of travelers. East-West travel has changed dramatically since the fall of the Berlin Wall. Cuba, once discouraging foreign visitors, now promotes them.

Tension between wealthy and poor nations influences tourism policy throughout the world. Some believe that the industrialized generating nations are obligated to support tourism in the poorer host nations. Tourism is desired for economic growth but often financial support is unavailable except with the aid of wealthier nations. In the future, as so many nations revise their forms of government and modify traditional policies, tourism may lose or gain in its priority position. Domestic and international issues—economic, power struggle, standards of living, social conflict, and sovereignty—may force a dramatic change in national tourism policies.

The Helsinki Accord of 1975 was a freedom-of-travel agreement among thirty-five nations, including the United States and Russia. Among items agreed upon that have formed the foundation for much greater ease of travel were the following: (1) intent to increase tourism, (2) recognition of research needs, (3) assurance of protection of historic and cultural heritage, (4) encouragement of more personal and professional travel, (5) reduction of entrance fees and official documents, (6) increased cooperation on tourism development, and (7) promotion of visits to respective countries.

The U.S. National Tourism Policy Act of 1981 for the first time in this country detailed national policy for tourism development and promotion. The provisions were broad and concerned both international and domestic travel. However, because of limitations on funding, emphasis has been placed primarily on promotion of travel to the United States (Gunn 1983). The U.S. has negotiated tourism agreements with several countries— Mexico, Venezuela, Egypt, the Philippines, Hungary, Poland, Morocco, and Canada.

Tourism policy is also influenced by several international organizations. The Organization of American States (OAS) provides development assistance to member countries in areas such as financing mechanisms, facilitation, statistics, education, and training. The Organization for Economic Cooperation and Development (OECD), headquartered in Paris, provides a forum for discussion of economic issues including tourism. It has fostered the reduction of border customs and restrictions. The World Tourism Organization (WTO), with main offices in Madrid, fosters meetings and technical assistance, and sponsored the major World Tourism Conference in Manila in 1980.

At all levels, national to local, policies set by public agencies have a great bearing on how tourism is planned, developed, and managed.

Cooperation/Collaboration

Finally, a tourism planning antecedent is *cooperation and collaboration* with other related planning. All other agency and organizational planning must be reviewed to discover important relationships. Mechanisms need to be developed so that tourism does not conflict with and can be integrated into these other plans. Urban planning, industrial planning, rural planning, transportation planning, and other planning can greatly affect all tourism development. Tourism planning must be integrated with all other planning activities.

BACKGROUND

Years ago a few scholars, planners, and geographers expressed interest in how tourism was being developed and responded with new models and processes for planning tourism. A few of these that have influenced modern thinking on the topic of tourism planning follow.

Recreation Areas

Romsa (1981, 343) has described a planning model prepared by Kiemstedt (1967) that measures and maps three sets of factors to determine areas best suited for recreation development. Factors investigated are inherent physical attributes, available leisure facilities, and the cultural milieu of the region. Each set is summarized to arrive at an index of attractivity. The measurement problem was solved by use of a delphi technique evaluation.

The process includes several steps beginning with measuring the relevant subcomponent variables for a given quadrant of land. From an attractivity function, the attractivity value for each variable is calculated. The attractivity value is then multiplied by a weighting factor and the resultant values form an index. Kiemstedt describes this function in the following formula:

$$\text{Ar I} = \sum_{i=1}^{m} i = \sum_{j=1}^{n} j \cdot aj \cdot wj$$

where Ar I = attractivity index of region I
    i = quadrant
    aj = the attractivity value of variable j
    wj = the weight assigned to variable j

Overlay maps are then prepared for each component. Those land areas that fall into the upper categories for all components are deemed the most attractive for recreation development.

Further modifications were made by others in an attempt to gain greater insight into analysis for planning.

Product's Analysis Sequence for Outdoor Leisure Planning

Lawson and Baud-Bovy (1977) created an approach to planning outdoor recreation and tourism development called Product's Analysis Sequence for Outdoor Leisure Planning (PASOLP). Baud-Bovy (1980, 1982) later elaborated on his earlier experiences of applying some of his concepts and principles of tourism planning in several countries. He stressed integrated planning—planning that breaks from the traditional technical planner's approach. By integration, he asked that tourism planning be integrated with the nation's policies, physical environment, and related sectors of the economy; into the public budget and international tourism market; and with the structure of the tourist industry.

His experimentation with an updated PASOLP approach in Niger has resulted in the concept shown in Figure 5-1 (Baud-Bovy 1982, 312).

Baud-Bovy emphasized that planning should be a continuous process because of the vagaries of tourism over time—economy, politics, and fashion. Required is a regular monitoring system. He conceived a four-phase planning process:

A. Scientific investigation and analysis
   • Principal tourism flows (existing and potential) are compared with attractions and resources.
   • The nation's structures, politics, and priorities are analyzed.

B. Identification of development objectives
   • Each market segment is examined.
   • Existing tourism products are compared to market segments.
   • Destination attractions are examined.
   • Feasibility, as well as socioeconomic and environmental impacts of new development are examined.
   • Priority development is identified.

C. Creation of physical plan
   • Three preliminary studies are made: needed new facilities, estimated impact on sites, and preferred destinations.

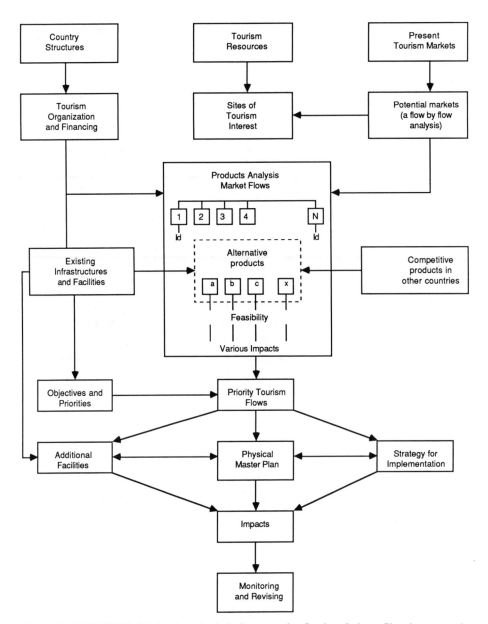

Figure 5-1. PASLOP Model. Product Analysis Sequence for Outdoor Leisure Planning, an early process applicable to tourism planning. (Baud-Bovy 1982, 313).

- Based on results of Phase B, conclusions and recommendations for needed planning are stated.

D. Impacts
   - Socioeconomic and environmental impacts of proposed development are assessed.
   - Resource issues and problems are given particular attention.

Market-Plant Match

An important process step for planning tourism in a region is to match development with needs and desires of travel markets as described in Chapter 2. As an experiment, Taylor (1980, 96) applied market analysis in several countries to the Canadian tourism plant. It was found that of the six segments of Swedish travelers, the Canadian plant could satisfy only one segment. West German markets were matched by only two. All American market segments, however, matched the available Canadian plants.

A special contract to develop a market-plant model for Canada was offered by Canadian Government Office of Tourism (CGOT). The objectives were to:

Assemble and store key data on tourism market and plant.
Find where markets should be directed to meet expectations.
Show gaps in tourism plant.
Show Canada's position in world plan.
Relate CGOT's program to market/plant. (DPA Consulting 1981, 1)

Running parallel with that investigation was a second study directed toward elaborating a federal perspective on tourism destinations throughout Canada. Particular reference was to be made to four markets: the United States, overseas, interregional Canada, and intraprovincial. The investigation was limited to review of existing documents on planning and zones. The study (Gunn 1982) resulted in two main conclusions. First, several functioning destinations have developed even though they are not necessarily the result of plans. Market data for the four market thrusts of the project were applied to known Canadian resources, access, and developed destinations. The ideal criteria used for new delineation of zones were access, service centers, natural resource base, cultural resource base, other resource factors, and program-management factors.

Second, in the effort to delineate zones based on these criteria, several observations suggested that a new approach to planning was needed. The existing basis for destination delineation seemed to have several weaknesses: (1) provinces used different criteria, (2) definitions of destination zones were not uniform, and (3) dates of basic data of provinces and federal government varied considerably.

It was concluded that a new methodology for identifying destination zones within the entire nation was needed. This resulted in a three-phase planning approach to discover zones of potential: (1) research of physical factors, (2) research of program factors, and (3) conclusions for destination potential (Gunn 1982).

Spatial Patterns

At the same time that planning consultants and governments awakened to the need for tourism planning, several geographers began to take interest. Pearce (1981) built upon earlier work of Gilbert in England, Miege in France, and Poser in Germany to identify structures and processes of tourist development, evaluation of resources, and analysis of impact of tourist development.

Pearce (1981, 6) identified five elements of tourism supply as attractions, transport, accommodations, supporting facilities, and infrastructure. He divided attractions into three types: natural features; man-made objects; and cultural, such as music, folklore, and cuisine. Transportation for travelers has shifted, causing spatial changes in tourism development. Accommodation patterns have diversified and a wider range of other services are in demand. While infrastructure is not revenue producing, it is essential to tourism. "Successful tourist development depends in large part on maintaining an adequate mix, both within and between these sectors" (Pearce 1981, 9). Developmental factors of interest to geographers include location, land tenure and use, carrying capacity, and analysis of tourism impacts. With these foundations, spatial planning issues identified are: areas with greatest developmental potential, the need to foster growth in dispersed areas, and the need to ameliorate local cultural disruption.

Pearce (1981, 83) concluded that there are many constraints on planning for tourism. One problem, particularly in developing countries, is the temptation to use models from elsewhere due to lack of data and expertise. This may lead to highly inappropriate development. Implementation is also an issue, especially when roles of the several sectors are not clearly understood. Coordination between agencies is often difficult. Planning as a process is preferred over a plan due to the dynamics of tourism. Feedback, monitoring, and flexibility to meet changing conditions are needed.

Because tourism involves elements of great interest to geographers—spatial differentiation and regularities of occurance (Pearce 1979, 247)—few disciplines have contributed as much to the literature of tourism development. Pearce identified interest topics such as spatial patterns of supply (Thompson 1971; Wolfe 1951; Piperoglou 1966; Pearce 1979), spatial patterns of demand (Wolfe 1951; Deasy and Griess 1966; Boyer 1962, 1972), the geography of resorts (Pearce 1978; Pigram 1977; Relph 1976), tourist movement and flows (Williams and Zelinsky 1970; Guthrie 1961; Archer and Shea 1973; Wolfe 1970; Campbell 1966; Mariot 1976), impacts of tourism (Christaller 1954, 1964; Coppock and Duffield 1975; Archer 1977; Pearce 1978; Odouard 1973; White 1974; Smith 1977), and models of tourism space (Miossec 1976, 1977; Yokeno 1977). Van Doren and Gustke (1982, 543) analyzed shifts over time (1963–1977) of the growth of hotel development with particular reference to the Sun Belt of the United States. This sampling of scholars and topics emphasized the fact that economics and promotion, while dominating political interest in tourism, are not the only topics of study important to planning.

Other geographers have studied special aspects of tourism. Demars (1979, 285) traced the development and distribution patterns of resorts in North America and Great Britain. Murphy (1979, 294) investigated the spatial imbalance in travel patterns and the place of camping in market development strategies in Canada. He concluded that market plans must be much more aware of specialized behavioral preferences for destinations. Britton (1979, 326) in his study of Third World tourism concluded that "Host governments must convince an arrogant and powerful industry that local citizens *and* tourists would benefit from the honest representation of places." Geographical studies in developing countries have been made by many geographers including Helleiner (1979, 330), Hyma and Wall (1979, 338) and Collins (1979, 351).

Insight on the spatial aspects of tourism planning was brought forward by Fagence (1991). His focus was on frameworks that help identify destination zones that have special suitability for tourism. His basic working premise was:

> that locations, regions, resources, amenities and infrastructures have an unequal potential and capacity for particular forms, types and scales of development. (Fagence 1991, 10)

Based on this premise, he advocated a coordinated and collaborative approach among all public and private interests, especially to stimulate entrepreneurial initiative. This geographically referenced framework could provide tourism planners and developers with a tool that would be able:

1. To express the spatial aspects of any national or regional policy—locations, concentrations, geographic linkages, travel routes and networks, areas of amenity, distributions, and so on;
2. To monitor the evolving patterns of geographic suitability—i.e., beyond the status of mere physical capability for development as measured through impact assessments of various kinds—within such concepts and strategies as balance, diversity, complementarity;
3. To facilitate the geographical integration of the various types of tourism development, and of tourism development with other forms of economic activity—so as to avoid inharmonious relationships, creation of economic monocultures, incompatible forms and quantities of development and servicing need;
4. To assist the integration of tourism development with other forms of economic and regional restructuring;
5. To more efficiently identify locations or "zones" for tourism development so as to maximize the utilization of indigenous spatial, economic and environmental resources, and so as to pursue specialization and balance rather than duplication, replication, perhaps at the expense of sub-optimization of realistic opportunities; and
6. To formulate integrated strategies to accommodate local/regional/national government and entrepreneurial initiative, so as to provide a context of investment and development confidence, and so as to achieve a coordination of transport, communication, utility infrastructure, and other public capital works programmes. (Fagence 1991, 11)

Perhaps the strongest endorsement of the Fagence approach is its practical applicability. It again emphasizes the need for tourism management tools that are not only spatially sound but also are related directly to business success, environmental protection, and local social integration. His lucid paper offers further framework concepts that include *points, lines,* and *areas* as essential elements of tourism planning, development, and management (Fagence 1991, 14).

Regional Factor Planning

As early as 1950, Gunn identified factors important for tourist business locations in the state of Michigan. In his planning guide, *Planning Better*

Vacation Accommodations (1952), he advised investors to consider locations with favorable natural resource factors, such as water, wildlife, land forms, forests, and climate; and man-made factors of markets, transportation, competition, history, and neighborhood. These factors for success had grown out of observation and study of tourist business places in connection with the Tourist and Resort Extension Service of Michigan State University.

Further study revealed the need for planning concepts and principles at the regional scale and were contained in the dissertation, *A Concept for the Design of a Tourism-Recreation Region* (Gunn 1965). This work was coincidental to the Michigan's Upper Peninsula planning project described in Chapter 6. The study identified a planning process with these major phases: (1) research of geographic position, geographic content, and landscape expression; (2) evaluation of potential, including demand, owner's rewards, and synthesis; (3) application of a design-planning concept; and (4) implementation.

The *environmental research* phase first recommended an analysis of a region's *geographic position,* as illustrated in Figure 5-2. Proximity to markets, A, can influence greatly both volume and other characteristics of how travel demand will impact a region. At the time of the study, based on Michigan's travel situation, the position of the state made it vulnerable to new attraction development in the Kentucky region (Figure 6-2). B (Figure 5-2) illustrates further geographic relationships that can influence travel flows and anticipated demand impacts.

Another step in the research was analysis of *geographic content.* Figure 5-3 illustrates eight characteristics of the Upper Peninsula's geographic content: geology, soils, land relief, forests, water, climate, development, and historical background. Identification of land uses, distribution of cities, and size and shape of the region were included in this analysis.

A third aspect of the research was *landscape expression* as illustrated in Figure 5-4, as applied to Michigan's Upper Peninsula. The dominance of common characteristics is shown in part A, universality. However, considering other factors of the land, the region could be described as being made up of two halves, each with its own set of interrelated land characteristics, B. When analyzing the region for special characteristics lending distinction to places, several locations can be delineated as shown in part C.

The next phase, *evaluation of tourism-recreational potential,* included a synthesis of the environmental research results with findings regarding *demand* and *owner's rewards.* This process step to determine demand suggested use of market survey research to identify differences between activities sought while touring or for longer stays. Results of demand research were to be representative of the demand area, current—not

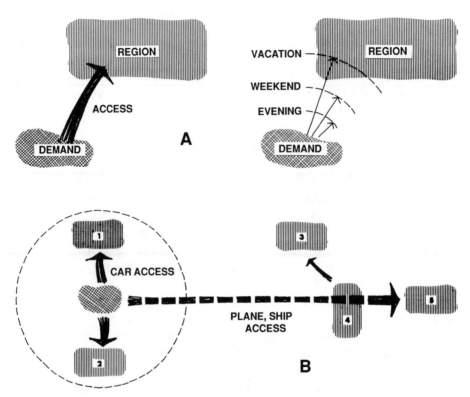

Figure 5-2. Geographic Position. Future development depends greatly on market proximity. A illustrates comparison between evening, weekend, and vacation distances. B suggests different demand for five destinations: 1 and 2 are accessible by automobile whereas 3, 4 and 5 are reached only by ship or plane. Dominant travel to 4 and 5 help provide access to secondary location 3 (Gunn 1965, 7).

based on outdated study, representative of present users of the region, and indicative of trends in competitive regions.

Study of ownership and owner rewards was considered (Gunn 1965, 20) an important factor of this phase. Development would vary depending on whether the anticipated rewards to owners would be toward social goals or profits.

The final stage in the evaluation phase was that of *synthesis*, combining the study results to determine meaning for planning. Some of the questions resolved at this step include:

> What is the land character and points of entrance to the region?
> How does the present development compare with what the resource assets suggest could be developed?
> What types of new recreation-tourism activities are suggested by the land analysis?
> What are the seasonal opportunities and limitations?
> What special qualities of communities suggest expanded tourism-recreation there?

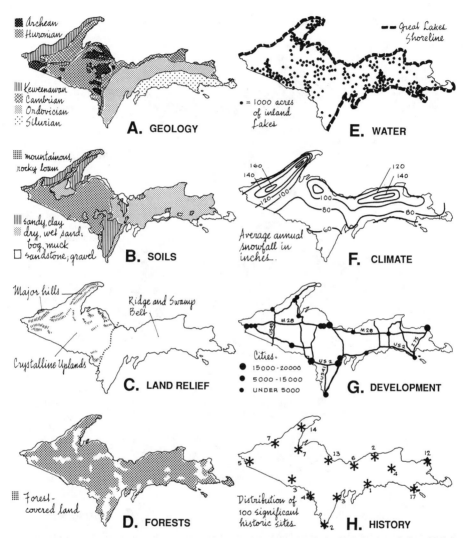

Figure 5-3. Geographic Content. Eight factors derived from study of physical characteristics of Michigan's Upper Peninsula were used as foundation for the example described in Chapter 5 (Gunn 1965, 10).

> How does the distribution pattern of communities relate to the entire region and resource assets? (Gunn 1965, 24)

The next phase was the creation and application of *planning concepts*. Figure 5-5 illustrates a model of the key elements important to planning a region for tourism put forward in 1965. These include:

> A definable regional boundary
> Access from markets and internal circulation corridor

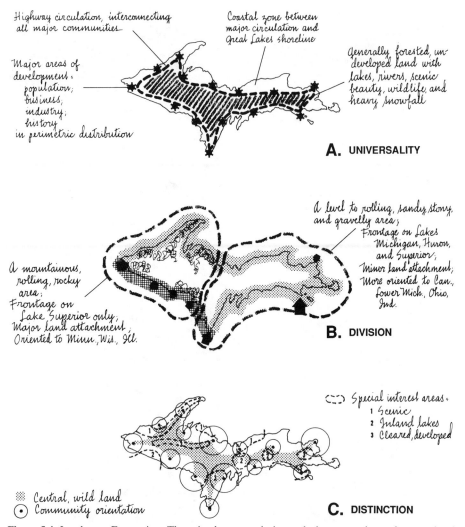

Figure 5-4. Landscape Expression. Three landscape analysis conclusions were drawn from study of Michigan's Upper Peninsula: "A" universality, "B" division, "C" distinction (Gunn 1965, 13).

Community attractions complexes
A "non-attraction hinterland"
Critical entrances to region

All of these have special design and planning concerns but especially important is how they fit into the whole.

Details of remaining steps in the application of this planning concept and process are described in Chapter 6. For example, several natural and cultural resource characteristics were studied and conclusions were reached regarding their adaptability to tourism development. Further

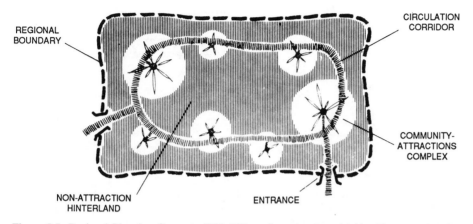

REGIONAL
BOUNDARY

CIRCULATION
CORRIDOR

COMMUNITY-
ATTRACTIONS
COMPLEX

NON-ATTRACTION
HINTERLAND

ENTRANCE

Figure 5-5. Regional Planning Concept, 1965. This early regional model identifies several major elements for tourism planning purposes: regional boundary, access and circulation corridor, entrances, community attractions complexes, and a nonattraction hinterland (Gunn 1965, 26).

study identified nine zones with greatest potential, and key development themes and projects were identified for each. Conceptual planning was also performed for several specific locations. This early regional planning could be called an integrative process because it was performed jointly by tourism specialists of Michigan State University, governmental agencies, and representatives of local people including tourism interests. Although computer mapping was not yet available, the principle of analyzing physical factors as well as market characteristics was utilized.

This regional planning concept model was then refined as illustrated in Figure 5-6, published in Gunn (1972, 71). More recent interpretation of the "community-attractions complex" suggests that it may be more correctly labeled "destination zone." Models of relationships between communities, services, attractions, and access were diagrammed for several types of travel objectives (Gunn 1972, 73–97): vacation home use, attending conventions, organization camping, resorting, attending events, visiting friends and relatives, hunting/fishing, winter sports, special uses, and touring/sight-seeing. The models have been useful for nations and regions to conceptualize the planning of the overall tourism system.

Although the model illustrated in Figure 5-6 is basic to all regions, further study reveals several patterns of destination use by travelers. Figure 5-7 illustrates results of a study by Lue, Crompton and Fesenmaier (1993) that revealed at least five different spatial configurations:

1. *Single Destinations*—most activities within one destination.
2. *En Route*—several destinations visited en route to a main one.
3. *Base Camp*—others visited while at a primary destination.

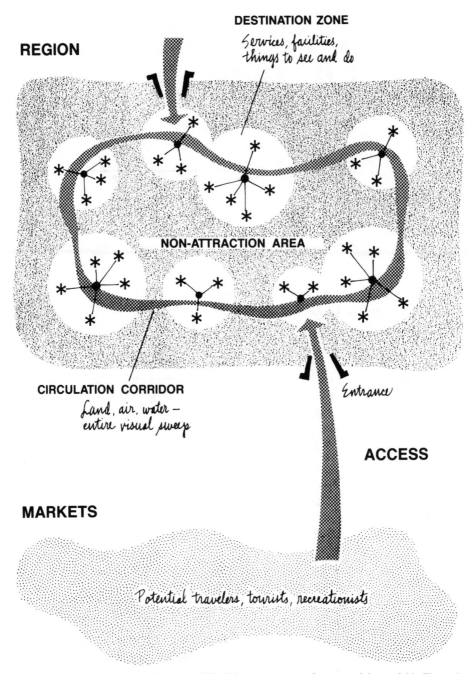

DESTINATION ZONE
Services, facilities, things to see and do

REGION

NON-ATTRACTION AREA

CIRCULATION CORRIDOR
Land, air, water — entire visual sweep

Entrance

ACCESS

MARKETS

Potential travelers, tourists, recreationists

Figure 5-6. Regional Planning Concept, 1972. This represents a refinement of the model in Figure 8-5 (Gunn 1972, 71).

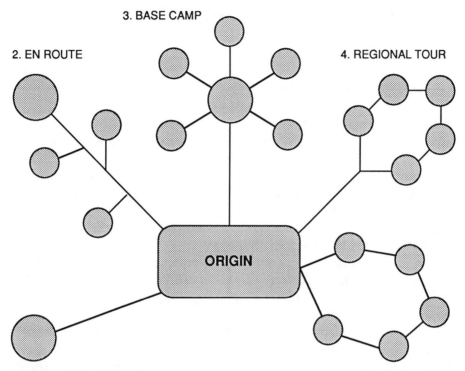

Figure 5-7. Geographic Pattern of Destinations. Typical destination zone types: single, en route, base camp, regional tour, and trip chaining (Lue, Crompton and Fesenmaier 1993, 294).

4. *Regional Tour*—several destinations visited while in a target region.
5. *Trip Chaining*—a touring circuit of several destinations.

From a planning perspective, the patterns again endorse the need for planners, developers, and managers at all levels to work together. Spatial patterns are influenced both by distribution of resources within a region and market interest in travel to and within the region. Smaller and rural destination zones can benefit from cooperating with larger ones for development and promotion. Destinations visited for only a short time can benefit from food service, retail sales, and admissions whereas lodging may take place in larger destinations. These patterns are useful in evaluating the potential based on resource factors—some with abundant natural and cultural resources may be favored over others. When an individual community seeks to develop tourism, it should consider these patterns in determining relationships to others and emphasis upon special resource characteristics for attractions.

Before planning techniques are discussed later in this chapter, it is useful to provide a foundation based on market and resource factors.

REGIONAL DEVELOPMENT HIERARCHY

Based on past tourism experience, a dependence hierarchy, such as diagrammed in Figure 5-8, can provide a useful foundation for planning. This heirarchy summarizes many of the topics and principles stated earlier in this book, such as the tourism system and influential factors in Chapter 2.

Regional development of tourism (A in Figure 5-8) generally must have an increase in the volume of participation (B in Figure 5-8). More people must go to a region and spend money on tourism activities in order to generate new jobs, new incomes, and new tax revenues. However, increased participation depends upon two very important factors.

First, there needs to be a heightened demand (C1) to visit the given region. In this context it means that more people at their home origins must be able to exhibit both the *desire* and the *ability* to travel to the region and participate in its offerings. If prospective visitors do not have a desire to visit the given region, it is doubtful if they will. In addition to desire, they must have the time, money, transportation, and equipment necessary to make the visit.

Second, if more people are to do this, changes in present levels of offerings—the supply—must take place (C2). Either the capacity of the present physical plant or the total number of offerings must be increased. In other words, either more people or shifts of markets must be accommodated at more attractions, lodging, food service, transportation, and retail sales and services. Furthermore, if the region has a reputation of low attractiveness or poor service, this image must be reversed. From an economic point of view, the local system servicing tourism should have the highest export ability; that is, it should import the fewest services and goods. Finally, whatever changes are made must be appropriate to both national and local political and social goals. For these accomplishments to happen, there need to be changes in both markets D1 and resource development D2. Some of the changes can be manipulated from the standing of the region; others cannot.

Expanded Markets

Changes in D1 are often influenced by overall cultural and economic trends of the nation (for domestic tourism) and the world (for foreign tourism) and are not subject to easy manipulation by a tourism region. Some, however, can be influenced. A review of some of the important factors within markets D1 may provide some insight into the opportunities and limits of market manipulation.

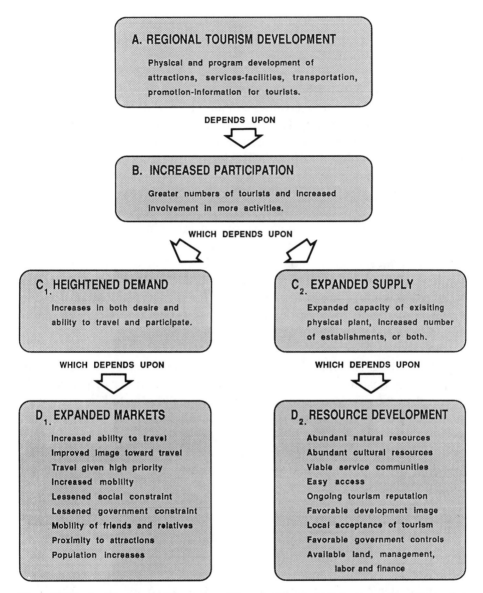

Figure 5-8. Tourism Development Dependence Hierarchy. If tourism is to be increased, greater market stimulation and greater development of tourism supply must take place. This diagram emphasizes the need for understanding fundamentals of resources and markets.

Ability. Shifts in the ability of people to travel and to spend moneys on travel objectives can have a very important impact on a region. Factors such as increased incomes, greater job security, and discretionary incomes can also have great impact. These, however, are not easily manipulated by the tourism region as they are general conditions of a total society and economy at the source of markets. Sometimes the lowered pricing of transportation and destination services can increase a market's ability to travel to the destination.

Image. Markets have either negative, neutral, or positive image values toward regions. These image values can have a good or bad influence upon the popularity of a region. Their creation is extremely complicated and not easily manipulated, as has been discovered by tourist agencies who have been disappointed with massive image-changing programs. In the long run, better supply development at destinations can enhance the region's image, providing increased word-of-mouth recommendation.

Priority. People must place high priority on travel in their expenditure of time and money if tourism is to thrive. If society shifts its priorities into other consumer targets—homes, automobiles, and education—tourism will lose. Although advertising and promotion may have some impact, it is difficult to change the priority ratings of families and individuals. While some modification of priorities on personal expenditures can be determined from the standing of a region, it is very limited.

Mobility. Obviously, mobility of the market—opportunity to travel from home to the destination—is very important. The number of people able to travel to tourist destinations may be drastically affected by continued changes in costs of automobile, bus, and air travel. To some degree, mobility both within and relating to a region can be changed by influence from a destination area. However, increased ownership of automobiles and controls of gasoline and plane ticket costs are difficult to influence from the standing of a region.

Social Constraint. Over history, social controls have been increasingly liberalized. Changes in dress, conduct, and an increase in the variety of recreational activities have influenced travel land use in recent decades. However, such cultural shifts come from market sources and are not easily manipulated by the destination region. A local society may even have values in conflict with those of visitors. Better information and educational programs can be used to lessen social conflict between hosts and guests.

Governmental Constraint. Generally, there are few direct governmental constraints to travel, but governmental policy and regulations do have an impact on travel and tourism development. Taxes on gasoline, air travel, and properties exert constraints on certain recreational activities. Governmental distribution of subsidies to highways, airports, reservoirs, and recreation areas may favor some activities over others. In some areas "Blue laws" place constraints on purchases of recreational goods on Sunday. Land use regulations and environmental controls are of increasing importance. Political agreements (or disagreements) between nations, such as for control of disease or terrorism, can foster (or restrict) travel. To some extent tourism regions can exert control over governmental constraint.

Friends and Relatives. A major category of the tourism market activity is the visiting of friends and relatives. The habitat shifts of these people make a difference in the destinations of this segment of travelers. Knowing the locations and changes in locations of friends and relatives is important but it is difficult for a tourism region to have any influence over this factor.

Proximity. Generally, the shorter the distance between home and the tourism region the better. Markets nearby or within a region are usually the ones most productive. One way a region can affect this proximity is by favoring destination development at locations most accessible from markets. Another way is to tap new market segments within the market area. Improving the time-distance relationship, such as discount air travel, between home and destination can sometimes improve the effect of proximity.

Volume. Given today's burgeoning environmental issues, it is fanciful to suggest increasing the population in market areas in order to increase tourist business. However, for certain destinations, it may be within a region's power to tap increasing volumes of new market segments in cities of origin within their market range, especially those that exhibit elements of growth.

Resource Development

Although market manipulation is not the subject of this book, it has been introduced to more clearly identify the relationship to the role of resource development (D2) in changing the economic and social impact of tourism. In other words, if anything major is to take place within a tourism region the changes in the supply—providing more for people to see and do—become very important. If numbers of attractions, transportation facilities, accommodations, food services, and retail sales and services—those economic-impact generators—are to increase, upon what factors do they depend?

Natural Resources. The given natural resource assets that lend themselves to development are important if growth of development is to take place. If a region has an abundance of usable surface water, esthetic and game-laden forests, interesting topography, buildable soils and favorable climate, it has greater potential for tourism development than one without these assets. Of course reservoirs can be built, forests can be planted, wildlife can be increased with controlled management, and hostile climates can be ameliorated (enclosures with heat in winter and with air-conditioning in summer). However, these come at a cost, a cost which often can be lessened by avoiding areas needing environmental modification and by selecting areas with the most suitable natural resource assets. Certain rare natural resource assets cannot be replicated and therefore demand special consideration. Many developed attractions, such as natural resource parks, scenic overlooks, resorts, scenic tours, and hunting and fishing areas, depend greatly upon natural resource assets.

Cultural Resources. Many participants seek their travel objectives less from developed natural resource assets than from those that are the result of man's cultural imprint. Religious, scientific, and educational institutions, trade centers, national shrines, engineering feats and manufacturing processes, as well as historic and archeological sites, buildings, and artifacts are examples of the wide range of cultural resources important to tourism development. These often already exist within a region but have not been developed for tourism.

Viable Service Communities. Generally, the cities that lie within a region being considered for tourism development serve two functions. First, they frequently contain attractions or resources with potential for attraction development. Second, they provide many needed services, facilities, and products. The primary ones, of course, are lodging and food service, but equally important for many tourists are other services, such as police, communications, medical aid, shopping, and banking. In addition, cities offer the infrastructure—water, waste, fuel, and electrical power—necessary for tourism development. Tourism expansion, therefore, depends upon the distribution and viability of cities. Generally, the larger the city, the more complete will be its ability to provide these functions.

Easy Access. Tourism expansion depends heavily on access and not all regions are equally served by transportation and access. Within the continental United States, the highway system is very important because automobile travel dominates. However, for certain localities and activities, air (and even ship) travel are important access factors for tourism. Even when expansion is considered, existing routes generally are favored over new ones.

Existing Development. An area that already possesses an ongoing tourism development has a stronger factor in its favor for future expansion than does raw and undeveloped land. The existing development may have established a reputation that is well known in the market place. Existing development, such as public parks, theme parks, historic sites, and beaches, can provide many clues to the relative importance of resource potential of an area.

Favorable Development Image. Image is a product of both the supply and user attitude and therefore cannot be dealt with only on a resource development basis. However, if an area, no matter the reason, now has a reputation of poor (or excellent) quality of tourism participation experience, it can deter (or favor) further expansion greatly. Changes of development can alter this image but not without massive change.

Local Acceptance of Tourism. Expansion of tourism depends greatly upon the local attitude toward expansion. If the local electorate and leadership fully understand the implications of tourism and favor its development, further expansion has support. However, if attitudes are antagonistic or hostile, it will be difficult to develop tourism.

Favorable Governmental Controls. Tourism development can be accomplished best with the least governmental constraints. If too many legislative controls are enacted against it, certainly development is restricted. Legislation, however, is an act of man and can be changed. Jurisdictional problems can sometimes limit full opportunity of developing legislation that gives tourism greater chances of growth. Care needs to be exercised in evaluating controls. Many of the recent environmental controls may appear to work a hardship on some development but, upon deeper examination, may be protecting and perpetuating tourism attraction assets.

Available Land for Development. Tourism development certainly depends upon space for development. Some segments use more land than others. Beach use may be very intensive, whereas hunting and wildland recreation are probably the most extensive. Vacation home development uses relatively large areas of land. Probably a greater constraint is not being able to purchase land that is properly located. Since modern concepts of ecology do not allow any land to be classified as waste, new tourism development must be a tradeoff from existing or other potential land use. Land price and purchasability are important. Therefore, tourism development depends upon the availability of suitable land for expansion—suitable in both quantity and quality.

Availability of Entrepreneurs and Managers. The tourism development of a region will depend upon the availability of entrepreneurs and managers. If a region does not have these resources, they will have to be imported. However, this can cause conflict with local aspirants who thought they could qualify for the positions. The greater the supply of several types of developers and managers—for attractions, transportation, and lodging—the more favorable a region is disposed to development.

Availability of Labor Pool. Tourism employs a wide range of job categories from highly skilled to unskilled. The nature of development will determine the labor needed and whether the region will have to import labor or supply its own. If new labor is imported, local underemployed or unemployed people may resent their coming and resist tourism expansion. Therefore, source of labor is an important factor in tourism development.

Availability of Finance. Tourism development demands great amounts of capital investment. Perhaps it would appear that the means of finance would not matter as long as development takes place. This may be true in the economic sense that some additional development is better than none. However, investment sources often carry with them contingencies that may or may not be compatible with local interests. For example, local residents may realize the value of certain land use controls to protect resource assets. An outside investor may refuse to invest under such conditions. Availability of finances is important from many standpoints.

This hierarchy of dependency identifies a number of variables, any one of which can make considerable difference in opportunities for tourism development. Some are geographic; others are not. Some are slow to change; others change very rapidly. Some are subject to legislative control; others are determined—sometimes permanently—by given environmental conditions. Some are subject to the caprice of society—either that population who lives in and controls land use of a region or that coming in as visitors. Some can be maneuvered from the standing of the region; others cannot.

Study of this hierarchy can reveal a number of factors that are within the realm of regional planning possibility.

PLANNING TECHNIQUES

Existing Situation

Even though planning approaches have varied in the past, all planning processes have begun with some study of existing characteristics of land and development. Often, this is called inventory. Regional studies often begin with lists of services and facilities—numbers and categories of lodging, food service, and attractions. Others begin with statistics on economic impact—numbers of people employed in tourism, income, and tax revenues produced. Still others identify a broad range of resource factors, both natural and cultural.

These studies are intended to lay the foundation for the creation of plans that move forward from the existing situation. Mere listing is of limited value unless it is done for fostering planning. The studies should reveal issues, deficiencies, and opportunities when analyzed for this purpose.

Coastal Tourism Resource Inventory Project

The province of British Columbia, Canada, has initiated a thorough technical computerized approach to resource analysis for sustainable tourism development (British Columbia 1991). The technique is being tested on the coastal region to determine its future applicability elsewhere. Coastal tourism here already has an estimated economic value of $220 million annually. The focus is that of inventory as a foundation for future policy and planning by both private and public sectors. Figure 5-9 illustrates the major steps in the process for phase I. The objectives of the Coastal Tourism Resource Inventory Project (CTRIP) are as follows (British Columbia 1991, 1–2):

1. To develop and implement a rigorous and credible tourism resource mapping methodology that:
   - identifies and maps tourism resources based on the needs and expectations of tourism operators and consumers;
   - reflects the present and future resource needs of the coastal tourism industry;
   - documents existing tourism resource use and infrastructure;
   - respects, where appropriate, the need for confidentiality of data; and

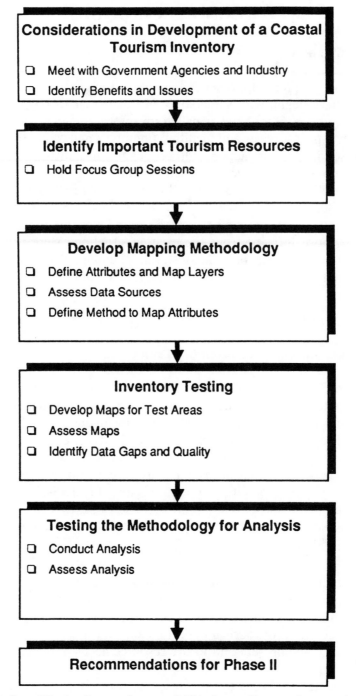

Figure 5-9. Coastal Tourism Resource Inventory, I. This diagram illustrates the steps taken in Phase I to develop, test, and refine the inventory methodology for coastal assessment for tourism (British Columbia 1991, Ex. 1.1).

- is compatible with emerging provincial government Geographic Information System (GIS) standards.

2. To ensure that the inventory provides a cost effective tool to support tourism planning and specifically:
   - enables the derivation of tourism resource values in a credible and technically sound manner;
   - highlights areas requiring land and resource use protection and/or management to maintain present and future tourism development options;
   - increases the capacity of the Ministry to represent tourism interest in integrated resource management processes; and
   - provides the basis for preparation of a coastal tourism plan.

Resource Identification

In order to identify key resources to be studied, a three-step process was followed with representatives of 57 existing and potential products, operators and recreationists, and consultants:

1. Consultants prepared tentative list of products.
2. Focus group sessions were held.
3. Interviews with those unable to attend sessions.

Findings

Results include two sets of information: information on resource attributes and consensus on those most important for each of eight categories:

Sportfishing—Overnight	Kayaking
Sportfishing Day Charters	Scuba Diving
Coastal Overnight Cruising	Marinas
Coastal Cruising—Day	Cruise Ships

For example, for marinas, the following requirements were identified:

1. Site protection—from wind and wave action.
2. Site location—dependent on the market and type of marina facility.
3. Availability of activities—depends on user type.

Mapping Methodology

Based on available secondary data, aerial photographs, anecdotal information, fish landings, and minor site inspection, the consultants were able to create maps for a series of resource factors:

Physical oceanography

Shoreline configuration and features

Mammals

Birds—spectacles and locations of unique species

Heritage/cultural resources

Access

Existing tourism use

Shoreline type

Climate

Fish and shellfish

Vegetation

Scenic resources

Land status and use

Potential Capability

Future uses can now be guided by this map series because they show the relative importance of each factor in all locations. This method was tested first in two areas along the British Columbia coast, Broughton and Juan de Fuca. Figure 5-10 illustrates the essential elements of this process and its application. The governmental agency, with its consultants, is establishing itself as the catalyst for assisting developers and managers of tourism development in their land use decisions.

Bekker (1991, 84) points out that the Geographic Information System (GIS) computer overlays of factors can be selected for specific future purposes. For example, managers of large ship cruising can use only those factor overlays deemed important to their "product" activity. When superimposed these overlay maps can produce a composite map showing relative capability distribution. Such maps can also reveal relationships between resource protection areas and concentrations of tourist services. Although still in an experimental stage, this process is already demonstrating its utility. Again, it should be emphasized that it is a tool and not a legal determinant and is being developed jointly between the public and private sectors. Planned is application for the entire province following completion of the coastal project.

Discovery of Potential Zones

At the regional scale, the identification of potential destination zones is of great help to planners and developers. Examples of accomplishing this are described in Chapter 6. For the Upper Peninsula project in the 1960s, the process used was based on generalizations of markets and resource factors

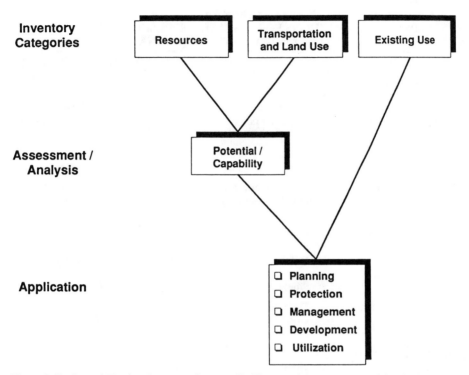

Figure 5-10. Coastal Tourism Inventory Process, II. Three major steps are used for the inventory process and application in British Columbia (British Columbia 1991, Ex. 6.1).

of the region. By studying characteristics of the resource factors, deductions were made by the planning/design team and local representatives to identify destination zones—areas where the factors were in greatest abundance and best quality. Computer techniques were unavailable at that time.

Computer Mapping

With the advent of computer mapping, using GIS programs, the speed and accuracy of performing this task are improved greatly. The use of this computer aid is explained in more detail in *Tourism Potential—Aided by Computer Cartography* (Gunn and Larsen 1988). The *Upcountry South Carolina* analysis for destination zones in Chapter 6 utilized the technique of computer overlay maps as illustrated in Figure 6-19:

- Before each map was digitized, each resource area was drawn oversize to assume influence of the factor on the surrounding area. The assumptions used for this were based on general relative importance of each factor and are listed in Table 5-1. For example, reservoirs

TABLE 5-1
SPATIAL ASSUMPTIONS FOR GIS MAPS OF RESOURCE FACTORS,
UPCOUNTRY SOUTH CAROLINA

FACTOR	CATEGORY	RATING	ASSUMPTION
Water, waterlife	Large lakes	A	Boundary + 4 mi.
	Small lakes	B	Boundary + 2 mi.
	Major rivers	B	3 mi. wide area
	Small rivers	C	2 mi. wide area
Vegetation, wildlife	Best forests/game	A	Boundary + 2 mi.
	Good forests/game	B	Boundary + 2 mi.
	Fair forests/game	C	Boundary + 2 mi.
Topography, soils	Best topography/soils	A	Boundary + 2 mi.
	Good topography/soils	B	Boundary + 2 mi.
	Fair topography/soils	C	Boundary + 2 mi.
Existing natural resource development	Parks	A	Boundary + 2 mi.
	Ramps, camps, game areas, FS land	B	Boundary + 2 mi.
	Single sites	C	Approx. 2 mi. r.
Archeology, prehistory	Dominant sites	A	Area + 2 mi.
	Good sites	B	Area + 2 mi.
	Fair sites	C	Area + 2 mi.
History, ethnicity	Dominant sites	A	Area + 2 mi.
	Good sites	B	Area + 2 mi.
	Fair sites	C	Area + 2 mi.
Economic development	200+ industries	A	City + 6 mi. r.
	100–200 indust.	B	City + 4 mi. r.
	2–50 industries	C	City + 2 mi. r.
Existing cultural resource development	Greatest mass	A	Area + 4 mi.
	Good mass	B	Area + 3 mi.
	Fair mass	C	Area + 2 mi.
Transportation	Interstate highways	A	8 mi. wide area
	US highways	B	6 mi. wide area
	Major airport	B	10 mi. r.
	State highways	C	4 mi. wide area
Cities	25,000+ population	A	9 mi. r.
	10,000–25,000	B	5 mi. r.
	2,500–10,000	C	4 mi. r.

Source: Gunn 1990, 35

generally have broader influence than streams; expressways broader than secondary highways; and large cities broader than small ones.

• Because the factors are not equal in their influence in potential for future development, they were weighted according to Table 5-2. These weightings were used in a computer aggregation of each series of maps.

TABLE 5-2
WEIGHTED FACTORS, UPCOUNTRY SOUTH CAROLINA

FOR NAT. RES. DEVELOPMENT		*FOR CULT. RES. DEVELOPMENT*	
Water, waterlife	30	Archeology, prehistory	6
Vegetation, wildlife	22	History, ethnicity	18
Topography, soils	16	Economic development	20
Existing natural resource development	10	Existing cultural resource development	20
Transportation	18	Transportation	15
Cities	4	Cities	21
	100		100

Source: Gunn 1990, 36

Discussion

Several caveats need to be mentioned regarding the application of this methodology for discovering zones of potential—destination zones. First, these zones are *temporal* and should not be delineated in ways that imply permanence. They are instead dynamic because both market influences and resource development change over time. Second, each zone must be studied in greater detail to determine *capacity* for further development. Each zone may contain abundant and high quality resources but already has been so intensively developed that it has no capacity for expansion. However, investigation may reveal that with better planning and management, further growth is possible. Third, this identification of zones does not assure viable *feasibility* of projects. All three development sectors—governments, nonprofit organizations, and commercial enterprise—will need to review the zone for their own opportunities for development. Finally, this technique is just one *part of an overall planning process.*

Perhaps the greatest significance of this methodology is to assist governments and the private sector in planning for the nation's or region's future. It should help governments in policy formation and implementation, such as technical assistance or grants for development. The private sector is assisted by the identification of service areas where new investment is most feasible and not dispersed along highways or among valuable resources, spoiling their scenic and recreational value.

PLANNING PROCESSES

Regional plans and planning for tourism take on many forms. Some are skewed heavily toward *promotional plans.* Often, these are improperly labeled marketing plans because they focus mostly on how more travel can be sold. Some nations develop *marketing plans* that include both improved supply side development as well as how to merchandise it.

Supply side planning, the primary focus of this book, can range from policies and guidelines to specific action strategies for physical and program development. For this, today's planning suggests there is value in a nation or region performing two types in concert—*a supply side plan*, updated regularly (perhaps every five years) and *continuous planning action*. Descriptions of these two approaches follow.

Supply Side Plan Project

Figure 5-11 illustrates key steps in the process for developing a regional tourism plan. It must be emphasized that the five-step process assumes that it has been preceded by several important antecedents. First, a well-represented public-private commission or organization must sponsor the process. Second, the goals of visitor satisfaction, economic improvement, resource protection, and local integration must be equally balanced moti-

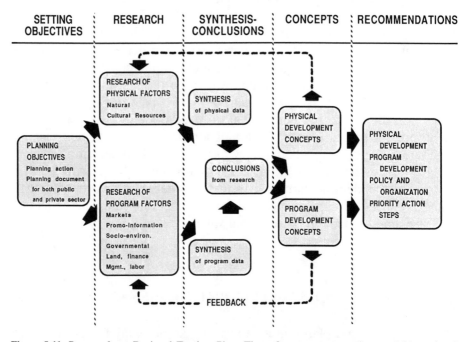

Figure 5-11. Process for a Regional Tourism Plan. These five steps can produce a viable regional tourism plan when prepared jointly by planning professionals and regional representatives of public and private sectors. It should be accompanied by a continuous planning process.

vating forces for planning. Third, all parties must have agreed to involve local constituencies throughout the process. Fourth, recommendations must be directed toward all three sectors involved in tourism development in the region—governments, nonprofit organizations, and commercial enterprise.

Step 1. Setting Objectives. The key objectives of a regional plan would be to provide planning action on (1) solutions to constraints and issues, (2) identification of destination zones with greatest potential, and (3) action objectives and strategies. Optional objectives might include concepts for projects and new policy statements. Upon completion, these objectives should be expressed in two major ways—a document and public forums.

Step 2. Research. This step can usually be accomplished through use of secondary data—existing reports, maps, and literature. However, the planning team will benefit from reconnaissance and public workshops throughout the region.

Two sets of factors need to be studied. An understanding of the *physical factors* is necessary for five reasons. First, it is essential to determining *potential destination zones.* Second, as these resources are studied, the planning team should be stimulated to *identify concepts, projects, and solutions to issues.* Third, this study helps to place the region in proper *geographical and competitive context..* Fourth, information thus derived for physical resources is essential to the establishment of *new and improved attractions,* usually the first order of tourism growth and expansion. Fifth, such an examination of resources identifies existing *threats to the environment* and guidance for future expansion capacity limits.

A prevalent fallacy of tourism development is the popular notion that all areas and communities have equal potential. The strong desire to improve local economies tends to overlook the many differences among areas. An assumption is made that the sole factor for tourism growth is promotion, and that with greater expenditures on advertising, any area can enjoy the fruits of tourism. This fallacious belief has resulted in many disappointments when communities discovered that even increased advertising could not make up for deficiencies of basic foundations. Sometimes governmental policy has provided financial incentives for tourism development in sterile geographical locations. Fagence (1991, 10) has put forth the working premise "that locations, regions, resources, amenities, and infrastructure have an unequal potential and capacity for particular forms, types, and scales of development."

The examples described in Chapter 6 contain application of processes that seek to identify zones that contain the best and most abundant factors that support tourism development. Of the many physical factors, experimentation has resulted in using a series of factors that can be generalized and aggregated to produce composite maps illustrating areas where the several factors occur in greatest mass (Figure 6-22). This process is based on the assumption that travel market interests can be generalized into two overall categories—those activities based on development utilizing natural resources or those utilizing cultural resources.

Several *program factors* require study. Essential is basic information on market preferences and other characteristics to determine gaps in present developed supply. National and international trends are also part of the study. An evaluation needs to be made of the present *promotional* and *informational* systems. An identification of *constraints* and *issues* is also part of the study. During this process, the planning team should obtain a sense of socioenvironmental concerns in the region as well as special influences of government, labor, finance, and available management and policies.

Step 3. Synthesis and Conclusions. Many consultantancy projects omit an essential step at this point in the planning process. Instead of going directly into the stage of recommendations, it is wise to evaluate what the research step has revealed. For example, the nine statements of "conclusions" for the Upper Peninsula study (Chapter 6) provided a basic foundation for the creation of recommendations and concepts. The main purpose of this step is to derive meaning from mixing together the findings from the research stage. Conclusions from both program and physical data are then derived.

Step 4. Concepts. It is at this step that creativity and ideation have full sway. Because tourism planning is more art than science, the first three steps are not determinants—they suggest and stimulate propositions. It is at this step that local citizens, and public and private developers and professionals review the findings and conclusions. This requires many meetings and workshops throughout the region. The final recommendations depend on how well all parties can visualize change in order to produce desired results.

A major aid to the development of concepts is the discovery of destination zones with greatest potential. Local areas will benefit from a regional assessment that will place them in proper perspective. The process utilizes the following steps: (1) mapping natural and cultural resources, (2) weighting and aggregating these maps by computer, (3) interpreting zones with highest quality and quantity of resource factors.

Step 5. Recommendations. At the regional scale all recommendations must be generalized but not necessarily vague or weak. To the contrary, the focus is on planning toward making the tourism system function more smoothly and more productively. Actors in all parts of the region will then see how their efforts can be helped by contributing to the success of the whole.

Recommendations on four aspects of tourism development are suggested here.

a. Physical Development. At this step, the kinds of development needed in order to improve the supply side match with demand will be described. Because this is at the regional scale, these would be generalized but would suggest types in the following categories: attractions, transportation, and services. By identifying types of development and management changes needed, actors within all three sectors would discover opportunities for their following through with development plans at the destination and site scales. In addition there would have to be recommendations on the infrastructure (water supply, waste disposal, police, and fire protection). Finally, the issues of capacities and environmental impacts would be addressed.

b. Program Development. Recommendations would be provided on the need for improvement in tourist information systems—information centers, descriptive literature, videos, tape narratives, maps, and directional systems. Assessment of the promotional program would suggest recommendations for improving advertising, publicity, public relations, and incentives. This final step would also include recommendations to resolve issues and eliminate or ameliorate constraints on tourism development.

c. Policies. Most regions lack a policy statement that provides a framework for tourism development throughout the region. This policy would be the result of joint agreement by public and private sectors. All destinations and individual enterprises can then have a sense that they are part of a whole that has agreed upon overall dimensions of tourism development. The policy should set forth the importance of the four goals addressed in Chapter 1—enhanced visitor satisfactions, resource protection, economic expansion, and integration into the local environment and economy. It should also clarify the roles of government and the private sector and especially within each destination zone. How will the roles of promotion, research, and education be allocated? What public agencies are involved, and how will their policies support tourism? How do regional taxation and governance issues relate to tourism? Are new public and private institutions needed? These and other policy questions may need to be addressed.

d. Priority. A major concern of tourism planning, especially at the regional scale, is that the volume of recommendations is so great that the task seems formidable. Probably this is the greatest reason that many well-thought-out plans remain unimplemented. A solution is to review all recommendations with the purpose of assigning priority. Some will take much greater funding and a longer time span than others. Top priority should be given to those that can be accomplished most readily in order to demonstrate improved tourism at the regional level. High priority must be allotted to organizing destination zones for their own planning and development.

The five steps can produce a region's blueprint for improved tourism. Major emphasis is based upon action strategies that regional organizations and agencies can and should implement. If the planning antecedents were properly considered at the start, implementation of the recommendations should be well under way.

One of the major outcomes will be identification of destination zones. Having accomplished this at the regional scale, the next question to be dealt with is getting the zones organized so they can initiate their own planning, as described in Chapter 7. The final step requires close collaboration between those responsible for planning at all levels—regional, destination, and site.

The final report resulting from the regional planning effort may best be presented in two kinds of publications. First, there may be need for a full report that describes completely all steps taken and the documentation to support them. This is not publicly distributed but is placed on file with all principals for future action and reference. From this a second report—condensed, clearly written, and action oriented—would be prepared for widespread distribution. Emphasis would be placed on the action strategies needed at the regional level with follow-up recommended for the proposed destination areas. This publication can be a useful tool to stimulate involvement by both regional and local levels.

It must be emphasized that such a plan, although of great value, is bound to the time period during which it was prepared. For this reason, such a plan should be revised at some future date and be accompanied by continuous planning, as described in the next section.

Continuous Planning Action

In recent years, planners and scholars of planning theory have been giving increasing attention to planning as a continuous process. Much of this activity is reaction to the inadequacies of the project or plan approach (sometimes master plan) "which gave a detailed picture of some desired future and state to be achieved in a certain number of years" (Hall 1975, 269). The project approach grew out of architecture and landscape architecture which dealt with specific buildable site development. Today, it is increasingly recognized that in addition to this approach, planning as an *ongoing process* has great merit.

The process that checks back upon itself has grown out of the science of cybernetics, coined by mathematician Norbert Wiener in 1948. This process was presented as a means of controlling complicated mechanisms by interrelating important information. It was applied not only to internal control exercised by the nervous system in an animal but also to the engineering control of equipment such as guided missiles. An important aspect of cybernetics is feedback, in which corrections are made as necessary in the functioning of a system, such as the path of a missile. From this the concept of systems planning developed, the integrated and operational planning of the entire system as a whole composed of interrelated parts. The concept of continuous planning is an application of systems planning to existing agencies, organizations, and the private sector.

Within each component of the tourism functioning system is massive involvement by public agencies. In addition, many organizations outside government exercise great influence on functions of each component. Seldom, however, are these ever integrated. In fact, they are frequently counterproductive. Certainly, for the sake of diversity and countercheck, it is desirable to have such an array of agencies and organizations. But there are instances, particularly at the planning stages, when even a small amount of collaboration and cooperation would be constructive.

Not only must the tourism system receive better continuous planning but also tourism must be integrated with all other planning for social and economic development. Many governmental agencies at the federal to local level are engaged in programs fostering new jobs, housing, and general social welfare. However, seldom do these programs include tourism. A review of structure plans (official planning documents) in England (White 1981, 40) revealed that tourism was seldom mentioned. Tourist agencies and enterprises apparently have not yet raised tourism to the needed level among the body politic. Undoubtedly, this general lack of integration of tourism into overall social, economic, and environmental planning is typical the world over, not just in England.

A continuous tourism planning function could be modeled as an interactive system whereby each sector is not subjected to a superior level of planning. Instead, each sector *on its own initiative* interacts with all others in its own decision making. Since this is not a legislated planning model, it does not depend on a planning bureaucracy or hierarchy. It capitalizes on its own self-interests to benefit from communication and interchange with other sectors.

For example, the accommodations sector (entrepreneurs, managers, and organizations), in order to stimulate greater occupancy, would on its own initiative interface with the historical restorers, festival backers, park owned recreation interests, and entertainment sectors because they are the ones who stimulate more visitors. Because accommodations can be affected by the policies and decisions of the other sectors, leaders would open up communications with them. While some overall committee, council, and other structure may be needed to integrate action, it would seem that the greater each sector increases its own sophistication regarding tourism integration, the more it will contribute to overall integrated planning for tourism.

Such an approach may be getting closer to Lang's call for better integrated planning—". . . to create a new sense of commonality which may then motivate actors to seek new forms of collaborative action; and to build capability to respond effectively to change as well as to generate change when that becomes necessary" (Lang 1988, 98). Lang utilizes the concepts of "domain" (Trist 1985), used to describe a set of interdependencies among stakeholders in a transactional (shared) environment. Collaboration begins by stakeholders recognizing that they have mutual interests and that their problems are too complex and too extensive for organizations to go it alone. Each one may be willing to engage in a give-and-take exchange on the basis of mutual gain. Only when each sector sees the advantages of interactive functioning will it reach out beyond its traditional and mandated turf.

In order to activate such interagency and intersector cooperation a detailed review of existing practices, policies, and legal mandates may be necessary. If, for example, a federal agency's enabling act makes no mention of tourism in spite of its actions impinging greatly on tourism development, it may be necessary to amend the legislation. To illustrate further, a highway department may have great competence in engineering construction but lack planning data on human tourism trends that influence future highway planning. Until the department's official mandate is amended to include greater responsibility to traveler needs, it may be expecting too much of officials to reach out and cooperate with tourism developers on a voluntary basis.

Even though a continuous planning process ideally would encompass great integration of all actors, it may be necessary to empower a central tourism agency at the highest level of government to be the catalyst for continuous planning. Most tourism agencies today at the federal level are promotion oriented and do not have powers of coordination and integration of overall tourism. When the key tourism agency is given responsibility for more than promotion, more effective planning and decisions can be made by both public and private sectors. One way of accomplishing this is for a regional public-private tourism consortium or council to sponsor annual reports of planning opportunities. Following is the recommendation made to Canada in 1982 (Gunn, 39) for annually publishing and distributing widely a three-part set of tourism development guidelines.

1. Resource Foundation for Potential Tourism Development. One well-illustrated and brief bulletin would contain descriptive information delineating the geographic distribution of resource factors. A generalized description of potential destination zones would be included. This publication would serve as an educational tool for local and provincial understanding of tourism's foundations.

2. Market-Economic Foundations for Tourism Development Potential. A second bulletin would contain information on current economic and travel market trends for the region. Market information would be for overseas, U.S., inter-Canadian, and provincial markets.

3. Tourism Potential. The third publication would be a combination of the two above, providing guidance on matching market trends with new supply development. Included would be guidelines regarding destination, attraction potential, services, transportation, information, and promotion. It would be directed toward the three action sectors—governments, non-profit organizations, and commercial enterprise.

These popular publications would be based on ongoing research essential to the information needed. Local as well as federal input would be essential. The first bulletin would not need to be revised annually because the foundation factors change more slowly.

Figure 5-12 illustrates a continuous planning process that obtains input from three sources. If it were a public-private organization sanctioned by the federal or state tourism office, it could carry on regular monitoring of supply side development. Such action would stimulate integrated action by private organizations and governmental agencies at the regional level. A major input would be from a supply side planning project at intervals depending on conditions of markets and supply, perhaps every five or ten years. These projects would be sponsored by the central agency but carried out by consultants and representatives of tourism. Detailed recommendations on overall policies as well as trends in destination zones would be provided. Another major input would be the production of destination

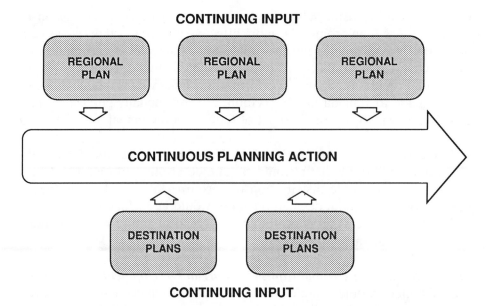

Figure 5-12. Continuous Planning Action. When combined with periodical regional and destination zone plans, a continuous planning action can provide needed monitoring of change and implementation.

zone plans. Such plans are now being initiated in many locations and are often called area, county, or community action plans. The regional agency would be the catalyst and coordinator for such plans.

CONCLUSIONS ON INTEGRATED REGIONAL PLANNING

If either the supply side plan project or the continuous planning action approaches are to be meaningful, new planning integration at the regional level (national, state, and provincial) is necessary. For example, from the earlier discussions and case studies new planning integration must encompass all three sectors of decisionmakers—governments, nonprofit organizations, and the commercial enterprise sector. New organizational structures must be sought so that all can take part in guiding tourism's future.

All sectors need to develop new ways to integrate their development of the supply side toward common goals. For a better future, the several goals are equally valid for all sectors—enhanced visitor satisfaction, improved economy and business success, protected resource assets, and community and area integration. All regional planning for tourism must allow and even stimulate action by all sectors toward these common goals.

National planning must have continuing and accurate information on both the market and supply sides, especially on how well they are in balance. The dynamics of this relationship requires ongoing planning of tourism as a system. If the components of the supply side—attractions, services, transportation, information, and promotion—are to be most successful, national planning must foster their integration as well as individual success.

Further examination of integrated planning at the regional scale reveals the need of addressing several important issues. For discussion, these issues are grouped as they relate to international or domestic planning even though they may demand the same policies and actions.

DOMESTIC TOURISM ISSUES

As a nation looks toward its own territory, several planning issues need to be addressed.

Interagency Cooperation

National governments everywhere have established many departments (ministries) to carry out rules important to their nation's welfare. Departments of conservation, forestry, agriculture, transportation, and industrial development and their many subdivisions are common. In the United States, for example, each of the dozens of agencies that own and control lands used by tourists was created for other than tourist purposes. Needed at the national, state, and provincial levels in most nations is some method of (1) identifying and clarifying its policies and practices that relate to tourism and (2) establishing mechanisms to foster cooperation and integration among these agency roles for tourism.

An effort in this direction was mandated by the U.S. National Tourism Policy Act of 1981 by establishing a Tourism Policy Council. This interagency council is directed to "coordinate policies, programs and issues relating to tourism, recreation or national heritage resources involving Federal departments and agencies" (Edgell 1990, 7). Included is the Secretary of Commerce, who serves as chairman; the Under Secretary of Travel and Tourism; the Director of the Office of Management and Budget; a representative of the International Trade Administration; the Secretary of Energy; the Secretary of State; the Secretary of Interior; the

Secretary of Labor; and the Secretary of Transportation. This council fosters greater coordination of all plans that impact tourism.

Public-Private Cooperation

Even more complicated, but necessary, is greater integration of policies and practices relating to tourism planning by the public and private sectors. Too often the public sector, because of its regulatory and administrative functions, is viewed as obstructionist and the enemy of the private sector. Conversely, because the private sector has sometimes abused its societal role, it is viewed by government as needing greater control.

From a planning perspective, both sectors depend greatly upon each other's tourism planning, development, and management. Needed is stronger national policy by both sectors that fosters integration of their practices. The many private trade associations—hotel, airline, automobile, restaurant, tour, and travel agency—have the opportunity to take a stronger proactive stand on planning tourism in cooperation with government agencies. Governments have an equal opportunity to open up the communication lines with the private sector for mutual gains from integrated planning.

Discovery of Potential

A major planning need at the national, state, and provincial level is to identify and assist destinations that have greatest developmental potential. Techniques and processes are now in place but application has lacked support. Future promotional programs at the national, state, and provincial levels can be much more effective when destinations have been planned and developed properly to receive visitors. Although the responsibility for this action lies heavily upon the destination zones, a major regional step should precede local action. Viewing the region as a whole, recognizing the geographic differences, can be a great aid to local constituencies. Some areas may then realize they should place their funds and energies behind other forms of development whereas some others may be stimulated to take further steps to plan for a tourism future. Knowing the areas of greatest potential, governments can allocate much more efficiently their incentives for planning and development.

Inter-Destination Cooperation

It is only at the higher level, the region, that inter-destinational issues can be assessed. For example, national highway or airway travel policies may foster or inhibit the potential of some destinations. National park and resource development decisions can seriously impact the potential of some areas for destination status.

Because destination zones vary greatly in size and location, certain forms of tourism can be integrated through greater inter-destination cooperation. The several patterns of touring destination use suggest that there are opportunities for several destinations to cooperate on promotion and management. Following decisions on touring routes, some areas may newly discover their destination potential.

The regional overview can assist greatly in resolving conflicts among destinations. For example, many regions have established festival calendars in order to avoid overlap of dates.

Environmental Issues

Although environmental protection is a responsibility at all levels, it is at the regional level that greatest planning integration can be realized. It is at this level that a balance between tourism and other resource uses can be obtained. Without national laws and enforcement, many of the natural and cultural resource assets may be so damaged by other development that tourism is precluded. Only with strong national policies and actions can sustainable resource development be assured.

The very foundations of tourism—cultural and natural resources—cannot continue to be threatened by political leadership that ignores its own environmental laws. In spite of protective environmental legislation, political greed for tourism's economic impact can devastate wildlife, encourage poaching, and allow pilfering of rare archeological artifacts. Public agencies that continue to allow municipal and industrial waste pollution must be held accountable if tourism is to function.

Seasonality

For many destinations, seasonality continues to inhibit healthy tourism development. At the national level, both the market and supply sides need attention. Perhaps changes can be made in school and industrial legislation to allow greater diversity of vacation periods. The growing market demand from retirees and those interested in cultural attractions suggests greater travel potential in winter and shoulder seasons. A more year-round demand could greatly increase the viability of service businesses by maintaining higher staff employment and meeting regular year-round capital costs.

Equally important is stimulating supply side entrepreneurs to be more creative in resource use at all seasons. Grants and other incentives could reward businesses that find new ways of providing attractions and services that do not depend on summer weather. In northern regions progress has already been made on creating more tours, winter sports, festivals, and cultural attraction development for more visitors in fall, winter, and spring.

Many opportunities are available at the regional level for alleviating seasonality constraints.

Information/Direction

A major obstacle for travelers is gaining proper directions for finding and understanding attractions. Excellent attractions and traveler services are of little value if the traveler cannot find them. Maps, guide books, and descriptive information are needed by the traveler but in most regions are inadequate. The millions of dollars spent on flashy advertising do not solve this issue.

Instead, at the regional level a uniform traveler information system is needed. A few nations such as the United Kingdom and Australia have resolved this issue with uniformly labeled information centers. A simple "I" sign on the highway and center, coordinated with symbols on maps, direct the traveler to centers where assistance and descriptive literature about attractions can be obtained. Many provide personal counseling—information on medical help, shopping, food service, and entertainment.

Funding for information centers is often a federal responsibility. In small towns, Western Australia has provided part-time funding to small business operators to provide some space and time for information within a strategically located shop or restaurant. Travelers deserve better guidance and information to realize their travel objectives.

Promotion

At the regional scale, much reform is needed to sort out promotional roles at all levels. Advertising and other promotional efforts frequently overlap among sponsors—states, destinations, cities, and attractions. Because of the millions of dollars of support, the amount of material available to the travel consumer is overwhelming.

Equally important is the challenge of truth in advertising and promotional ethics. National private and public agencies and organizations need to set standards of performance to assure the traveler that promises will be fulfilled. Again, viewing tourism as a system reveals the need for promotion to realistically reflect true conditions in all the supply side components. Promotional adjectives such as "the original," "the first," and "the only" may be duplicated in several locations unless controlled at the regional level.

Research/Education

Although the support for research and education must be shared at all levels, there are several needs and opportunities at the regional scale. Small businesses have neither the time, money, nor expertise to mount such programs. Differences in research measures, such as for economic impact, among the many destinations often makes comparability impossible. Uniform economic modeling can produce meaningful data for use throughout a region. Many issues, such as capacities and environmental degradation, can be resolved best with regional leadership.

Incentives and grants at the regional level could elevate and expand needed tourism education. Although university and community tourism education has grown it is still sporadic and lacking in many regions. A portion of promotional moneys might better be directed toward now nonexisting educational programs in tourism planning.

Education and training at the primary and secondary levels are needed in two directions. First, young people need greater understanding of career opportunities in the field of tourism. For those not bound for university education, vocational programs are needed for many occupations in tourism. Second, young people need education in how to travel so that when they become adults they understand travel procedures, etiquette, and how to get the most personal satisfaction from the travel experience.

Processes and Techniques

As beter models and processes for planning tourism are generated at the regional scale, they will be of no avail if not utilized. A great amount of communication and education is needed to increase awareness and need.

At the federal, state, and provincial levels, the continued preoccupation with promotion disproportionately skews budget allocations away from improvements of planning models and techniques. Ongoing research and experimentation are needed to create new and better planning processes for tourism.

Both a regional plan and a continuous regional planning process are needed if tourism is to be developed properly. A specific plan, renewed periodically, can document strengths, weaknesses, and desired action at the macro scale. However, because both markets and supply side development are dynamic, such plans must be accompanied by ongoing planning from all public and private decisionmakers.

INTERNATIONAL ISSUES

With the great expansion of interstate, interprovincial, and international travel, new regional policies and practices are needed to foster better tourism planning.

Transportation Linkage Between Regions

At the regional level, governments and the private sector must maintain close monitoring and support of transportation systems for travelers. Air, rail, highway linkages are very critical to market decisions. Costs, ease of access, reliability, and security are of increasing importance. There is little point in promoting travel to or from regions where transportation fails to meet these criteria. Much can be done through greater cooperation and understanding at the regional level.

Although many nations control air travel at the federal level, deregulation has increased worldwide, stimulating greater competition within the private sector. Greater study is needed to determine the positive and negative results from such deregulation. At the same time that travelers may have benefited from lower rates on some trips, service may no longer be available on other routes. Future regional policy may include stronger public-private mechanisms for maintaining service at the same time protecting freedom of competition.

Health and Safety

With political unrest occurring in many regions, travelers often face threats to personal health and safety. New policies at the regional level are called for that can assure freedom from crime, sickness, and accidents. Feedback from travelers who experienced such difficulties is devastating to market interest in travel to some destinations and regions. Especially critical are food and potable water standards and controls. Unless a region can assure high quality, no amount of promotion can entice travelers to it. Pickpocketing and mugging are threats that deter travel to many regions. Corrupt law enforcement in some regions soon develops negative reputations for the regions as places to visit. Unmarked and dangerous attractions tend to create visitor accidents. Issues of visitor safety and health are frequent agenda items at international tourism conferences and negotiations.

International Agreements

The communications revolution has helped shrink the world. International barriers continue to break down, stimulating greater international travel. However, this growth demands a greater number of and much stronger intergovernmental agreements on travel.

In other instances, regional policy has been primarily directed toward domestic tourism. Although this may be a market that is more visible and easier to promote, it precludes some interesting and productive opportunities from international travelers. In nations such as the United States and Canada, destinations that contain a dominance of foreign, ethnic, or national influence could be marketed to nations of origin.

However, in many instances new international travel agreements will be required for greater international travel. Visa and customs procedures often inhibit travel between nations. Regional agreements can greatly foster the reduction or elimination of travel barriers.

REFERENCES

Baud-Bovy, Manuel (1980). "Integrated Planning for Tourism Development." Presentation, CAP/SCA Seminar, Colombo, Sri Lanka, May 8–18. Madrid: World Tourism Organization.

Baud-Bovy, Manuel (1982). "New Concepts in Planning for Tourism and Recreation." *Tourism Management*, 3(4), 308–313.

Bekker, Pieter (1991). "Tourism Resources and Protected Areas Along British Columbia's Coastline." *Tourism-Environment-Sustainable Development: An Agenda for Research,* proceedings of the Travel and Tourism Research Association Conference Canada. October 17–19, pp. 83–88. Hull, Quebec.

British Columbia (1991). *Coastal Tourism Resource Inventory, Phase I: Mapping Methodology*. Victoria, British Columbia: Ministry of Tourism.

Britton, Robert (1979). "The Image of the Third World in Tourism Marketing." *Annals of Tourism Research*, 6(3), 318–329.

Collins, Charles (1979). "Site and Situation Strategy in Tourism Planning: A Mexican Case." *Annals of Tourism Research*, 6(3), 352–366.

Demars, Stanford (1979). "British Contributions to American Seaside Resorts." *Annals of Tourism Research*, 6(3), 285–293.

DPA Consulting (1981). "Plant/Market Match Model," unpublished report, November 24, to Canadian Government Office of Tourism, Ottawa.

Edgell, David L. (1990). *Charting a Course for International Travel*. Washington DC: U.S. Travel and Tourism Administration.

Fagence, Michael (1991). "Geographic Referencing of Public Policies in Tourism." *The Tourist Review*, March, 8–19.

Gunn, Clare A. (1990). *Upcountry South Carolina Guidelines for Tourism Development*. College Station, TX: author.

Gunn, Clare A. (1952). *Planning Better Vacation Accommodations*, Cir. R-304, Tourist and Resort Series, Cooperative Extension Service/Agricultural Experiment Station. East Lansing: Michigan State University.

Gunn, Clare A. (1965). *A Concept for the Design of a Tourism-Recreation Region*. Mason, MI: BJ Press.

Gunn, Clare A. (1972). *Vacationscape: Designing Tourist Regions*. Austin, TX: Bureau of Business Research, University of Texas.

Gunn, Clare A. (1982). *A Proposed Methodology for Identifying Areas of Tourism Development Potential in Canada*. Ottawa: Canadian Government Office of Tourism.

Gunn, Clare A. (1983). "U.S. Tourism Policy Development." *Journal of Physical Education, Recreation & Dance*, 54(4), 32–35.

Gunn, Clare A. (1990). *Upcountry South Carolina Guidelines for Tourism Development*. College Station, TX: author.

Gunn, Clare A., and Terry R. Larsen (1988). *Tourism Potential—Aided by Computer Cartography*. Aix-en-Provence, France: Centre des hautes Etudes Touristiques.

Hall, Peter (1975). *Urban and Regional Planning*. New York: John Wiley & Sons.

Helleiner, Frederick (1979). "Applied Geography in a Third World Setting: A Research Challenge." *Annals of Tourism Research*, 6(3), 330–337.

Hyma, B., and G. Wall (1979). "Tourism in a Developing Area: The Case of Tamil Nadu, India." *Annals of Tourism Research*, 6(3), 338–350.

Kiemstedt, H. (1967). "Zur Bewertung der Landschaft fur die Erholung." *Bertrage zur Landespflege*. Sonderheft 1, Stuttgart.

Lang, Reg (1988). "Planning for Integrated Development." *Integrated Rural Planning and Development*, F. W. Dykeman, (ed.), pp. 81–104. Sackville, New Brunswick: Rural and Small Town Research and Studies Programme.

Lawson, F. and Manuel Baud-Bovy (1977). *Tourism and Recreation Development*. London: Architectural Press.

Lue, Chi-Chuan, John L. Crompton and Daniel R. Fesenmaier (1993). "Conceptualization of Multi-Destination Pleasure Trips." *Annals of Tourism Research*, 20(2), 289–301.

Murphy, Peter (1979). "Tourism in British Columbia: Metropolitan and Camping Visitors." *Annals of Tourism Research*, 6(3), 294–306.

Pearce, Douglas G. (1979). "Towards a Geography of Tourism." *Annals of Tourism Research*, 6(3), 245–272.

Pearce, Douglas G. (1981). *Tourism Development*. London: Longman.

Romsa, Gerald (1981). "An Overview of Tourism Planning in the Federal Republic of Germany." *Annals of Tourism Research*, 8(3), 333–356.

Taylor, Gordon D. (1980). "How to Match Plant with Demand: A Matrix for Marketing." *Tourism Management*, 1(1), 56–60.

Trist, Eric (1985). "Intervention Strategies for Interorganizational Domains." In R. Tannenbaum, et al. (eds.), *Human Systems Development: New Perspectives on People and Organizations*. San Francisco: Josey-Bass.

Van Doren, C. S., and Larry Gustke (1982). "Spatial Analysis of the U.S. Lodging Industry." *Annals of Tourism Research*, 9(2), 543–563.

White, Judy (1981). *A Review of Tourism in Structure Plans in England*. Centre for Urban and Regional Studies. Birmingham, England: University of Birmingham.

Chapter 6

Regional Planning Cases

Introduction

Today, many nations, states, and provinces are seeking investment in tourism, just as they would seek investment in manufacturing or processing plants. But, as described in Part I, tourism cannot be accomplished the same way as obtaining investors in plants. All three sectors—government, nonprofit organizations, and businesses—invest in tourism and have different needs. But, these investors need a great amount of information before they will be convinced that tourism development is feasible. Even though tourism leaders may have some ideas on what needs to be developed and where, this is usually based on opinion and a limited factual base. Experience has shown that some areas are far better suited to tourism development than others, but only after failures and successes have become evident. It would seem that the time is way overdue to have more sophisticated approaches that can at least provide guidelines for best development. The following discussion includes some of the attempts that have been made toward giving regional leaders insight into the general areas suited to development and the types of development that are most appropriate. Again, the emphasis here is on the main physical components of the supply side—attractions, services, and transportation. Information and promotion follow the physical development phase.

Experimentation continues in the search for approaches toward improved tourism development. Individuals, governments, scholars, and consultants have entered into planning in many ways. But, as yet, no universally accepted methodology has emerged. So, in order to provide a base for improved approaches in the future, this chapter includes both older and newer cases of planning tourism at the regional level.

MICHIGAN'S UPPER PENINSULA

In 1945, Michigan established the Tourist and Resort Service, an advisory extension program based at Michigan State University. An outgrowth of

161

study and counsel with tourist business people was a planning project for recreation and tourism growth in the Upper Peninsula (Blank et al. 1966). A loosely knit organization, the Upper Peninsula Committee on Area Progress, and the regional Cooperative Extension Service under the direction of Uel Blank, sponsored a project to analyze and make recommendations for future development. The approach was to activate planning committees in all fifteen Upper Peninsula counties, utilize university staff specialists, and engage a planning-landscape architectural firm, Johnson, Johnson & Roy.

Preceding this project was a special program to stimulate local interest called the "It Pays to Know" campaign (Gunn 1964). The program came in response to surveys that showed visitor hosting was less than desirable. Although the focus was on improved hospitality (6,000 people attended the host training seminars), it was the first program to break tourism lethargy in the region. It served well as a foundation for the guideline project.

The regional planning project begun in 1963 was organized in three phases. First, the resource assets, economic development, tourism sectors, and travel markets were studied. Little sophisticated data was available so information was gathered from chambers of commerce, tourist associations, government agencies, and interviews with involved citizens. An important part of this phase was the creation of County Tourism Planning Committees for local public involvement. Second, the study team derived conclusions in concert with planning specialists and the county committees. This local involvement was a key element in the process. Finally, the study team developed two general types of recommendations: broad scale project development, and concepts for specific areas based on local initiatives. Figure 6-1 illustrates the framework used for this project.

Review of secondary information on *markets* produced generalizations useful to planning. Their geographical relationship is shown in Figure 6-2. Sources indicated that recent market trends were shifting. Some of the Chicago-Detroit-Milwaukee-Minneapolis markets were becoming interested in travel to the Ozarks and Kentucky lakes regions because of two factors. First, new Interstate highways provided easier access, and second, more modern facilities, including air conditioning, were breaking down the tradition of going north and the resistance of going south. These market findings suggested the need for new and better attractions and facilities in the Upper Peninsula.

Study of existing *supply* revealed some fine examples of resorts, state parks, national forests, wilderness areas, festivals, and motels and other travel services. Reasonably good access was available—98 percent of travelers arrived by automobile.

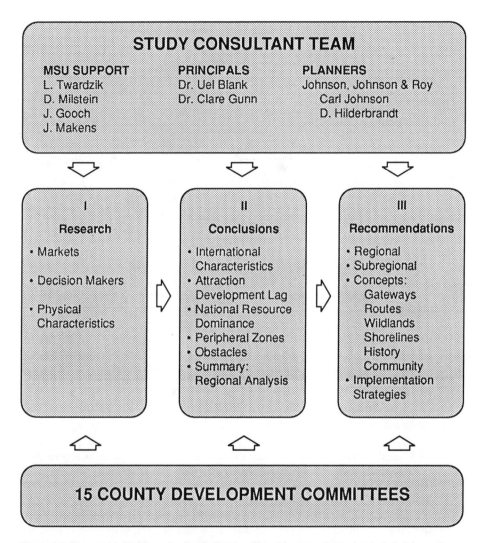

Figure 6-1. Framework for Upper Peninsula Tourism Plan. The core of planning included three phases: research, conclusions, and recommendations. Throughout the planning process, input was obtained from two major players: the study consultant team, and local development committees from the fifteen counties of the region.

Analysis of the *decisionmakers* for development showed that hundreds of separate land owners controlled tourism. Over 38 percent of the region was under governmental ownership: 1,921,000 acres federal; 2,094,000 acres state; 51,000 acres local. Many of these lands were developed for outdoor recreation—parks, hunting areas, scenic tours, and fishing sites. A large portion of privately held land was in the hands of forest and mining corporations. Tourist services were dominantly small business.

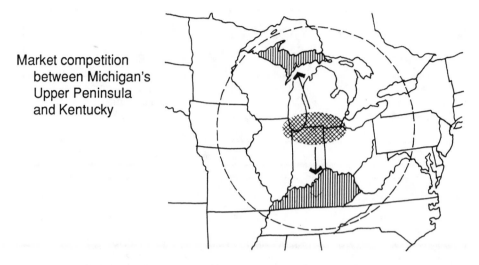

Market competition between Michigan's Upper Peninsula and Kentucky

Figure 6-2. Market-Regional Relationship: Michigan's Upper Peninsula. Because of new Interstate highways and greater use of air conditioning, many travel markets traditionally bound for the Upper Peninsula began going south to Kentucky and the Ozarks (Gunn 1965, 7).

Regional *physical characteristics* (see Figure 5-3) were derived from study of geological survey maps, highway and aerial reconnaissance, review of documents, and interviews of knowledgeables. A summary analysis is illustrated in Figure 6-3.

The key *conclusions* reached jointly by the county committees and the planning team were:

1. Visitation to the Upper Peninsula for pleasure already is great, comes primarily by automobile, and is mostly from heavily populated areas one day away. Visitors come for a variety of recreational reasons but primarily those related to the original natural (not man-made) resource base.

2. The region, as never before, is now caught up in inter-regional competition, especially with the new and massive man-made and nature-interpretive attractions equally available to its markets. This appears to be the major cause of the present arrested growth of tourism there.

3. Investigation showed many possible reasons for stagnation, chief of which are: a lag in development of powerful attractions, voids in certain services (especially those catering to socioeconomic brackets), and proliferation of natural resource use.

4. The bulk of recreation land development policies and practices (and therefore the dominant control of decisionmaking) now lies in four main groups: small commercial tourist enterprises, private personal land holdings, large private nontourist-oriented businesses and government (state, federal, local) forest and recreational agencies.

5. If there is any one dominant characteristic which sets the Upper Peninsula apart from its surrounding competitive regions, it is its wild vastness of undeveloped forests and water-blessed land.

6. Investigation revealed clues to promise for growth in spite of recent relative lag: its fortunate geographic position relative to markets, its ease of access, its abundance

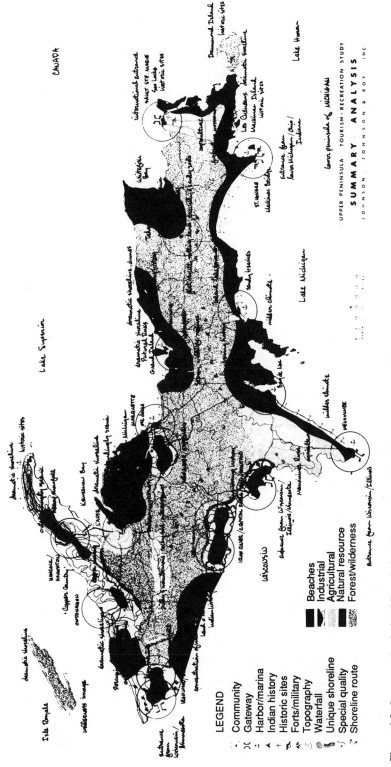

Figure 6-3. Summary Analysis of Foundation Factors. Based on interviews, research of documents, and reconnaissance of the region, resource characteristics were identified and mapped. This reproduction is a summary graphic used in the study (Blank et al. 1966, 42–43).

165

of natural resource assets, its unspoiled frontier, its unique and rich historic development and a very desirable distribution of fine community service centers.

7. The greatest amount of existing development for tourism and the greatest potential for future expansion appears to lie most heavily in the peripheral zone, leaving the interior a dominantly undeveloped region. Yet within this outer zone, a variety of resource base suggests varied and interesting development potential.

8. The major obstacles to expansion, therefore, are not those imposed by nature, nor by gross errors in development to date. Rather, the growth of visitation and its economic corollaries appear to lie in major new development—both quantitative and qualitative.

9. The greatest opportunities shown by this search are in the design, location, investment and management of new attractions clusters and their supporting services and facilities, but developed in a manner to enhance the valuable natural and man-made resource assets.

The last phase, recommendations, encompassed several sets of guidelines that were derived from the first two phases.

Regional recommendations centered primarily on the opportunities for attraction development in nine destination zones, as illustrated in Figure 6-4. The identification of these zones was based on the following criteria as well as their individuality:

- A series of attractions, including existing ones, as well as new ones— some urban, some rustic, some refined, and all based upon existing resource assets.
- At least one, possibly several, community service centers, first utilizing existing communities with the possible necessity of developing new ones.
- Linkage by road, waterway, airway, or trail between and with the overall regional circulation system.
- A subregional unity derived from community influence, natural and man-made resource base, and a unity of attraction theme.

An example of the findings of one area, Zone A, included the following (Blank et al. 1966, 53):

> The theme of subregion "A" could well be "Voyageurland" because of the dominance of historic fact and lore, perhaps in greater concentration than anywhere else in the Upper Peninsula. Major historic complexes at St. Ignace and Sault Ste. Marie could depict: early exploration, Indian occupation, French claims, missionary activity, fur trading activity, forts and battles, British Control, War of 1812, American settlement, and the heyday of the Victorian resort era. When land and waterway interpretive tours as well as pageantry and festivals are added these can be outstanding attractions. Additional attraction potential of this subregion includes:
> Gateway complex at both St. Ignace and at Sault Ste. Marie.

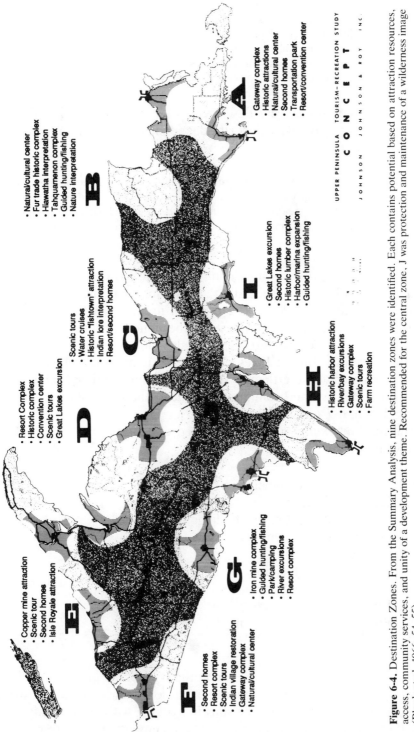

Figure 6-4. Destination Zones. From the Summary Analysis, nine destination zones were identified. Each contains potential based on attraction resources, access, community services, and unity of a development theme. Recommended for the central zone, J was protection and maintenance of a wilderness image (Blank et al. 1966, 54–55).

A natural resource culture center
Major marina development
Second homes subdivisions
A "Soo Locks" transportation park
A year-around resort complex and convention center

The eight other zones were described in the same manner. The central zone of the region was described as "deserving of restraint and conservation."

> Because it is farthest from established community centers, and because the other subregions contain the strongest resource potentials for tourism and recreation development, this area could be injured by scattered and haphazard development. For the time being, it may be best suited to other economic uses, such as mining, forestry, and agriculture. (Blank et al. 1966, 57)

Built into the project was a commitment to provide *conceptual plan ideas* for specific areas, especially those where local interest already had stimulated some directions. The types of areas given this extra design input included: gateways (entrances to the region), routes (expressways, secondary routes, scenic auto routes, trails, and waterways), natural wildlands, shoreline (inland lakes and streams), historic appeal (Indian, French explorers, first settlement, military, mining, lumber, fishing village, and ethnic village), and community. Some of these are illustrated in Figures 6-5, 6-6, 6-7, 6-8, and 6-9.

The *implementation* was to be carried out locally and to include the following topics:

1. Attraction development
2. Regional Committee
3. Dissemination of report findings
4. Specific development tasks
5. Subregional action
6. Training and education
7. Marketing study and analysis
8. Upgrading and analysis
9. Promotion and advertising
10. All-season activities

The implementation phase began at the start of the project in 1963 and continues yet today. The 15 county extension agents, by administrative request, were involved from the start in working with local constituencies and the planning team. As the project recommendations were being for-

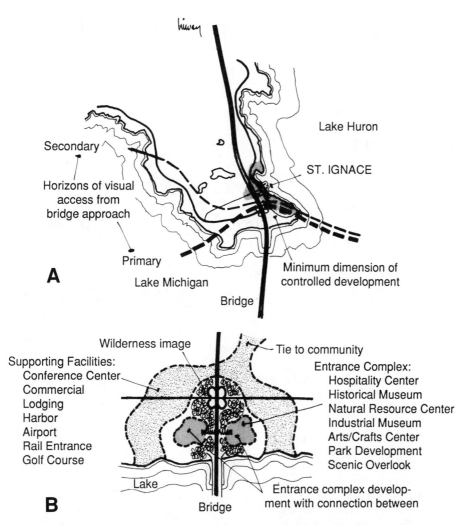

Figure 6-5. Concept for Gateway at St. Ignace. The main travel market approach to the Upper Peninsula was at the north end of the Mackinac Bridge. A, diagram of relationship between bridge, St. Ignace, and highways. B, conceptual diagram of features: hospitality center, museum, park, scenic overlook. Mental imagery of entering was a dominant design theme (Blank et al. 1966, 63).

mulated, two types of air tours were held. One invited several travel writers from major cities to fly the region so that they could see first-hand, and then write about, investment needs and potential. The other flight included investors who were exposed to the regional and local representatives at several stops throughout the Upper Peninsula.

An assessment was made of progress after ten years from the start of the project. The following are some of the major items that had been started or established (Gunn 1973) as reported by Ray Gummerson, area development specialist of the Upper Peninsula Extension Service.

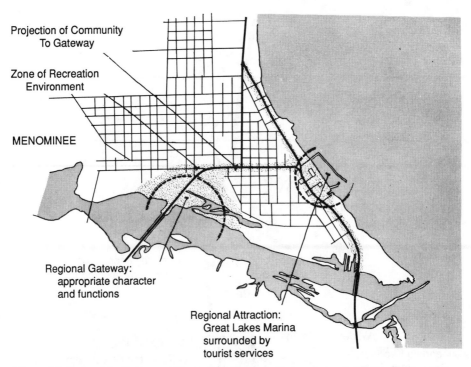

Figure 6-6. Concept for Gateway at Menominee. Suggested gateway planning for market access from Wisconsin. Waterfront regional attraction of Great Lakes Marina along Lake Michigan in the heart of the city is linked to main access by means of a park/recreation corridor (Blank et al. 1966, 91).

- A 1600 acre lake with canoe liveries and guides.
- Big Sea Development of the U.S. Forest Service.
- Pictured Rocks National Lakeshore established—new marinas, boat tours, renewed fishing.
- Memorial statue to Bishop Baraga as part of historic complex.
- New convention center complex at Marquette.
- Restoration of Carp River Forge.
- Quincy Hoist (copper mine) has been restored.
- New ski-flying facility was installed.
- Large forest-lake tract, Sylvania, established by Forest Service.
- Mystery Ship and Memorial Marina established at Menominee.
- Overlook and interpretive tower established at Sault Ste. Marie.
- Many new motels, food services, and other travel services.

Reflection on this project reveals several implications. Planning implementation takes time; it cannot be expected to produce immediate results. There is much value in bringing together local constituencies *and* professional planners-designers. As Blank described it, "there is not a simple linear-research-education continuum. Rather, there is a multidimensional matrix, with study-action as one facet, the range of local-state-federal as another, public-private decision makers as yet another facet, plus many

Landscaped streetscape

Entrance to community

Shopping

Public Square

Parking

shopping

traffic rerouted and street vacated to create pedestrian environment from shopping area, through Marina Park to water's edge.

Lake Michigan

View to water

Marina Chapel

Plaza

Park

Figure 6-7. Detail of Gateway Attractions. This concept features waterfront business restoration at Menominee and new vistas toward water over a plaza, a marina chapel, a park, and a restored historic ship. Downtown street segments are to be closed to traffic to allow pedestrian access and enjoyment (Blank et al. 1966, 93).

others" (Gunn 1973, 3). This project allowed practical application of the theoretical concepts of planning developed by Gunn (1952, 1965) (see Chapter 5). It dramatized the value of analyzing several geographical factors to determine how they combined into potential destination zones— an aid to discovery of potential. Finally, there was great value in spreading the project over a three-year time span to allow maximum interchange and communication between all planners and stakeholders. (See "Great Lakes Crossroads Museum and Welcome Center," Chapter 10, as further follow-up of this project.)

SOUTH CENTRAL TEXAS

Experimentation in regional tourism planning methodology has taken place for several years in selected regions of Texas by Texas A&M Uni-

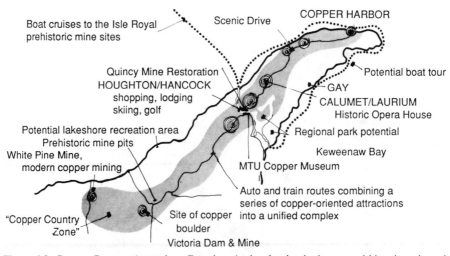

Figure 6-8. Copper Country Attractions Complex. A plan for developing several historic and scenic attractions related to early copper mining in the area traditionally known as the Copper Country. Both highways and program theme would link many attractions together (Blank et al. 1966, 83).

versity in connection with graduate classes in the Department of Recreation, Park, and Tourism Sciences. The objective was to continue to refine the techniques and, especially, to utilize new computer mapping programs.

One of the projects was for the 20-county region in south central Texas, from San Saba to the Gulf of Mexico coast at Port Lavaca, as illustrated in Figure 6-10 (Gunn and McMillen 1979). This project refined greatly the technique used in the Upper peninsula study. Major revisions included dividing potential development into touring circuit and destination categories, weighting the factor maps, and using the synagraphic computer mapping program (SYMAP) (Dudnik 1971) for overlays of factor maps.

First, it seemed useful to identify zones and routes that had touring circuit potential, if and when appropriate attractions were developed. This, together with destination potential, would identify local areas with both kinds of potential. Touring circuits were defined as highway routes that connected a series of attraction locations and service centers (communities). Destination potential would occur where longer stay development would be appropriate—resorts, parks, organization camps, convention centers, and vacation home use.

Second, it seemed that each resource factor would have slightly different value in assessing potential. Therefore, some method of weighting the several factors was needed. Because research literature had not yet identified the basis for such weighting, the technique used was a panel of knowledgeable people to reach consensus on relative weights for each factor. These are illustrated in Table 6-1 and 6-2.

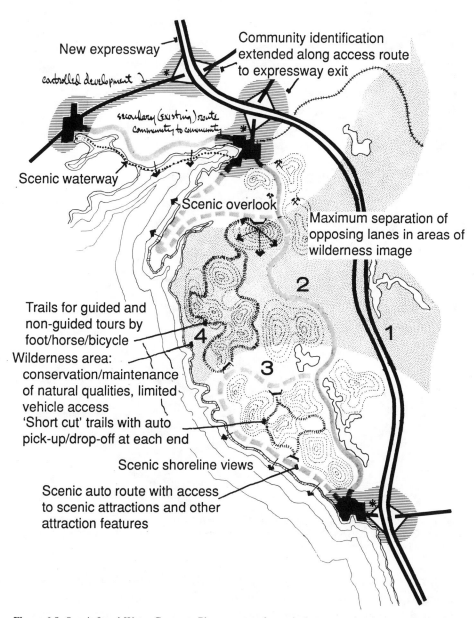

Figure 6-9. Scenic Land-Water Concept. Plan concepts for typical resource development for tourism: (1) Highway design through wilderness; (2) scenic forest drive; (3) scenic drive access to wilderness trails and water overlooks; (4) conservation area accessible only by trail (Blank et al. 1966, 69).

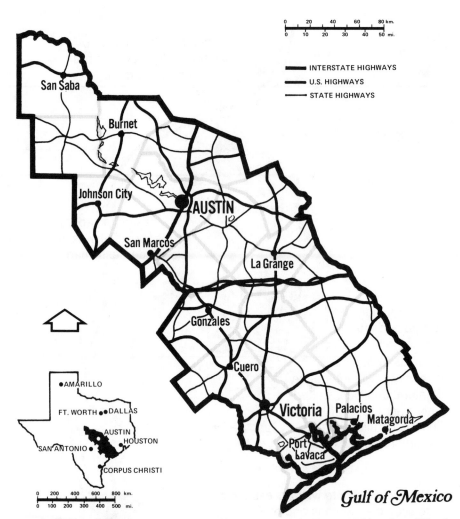

Figure 6-10. A Texas Tourism Study Region. A 20-county area in Texas, reaching about 275 miles from the Gulf of Mexico, was studied for its tourism potential. Shown are principal communities and highway network (Gunn and McMillen 1979, 3).

Third, by using the SYMAP program (Synagraphic Mapping System, designed at the Laboratory for Computer Graphics and Spatial Analysis, Harvard University) the several factor maps could be added together to identify zones where the factors are the best and most abundant. The location of each factor was the same for touring and destination objectives but the weighting was different as illustrated in the tables.

The theoretical foundation for the process of assessment used included:

1. Tourism development is most frequently promoted because of its estimated economic impact, derived through service businesses and facilities.

TABLE 6-1
WEIGHTED FACTORS FOR TOURING TOURISM

				Scale		
Factor	*Index*	*Very Weak*	*Weak*	*Moderate*	*Strong*	*Very Strong*
Water, waterlife	8	0	1–2	3–4	5–6	7–8
Topography, soils, geology	10	0–1	2–3	4–6	7–8	9–10
Vegetative cover, wildlife, pests	7	0	1–2	3–4	5–6	7
Climate, atmosphere	3	0	1	1	2	3
Esthetics	13	0–1	2–4	5–7	8–10	11–13
Existing attractions, industries, institutions	10	0–1	2–3	4–6	7–8	9–10
History, ethnicity, archeology, legend, lore	9	0–1	2–3	4–5	6–7	8–9
Service centers	15	0–2	3–5	6–9	10–12	13–15
Transportation, access	25	0–4	5–9	10–15	16–20	21–25
Total	100					

Source: Gunn 1979, 3

2. These service businesses depend upon tourists seeking things to see and do, attractions (parks, recreation areas, theme parks, events).
3. Attractions, while eliciting personal responses in tourists, are primarily physical land developments.
4. Attractions and other tourism developments depend, in varying degrees, upon both physical and program factors.
5. When these factors are studied and mapped, a better understanding of the future potential of tourism can be determined. When this is done at the regional scale, better assessment for policy decisions can then be made at the destination and site scales. (Gunn and McMillen 1979, 1)

TABLE 6-2
WEIGHTED FACTORS FOR DESTINATION TOURISM

				Scale		
Factor	*Index*	*Very Weak*	*Weak*	*Moderate*	*Strong*	*Very Strong*
Water, waterlife	24	0–4	5–9	10–14	15–19	20–24
Topography, soils, geology	10	0–1	2–3	4–6	7–8	9–10
Vegetative cover, wildlife, pests	8	0	1–2	3–4	5–6	7–8
Climate, atmosphere	13	0–1	2–4	5–7	8–10	11–13
Esthetics	7	0	1–2	3–4	5–6	7
Existing attractions, industries, institutions	5	0–1	2	3	4	5
History, ethnicity, archeology, legend, lore	3	0	1	1	2	3
Service centers	10	0–1	2–3	4–6	7–8	9–10
Transportation, access	20	0–3	4–7	8–12	13–16	17–20
Total	100					

Source: Gunn 1979, 3

The study included review of maps and other documents describing the following physical factors:

1. Water, waterlife
2. Vegetative cover, wildlife, pests
3. Climate, atmosphere
4. Topography, soils, geology
5. History, ethnicity, archaeology, legends
6. Esthetics
7. Institutions, industries, existing attractions

The program factors studied were:

1. Markets, promotion
2. Information, direction
3. Socioeconomic characteristics
4. Implementing agents (Gunn and McMillen 1979, 2)

A major feature of the study was to describe the assets and liabilities of each of these factors, revealing conclusions important for future development.

Assets	*Liabilities*
The region has an abundance of resource assets, reasonably accessible by markets, and fairly well served by businesses with some implementing agents available.	Some cities (smaller ones) have inadequate facilities; few tours are available; promotion and information are weak; some environmental degradation; no overall organization.

The results of aggregating the several resource factor maps by SYMAP resulted in Figures 6-11 and 6-12 for touring and destination potential, respectively. By means of interpretation of these maps based on reconnaissance and study of the region, recommended development was identified as shown in Figure 6-13 and 6-14.

This study represented an advancement of technique over the Upper Peninsula study. By identifying and mapping the several factors in greater detail, the results were based on a rather sound foundation. However, as an action project, it lacked public involvement because it was performed as a university class project. For the first time, the tourism leaders in communities and counties had sound information available for guiding their future. In addition to revealing areas of greatest potential, the project called attention to areas where new investment had less chance of success. One area, Gonzales county (see Chapter 8), was stimulated to

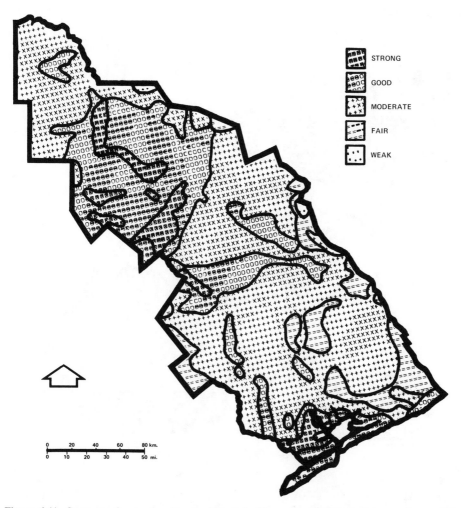

STRONG

GOOD

MODERATE

FAIR

WEAK

Figure 6-11. Computer Composite—Touring Potential. When nine physical factor maps for touring potential are aggregated, a composite map is the result. The darker areas show where the factors are the most abundant and of best quality to support touring attraction development (Gunn and McMillen 1979, 10).

enter into a special study of its tourism potential. The report emphasized the need for greater cooperation and collaboration between the public and private sectors. With the focus on natural and cultural resource foundations, opportunities for indigenous attractions were identified, setting the areas and region apart from others.

OKLAHOMA

In 1987, Price Waterhouse was engaged as consultant to investigate and prepare a master plan for tourism in the state of Oklahoma. Subcontrac-

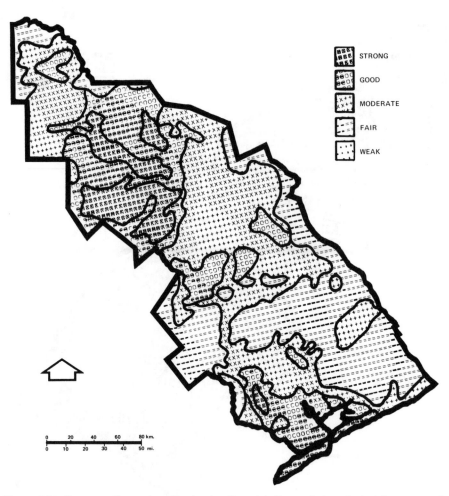

STRONG

GOOD

MODERATE

FAIR

WEAK

0   20   40   60   80 km.
0   10   20   30   40   50 mi.

Figure 6-12. Computer Composite—Destination Potential. By overlaying physical factor maps for longer-stay potential, a composite map is the result. The darker areas illustrate the areas best suited to longer-stay tourism development (Gunn and McMillen 1979, 10).

tors were Grey Advertising for a marketing study and Clare A. Gunn for regional analysis of tourism potential. It was reported in *Proposed Master Plan for Travel Marketing and Development for the State of Oklahoma,* October 1, 1987. Figure 6-15 highlights the content of this project.

The overall goals were to:

• Increase employment.
• Increase personal and business income.
• Increased tax revenues from increased travel activity.
• Diversify and stabilize the state's economy.

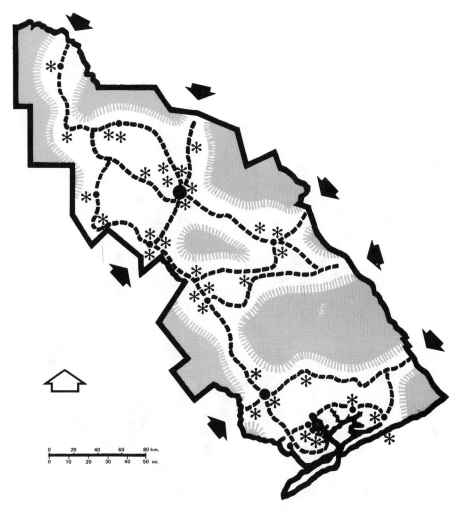

Figure 6-13. Areas Best Suited to Touring Tourism Development. An interpretation of the computer-generated composite map showing zones of best potential. Attraction potential (stars), touring route potential (dotted), and market access (arrows) are shown (Gunn and McMillen 1979, 11).

Specific objectives included:

- Increase travel employment 2 to 4 percent per year by 1993.
- Increase average travel wage by ten to fifteen percent.
- Increase sales tax revenues by ten to fifteen percent.

Private and public sector roles were defined:

> Specifically, the *public sector* should promote the State or areas of the State as a travel destination and serve as a catalyst for private sector development of travel

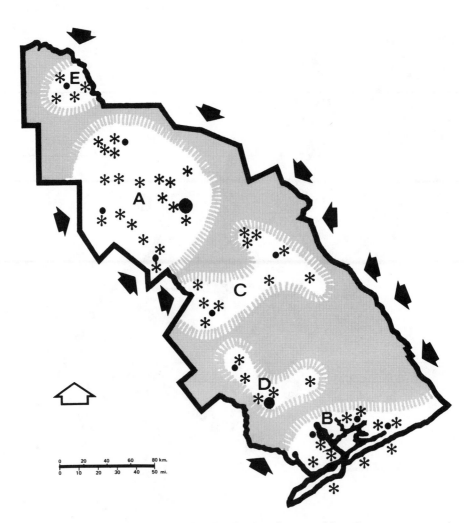

Figure 6-14. Areas Best Suited to Long-Stay Development. Interpreted from the computer composite, this map shows zones with best and most abundant factors in support of longer-stay development. The stars illustrate locations of attraction potential; dots show service communities; arrows show market access. (Gunn and McMillen 1979, 11).

> products and resources. The *private sector* should be responsible for promoting its own products and providing investment capital for financing development and enhancement of its travel products. (Price Waterhouse 1987, 5)

A regional analysis of potential was part of the Product Development Plan. It utilized a process similar to that of the central Texas project but employed a more contemporary computer mapping program called Compass, developed by the College of Architecture, Texas A&M University. The complete report of its application to the Oklahoma project is

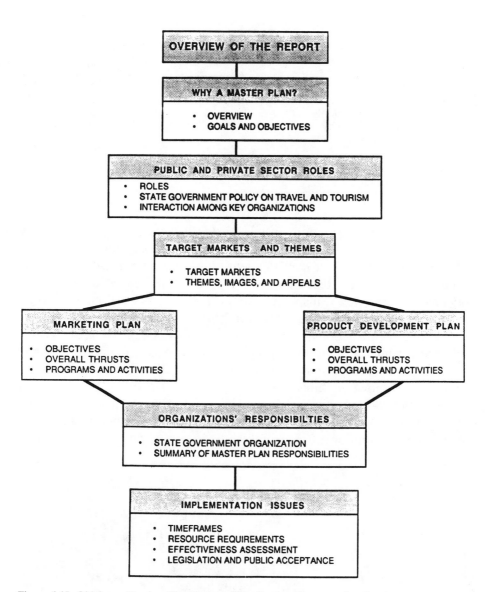

Figure 6-15. Oklahoma Tourism Plan Process. This diagram illustrates the planning approach used to develop a master tourism plan for the state of Oklahoma. Focus was primarily on product development, policy, and organization (Price Waterhouse 1987, Ex. 2).

described in *Tourism Potential—Aided by Computer Cartography* (Gunn and Larsen 1988).

Study of travel markets revealed those seeking outdoor recreation, touring, city amenities, close-to-home attractions, and visiting friends and relatives. Pass-through tourists were particularly important because of the state's geographic position between markets in the eastern part of the

TABLE 6-3
WEIGHTED FACTORS FOR OKLAHOMA PLAN

Factor	Index
Water	15
Topography	8
Vegetation/Wildlife	8
History/Ethnicity	15
Attractions	12
Cities	20
Transportation	22
Total	100

Source: Gunn and Larsen 1988, 30

United States and attractions in the West. Business-convention travelers included those going to business meetings, conventions, and trade shows.

As part of the Product Development Plan, a study of the development potential was made. Resource factors were studied based on review of documents, interviews, inspection tours, and several local citizen workshops. The seven factors were water, topography, vegetation/wildlife, history/ethnicity, attractions, cities, and transportation. First, generalized maps to a common scale were prepared by hand showing areas of high, medium, low, and poor resource importance. Then, the factors were weighted, as shown in Table 6-3.

Through use of the Compass overlay program these factor maps were aggregated, producing the mosaic illustrated in Figure 6-16. The figure shows the distribution of the combined resources and for total tourism

Figure 6-16. Composite of Tourism Factors for Oklahoma. This map is the result of combining computer maps of seven resource factors. Darker areas indicate greater potential for tourism development (Gunn and Larsen 1988, 32).

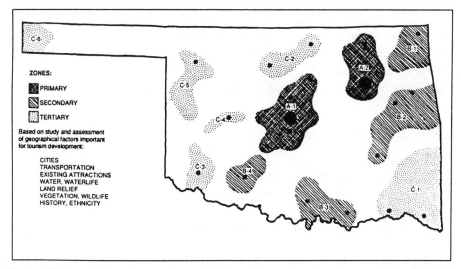

Figure 6-17. Potential Development Zones, Oklahoma. Interpretation of research and computer map composite resulted in identifying primary, secondary, and tertiary zones of tourism development potential (Price Waterhouse 1987, Ex. 8).

(not separated for natural or cultural factors). By means of study and interpretation of this map and other research material, destination zones were identified, as illustrated in Figure 6-17. "Primary" zones are areas where the best and most abundant resource factors are in greatest combination. "Secondary" zones are those areas where several factors show significant potential for development based on a combination of several factors. "Tertiary" zones have a combination of a few factors in sufficient strength to indicate some potential. Brief summaries of these zone potentials are listed below:

A. PRIMARY ZONES

A-1 *Oklahoma City Zone*
- Major improvements in conference, convention facilities.
- Better massing of existing attractions, tours.
- Greater exploitation of pass-through tourists.
- Major enhancement of downtown amenities.
- Major cowboy entertainment complexes.
- Agricultural/range history museum and center.

A-2 *Tulsa Zone*
- Major national class folklore institute (Indian and other ethnic center, entertainment, events).
- Enhanced development of historic sites (Indian, Civil War).
- Improved existing attractions, tour packaging.

- Expanded meeting, conference programs.
- Greater exploitation of pass-through travelers.
- New Will Rogers Entertainment Center.
- Redevelopment of Osage, Chickasaw capitals.
- Osage ethnic museum and visitor center.

B. SECONDARY ZONES

B-1 *Miami Zone*
- New national class prehistoric museum.
- Major new petroleum interpretation center.
- Expanded lake resort development.
- Greater exploitation of pass-through travelers.

B-2 *Muskogee Zone*
- Major redevelopment of several Civil War forts (with interpretation, pageants).
- Major prehistoric museum and institute (Spiro).
- Expanded Cherokee theme—historic sites, events.
- Tourist tour redevelopment of first Oklahoma railroad.

B-3 *Ardmore Zone*
- Expanded private resort development.
- Redevelopment of historic forts.
- Redevelopment of Chickasaw capital.
- Redevelopment of trail towns near I-35.
- Expanded Arbuckle Mountain resorts, scenery.

B-4 *Lawton Zone*
- New military visitor center, museum (Ft. Sill).
- Prehistoric museum and interpretation.
- Redevelopment of Chisholm Trail (Duncan-Enid).
- Expanded Indian culture centers, tours.
- Expanded private sector outdoor recreation.

C. TERTIARY ZONES

C-1 *Ouachita Mountain Zone*
- Redevelopment of scenic routes.
- Expanded outdoor recreation development.
- Restored forts and historic trails.
- New major fishing events, festivals.

.C-2 *Enid Zone*
- Chisholm Trail redevelopment (Enid-Duncan).
- Outdoor drama: "The Run."
- New guest ranch developments.

C-3 *Altus Zone*
- Expanded Quartz mountain development.
- Prehistoric Plains Indian Museum, interpretation.
- Redeveloped "Doan's Crossing," Red River trip.
- New cowboy-cattle trail recreation.

C-4 *Weatherford Zone*
- Greater exploitation of pass-through travelers.
- Development of tour packages.
- Cowboy entertainment, guest ranches.

C-5 *Woodward Zone*
- Expanded cowboy-ranch development.
- Restoration of historic casino, entertainment.
- Outdoor recreation trails.
- New hunting ranches.

C-6 *Black Mesa Zone*
- Prehistoric museum, interpretation.
- Greater exploitation of pass-through travelers.
- Western wildlife museum and interpretive center.

Project director Eugene Dilbeck, then director of the Department of Tourism and Recreation of Oklahoma, reprinted the overall Price Waterhouse report plan, distributed it widely, and held tourism development workshops throughout the state. This action has stimulated much greater interest in Oklahoma's tourism potential than even before.

Regarding the regional analysis phase, some evaluation should be noted. This application again exposes the need for a better means of weighting the several factors. Researchers need to accept this challenge. Because tourism is dynamic, the zones delineated must not be considered permanent. They suggest to the local political and tourism officials that there are areas where the potential is better than other locations. Finally, areas indicated as having greatest potential need to be examined carefully to determine capacity limitations. Development already may have reached saturation.

The project gave priority to development recommendations as follows:

- Emphasis on enhancement and new development in primary zones and, to a less extent, secondary zones.

- Emphasis on enhancement and development of festivals and events, rather than attractions, in tertiary and non-zone areas.
- Development of one or several lake development areas.
- Emphasis on grouping attractions within city or area.
- Increase usage of existing facilities and attractions, by extending hours of operation, extending seasons, and identifying other methods to utilize facilities and attractions more intensively during prime seasons.
- Improve quality, and number of attractions overall, and specifically those based on Western Heritage/Native Americans for which Oklahoma may become a travel destination. (Price Waterhouse 1987, 23)

UPCOUNTRY SOUTH CAROLINA

A more recent application of regional analysis for tourism potential took place in 1989 for a six-county region in northwestern South Carolina known as Upcountry. This was cosponsored by the Discover Upcountry Carolina Association, the Pendleton District Historical and Recreational Commission and the Department of Parks, Recreation and Tourism Management, Clemson University (Gunn 1990). The project work was directed by C. A. Gunn who was assisted by students of the university and members of the Regional Resource Development Institute. It is cited here especially because it utilized a later generation of a computer overlay program.

The process included (1) setting goals and objectives, (2) researching basic factors, (3) synthesizing research results, and (4) identifying new opportunities in destination zones best suited to development. The study region (Figure 6-18) is located in the Appalachian foothills region, is 3,849 square miles in size, and is bordered on the north by North Carolina, on the west by Georgia, and on the south and east by the Piedmont area of South Carolina.

The technical and theoretical foundations for this application to tourism are based on the following principles:

1. That the greatest economic impact of tourism occurs within metropolitan areas because these areas contain the greatest number of commercial services for tourists;
2. That these services, in turn, depend upon business and pleasure attractions in and around the cities that draw visitors to the region;
3. That the attractions are owned and managed by three sectors: governments (parks, marinas, campgrounds, and beaches), nonprofit organizations (museums, historic sites, and youth camps), and commercial enterprises (theme parks, resorts, and guided tours);

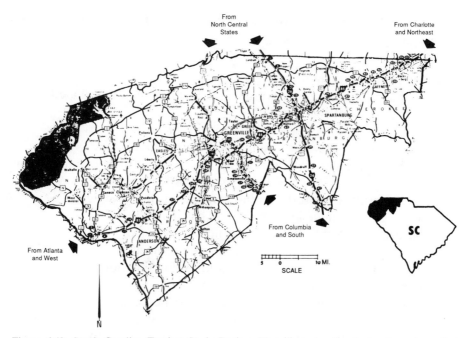

Figure 6-18. South Carolina Tourism Study Region. Map illustrates the six-county region called Upcountry South Carolina. Primary and secondary highways, cities, and principal travel market entrances are shown (Gunn 1990, 7).

4. That the future growth of tourism depends greatly on improvement in the number, size, and quality of attractions;

5. That expansion of attractions depends largely on several important factors: natural resources, cultural resources, transportation, information, promotion, and community acceptance; and

6. That when new and better attractions are in place, better access is provided, greater information is available, and better services are provided, then these products can be promoted in the areas of prime market potential.

The *research* phase included review of existing documents, maps, reconnaissance of the region, and a limited number of interviews. It included obtaining descriptive information suited to both narratives and maps. The following program factors were studied: markets, information, promotion, socioenvironmental issues, and planning action agencies. The physical factors included water and waterlife resources; vegetative cover and wildlife resources; topography, soil, and geologic resources; existing natural resource development; archeological and prehistoric sites; historic and ethnic resources; economic development; existing cultural resource development; transportation and access; and cities and towns.

The *synthesizing* step of the project resulted in the following conclusions:

- Significant tourism already exists in the region.
- Abundant natural and cultural resources remain undeveloped, especially for new attractions.
- Access is very good—good linkage with markets.
- Key urbanized areas are well served by transportation.
- Services are generally good but appear deficient in some parts of the region.
- Much literature is produced but some needs improvement.
- New regional leadership for tourism has begun.
- Tourism is well-balanced with economic diversity.
- Resources need stronger safeguards and protection.
- Promotion has a good base but requires coordination.
- Human resources are a valuable asset.
- Travel market segments are assumed to be: markets interested in natural resources attractions, markets interested in cultural resource attractions, longer-stay visitors, and pass-through visitors.

An important part of this synthesizing step was mapping the physical resources and aggregating them by means of a geographic information system called ARC/INFO, developed by the Environmental Systems Research Institute, Inc. The following steps were used for mapping:

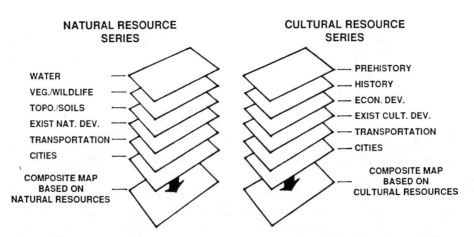

Figure 6-19. Map Overlay Process. For each map series—natural and cultural resources—six factor maps were combined to form two composite maps. These composite maps were used as foundations for interpretation into potential development zones (Gunn 1990, 17).

hij hurays
+
Communities

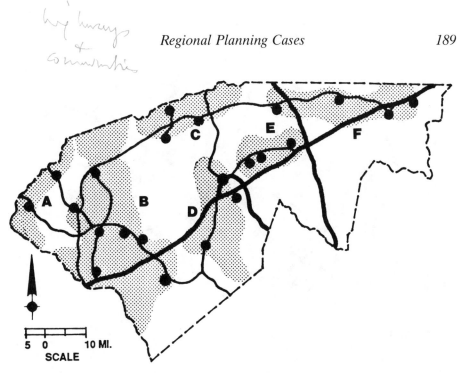

Figure 6-20. Destination Zones Based on Natural Resources. Interpretation of the computer composite map reveals tourism development potential in six destination zones. Shown also are main highways and service communities. (Gunn 1990, 19).

1. Each of the ten physical factors was mapped in a generalized way to show areas of four levels of importance: maximum, good, poor, little, or none.
2. Each map was then digitized by computer.
3. The ten factors were weighted to reflect relative importance.
4. Computer maps were then aggregated to show zones of greatest combination of factor influence (Figure 6-19).

By means of review of all research data for the region and inspection of the two composite maps, conclusions were reached on how these might be generalized into potential destination zones. Figure 6-20 illustrates six destination zones that have greatest potential for tourism development based on *natural resources*. Figure 6-21 shows four zones that have greatest potential based on *cultural resources*. Figure 6-22 is a combination of these two, illustrating zones of greatest *total potential*. Following is an excerpt from the report recommendations and includes opportunities in five categories.

    A. Opportunities Based on Natural Resources. The following are suggested in order to tap new markets interested in natural-resource-oriented travel.

    ZONE A: • Major Forestry Interpretive Center
                  • Chattooga Hiking Trail

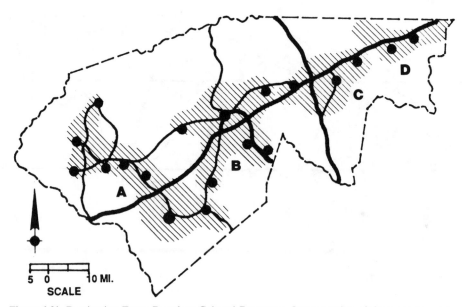

Figure 6-21. Destination Zones Based on Cultural Resources. Interpretation of the computer composite map reveals tourism development potential in four destination zones. Included are main highway access and key service communities (Gunn 1990, 22).

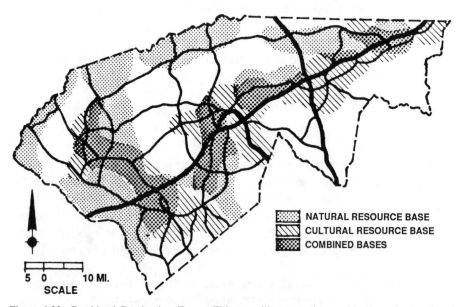

Figure 6-22. Combined Destination Zones. This map illustrates the combination of natural and cultural-based destination zones (Figs. 6-20, 21 combined). It is in these areas that local and regional leaders and developers need to concentrate their planning and development efforts for greatest success (Gunn 1990, 26).

- Wildland Environmental Training Center
- Timber Festival

ZONE B:
- Resort Complexes
- New Major Marinas
- Scenic Lake Drive
- Commercial RV Parks

ZONE C:
- Scenic Mountain Tour
- Mountain Resorts
- Wildland Recreation Area
- Natural History Interpretive Center

ZONE D:
- Golfland Complex
- Expanded Roper Mountain Science Center
- Mountain Resorts

ZONE E:
- Farm Guest Ranches
- Lake Cooley Recreation

ZONE F:
- Lake Bowen-Blalock Resorts
- Riverine Recreation

B. Opportunities Based on Cultural Resources. The following suggested attractions are intended to tap new markets interested in cultural-based travel to this region.

ZONE A:
- Major Cherokee Interpretive Center
- Newry Restoration
- Expanded Pendleton Area
- New Recreation-Tourism Institute

ZONE B:
- The Textile Place Interpretive Center
- Convention Center
- Fitness Resort
- Living History Park
- Moonshine-Clogging Festival

ZONE C:
- Restored Cattle Drive
- Expanded Walnut Grove
- Equestrian Ranch

ZONE D:
- Tree Rental Farms
- King's Mountain Historical Complex

C. Opportunities for Regional Tours. The research and mapping of this region suggested that the resource distribution lent itself well to new shorter and longer tours. The following would be possible only after the several recommended additions to attractions have been developed.

- Regional Attraction Tour
- Salem-Anderson Historic Tour
- Restored "Great Indian Road "
- Business-Science-Educational Tour
- Scenic, Wildland Tour
- Regional Historic Tour
- Restored Carriage Trail
- Railroad Excursions
- Old Rail Trails

D. *Need for Regional Leadership and Cooperation.* In order to strengthen tourism development in this region it became apparent in this study that there were several opportunities for stronger leadership and cooperation. Following are the key topics to be considered.

- *Integration of separate entities.* The great many separate decisionmakers and developers could gain by cooperating with one another to a greater degree. Especially important is better public-private cooperation on all regional tourism matters. Regional leadership could provide the catalyst for forums on matters of mutual interest.
- *Resource protection.* Throughout this study, it became clear that new development must be done with great care and sensitivity to the environment. Greater engagement of professional landscape architects and planners is essential. New leadership may be necessary to place tourism in a proactive position regarding environmental protection.
- *Clustering.* The principle of clustering is one way of protecting the environment at the same time development takes place. When businesses are clustered, each one gains from engineering efficiency and more effective promotion. Attraction clusters concentrate development, leaving more of the natural resources unharmed.
- *Implementation.* The implementation of better tourism plans and action will require strong leadership. The Discover Upcountry Carolina Association and the Pendleton District Historical and Recreation Commission can be effective agents for introducing new development concepts and programs. For all tourism development, public support is essential.

E. *Opportunities for Program Development.* In addition to physical development of tourism, several program topics need consideration.

- *Information.* Suggested is installation of new information centers and systems in order to provide better guidance for visitors—directions and needed data on lodging, attractions, and routes. Many new interpretive centers are needed. Interactive video equipment, a toll-free telephone line, and new visitor guides should be considered.
- *Promotion.* Future consideration should be given to a balanced program of promotion that includes not only advertising but also publicity, public relations, and

incentives. Special attention should be given to targeting promotion to specific market segments.

- *Service Businesses*. Although most tourist service businesses are of good quality, some communities lack adequate response to need—food services, travel guidance, and adaptation to travel markets.
- *Transportation*. Only minor changes seem to be needed in transportation—better signage and improved standards for some highways that are narrow and tend to be unsafe with increased traffic. New policies of highway design may be needed to protect roadside scenery.

Conclusions

The overall conclusions from this study and analysis are listed as follows:

- Significant tourism development is already in place.
- Region has opportunity to compete well with others.
- Growth and popularity depend on good planning and design.
- Greater cooperation within and among zones is needed.
- Stronger linkage between rural attractions and cities needed.
- Greater outside cooperation would help region.
- Small-scale and slow growth is more adaptable.
- Market research, training, education, public cooperation, stronger regional leadership and integration, and greater protection of resources are needed.

This planning study produced a comprehensive guide for future tourism development in a region. In addition to the use of traditional planning process steps, a computer mapping technique was used as an effective tool to aid in consolidating geographical information. Emphasis was placed on new attraction development to stimulate greater volumes of visitors. Because most of these attractions depend on natural and cultural resources, environmental sensitivity must dominate all planning and design policies and practices. The implementation of the recommendations is now before the many decisionmakers and developers at the regional, destination zone, and site scales. This study demonstrated that effective planning guidance can be produced within a relatively short time and within a small budget, provided that it is properly organized.

THE ADIRONDACKS

In a 1986 report Roger Trancik described a planning framework for recreation and tourism that identified destination zones within the region of

Adirondack Park, a state-managed region of six million acres in northern New York state. This report is part of a five-year study entitled "Hamlets of the Adirondacks" performed by Trancik and a team of state and county planners in the Adirondack region. [see also by R. Trancik, *Hamlets of the Adirondacks* (1983) and *Hamlets of the Adirondacks: Development Strategies* (1985).]

It is the largest park in the lower 48 states and the biggest nature preserve east of the Mississippi River. It contains mountains, lakes, streams, wildlife, and forests. But unlike other parks, only one-third of the area—2.3 million acres—is under administration by the Adirondack Park Agency (APA) as the Adirondack Forest Preserve. The balance is a mixture of land owned by paper companies, state-owned lands, private individuals, and municipalities. Scattered throughout the region are many hamlets, some established in early 19th century for timber production, and others for military, mining, resorting, and health spas.

A planning framework included study of the region in order to identify subregions with community centers, amenity areas (destination zones, as defined here), and tourism routes. Study was accomplished by means of mailed questionnaires, site visits, workshops, historic research, and other available data sources. Data sets were compiled on a matrix containing factors such as geography (including natural resources), function (including demographic economic factors), and physical characteristics. As a result, the major destination zones, shown in Figure 6-23 were identified. With this concept and plan, the remaining portion of the region could be administered as a protected natural resource area. The following recommendations were derived from this study (Trancik 1986, 9–15) and are excerpted from the report.

Strategies for Recreation and Tourism

The recreation and tourism program involves park-wide, subregional and local development strategies. Three park-wide concepts are essential for the development of a tourism and recreation plan:

1. *A regional network of tourist information and interpretive centers* strategically located to contain interpretive exhibits on the cultural and natural history of the region.

2. *The identification of amenity areas* which divides the Park into recreation zones.

3. *Development of recreation and tourism routes* which tie the network together. These routes could include roadways, bicycle touring circuits, river canoeing, skiing, hiking and snowmobile trails, etc.

Tourist Information and Interpretive Centers

A network of visitor centers would add greatly to the undetstanding and appreciation of the Adirondack Park in obvious ways. There should be a major regional

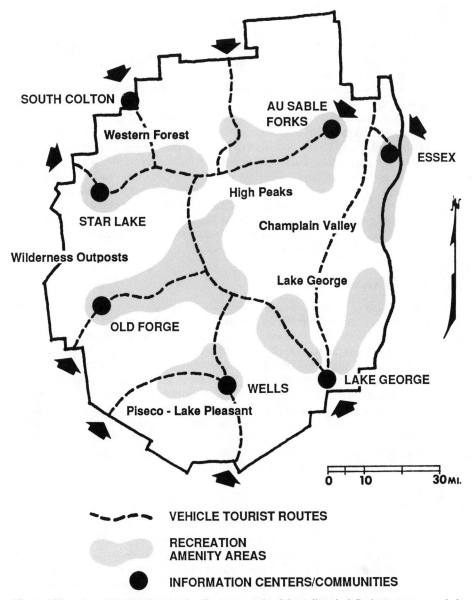

Figure 6-23. Adirondack Park Destination Zones. A study of the Adirondack Park resources revealed destination zones of primary importance. Illustrated are the zones (recreation amenity areas), vehicle tourist routes, communities (information centers), and market acccess entrances (Trancik 1986, 9).

facility near the center of the park which would become a destination point for visitors. This center would highlight the natural and cultural resources of the region and serve as a major information dissemination point. Special events, plays, historical pageants, interpretive slide shows, and other similar activities could be held here regularly.

The regional destination facility should be complemented by eight or ten gateways facilities in strategic communities. These would inform visitors of arrival at the park and offer a variety of information on events, activities, and their locations. Small information kiosks in numerous other Adirondack hamlets throughout the park would be the most local of tourist-centers. These would help visitors identify travel routes and tours, camping sites, and scenic highlights. An information kiosk in a hamlet would become an important point of interest which would encourage tourists to stop, tour the community on foot, and enjoy local shops and restaurants. It could be a part of some new public space improvements, such as a park, town square or village green and serve as a generator of other hamlet development and revitalization projects. Such a coordinated group of information centers would also create a sense of park unity for the traveler visiting different areas of the region.

Amenity Areas

Identifying major recreational amenities and grouping similar types by geographic locations and seasonal importance suggest another parkwide strategy. For example, if one or two regions within the park are ski regions (e.g. Whiteface and Gore Mountain), these would be identified as a major amenity area. This concept, described as "amenity frontage" encourages hamlets within or adjacent to such areas to use this classification in their own marketing and development programs and capitalize on proximity. Another area might be identified as a major hiking, camping or wilderness experience area. Again, hamlets in this region would emphasize proximity to trails and campsites, encourage bed and breakfast inns, and develop other services appropriate to these activities. Numerous amenity areas throughout the park not only strengthen and clarify its image as a major recreational and sports destination, but also give a clearer focus to hamlets as they develop local marketing information.

Tourism Routes

Tourism routes could offer unique experiences to visitors moving through the Adirondack Park. Whether such tours are made by individuals on foot, on bicycles, or in cars, or enjoyed as an organized bus tour, carefully designed routes through the area would extend a visitor's enjoyment and opportunities while in the park. Due to its large size, the Adirondack Park is usually not experienced in its entirety by any one visitor on a single trip. Interesting and more informative tours would encourage travel, additional sightseeing and longer average stays by visitors to the Park. The local hamlets could be logical stops along a tourism route and could benefit significantly from such a comprehensive system.

Subregional Approaches

The sharing of resources in relation to tourism and recreation development allows individual hamlets to identify and embellish their own outstanding offerings while at the same time supporting the activities based in adjoining communities. Increased interaction among hamlets would eliminate the repetition of similar activities while allowing individual activities to be more fully developed within a single hamlet. With the subregional formula, the population needed to support certain recreational facilities is expanded, including increased cooperation and the potential for shared advertising. An example of the subregional grouping concept is elaborated below for the Wilderness Outpost Hamlets.

Wilderness Outpost Hamlets Strategy

The Wilderness Outpost Hamlets offer the perfect setting and activities so often envisioned by the visitor to the Adirondacks. The communities of Indian Lake, Blue Mountain Lake, Long Lake and Raquette Lake have a special opportunity to pool their unique resources into an expanded and extraordinary recreational experience. Many of the activities and their necessary facilities are already present in these hamlets. The key, however, is to see this group as a whole which can expand individual opportunities to create a major tourism and recreational area. The resources and activities to be emphasized in this subregion are those characteristic of the Adirondack wilderness: hiking, camping, canoeing, swimming and, in winter, cross-country skiing and snowmobiling. The major concept is to develop these hamlets as stops along recreational trails emphasizing the interconnected system and developing complementary services and facilities.

Hiking trails are the most obvious forms of pedestrian systems. The existing Northville-Lake Placid Trail is a major hiking route bisecting the region, and numerous public trails such as Cascade Lake Trail and Owl's Head have been developed in specific areas. This scheme would expand the connections of the individual trails and identify accommodations by both location and type. A guide or brochure could identify these for the hiker and list services offered. Such a study would also pinpoint areas where services are lacking or where facilities exist. This information would allow for the development of a major hiking network between the outpost hamlets, rather than isolated trails and uncoordinated services in indivudual communities.

An identical strategy could be used to interconnect canoe trails, cross-country ski trails, white-water rafting trips, etc. If the outpost communities acted in concert, a much more desirable system of amenities and service facilities would result. The recreational opportunities could also be publicized more economically and effectively as the offerings of a group of hamlets rather than an individual community.

Within this interconnected group of recreational activities, each hamlet could highlight its unique attractions to visitors. Long Lake has spectacular views and a fine beach which travelers to this hamlet can enjoy. It also has one of the few seaplane services in and out of the Adirondack Park. The Raquette Lake area is renowned as the home of William Durant's great camps, including Pine Knot, Sagamore, and Kamp Kill Kare. These are regularly open for tours and would offer tourists a unique Adirondack experience. Indian Lake has a fine beach and a municipal golf course. Adirondack Lake is known for its floating bog islands, an unusual natural phenomenon. As the central hamlet in the group, Blue Mountain Lake has a special position among park hamlets as the home of the Adirondack Museum. One of the nation's outstanding museums, the facility's grand setting overlooking the lake and creative interpretation of Adirondack history affords travelers a stimulating visit. Arts and crafts shops and a local craft guild, in addition to the museum, make Blue Mountain Lake a cultural center in the central Adirondacks as well as a critical element in the Wilderness Outpost recreational and tourism subgroup.

The Boquet River Interpretive Trail

Another example of a subregional strategy is the Boquet River interpretive trail. It should be recognized that many waterways are corridors which link historic cultural sites and serve to create subregional groupings along waterway systems. Because of the history and industrial development associated with these systems, an interpretive trail highlighting this history offers one opportunity for utilizing the riverfront resources found in many Adirondack communities. While an interpretive trail along a river can be organized within a single community and take advantage of local resources, a more diversified trail could be created by linking several hamlets. Such a possibility exists along the Boquet River in northeastern Essex County. Connecting these hamlets by an interpretive trail would not only enhance the public space within the hamlets, but would also encourage visitors to the Park to spend time in these communities.

The movement along such an interpretive trail from hamlet to hamlet could be accomplished in several ways. One would be the creation of canoe trails along the river. In each community, a small park or open space would allow canoeists to stop, use the facilities, wander through the hamlet, and read over the interpretive brochures or plaques in the park. Another strategy would be bike trails, either along the river or along existing roads with identifiable stops in the hamlets.

In such a group, one could organize a trail which would be unique in each entire region. In the Boquet group, the trail could begin in Elizabethtown with a discussion of community government and the early history of the river valley. Wadhams could demonstrate the role of water power in the industrial history of the area with a possible tour of the restored hydro plant in the hamlet. Whallonsburgh would illustrate the role of agriculture in the Champlain Valley region, with its nearby farms and its farm-service businesses as contemporary examples. A stop at the Boquet schoolhouse and a short trip into Essex could highlight the cultural and social history of the area with its beautifully restored shops and homes. A final stop in Willsboro could relate both the historic significance of the hamlet as a milltown and early military settlement and its emerging role as a recreation center on Lake Champlain. At this time, a Boquet River interpretive trail map and short history containing many of these features is nearing completion.

Local Approaches

Local approaches to developing recreation and tourism in the hamlets are often the easiest to conceptualize and most difficult to implement. The first step in establishing such a concept is understanding the negative and positive points of the hamlet in terms of recreational offerings. Does the hamlet have a beachfront, ski area, good fishing river or other amenity? The physical setting and landscape characteristics and features will determine to a great extent what a particular hamlet can offer.

An individual hamlet should be viewed in terms of the park-wide and subregional approaches just discussed. Is the hamlet located within a group of hamlets that together could create a strong recreational amenity group? Or does a nearby hamlet have a strong recreational or tourism emphasis which could be complemented or enlarged upon? Some of these questions will be answered by determining the way in which a hamlet functions for tourists in the Park. Three general classifications of hamlets with regard to local recreation and tourism attributes are defined below.

Gateway Communities: hamlets located on important transportation routes on the edge of the Park announcing a visitor's arrival, such as the community of Star Lake where detailed design plans have been prepared for tourist service centers and related open space development.

Destination Resorts: communities and attractions which are the places travelers head for in the Park. Lake Placid, with its Olympic facilities and nearby skiing areas, is a well-known destination resort community. So too, is the Adirondack museum in Blue Mountain Lake and the Camp-in-the-Woods religious retreat in Speculator. Outstanding natural amenities and theme parks become designations as well. Santa's Workshop greets many summer visitors as does High Falls Gorge between Wilmington and Lake Placid. Visits to the great camps entice others to head for Raquette Lake or Enchanted Forest in nearby Old Forge. These communities all have some special feature which people come to see or experience and which usually establishes a tourist market of its own.

Flow-through Hamlets: communities along major transportation routes which serve neither as gateways nor destinations but are "market-following" places. They are hamlets which travelers drive through on their way to other destinations in the Park. Often the form of such hamlets reflects clearly this pass-through function—long, linear settlements lacking a central core while offering numerous highway services. This pattern of development is rather common in Adirondack hamlets. Wilmington illustrates this type of community perfectly. Strung out along Route 86, the village has no identifiable core, no clear edges, and an overabundance of underused motels and abandoned gas stations.

Local tourist and recreation attributes determine what kinds of redevelopment approaches should be considered in a hamlet. A gateway community needs to work at acquiring a Park visitors' center around which a public open space for visitors can be created—located as close to the center of the community as possible. An attractively developed site would encourage travelers to stroll through the core area and would create the need for shops and restaurants.

Destination resorts need to address at least two issues: the drawing feature of the hamlet and the quality of the hamlet itself. Again, this would suggest improving the visual environment of the area. In terms of a unique amenity, such as a large beach or amusement park, this might suggest improving or updating facilities, including access. Destination resorts also need to market the unique features that attract visitors.

Flow-through hamlets have a more difficult task, because they have no direct attraction for tourists. They should attempt to give the community an identifiable core by encouraging centralized development rather than allowing sprawl to occur at the hamlet edges. An attractive public space in the central area of the village would also encourage visitors to stop. A small park with an information booth, rest room facilities and perhaps a scenic view would be such an amenity. Highway services should also be improved to promote more activity in the community.

This planning project represents sustainable development principles for tourism growth. It encourages facility development in the hamlets, managed visitor contact with resources, and protected resource policies outside these functional areas. Recommendations include the value of greater cooperation and collaboration among developers. For greater information, education, and enjoyment of visitors and greater resource protection, the concept recommends increased use of visitor interpretive trails and visitor centers. Throughout the plan, the uniqueness of place is protected. Because local people have been involved in the planning process, the concepts for future development and management have a much greater chance for implementation.

FINGER LAKES REGION

In 1989, the Finger Lakes Association, a nonprofit agency for tourism development and promotion, initiated through its executive director Conrad Tunney, a project to plan the future for this 14-county region in west-central New York state (Figure 6-24). The project was a follow-up to an overall statewide tourism plan prepared by Price Waterhouse in 1987.

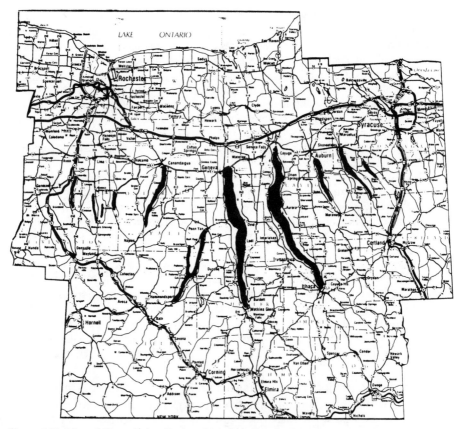

Figure 6-24. Map of Finger Lakes Region. Map including the fourteen counties (9000 sqare miles) within the scope of the Finger Lakes Association of New York. Illustrated are highways, cities, and lakes of the region (Finger Lakes Region 1991, 20).

The project (Finger Lakes Region 1991) differed from many others because of its approach. First, it was to be performed by a Finger Lakes Association Planning Development Committee including representatives of the Finger Lakes Association and four regional planning and development boards having jurisdiction over counties within the region. Second, leadership was assigned to Bill Hess, director of the Southern Tier Central Regional Planning and Development Board. Third, public input from over 125 representatives of local tourism through survey questionnaires and areawide workshop meetings was obtained. Fourth, tourism consultant Clare Gunn was engaged to provide technical assistance. And, finally, the project was funded by the planning and development boards, the Finger Lakes Association, but primarily by a grant from the New York State Urban Development Corporation.

The Finger Lakes region is approximately 9,000 square miles in size and is one of the "vacationland" regions designated by the state tourism authority. The purpose of the project was to: (1) document the economic impact of tourism; (2) identify those involved in tourism, including their roles, responsibilities and resources; and (3) identify the constraints and opportunities for enhancing regional tourism (attractions, events, and supporting facilities). The study focused primarily on identifying opportunities and action needed but did not involve geographic analysis to determine locations and characteristics of destination zones. The process included the following five tasks:

1. Obtain consensus on goals.
2. Inventory attractions, facilities, services.
3. Identify organizations and their roles.
4. Identify constraints and opportunities.
5. Recommend implementation strategies for goals and objectives.

Task 1. The goals agreed upon were:

1. Enhance the provision of visitor satisfactions.
2. Increase the rewards to the region's economy and all sectors involved in tourism development.
3. Protect the region's natural and environmental resources.
4. Integrate tourism into community social and economic life throughout the region.

Task 2. This task included summarizing existing market information and inventorying the following:

Attractions	553
Lodging facilities	458
Food and beverage	1605
Marinas	67
Events	1601
Transportation (highways, airports, rail)	

Task 3. The several private, quasi-public, and public organizations were identified and their tourism roles were analyzed. Generalized categories were named for the several jurisdictional levels as shown in Figure 6-25. Their roles included planning, development, operation, and promotion.

Task 4. Through surveys and workshops, the four major areas of constraints impacting tourism in the region were:

A. Inadequate financial assistance
B. Poor local support of tourism
C. Lack of cooperation among tourism sectors
D. Insufficient promotional and marketing efforts

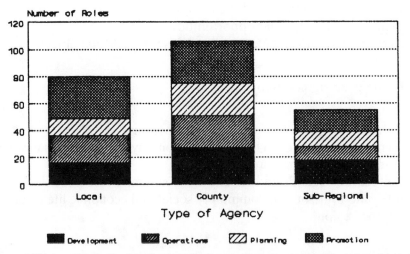

Figure 6-25. Agencies Involved in Tourism. The graph illustrates comparative roles of agencies for tourism in the Finger Lakes region at the local, county, and subregional levels. These roles are directed toward development, operations, planning, and promotion (Finger Lakes Region 1991, 32).

TABLE 6-4
ORGANIZATIONS RESPONSIBLE FOR ACTION

Organizations	Economic A			Support B			Coopera-tive C			Promotion D		
	1	2	3	1	2	3	1	2	3	1	2	3
Regional Tour Association	●	●	●	●	●	●	●	●	●	●	●	●
Regional Planning Boards	●	●	●	●	●	●	●	●	●			
Tourist Promotion Organizations			●	●	●	●	●	●	●	●		●
Visitors and Convention Bureaus			●	●	●	●		●	●	●	●	●
Other Planning Organizations			●	●	●	●	●	●		●		
Economic Development Organizations	●	●	●	●	●	●		●				
Chambers of Commerce	●	●	●	●	●	●		●	●	●	●	●
Public Open Space Agencies		●	●				●	●	●			●
New York State Department of Econmic Development	●						●				●	●
Tourism Businesses	●	●	●							●	●	●
Legislatures		●			●		●	●	●			
Cooperative Extension Services						●	●	●	●		●	●
Civic Organizations					●	●	●	●				
Regulatory Agencies		●					●					
Financial Institutions	●		●									

Source: Finger Lakes 1991, 14

Task 5. Study of the findings and deliberations among the principals of the study resulted in naming *objectives* and *strategies* to meet the challenge of the four constraints identified in Task 4. These are identified in the following description excerpted from the Executive Summary of the report *Finger Lakes Region Tourism—Development Opportunities* (1991), pp. 6–12. Table 6-4 presents a matrix of the main organizations that would be responsible for leadership for each objective.

Development Opportunities

The study's survey of organizations impacting the region's tourism industry identified many opportunities to enhance tourism in the Finger Lakes. Some of these opportunities were development projects, such as a marina or a museum at a specific site. Others focused more on the processes involved in attracting and serving visitors. Frequently, these broader opportunities were related to the issues and constraints identified earlier.

The review of survey information with study participants in workshop settings and with the project consultant led to the formulation of the following goals, objectives, and strategies for enhancing the region's tourism (Finger Lakes Region 1991, 6–12).

GOAL A: IMPROVE ECONOMIC VIABILITY OF TOURISM

OBJECTIVE 1: *Enhance Business Finance*

STRATEGIES:
- Create investment incentives and tax incentives for tourism physical plant upgrading, expansion, and new development.
- Legislate dedicated tax revenues for tourism development.
- Increase public seed monies for attractions and service businesses.
- Hold educational seminars for the financial community (banks, loan agencies, financial institutions and tourism entrepreneurs) for the purpose of broadening their understanding of tourism economics.
- Modify credit and banking requirements to encourage feasible tourism development.
- Establish a venture capital fund and loan program, including the expansion of existing matching funds programs.
- Encourage existing funding agencies to give higher priority to tourism funding, at least equal to other industrial development.

OBJECTIVE 2: *Reduce Regulatory Constraints*

STRATEGIES:
- Review and amend laws, regulations and administrative procedures (local to federal) that conflict, overlap, are obsolete, and unnecessarily constrain tourism development.
- Initiate local, state, and federal action to ameliorate and eliminate constrictive regulations.
- Review permitting processes to identify and propose elimination of excessive "red tape".
- Suggest new legislation that is needed for more viable protection and development of tourism in the Region.

OBJECTIVE 3: *Expand the Supply Side of Tourism*

STRATEGIES:
- Encourage existing travel-oriented attractions and service businesses to upgrade and adapt to shoulder and all-season markets. This will automatically encourage return visitations.
- Stimulate each county to review all proposed development opportunities recommended by participants in this study.
- Encourage local political jurisdictions to improve the infrastructure to current standards, especially those features that assure the quality of the public water supply.
- Encourage each county to study the potential for more and better attractions, services, information, and promotion.

- Improve, coordinate and expand transportation access (including signage) to attractions and services wherever there is evidence of need.
- Encourage each county and community to determine how well present tourism supply meets the needs of market demand, especially changing market trends. An enhanced product will also tend to lengthen stay.

GOAL B: ADVANCE LOCAL SUPPORT OF TOURISM

OBJECTIVE 1: *Create an Area Tourism Plan and Obtain Local Commitment to its Implementation*

STRATEGIES:
- Within the framework of regional goals and objectives, and by analysis of resource needs and market trends, determine potential "touristic impact zones" within the Finger Lakes Region. (A touristic impact zone is the area in which all elements supporting tourism combine in the greatest number and strength and are not necessarily confined to jurisdictional boundaries.)
- For each touristic impact zone, identify the communities best able (by interest capability) to serve tourism.
- Charge each touristic impact zone (including its service sommunity) to develop a set of project guidelines, addressing issues such as zoning, resource protection, growth limitations, etc.
- Identify the groups (agencies, organizations) best able to champion the recommended guidelines and create a network linking local touristic impact zone guidelines to regional goals and objectives.
- Encourage necessary zoning codes to identify localities best adapted to tourism development and those needing resource protection.

OBJECTIVE 2: *Integrate Tourism into all Local Plans for Development*

STRATEGIES:
- At the Regional Planning Board level, integrate all tourism development projects into the planning process.
- Encourage all planning entities and officials to consider tourism implications in all plans and decisions.
- Charge tourism agencies with the responsibility of considering all community impacts resulting from their decisions on developmental and promotional matters.
- Place tourism development issues on the agendas of regular meetings of county and community legislatures.
- Identify the tourism image and theme that best describes the character of the area.
- Establish stronger local leadership and broader involvement of the many constituencies in tourism.

OBJECTIVE 3: *Establish a Local Tourism Awareness and Educational Program*

STRATEGIES:
- Provide research and support to local educational institutions (schools, colleges, universities) for extension-type educational programs on tourism issues, including technical assistance for small tourism businesses.
- Hold public meetings between tourism proponents and residents regarding the economic, social, and environmental implications of tourism.

- Use local media (radio, TV, press) to publicize tourism and its importance locally.
- Provide informational lectures on tourism at regular meetings of civic and other local organizations.

GOAL C: INCREASE COOPERATION AMONG ALL SECTORS

OBJECTIVE 1: *Foster Better Inter-public Agency Cooperation*

STRATEGIES:
- Encourage better working relationships by defining and agreeing upon roles and responsibilities.
- Revise legislative mandates regarding tourism roles and policies for each public agency (federal to local) that impacts tourism.
- Establish inter-agency tourism councils at the city, county, and regional levels.
- Establish a program of educational seminars to enhance inter-agency under-standing of tourism.
- Develop conflict resolution between agencies by means of catalytic educational leadership and program.
- Encourage private sector representation of the tourism industry to participate on boards of public and non-profit tourism-related agencies.

OBJECTIVE 3: *Establish Better Joint Planning*

STRATEGIES:
- Involve private tourism sector in all public tourism planning efforts (e.g., park location planning and design decisions).
- Encourage planning agencies with responsibilities for producing joint public-private tourism development plans to communicate such plans on a Finger Lakes regional basis.
- Incorporate tourism objectives in all Main Street and other downtown renovation plans.
- Address water and waste disposal system needs in all tourism development opportunities surrounding the Region's lakes and waterways.
- Encourage the incorporation of historic and natural resource parks in development plans to provide greater utilization of the many assets of interest to visitors.
- Plan for integrating scattered small attractions into larger, visible, and more meaningful and promotable entities.

GOAL D: ENHANCE PROMOTIONAL AND MARKETING EFFORTS

OBJECTIVE 1: *Integrate and Coordinate All Promotional Programs*

STRATEGIES:
- Establish a Finger Lakes Promotional Advisory Board to facilitate integration of state, regional, county, community and local promotional programs (i.e., publicity, publications, advertising, public relations, and incentives) to maximize resources and minimize duplication of efforts.
- Establish a Finger Lakes Tourism Research and Information Center to conduct market research and function as an informational clearinghouse.

- Regularly publish findings on Finger Lakes tourism market research, characteristics and trends, and other topics of interest to the tourism industry.

OBJECTIVE 2: *Improve Tourist Information*

STRATEGIES:

- Strengthen regional network of information stations and identify on tourist promotional materials (e.g., maps).
- Develop a recognizable symbol (logo) to identify information stations for the traveling public.
- Publish informational literature, tour guides, and directories and make available to travelers (separate from promotional materials).
- Promote utilization of modern electronic technology (computers, video equipment, etc.) in strategic locations to better communicate with the traveling public.
- Expand tourist hospitality training programs to include interpersonal techniques and information on local attractions and services.
- Maintain and update the database created as part of the Study.
- Encourage promotional agencies to improve use of public media, (e.g. newspapers and television) to promote tourism events and attractions both inside and outside the Region.

OBJECTIVE 3: *Target Marketing to Specific Segments*

STRATEGIES:

- Utilize most recent tourism market research to identify specific market segments.
- Make more efficient use of promotional funds by targeting them toward the identified market segments.
- Focus promotion on the indigenous natural-resource, outdoor recreation, and ecotourist market.
- Focus promotion on the indigenous cultural resource, historic, ethnic, entertainment market.
- Focus promotion on the "pass through" market, identifying worthwhile travel experiences at focal points enroute to extend traveler stay.
- Focus promotion on those market segments that will enhance shoulder and off-season tourism business and encourage return visitation.

In addition to these objectives and strategies, the principals of the study presented two more recommendations—a policy statement and an action process.

The *policy statement* charged the Finger Lakes Region Planning and Development Committee with the responsibility for future implementation and leadership because it represented the main regional tourist association and was a major actor in the study. Following is the text of the Policy Statement (Finger Lakes Region 1991, 13).

"To guide and coordinate the development and promotion of overall tourism within the 14-county area of west/central New York State, identified as the Finger Lakes

Region, in order to improve the economic viability of tourism, advance local support, increase cooperation, and enhance the promotion and marketing of the Region."

This policy defines "tourism" as the varied business and pleasure activities pursued by travelers; the attractions that entice travelers to the Region and provide satisfaction therefrom; the travel and transportation systems; the services and facilities for travelers; the travel information systems; and the promotion and marketing of tourism.

This policy recognizes the tri-sector organizational structure of tourism, including governments, the nonprofit sector, and the private commercial enterprise sector.

This policy encourages the development of tourism in a manner compatible with other local economic, social, and environmental activities in order to protect natural resources and the quality of life throughout the Region.

And, this policy includes the fostering of high quality natural and cultural resource assets as important foundation factors for sustaining development of tourism.

Finally, the Regional Planning Development Committee agreed upon a process of implementation that built upon present conditions but started action on the recommended strategies. First, this included wide dissemination of the Executive Summary of the report findings that stressed the objectives and strategies for action. Second, the region was advised to take advantage of the momentum of new cooperation within the region that had been stimulated by the project. Finally, the region should initiate a procedure to adapt the recommendations to local conditions. Recommended was a tourism action workshop with widespread participation, with the following purposes (Finger Lakes Region 1991, 15):

- To review and refine regional strategies to address subregional needs and opportunities.
- To identify priorities for the refined strategies, and those which will require regionwide cooperation for effective action.
- To establish "action teams" for strategy implementation.
- To develop a timetable to initiate each strategy.

It was the consensus of the committee that the project had (Finger Lakes Region 1991, 16):

1. Established or enhanced communication among the organizations involved in the region's tourism industry;
2. Produced base-line data describing key features of tourism as a benchmark for future reference;
3. Created the foundation of a tourism data system to electronically link principal organizations supporting tourism; and
4. Produced significant strategies for enhancing the region's tourism based upon grass root's input.

Within one year, several steps have been implemented (Tunney 1992). Regarding Objective 1 (Goal A), a subsidiary of the Finger Lakes Association—a revolving loan fund—has been established to assist small business, especially attractions. In cooperation with the U.S. Travel Data Center, a regional research and information center is being established (Goal D, Objective 1). In response to Objective 3, Goal A, a special study of the attraction potential of the Seneca/Cayuga Sections of the New York canal system is in process. It demonstrates new cooperation among the four regional planning boards, the counties involved, the three economic councils, the Thruway Authority, and the Regional Economic Development Partnership Program, Urban Development Corporation.

This regional tourism project differs from a typical consultant plan by being organized, led, and performed by organizations within the region. The consultant acted only as adviser. In this case, the emphasis was more on program action than on geographical analysis for physical development. It promises a high degree of implementation in the future because the responsibility for action lies with existing agencies and organizations. It represents a bold and innovative approach by a tourist organization that has been focused primarily upon promotion.

JAPAN

The national tourism organization of Japan dates back to 1930 when the Board of Tourist Industry was established by the Ministry of Transport. After several reorganizational changes, especially in 1984, the Department of Tourism now functions under the Transport Policy Bureau, Ministry of Transport. (Tourism in Japan 1991, 51).

Department of Tourism

The department has three divisions: Planning, Travel Agencies, and Development.

The key functions and responsibilities within the *Planning* Division are:

Overall coordination and planning of tourist administration.
Supervision of the Japan National Tourist Organization (JNTO).
Improvement of reception services for foreign visitors.
Research and study on tourism.
Subsidies to the tourist industry.

Matters relating to the acquisition of stocks by foreign investors in the
field of tourism.

Collection and compilation of tourism-related documents.

Handling of general affairs for the Council for Tourism Policy.

Within the Planning Division an International Affairs Office was established in 1978 to improve international relations of tourism. It is responsible for:

Liaison, cooperation and exchange of information with tourism administration authorities in foreign countries and international tourism
organizations.

Research and study on tourism policies and situations in foreign
countries.

Planning and guidance concerning international tourism publicity.

Collection and compilation of international tourism documents.

The *Travel Agencies Division* has the responsibility for supervision of
the travel agency business, supervision of travel agents associations, and
supervision of the guide-interpreter business.

The Development Division contains several subdivisions related to
development, recreation, youth and convention activity.

Responsibilities for development include:

Financial affairs and a taxation system relating to the tourist industry.

Registration of hotels and *ryokan* (traditional Japanese design), and
supervision of the registered hotels and *ryokan*. Improvement of tourist souvenirs in quality.

Promotion of tourist morality.

Planning and guidance concerning tourism publicity.

Planning of the development of tourist facilities.

Guidance for the improvement of tourist facilities in Japan including the
Youth Hostel Center.

The *Tourism and Recreation and Recreation Planning Office* was established in 1972 and is responsible for the following:

Investigation and improvement of tourist resorts.

Affairs relating to tourism promotion in the comprehensive national
land development plans.

Investigation, preservation, and utilization of tourist resources.

Planning and coordination for the improvement of the Tourism and
Recreation Areas and the Youth Travel Villages.

Planning of systems to be formulated for the consolidation of the Tourism and Recreation Areas.

Financial aid for the development of the Tourism and Recreation Areas. Investigation and research on tourism and recreational activities.

The *Youth Hostel Center* provides guidance for operation of youth hostels in Japan. A *Senior Planning Officer* for Tourist Industries was established in 1984 and oversees work with the tourist industry.

Council for Tourism Policy

In 1963 the Council for Tourism Policy was established. It is composed of 27 nonofficial civilians of learning and experience from private and academic areas. Its purpose is to provide tourism administration with opinions and information, either requested by administration or volunteered from the council. Examples are "Theory and Method of Forming Desirable Domestic Tourism" developed in 1982, and "For the Future Development of International Tourism in Japan" completed in 1984.

Inter-Ministerial Liaison Council on Tourism

In order to interrelate with several other ministries and agencies that have interest in tourism, an Inter-Ministerial Liaison Council on Tourism was formed. It includes 21 director-generals of related ministries and agencies.

Local Tourism

Local tourism development is shared with the Department of Tourism through the 47 prefectural governments. At this level, plans are prepared for regional tourism development, promotion programs, tourist facilities improvement, and park and cultural protection. Also at the local level, nine district bureaus of the Ministry of Transport cooperate on travel agency management, liaison with prefectural governments, and local organizations.

Private Bodies

Several private and quasi-private organizations have active roles in tourism development and management. The *Japan Tourist Association* was established in 1964 to promote domestic tourism. It holds seminars and programs to stimulate better local understanding of tourism. A nonprofit foundation, the *Japan Travel Bureau*, carries on tourism research, provides consulting service for tourism development, and offers personnel training. The *Japan Guide Association* offers training and coordination for all government-licensed guides. The *Japan National Trust* is a foundation that fosters protection of special resources. The *Japan Tourism Development Foundation* was established in 1971 to promote wholesome tourism and recreation, and is also responsible for the Youth Hostel Center in Otsu City. Additional non-profit organizations include the Japan Hotel Association, Japan Ryokan Association, Japan Tourist Hotel Association, Japan Business Hotel Association, Japan Minshuku Association, Japan Economy Accommodation Foundation, Japan Association of Travel Agents, Japan Association of Domestic Travel Agents, International Tourism Development Institute of Japan, Japan Convention Promotion Association, International Tourism Center of Japan, and Welcome Inn Reservation Service.

Japan National Tourist Organization

The Japan National Tourist Organization (JNTO) was established in 1959 (and reorganized in 1964, 1979, 1983, and 1985) to promote inbound travel to Japan and provide information to Japanese travelers on traveling safely overseas. It is administered by the Ministry of Transport and supervised by an Administrative Council of 28 members selected from among people of learning and experience in tourism, appointed by the president. Its work is done through six departments:

General Affairs Department
Finance Department
Planning and Research Department
Overseas Promotion Department
Tourist Assistance Department
International Cooperation Department (including Japan Convention Bureau, Overseas Offices, Representatives and Tourist Information Centers)

Tourist Information Services

The purposes of tourist reception working programs include to

1. Improve quality of information services.
2. Accommodate language problems.

3. Promote mutual understanding and friendship.
4. Develop international tourism in local areas.
5. Reduce travel costs.

The tourist information service is performed through the following services directed toward each of the above objectives:

1. Tourist information centers, teletourist service, "i" network, mini-guides.
2. Japan travel-phone, tourist's handbook, signage, good-will guide movement, national examination for interpreters.
3. Home visit system, "Explore Japanese Culture" system.
4. Model international tourist areas, survey of international tourist areas, international culture villages, seminars on international tourism.
5. "Reasonable accommodations" list, international tourist *Minshukus*, international tourist pensions, tourist restaurants, Japan rail-pass.

Comprehensive Resort Planning

Law (71) of 1987 provides for the planning and development of resort areas known as Specially Designated Areas. These are approximately 150,000 ha. in size; are areas where a variety of activities are possible; where land is easily obtained, where total development is feasible; in low population density areas; and includes Priority Development Districts, approximately 3,000 ha. in area.

The planning of the areas is done primarily by government but directed toward private investment. The planning steps include

1. Basic planning policy by government agencies.
2. Plan making, by federal government in consultation with city, town, and village authorities.
3. Plan approval, by appropriate ministers.
4. Project implementation:
   • special tax abatement to entrepreneurs
   • development of utilities by public agencies
   • public financial assistance, federal, and local
   • land use regulations
   • protection of natural resources
   • sound development of tourist businesses
   • stability of land prices

Improved Facilities

In recent years travel demand, both domestic and foreign, has stimulated the establishment of many new recommendations. These are classified as hotels, *ryokan*, lodging houses, and boarding houses. The government provides financial assistance for accommodations—30.8 billion yen in 1990. Recently, there has been great increase in numbers of Western-style and business hotels. Lodges and vacation villages are associated with national parks. These resorts provide for outdoor recreation and are generally subsidized by government but often are managed by private individuals or organizations. The central and prefectural governments are responsible for roads, parking, campgrounds, and public utilities. The vacation villages are managed by a nonprofit organization called the National Vacation Village Corporation.

New Sites of Discovery

Perhaps the most innovative program related to planning is the New Sites of Discovery project, set up in 1984. The aim is to assist lesser-known areas in developing their tourism potential. Location of New Sites of Discovery is shown in Figure 6-26. The Ministry of Transport has established standards for their selection. The area must:

Have great appeal for overseas tourists.
Have a well-developed public transport system.
Have readily available medical facilities.
Offer Western-style accommodation.
Have "i"-centers, or local tourist information centers for overseas visitors.
Contain a population that shows a strong interest in attracting foreign tourists and improving reception facilities for overseas visitors.
Need strong support from the central government.

Tourism Resources

The government has expressed strong interest in relationships between natural and cultural resources and tourism. They classify natural areas in three categories. *Natural parks* encompass 23 national parks, 53 quasi-national parks, and 298 prefectural natural parks. Fifty-eight *marine parks* include sea areas and underwater resource protection. *Hot springs* per-

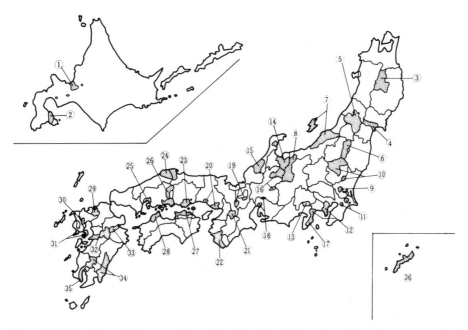

Figure 6-26. New Sites of Discovery. Japan. Map illustrates the location of lesser known areas that are being given special governmental assistance for tourism development because of resources, local government support, and local commitment (Tourism in Japan 1991, 26).

petuate the Japanese custom of bathing for therapeutic as well as recreational use. As of 1989, there were 2,302 spas in Japan.

The central government has classified cultural areas as follows (Tourism in Japan 1991, 33):

> Tangible cultural properties: constructions, paintings, sculptures.
> Intangible cultural properties; theatricals, music, craft work.
> Folkloric cultural properties: customs, historic artifacts.
> Monuments: ancient tombs, scenic areas, scientific areas.
> Clusters of traditional constructions; vernacular architecture.

The preservation of historical climate allows for designations of whole areas, such as ancient capitals and 7th century culture. By 1989, 39 "special areas" had been so designated. In both cultural and natural areas, mass tourism is planned and controlled, such as for traffic, so that the resources are protected.

This summary of tourism planning in Japan is based on *Tourism in Japan 1991,* a document that focuses primarily on policies, organization, administration, and regulation from the governmental perspective. As such, it does not describe the planning processes nor details of geographic characteristics used in identifying areas and sites with potential for development. Although this example is not a specific action plan, it demonstrates how one nation has accepted a strong federal role for planning, development, and management of tourism. Though it is heavily bureaucratized, there are many opportunities for input by local, area, and national organizations. This example shows how tourism is integrated into overall federal governance. It also represents new recognition of the important role of resources and the need for careful planning and design.

AUSTRALIA

At the federal level, Australia has launched a major tourism development plan (Commonwealth of Australia 1992, 1). The minister of tourism Alan Griffiths has stated, "There is need for careful planning to provide for sustainable industry development and a balanced approach to economic, environmental and social issues." The plan is designed to accommodate an additional 40 international flights per day as well as increased domestic tourism. The stated goals (Commonwealth of Australia 1992, 7) are to

> Optimize the tourism industry's contribution to national income, employment growth, and the balance of payments by creating a favorable economic environment for industry development.
> Provide for sustainable tourism development by encouraging responsible planning and management practices consistent with the conservation of our natural and cultural heritage.
> Enhance access to quality tourism experiences and ensure favorable social outcomes of tourism by diversifying the product base, raising industry standards, and protecting the public interest.
> Provide and encourage the necessary promotional, planning, coordination, research, and statistical support to assist the industry's development.

In order to plan and guide development toward these goals, seven major strategy themes have been described as governmental roles and responsibilities. They are paraphrased as follows (Commonwealth of Australia 1992, 7–15).

Marketing and Coordination

Enable Australian Tourism Commission to promote.
Target priority markets overseas.
Promote theme years, 1993–1997.
Facilitate coordinated development of overseas markets.
Assist operators on promotion.

Use expositions for promotion.
Create a National Tourism Awareness Campaign.
Ensure diverse representation in policy formation.
Support input from the Tourism Minister's Council (TMC) and the Tourism Advisory Council (TAC).
Assess scope of proactive TAC in planning.
Encourage development of States/Territories tourism plans.

Research and Statistics

Ensure effective functions of Bureau of Tourism Research.
Ensure production of statistics useful to government and industry.
Monitor structure of research.
Expand research scope in conjunction with States/Territories.
Establish forecasting consultative framework.

Economic and Business Issues

Help maintain a competitive environment.
Treat tourism as an economic export.
Encourage availability of long-term finance.
Permit foreign investment consistent with national interest.
Remove impediments to small business development.
Provide accelerated depreciation for tourism buildings.
Use Development allowances to encourage projects.
Support industrial agreements for tourism.
Minimize regulations.

Transport and Facilitation

Initiate reforms for airline competition.
Seek agreements for aviation sector to respond to market changes.
Implement policies for greater competition.
Recognize tourism interests in negotiations.
Link charter guidelines with tourism needs.
Minimize regulations for best fares within safety limits.
Facilitate new Sydney runway.
Foster domestic and international terminals at Melbourne and Brisbane.
Plan airport linkage with tourism.
Gain funds for improved highway standards.

Link road funding with tourism.
Review coach regulations for greater competition.
Improve coach terminals.
Increase competitiveness of rail.
Improve rail management for tourism.
Improve rail service to Perth, Brisbane, Sydney, and Melbourne.
Consider cruise potential along coastline.
Improve visa procedures.
Improve visitor entrance customs.
Improve travel agent effectiveness and service.

Training, Employment, and Standards

Assume role of training coordination.
Assess needs and provide funds for training and education.
Increase worker mobility, develop accreditation standards.
Provide scholarships.
Encourage educator emphasis on tourism training.
Increase employment opportunities for indigenous people.
Monitor special tourism skills needed.
Revise entry level requirements.
Encourage industry to take on overseas staff where needed.
Give priority to domestic labor training.
Relieve impediments to export of education services.
Stimulate private investment in education.
Encourage work reforms for better practices and careers.
Increase awareness of employment opportunities.
Reward excellence of service delivery.
Stimulate greater tourist shopping.

Environmental and Social Issues

Seek greater industry-conservation liaison.
Create, implement sustainable development policies.
Develop coastal policy.
Adopt plans for ecological sustainability of Great Barrier Reef, adopt
    zoning, education, and interpretive plans.
Review national park plans for tourism.
Implement a new tourism plan for Tasmanian Wilderness World Heri-
    tage Area and Wet Tropics World Heritage Area.
Ensure adequate funding for heritage area protection.

Promote ecotourism.
Consider Antarctic tourism development.
Facilitate tourism on Christmas and Cocos islands.
Support tourism environmental research.
Encourage regional tourism planning.
Assist State/Territories with their planning.
Cut red tape for tourism development.
Encourage evaluation of capacities.
Adopt "user pays" policy on public areas.
Consider other economic visitor controls.
Develop high standard interpretive facilities.
Raise visitor awareness of environmental impacts.
Develop adequate health and safety standards.
Improve opportunities for disabled visitors.

Accommodation and Market Segments

Refine a forecasting model for accommodations.
Increase diversity of accommodations.
Promote convention/incentive destination travel.
Encourage tourism-cultural relations.
Increase involvement of indigenous people.
Stimulate Aboriginal and Torres Strain Islander tourism enterprises.
Enhance and promote the arts.
Encourage greater historic-tourism cooperation.
Encourage more festivals, events.
Increase coordination of sport and commercial fishing.
Encourage marketing of adventure/wilderness holidays.
Encourage development of farms and rural tourism.

It is reported that this policy is the result of close public-private cooperation. Griffiths (1992, 2) said that key elements of this plan and policy are to encourage investment and promote Australia as an international destination. Furthermore, the intent is to encourage a competitive transport sector, develop skills, and provide for an ecologically sustainable development, especially for Aboriginal cultural tourism. His report provides a very comprehensive blueprint of objectives in order to enhance tourism nationwide. It does not, however, describe how this national program is to be integrated with state tourism plans. Nor does it identify specific strategies for reaching the objectives desired.

NEW SOUTH WALES

Independently from the national tourism plan, a task force was identified in the state of New South Wales, Australia, and charged with the responsibility of identifying tourism development needs and strategies. The effort was reported in *New South Wales Tourism Development Strategy: A Plan for the Future* (1990). The task force members included representatives of operators of tourism facilities, developers, local government, the conservation movement, trade unions, and other governmental units. The task force was assisted in more detailed study by six subgroups (New South Wales 1990, i):

Environmental Planning and Development
Government Support
Marketing
Training
Transport
Wages and Employment

Following are paraphrased excerpts from the report of the subgroup on Environmental Planning and Development (New South Wales 1990, x).

Major Recommendations

The subgroup identified the following as major needs in the region:

- Identify and increase the availability of sites and areas suitable for planned tourism development.
- Increase the efficiency of the environmental planning and development approval processes through the development of proper policies, guidelines, and practices.
- Improve the availability of information and increase knowledge and awareness relating to the requirements and benefits of tourism development.
- Increase cooperation and consultation between governments, the tourism industry and the community.
- Establish a tourism research program to provide the information base needed for adequate planning.

Planning and Land Use Policy

The report emphasizes that tourism development is not inherently detrimental to the environment and society but that it does require comprehensive study, analysis, and planning to assure orderly growth. It is at the destination scale that strategies and plans are needed. Each destination has its own character and yet its plans need to be coordinated with the overall regional plan. The study revealed that the following areas have the greatest destination potential and therefore require special planning (New South Wales 1990, 61):

Hunter Region
Illawarra Region
Murray Region
North Coast Region
Snowy Sub-Region
South Coast Sub-Region
Sydney Region (Inner and Outer)

At the present time, within these areas there is no coordinated planning except in the Sydney Region. There should be a clear, consistent, and meaningful framework of policies, plans, and guidelines upon which local councils, the tourism industry, and communities can develop and implement strategies for tourism development. Sites and areas for both protection and development potential need to be clearly identified. Equally important is to identify the types of development most appropriate for the locality, the terrain, and the several factors important to environmental protection and tourism success.

Currently, land use policy is not geared to tourism and often it is outmoded or unnecessarily complex. Needed are policies that stimulate creative and sensitive design for development. For example, even though the national parks are travel attractions, there is need for planning a better balance between protection of valuable resources and development of visitor services.

The subgroup recommends that within the destination zones, local tourism plans should be prepared. Local councils can exercise a very important catalytic role by promoting opportunities, assisting in resolving conflict and guiding growth. It is at this level that capacities can be determined and monitored.

The following specific action strategies are recommended (New South Wales 1990, 64–65):

- Appropriate government agencies identify areas most suited to planned tourism development.
- Prepare guidelines for use of governmental surplus lands.
- Prepare destination zone planning guidelines.
- Issue matching grants to local councils for tourism planning.
- The Department of Planning should prepare guidelines for:
    environmental protection,
    conservation (natural and built environment),
    design and layout of projects,
    transportation (provision and integration),
    utility services and public facilities, and
    planning and land use policies.

Environmental Planning Processes

The Environmental Planning and Assessment Act of 1979 is less than satisfactory for tourism. Reform must address the issue of delay in the process that imposes excessive costs on developers. Many of the statutory planning instruments are not responsive to change or innovation. Rezoning often takes an average of 33 weeks. Planning processes must be more flexible. Recommended changes (New South Wales 1990, 68):

    Clearly define objectives.
    Increase knowledge.
    Change attitudes.
    Allocate adequate resources.
    Undertake monitoring and *fine tuning*.
    Improve management skills.
    Take a holistic approach.

New manuals of procedure need to be produced by government agencies so that tourism developers can be properly informed. Governments should provide an advisory panel or officer to give advice on faster preapplication procedures. More flexible land use regulations are needed. Local councils should be encouraged to provide staff assistance in the processing of applications.

While these proposals do not constitute a regional plan, they identify many issues in New South Wales that must be dealt with if tourism planning is to improve. Experience indicates that similar problem resolution is needed in many nations and regions.

CONCLUSIONS

These nine case studies of planning tourism at the regional (national, state, and provincial) scale are offered here for several reasons. Although they are not necessarily representative of all worldwide tourism planning at this level, they offer a diversity of process and content.

Even with their differences, several common threads run through of all the cases. They show that tourism is driven by a demand and a supply side, and that planning's major role is to match needs of demand. Nearly all place great stress on the importance and location of natural and cultural resources for all future development. Such recognition of environmentalism is a relatively new application in regional plan practice. Virtually all cases provide guidelines for the discovery of destination potential. Some have utilized computer graphics as tools for destination identification. Planning goals have been stated or implied in all and include primarily the solving of issues and fostering of opportunities. Though regional plans such as these focus on the broad scale, recommendations are often made for destination and site development. However, feasibility of such projects is not provided until they are created by a potential developer. All of the examples demonstrate the need for integrating the many functioning components of tourism development at this scale of planning. Many of the planning processes exemplified here include the addition of public involvement in planning rather than it being solely a professional operation. Finally, all show the need for greater public-private cooperation on tourism planning and development.

REFERENCES

Blank, Uel, Clare A. Gunn, and Johnson, Johnson & Roy, Inc. (1966). *Guidelines for Tourism-Recreation in Michigan's Upper Peninsula*. East Lansing: Cooperative Extension Service, Michigan State University.

Commonwealth of Australia (1992). *Australia's Passport to Growth: A National Tourism Strategy*. Canberra: Ministry for Tourism.

Dudnik, Elliott (1971). *Symap User's Reference Manual for Synagraphic Computer Mapping*. Chicago: Department of Architecture, University of Illinois.

Finger Lakes Region—Tourism Development Opportunities (1991). "Final Report, Executive Summary." Penn Yan, NY: Finger Lakes Association.

Griffiths, Alan (1992). "Blueprint for Tourism Industry Growth." News release, June 5, 1992. Canberra, Australia: Ministry of Tourism.

Gunn, Clare A. (1952). *Planning Better Vacation Accommodations*. Circular: R-304, Tourist and Resort Series. East Lansing: Michigan State University.

Gunn, Clare A. (1964). "U. P. Tourism Expansion." *The Michigan Economic Record*, 6(7) July-August.

Gunn, Clare A. (1965). *A Concept for the Design of a Tourism-Recreation Region.* Mason, MI: B J Press.

Gunn, Clare A. (1973). "Vacationscape: A Case Study—Government, University, Landscape Architects." Presentation, Annual Meeting, American Society of Landscape Architects, Mackinac Island, Michigan, July 11.

Gunn, Clare A. (1990). *Upcountry South Carolina Guidelines for Tourism Development.* College Station, TX: author.

Gunn, Clare A., and J. Ben McMillen (1979). *Tourism Development: Assessment of Potential in Texas.* MP-1416. College Station: Texas Agricultural Experiment Station, Texas A&M University.

Gunn, Clare A., and Terry R. Larsen (1988). *Tourism Potential—Aided by Computer Cartography.* Aix-en-Provence, France: Centre des Hautes Etudes Touristiques.

New South Wales Tourism Development Strategy: A Plan for the Future (1990). Sydney, Australia: NSW Tourism Commission.

Price Waterhouse (1987). *Proposed Master Plan for Travel Marketing and Development for the State of Oklahoma.* Contributors: Grey Advertising and Clare A. Gunn. Washington, DC, and Oklahoma City: State of Oklahoma Tourism and Recreation Department.

Tourism in Japan 1991 (1991). Tokyo: Ministry of Transport, Japan National Tourist Organization.

Trancik, Roger (1983). *Hamlets of the Adirondacks: History, Preservation and Investment.* Ithaca, NY: Cornell University.

Trancik, Roger (1985). *Hamlets of the Adirondacks: Development Strategies.* Ithaca, NY: Cornell University.

Trancik, Roger (1986). "Hamlets of the Adirondacks; Regional Strategies for Recreation and Tourism," proceedings of Selected Educational Sessions 1986 American Society of Landscape Architects Annual Meeting. In *Landscape/ Land Use Planning*, Julius Fabos (ed.), pp. 1–16. Washington, DC: American Society of Landscape Architects.

Tunney, Conrad (1992). Personal correspondence, November 4, 1992, executive director, Finger Lakes Association.

Chapter 7

Destination Planning Concepts

Introduction

Even though the end products of regional tourism planning should include stimulation of tourism awareness, new interagency governmental cooperation, greater public-private collaboration, and identification of zones of greatest potential, seldom does this process immediately result in new brick-and-mortar tourism development. This can only take place at the destination and site scales and as follow-up to regional planning. It is in and around communities that tourism development can and will succeed. The vision, the policies, and the integration at the regional scale provide the blueprint for a systems planning approach, essential to the elimination of many obstacles and the determination of desirable directions. But, eventually, commitment and land use decisions at the destination and site scales are necessary in order to translate these guidelines into reality. It is at these levels that economies may be strengthened and visitors may be enriched.

The concept of destination—community, attractions, and traveler access—is used here (Figure 7-1) for several reasons. It recognizes the significant role of community in traveler flow, providing the majority of service needs. Communities also contain many of the attractions sought by travelers. All transportation modes lead to communities. But, in addition to these factors, the area around communities contains a great many resources and outlying attractions upon which the community travel services also depend. Using the concept of destination allows these important rural areas to be included in planning framework and principles.

It is no coincidence that this destination zone concept agrees with contemporary views of urban development. At one time, apparently in response to urban congestion, the principle of dispersion was put forward. Many conservation proponents still adhere to this principle. But, dispersion can reduce the indigenous value of both community and hinterland whereas combining a central city with its periphery into a single unit allows each to function in a symbiotic relationship. Gradus and Stern (1980, 418)

DESTINATION ZONE

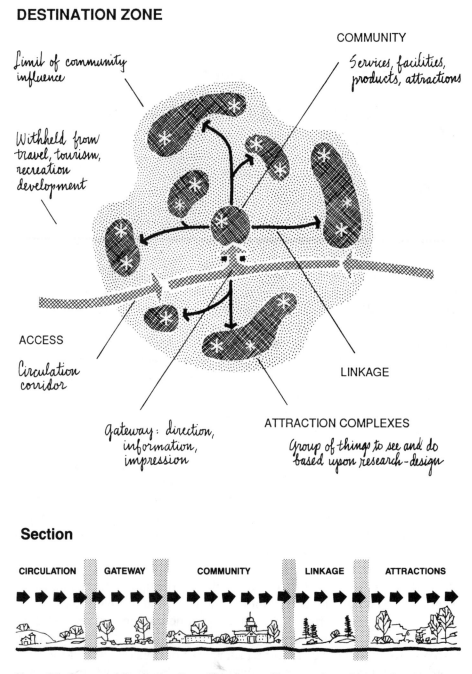

COMMUNITY

Limit of community influence

Services, facilities, products, attractions

Withheld from travel, tourism, recreation development

ACCESS

Circulation corridor

LINKAGE

Gateway: direction, information, impression

ATTRACTION COMPLEXES

Group of things to see and do based upon research-design

Section

| CIRCULATION | GATEWAY | COMMUNITY | LINKAGE | ATTRACTIONS |

Figure 7-1. Concept of Destination Zone. This diagram illustrates the major planning components and their relationship. Included are attraction complexes, linkage between attractions and community, community, access, and entrance gateway (Gunn 1972, 47).

called this a "regiopolis." The regiopolis combined the advantages of social, human, and economic development within and around communities. Likewise, the tourism destination concept allows retention of community identity but also recognizes the important interdependency of the surrounding area.

It is the intent of this chapter to put forward the fundamental of place for planning at the destination scale and offer models, concepts, and processes for planning tourism at this level.

THE IMPERATIVE OF PLACE

The greatest imperative for all of tourism is *place*. Throughout history, place has played a dominant role in society. Sovereignty of place continues to foster strong land protection, and even, to stimulate wars. For many peoples of the earth, the qualities of place mean survival or death. In spite of man's gargantuan efforts to reshape the earth, the land and its geographical differences remain. Every place on earth possesses its own peculiar characteristics, both as result of natural physical forces and acts of man.

As the topic of tourism planning shifts from the macro (the region) to the micro (destinations and sites), the importance of place dominates every concern. As tourism developers and promoters tend toward homogenizing the world with sameness, the opportunities for extracting the unique qualities of place so important to the traveler are being missed.

Characteristics of Place

Place, as defined by Motloch (1991, 279), "is the mental construct of the temporal-spatial experience that occurs as the individual ascribes meaning to settings, through environmental perception and cognition." Explicit in this definition are important meanings for tourism. All travelers must have a place to go. Simple as this may be, it is not well understood. Place qualities are absolute for all developers of services, facilities, transportation, information, and promotion—the components of supply.

Temporal aspects of place are critical to tourism planning. Visitor impressions and experiences vary greatly with the time a place is visited. When visitors report they have already visited a location and see no point in visiting it again, they may miss an entirely different experience at a different time. Weather conditions—brilliant midday sun, cloudy sunset time, snowclad winter, cold, heat, stillness, or wind—can give places quite different meanings. Places seen at night may be in absolute contrast when viewed in daylight. Not only will the landscape differ but also will the patterns and colors of activities and users be quite different. For example, a dramatically different experience results from visiting the French Quarter of New Orleans in the day as compared to night. Places of a singular year-round climate have different appeals to travelers as compared to places with seasonal change—spring flowers, summer green, autumn foliage colors, and a white landscape of winter. The new market surge of nature tourism selects places as much on the time of viewing wildlife as on their habitat location. Animal migrations are critical to viewing wildlife.

An equally important dimension of place is its *age*—ancient to new. Generally the older the place, the greater its amenities. An author of the southern region of the United States has stated: "Older places have accumulated more meaning, but they also very often are more tied to a specific setting or are simply more humane in scale or character—and thereby more engaging—than new places" (Morris 1990, 7). Viewing the ruins of Delphi on the wooded slopes of Mount Parnassus cannot help but evoke dramatically different images for the visitor than visiting the more recently planned cities of Canberra or Brazilia. Even within a lifetime, "the special places of childhood are not sacred but the memory of them is necessary for attaching sacredness to place" (Shepard 1967, 37). An enlarging travel segment seeks the experiences of visiting historic sites and places of prehistory. Planning for visitor use of these sites creates challenges never before faced by designers and managers—maintaining the integrity and patina of age at the same time providing for mass visitor use. For example, the removal of ancient skeletons from grave sites for display in museums is opposed by many native populations.

Spatial distribution of places around the earth has deep meaning for tourism and its planning. Each place has its own unique relationship to all other places, far or near. Analysis of geographic position and geographic content described in the last chapter for regional planning are attempts to identify spatial characteristics of importance. In modern context with changing air fares and access, spatial distribution of destinations takes on new meaning. What once was *far* may now be *near* in terms of ease of access, changing dramatically the competitive position of places.

Another important characteristic of a place is its *name*. "Landscapes without place names are disorienting; without categorical forms, awful" (Shepard 1967, 43). Place names call up fantasy and imagery. The names of places from northern Michigan to the Arkansas River in the United

States—Wisconsin, Peoria, Des Moines, Missouri, Osage, Omaha, Kansas, Iowa, Wabash, and Arkansas—stimulate recollection of French Jesuit explorers, Louis Joliet and Jacques Marquette's trip through this land in 1673 (Stewart 1967, 91). For settlers of Texas, religious themes dominated place names: San Antonio, San Jacinto, San Saba, Corpus Christi, and the Brazos River. Deeper analysis of market characteristics would probably prove that few travelers seek out places with unfamiliar or no names.

In spite of today's great mobility and migration of peoples, certain landscapes retain *people-place qualities.* A travel writer stated, "I believe you could exterminate the French at a blow and resettle the country with Tartars, and within two generations discover, to your astonishment, that the national characteristics were back at norm" (Durrell 1969, 157). Thus is the dominance of the landscape as place. Landscapes have special values, even when some cultural labels are the same. Durrell points out that the spirit of place has modified Catholicism to the extent that it is different in Ireland, Italy, Spain, and Argentina. The theology and practices result from modification due to place. Although these subtleties are not always readily available to travelers, with some time and introspection they become real. Visits to the Scottish landscape evoke the adventurous landscapes of Stevenson.

Of course, places can be described by *technical and scientific facts.* For example, Mount Everest is five-and-one-half miles (8.9 kilometers) above sea level, is located in the Himalaya range, and was named for a British surveyor-general of India, Sir George Everest. Madrid is located at latitude 40°24′30″ North and longitude 0°14′45″ West and occupies about 550 square kilometers. In resource analysis, as has been cited in the discussion of regional planning, the quantities of natural and cultural resource facts are listed: acres of forest land, sizes of lakes, lengths of streams, numbers and species of wildlife, and so on. Often, this is called *inventory*.

Human Attribution of Place

Although such inventorying is necessary in describing place, it is of little value unless interpreted and given meaning. *Human attribution* of resource facts is essential. "Neither the environment as such nor parts or features of the environment *per se* are resources; they become resources only if, when, and in so far as they are, or considered to be capable of serving man's needs. In other words, the word 'resource' is an expression of appraisal and, hence a purely subjective concept"

(Zimmerman 1933, 3). Resources are not; they become. For tourism and travelers, "The environment is encountered in a way in which self and place are related" (Shepard 1967, 34). Statistics of resources are of value to the planner only as anticipated visitor contact can be assessed. This intimate amalgam of place and human experience is again expressed by Shepard (1967, 43) as

> The desert is the environment of revelation, genetically and physiologically alien, sensorially austere, esthetically abstract, historically inimical. It is always described as boundless and empty, but the human experience there is never merely existential. Its solitude is not an empty void, a not-quite silence. Its forms are bold and suggestive. The mind is beset by light and space, the kinesthetic novelty of aridity, high temperature and wind. The desert sky is encircling, majestic, terrible. . . . The moon, sun and stars are perceptually exaggerated lower in the sky. Apparent motion in the horizontal plane is always greater.

An excellent example of place attribution is the concept of *scenery*. No such thing existed until after the Middle Ages. Forests were filled with demons and were of no value until felled for agriculture. Not until the painters and writers of the nineteenth century romanticized nature did vistas of landscapes become scenery. "The terrible awe of God was made into an esthetic—or, if you prefer, the forests and mountains of the earth came to be revered with religious intensity. The enjoyment of primeval wilderness had not been possible before" (Shepard 1967, 188).

Another aspect of human relationship to place is *social*. Cheek and Burch's (1976) early work emphasized the many social dimensions of leisure and place relations. There may be activities, such as picnicking, where the social group has higher priority than the location of place, as long as the needed amenities are present. Wilderness buffs often subscribe to Thoreau's tenet of seeking such places to find one's self. Certainly, the social context—solitude, friend, family, and lover—can evoke different visitor meanings even from the same place.

Perhaps the greatest lesson from this brief examination of place is the understanding of its powerful and almost inexplicable necessity for tourism. And, if its power and necessity are accepted, planning and design action must follow—*placemaking*. Areas that seek to become destinations for tourism have no choice but to become involved in placemaking. But, this process is not to be interpreted as artificially contrived. Quite the opposite. The challenge before the designer is to have sufficient understanding of both physical and human dimensions of place in order to design. Again, from Motloch (1991, 286), "placemaking should include the effective management of order and spontaneity for understanding and exploration."

Throughout the following discussion of planning destinations and sites for tourism, the importance of place is a continuing theme.

DESTINATION PLANNING ISSUES

Opportunities

Although much marketing of tourism is done at the regional (national, state, and provincial) scale, for most travelers this is too generalized. That size of geography is often too large to comprehend as being able to satisfy travel objectives. It may be open to question as to whether travelers really seek their rewards in the United States, Canada, and Australia, or in destinations such as in and around New York, Montreal, or Sydney. Communities and their environs—destinations—more frequently carry with them images of appeal for both business and pleasure travel.

At this period in the history of tourism, it would appear that so many destinations have already been developed that there are few opportunities left. This is a half-truth because of the dynamics of both the market and supply sides of tourism. Changes in markets—demographics, economics, lifestyles, fads, and interests—are constantly opening up new areas for development. Changes in transportation, attractions, information, services, and promotion are introducing new areas as having potential.

The destination discovery process described in Chapter 5 demonstrated how one can identify potential destination zones. In most instances, when current market trends are examined, communities will discover much greater opportunity than popularly considered.

The geographic model, illustrated in Figure 7-1 dramatizes a basic fundamental of all destination zones. They function for tourism only because of a *symbiotic relationship between focal cities and the surrounding area.* A destination function does not stop at the jurisdictional city limits. The surrounding rural area and small towns are an integral part of a destination zone. This symbiosis derives from tourist use which involves visiting attractions both inside cities and in surrounding areas and using tourist services—such as lodging, food service, and car service—primarily in the cities.

A great many traveler activities take place in the surrounding rural area, such as:

Picnicking	Canoeing
Camping	Cross-country skiing
Hiking	Swimming

Horseback riding	Outdoor recreation vehicle use
Bicycling	Resorting
Hunting	Retirement residence
Fishing	Historic touring
Boating	Scenic touring
Waterskiing	Festivals, events (Gunn 1988a, 238)

On the other hand, when travelers have participated in these activities, they seek lodging, food service, and other amenities and services of a focal city. Furthermore, feasibility of these service businesses favors city locations because they serve both resident and traveler markets.

Issues and Constraints

If opportunities for destination development are so abundant, why haven't more destinations occurred? One might glibly answer that this is due to lack of planning, but that is too simple because destination tourism planning is complicated. Because communities are the focal points for tourism destinations, it appears that there are several constraints for community action toward tourism development.

Blank (1989) outlines several salient limitations:

- Lack of comparative advantage (location, quality of potential).
- Carrying capacity limitations.
- Lack of community's acceptance of change—preference for status quo.
- Power structure's preference for other development.
- Myopic view of tourism.
- Fear of tourism—erosive characteristics.
- Environmentalist resistance to any development.
- Narrow and inflexible policies on public lands.

Canada has experimented with much planning for tourism, most of which has stimulated valuable development. Yet, in working with destination planning, a few researchers have observed some important constraints at the local level. Go et al. (1992) analyzed implementation of tourism strategies there and derived the following resistances:

- Tourism involves such a diversity of actors that clear mandates for development are lacking.
- Lack of local guidance and will.

- Mandates are unclear or in conflict.
- Local jurisdictions seek a quick fix and fail to provide financial and human resources to do the job.
- Lack of monitoring system to measure success.

A consequence of the geographic reality of a destination zone is that it *transcends political jurisdictional boundaries*. This fact complicates planning and development. Tourism leadership and political decisionmaking, such as for promotion, taxation, and development of amenities also usually stops at such boundaries. Within the several small towns, rural areas, and focal cities there may be different population characteristics and different traditions, attitudes, customs, and even conflict or animosity.

If tourism is to be developed, these barriers against cooperation must be removed or at least ameliorated. Tourism leaders and constituencies of all jurisdictions within a zone must be equally committed to tourism development or it will not take place. Conversely, *tourism may be the catalyst to bring peoples of these separate parts of the zone together* for a common cause.

Misunderstandings

The concept of destination, even as defined here, is plagued by several misunderstandings in field applications. They are related here only so that those involved in planning may avoid these problems (Gunn 1982).

1. Destination zones are singularly defined. Some writings refer to nations or continents as destinations. Certainly, this is a half-truth because images of these areas are often so defined in the minds of travelers. For example, Africa may have a stronger image than Krueger National Park. Destination zones are not uniformly defined. Some governments have divided regions into destination zones on the basis of administration. Such zones are suited to governance but have no relation to marketable or potential development areas. Sometimes marketing zones have been delineated but these lack consideration of resources yet to be developed. Zones based only on existing development and travel trends have been identified by Ferrario (1979). Ruest (1979) and others prefer to base destination zones on geographical resource factors, and this is the emphasis given in this book.

2. Destination zone boundaries are fixed. This fallacy needs special emphasis. As markets change and as development grows or decays, destination zones can take on new size and shape or even disappear. It is an error to publish maps of zones with the implication that the edges are well defined. Zones are generalized areas that have broad and soft edges. Even though some resource characteristics appear to be fixed, new interpretations may cause change in the future, such as today's new emphasis on ecotourism.

3. *Destination zones are of one type.* When one kind of development becomes popular and successful, there is a tendency to copy this development at other locations. There is room for repetition but within a different market range; witness the Disney attraction in Paris. However, there is usually a stronger competitive edge when each destination builds upon its unique characteristics of place creating a tourism theme of its own. Although the elements and principles of tourism development may be the same, they can be expressed differently, depending on the special resources of each place.

4. *The best zones are developed by the private sector.* Those who support a tourism industry philosophy are inclined to believe that private investment is the only solution to destination development. Although no one can deny the very important role of private investment and development, it represents only part of the formula for successful tourism destination zones. Even in capitalistic and industrialized nations, governments and nonprofit organizations continue to play important roles by providing many historic and natural resource attractions. Most isolated resorts, for example, fail not necessarily because of poor management but because they do not benefit from nearby attractions and government input in the form of roads, water supply, waste disposal, police, fire protection, and a governed community nearby. The best destination plan is created jointly by nonprofit organizations, government, and the private sector.

5. *Zones succeed the best where tourism is the only economic provider.* Experience has clearly demonstrated the fallacy of this statement. Areas dependent only on tourism are plentiful and many continue to survive. But, they are very vulnerable. Fads, fashions, politics, wars, competition, and economic changes can be devastating for tourism. Industrial developers for many years have promoted the principle of economic diversity. Such diversity provides a buffer against exigencies of change. A tourism destination can remain much more stable if the area includes a diversity of industry and services.

6. Zone identification assures success. Because basic factors are geographically clustered in a destination zone, all three developer sectors have better chances of success. However, it should not be construed that individual project feasibility is assured. If, for example, it is indicated that a historic site might be developed into a major attraction, the question of developer feasibility remains. If development fits the policies and abilities of government park and historic agencies, one may see that it is feasible. Or, it may be more feasible for a nonprofit organization or commercial enterprise to be the developer. Mere zone identification does not assure success. Many investment and management factors remain to be resolved.

DESTINATION PLANNING GUIDES

In recent years, governments and other organizations have prepared guideline manuals for public use at the local level. Often these are titled community planning manuals but in the context of definitions used in this book, they generally include an entire destination zone. The guides offer step-by-step processes that can be of great value to leaders and local population constituencies in their search for better tourism development.

Alberta Manual

An excellent example is the Community Tourism Action Plan Manual (Alberta Tourism 1988) developed by the provincial tourism agency of Alberta, Canada. It was prepared over several years of study by staff, outside consultants, and representatives of the private sector. It contains five main sections:

Book 1. Introduction. This section begins by defining tourism to include attractions, promotion, infrastructure, hospitality, and services. It emphasizes that deficiencies in any of these components can limit tourism. The content includes answers to questions such as, Where do we fit in? Who benefits? Who doesn't benefit? and Is it for us?

Book 2. Organization. This chapter opens with emphasizing the need for organization but only after full commitment to tourism. There must be first a strong desire for tourism by residents, businesses, and the municipal council. The first step following expression of commitment is to create a tourism policy and Tourism Action Committee. A sample policy would be stated as follows:

Tourism will be encouraged within _____ and its surrounding area in ways that will attract more tourists, increase their length of stay, increase the amounts of money they spend here, and ensure that any adverse social, economic and/or environmental effects are minimized as a result of activities to improve tourism. (Alberta Tourism 1988, 2/6)

According to the manual, the Tourism Action Committee should be mandated by local government with support from organizations such as the chamber of commerce and local tourism zone association (if one is in place). Members should include representatives of the following:

Chamber of Commerce	Economic Development Board
Hotel/motel operators	Service station operators
Restaurant operators	Historical society
Service clubs	Youth groups
Tourist zone representatives	Municipal administration
Recreation board	Tourist attraction operators
	Tourist event organizers
	(Alberta Tourism 1888, 2/9)

Members should meet the following criteria: knowledge of the community, commitment to tourism, ability to work in a group, ability to invest sufficient time in the committee and reliability.

Book 3. Process. Figure 7-2 illustrates the suggested flow of twenty-four action steps to develop a tourism plan at the local level. Step 1 is market analysis. Step 2 is gaining input from organizations and agencies. Steps 3–7 involve study of the area to determine assets and concerns. Steps 8–10 include identification of goals, objectives, and strategies for reaching objectives. Steps 11–18 involve completion of the plan, obtaining input from several publics, and gaining official approval. The final steps 19–24 consist of action implementation and reporting to the city council.

Book 4. Appendices. This book contains sources of assistance, such as private and governmental sources of grants as well as individuals and agencies that can offer technical and educational assistance.

Book 5. Workbook. The manual includes outlines for use in detailing the results of the several steps in the planning process.

As of September 1, 1990, approximately 250 of 429 eligible Alberta communities had developed tourism action plans. Based on the Alberta

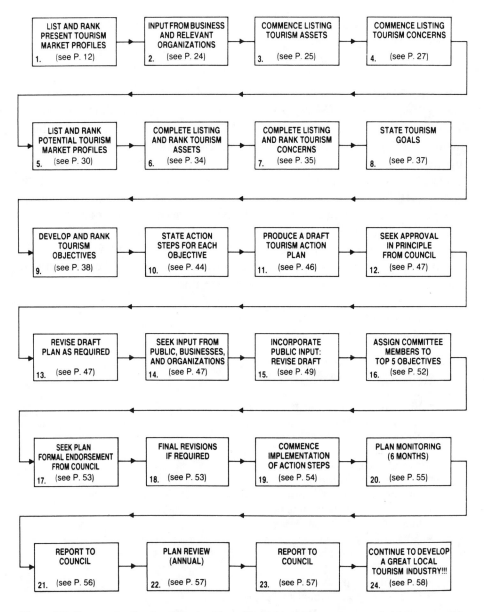

Figure 7-2. Community Tourism Planning Steps. These 24 steps are recommended for communities to take in the development of tourism action plans in Alberta, Canada (Alberta Tourism 1988, 3-1).

experience, Go et al. (1992) have identified five conditions for destination tourism development:

- A clustering of communities, each supporting the other.
- Avoiding duplication.

- Key players who are ready, willing, and able to cooperate.
- Resident cooperation.
- Finance for start-up is available.

Wight (1992), as a member of the provincial tourism agency, further emphasizes the need for local stakeholders to integrate their ideas with governmental agency initiatives. When communities waver in their involvement, progress bogs down. In recent years, developers have seen the new regulations of the Alberta Environmental Protection and Enhancement Act (AEPEA) and the Natural Resources Conservation Board (NRCB) as red-tape hurdles that are costly in both time and money.

A plan for the Calgary-Canmore destination zone (Pannell Kerr Forster 1985) identified many opportunities for tourism. Table 7-1 lists these together with potential impacts and funding support. Wight (1992) expands on the analysis and information required for public and private tourism development decisions, summarized as

- Tourism projects inventory
- Municipal financial impacts
- Transportation analysis
- Service and utility needs
- Private sector EIAs and NRCB
- Tourism market demand study
- Visual impact assessment
- Assessment of natural areas
- Needs of expanded public services
- Water quality evaluation of Bow River
- Analysis of environmental issues
- Environmentally significant areas
- Quality of tourism/recreation experience
- Baseline information summary
- Municipal operative workshops
- Annexation proposals
- Employee housing issues
- Rock industry study
- Recreation trails study
- Updates of general municipal plans
- Rock Mt. utilization study
- Sustainable wildlife study

Rural Tourism Guide

Based upon general decline in the U.S. rural economy, Congress in 1988 directed the Travel and Tourism Administration to sponsor a study of

TABLE 7-1
TOURISM DEVELOPMENT OPPORTUNITIES IN ALBERTA, CANADA

Opportunities	*Capital or Operations Emphasis*	*Potential Impacts*				*Primary Action or Funding Emphasis*
		Social	*Economic*	*Environmental*	*Cost*	
GENERAL						
Attract world class sports events before and after the Olympics	O	2	2	-1	C	Pr
Develop an annual winter festival	O	2	2	1	C	Pr
Develop a western heritage theme	O	2	2	0	C	Pr
Promote the scenery by making highways "visitor friendly"	C	2	1	0	D	P
Capitalize on linkages to attractions outside the zone	O	1	2	0	A	Pr
Prepare circle and exploration tour publications	C/O	1	1	0	B	Pr/P
Develop and promote major attractions in locations outside of Calgary	C/O	2	2	-1	X	Pr
Provide tax incentives and concessions for tourism developments	C/O	1	2	0	X	P/M
Develop and promote tours of Olympic facilities	O	1	1	1	B	Pr
Expand the variety of fixed roof accommodation available	C	1	2	-1	X	Pr
Improve and develop recreational vehicle (RV) parks	C	1	1	-2	B	Pr
Develop transportation services to destinations in Rural Zone 10	O	1	2	0	C	Pr
Adjust zone boundaries to include Cochrane, Highway 1A, and Stoney Indian Reserve	O	0	1	0	A	Pr

TABLE 7-1 (*continued*)
TOURISM DEVELOPMENT OPPORTUNITIES IN ALBERTA, CANADA

Opportunities	Capital or Operations Emphasis	Potential Impacts				Primary Action or Funding Emphasis
		Social	Economic	Environmental	Cost	
Develop adventure tours	O	1	1	1	B	Pr
Develop educational and industrial tours	O	1	1	1	B	Pr
Improve visitor information services to provide accurate and up-to-the-minute information on attractions, facilities, events, and services available in zone	C/O	1	1	0	C	Pr
Develop a central reservations system for zone accommodation, tours, sports, theater, events, etc.	C/O	1	2	0	C	Pr
Improve signage to attractions and services off major transportation corridors	C	1	1	0	B	P/M
Give Canmore and Rural Zone 10 higher profile in Calgary Tourist and Convention Bureau	O	2	2	0	A	Pr
Develop and deliver hospitality training programs	O	2	1	0	C	P
Improve operation of existing tourist services and facilities on Indian reserves	O	2	2	0	C	P
Develop public investment implementation strategy	O	1	2	0	A	P
Provide extra assistance to expedite application review and processing	O	2	2	0	B	P
Investigate the feasibility of developing first class casino in the zone	O	−1	0	0	B	Pr/P

TABLE 7-1 (*continued*)
TOURISM DEVELOPMENT OPPORTUNITIES IN ALBERTA, CANADA

Opportunities	Capital or Operations Emphasis	Potential Impacts				Primary Action or Funding Emphasis
		Social	Economic	Environmental	Cost	
CALGARY SUBZONE						
Develop attractions, facilities, and services in character areas and target tourist awareness programs at these areas	C	2	2	0	X	Pr
Coordinate marketing activities for major attractions	O	2	2	0	A	P/M
Implement more dynamic and experimental programs at major attractions	C/O	2	1	0	D	P/M
Organize nightlife and entertainment in character areas	O	2	2	0	C	Pr
Introduce design elements into the urban environment to promote tourism	C	2	2	0	X	M
Promote complementary or alternate activities for tourists	O	2	1	0	A	Pr/M
Promote tours and tour packaging	O	1	2	0	A	Pr
Develop boat cruise with entertainment on Glenmore Reservoir	C	2	1	−1	X	Pr
Plan and implement other world class events in Calgary	O	2	2	0	X	Pr
CANMORE AREA SUBZONE						
Promote Canmore area as the staging area for world class outdoor recreation events	O	2	2	−2	C	Pr
Develop arts community in Canmore	C/O	2	2	0	X	Pr/P/M

TABLE 7-1 (*continued*)
TOURISM DEVELOPMENT OPPORTUNITIES IN ALBERTA, CANADA

Opportunities	Capital or Operations Emphasis	Potential Impacts				Primary Action or Funding Emphasis
		Social	Economic	Environmental	Cost	
Develop a landmark or major gateway to attract people to the downtown area	C/O	2	2	0	X	Pr/M
Promote heritage design in Canmore	C/O	2	1	2	B	M
Capitalize on the Olympic Games and facilities in the area	O	1	2	0	X	Pr
Develop tours based on coal mining and forestry themes	O	1	1	0	B	Pr
Increase opportunities for water-based recreation	C	1	1	−1	B	P
Improve trails, trail signage, and access	C	1	1	−1	B	P/M
Attract major resort development to area	C	2	2	−2	X	Pr/P/M
Construct a gondola or tramway to a mountain viewpoint and restaurant	C	1	2	−2	E	Pr
Improve the visibility of facilities and services along Highway 1 and improve access awareness signage	C/O	1	2	1	X	Pr/P/M
Develop and promote nightlife and entertainment in town	C/O	2	2	0	X	Pr
Promote Canmore as a service center for surrounding resort and recreation developments	O	2	2	0	A	Pr
Prepare tourism action plan for Canmore	O	1	2	0	A	Pr/P

TABLE 7-1 (*continued*)
TOURISM DEVELOPMENT OPPORTUNITIES IN ALBERTA, CANADA

Opportunities	Capital or Operations Emphasis	Potential Impacts				Primary Action or Funding Emphasis
		Social	Economic	Environmental	Cost	
BOW VALLEY AND HIGHWAYS 1 AND 1A CORRIDOR SUBZONE						
Plan and promote the development of service centers and attractions at major intersections on Highways 1 and 1A	C/O	1	2	−1	X	Pr
Improve signage to attractions off Highway 1	C	1	1	0	A	P
Promote the development of resort and seasonal residential developments on patented lands south of Highway 1	C/O	1	2	−2	X	Pr/P/M/
KANANASKIS WEST SUBZONE						
Revegetate canal embankments	C	1	0	2	E	Pr/P
Develop campground/ cabin area with Nordic facilities on south end of Spray Lakes Reservoir	C	1	1	−1	X	Pr
Improve signage to Kananaskis Country	C	1	0	0	A	P/M
KANANASKIS CENTRAL SUBZONE						
Attract developers for Ribbon Creek Alpine Village	C/O	1	2	0	X	P/Pr
Develop campground at Bow Valley Provincial Park	C	1	1	0	E	P/Pr
Establish horseback riding and equipment rental concession	C/O	1	1	0	C	P/Pr
Develop trail and road systems to connect with resort developments in the Bow Valley	C	1	2	−2	X	P

TABLE 7-1 (*continued*)
TOURISM DEVELOPMENT OPPORTUNITIES IN ALBERTA, CANADA

Opportunities	Capital or Operations Emphasis	Potential Impacts				Primary Action or Funding Emphasis
		Social	Economic	Environmental	Cost	
KANANASKIS EAST SUBZONE						
Promote east entrance to Kananaskis Country	O	1	1	0	A	P/Pr
Upgrade Powderface Trail to a year-round road from Sibbald Flats to Elbow Falls Trail	C	1	1	−2	X	P
SARCEE SUBZONE						
Develop entrance to Rural Zone 10 and Tourist facilities and services on Sarcee Indian Reserve	C/O	2	2	−1	X	Pr

Source: Pannell Kerr Forster 1985, ix
Note. Study and analysis of the Calgary-Canmore tourism destination zone revealed many opportunities for tourism development. Potential impacts and funding support for each are listed in this table.

LEGEND

Capital or operations emphasis
C Capital
O Operations

Potential Impacts:	2 Significantly Positive	The impact scale represents an over-

Potential Impacts:
  2 Significantly Positive   The impact scale represents an over-
  1 Positive   view assessment by the consultants.
  0 No impact   Detailed impact assessments may be
  −1 Negative   required prior to development to
  −2 Significantly negative identify mitigative measures to be
  NA Not applicable   implemented.
  X Unknown

Costs potential order of magnitude:
(thousand dollars)
                            Cost potential is based on the first
  A Under 50   year of operation or the capital cost,
  B 50–99   whichever is applicable. Costs identi-
  C 100–499   fied represent minimal amounts as
  D 500–999   anticipated by the consultants.
  E Over 1,000   Actual cost will depend on specific
  X Unknown   development requirements.

Primary action or Fund- Pr Private
ing Emphasis: P Provincial
                          M Municipal

tourism potential in rural areas (Edgell 1990, 32). Their report, *The National Policy Study on Rural Tourism and Small Business Development* (Economic Research Associates) was issued in 1989. Another product was the preparation of a planning and development guide, *Rural Tourism Development Training Guide* (Koth et al. 1991), in cooperation with the Tourism Center of the University of Minnesota. It is a destination planning and development guide for rural areas and small towns and contains thirteen parts, including description of five cases of self-help. Although the manual covers other aspects, a planning process is outlined:

1. Getting organized.
2. Identifying community values.
3. Attraction inventory.
4. Attraction assessment.
5. Attraction packaging.
6. Organizational funding strategies.
7. Business inventory.
8. Marketing situational analysis.
9. Identifying a community tourism product.
10. Identifying target markets.
11. Setting market objectives.
12. Selecting promotional strategies.
13. (Optional) Tourism business retention and expansion.
14. (Optional) Community appearance.
15. Evaluation. (Koth et al. 1991, 1/17, 18)

The educational materials within the manual are directed toward a five step model, paraphrased as follows.

1. Values. Community groups must first explore the importance of their values, such as their geography, history, culture, and lifestyle. This is necessary to make sure tourism is not approached as an overlay or merely as a cosmetic treatment. Tourism should play an important role in enhancing and preserving basic community values.

2. Attractions. It is essential to identify the activities, cultural, arts, and historic resources, and developments that have the power to attract visitors. Both surrounding as well as internal community attractions are important. Attraction quality, drawing power, grouping, and management must be assessed.

3. Services. Both public and private services need to be evaluated. Water supply, sewage disposal, drainage, snow removal, fire protection, health control, police, and other public services by government need to be checked. Service businesses—lodging, food, transportation, entertainment, and retail trade—need to be offered in high quality. Entrepreneurship and business retention factors are important. New business should reflect the character of the community as well as fulfill tourism needs.

4. Marketing. Marketing is driven by traveler needs. Claims must be honest, accurate, and consistent with product delivery. Analysis of current programs should reveal efficiencies and need for change. Identification of market segments and use of most effective marketing strategies should be made.

5. Organization. Because tourism involves so many facets and political jurisdictions, it requires special organization and leadership. The tourism organizations need to

- Create a vision.
- Have a clear understanding of goals.
- Develop consistent leadership.
- Be adequately funded.
- Conduct periodic evaluation.

Cooperation with all other public and private groups is essential.

U.S. Community Guide

Sensing a need for guidelines for communities and areas to develop their tourism, the U.S. Department of Commerce, U.S. Travel and Tourism Administration, and the U.S. Economic Development Administration requested the University of Missouri to gather information and produce a manual. The first edition was published in 1978, and the second in 1986, and a revised and updated third edition in 1991 (Weaver 1991). The following discussion summarizes the contents of this guide.

Appraising Tourism Potential

This section of the guide provides information on how tourism can benefit communities with incomes, jobs, and tax revenues, especially as an aid to a diversified economic base. It also identifies costs of development: transportation, roads, parking, signs, water, sewage, restrooms, safety, health, and welfare. Included is the relationship of the community to attractions, services, and markets.

Planning for Tourism

Included here is the recommendation for leadership and organization. The need to coordinate the many components of tourism is addressed. The following planning steps are suggested:

1. Inventory and describe the social, political, physical, and economic development.
2. Forecast or project trends for future development.
3. Set goals and objectives.
4. Study alternative plans of action to reach goals and objectives.
5. Select preferred alternative(s) to serve as a guide for recommending action strategies.
6. Develop an implementation strategy.
7. Implement the plan.
8. Evaluate the plan. (Weaver 1991, 28, 29)

It is recommended that all segments of the community participate in all steps.

Assessing Product and Market

This chapter of the guide offers methods of market analysis—characteristics of visitors, expenditures, and activity preferences. Ways of inventorying and evaluating the match between market preference and attractions are presented. Forms for inventorying other elements of the supply side are included.

Marketing Tourism

Development of a promotional plan, target market advertising, local advertising and promotion, public and community relations, cooperative promotion, and souvenirs and promotional mementos are the main topics of discussion in this chapter of the guide.

Visitor Services

Visitor services are defined as all the normal city services together with those needed for hospitality. Recommendations on anticipating and planning service needs, coordination of visitor services, training for visitor services, hospitality training, public awareness, establishing tourist information centers, and evaluating visitor services are offered.

Sources of Assistance

Suggested help sources from federal, state, and local agencies as well as private consultant aid are recommended in this section. Examples of tourist organizational structures and tax legislation are included in the Appendix of the guide.

Community Tourism Guide

Another helpful guide for planning tourism development at the destination scale is *The Community Tourism Industry Imperative: The Necessity, the Opportunities, Its Potential* authored by Uel Blank (1989). This book is organized into twelve chapters and is directed to local individuals and organizations interested in development of tourism. Although all chapters provide basic guidance, of special value in planning are the following final three chapters of the book.

Chapter 10, Getting It Together—The Matrix of Decision Making, includes important topics, such as the process of decisionmaking, how to assess opportunities, the importance of long-term planning, and how to move from knowledge to action.

Chapter 11, Getting it Together—Tourism Development Policy, emphasizes leadership and relationship to state and federal tourism policy. The section on planning cites the need for several agencies, organizations, and individuals to exercise planning roles. Planning guidance must include:

- Attraction development
- Hospitality services
- Activities
- Promotion/advertising
- Transportation systems
- Community ambience and esthetics
- Local information, direction, and interpretive system
- Community infrastructures
- Financing of development
- Resource quality and management
- Agency responsibility and coordination
- Special market thrusts

- Seasonality
- Residents' living quality (Blank 1989, 185–186)

Chapter 12, Getting it Together—From Policies to Plans to Actions, provides guidance on preconditioning for action, bringing out the genius of the community, and the following action steps:

1. Initiative—recognition of need.
2. Set goals and objectives.
3. Collect needed information
4. Analyze information.
5. Develop concepts for future development
6. Develop specific strategies.
7. Carry out the plan.
8. Monitor and evaluate on regular basis. (Blank 1989, 196–197)

Local Government Tourism Policy

As an aid to destination zone planning and development for tourism, the Western Australian Tourism Commission has created a model policy statement to be implemented by the city council. Because of its value, it is quoted here in its entirety (Western Australian Tourism n.d.).

Objectives

In establishing a tourism policy, the council has as its major objectives:

1. To recognize tourism as a social and economic force and as a major or potential major employer within the Council area.
2. To foster and create a community awareness of the benefits of tourism within Council's area.
3. To ensure that Council will guide and influence the development of tourism in the Council area.
4. To provide the basic facilities and infrastructure sufficient to encourage development.
5. To ensure that facilities within the area are adequate to cater for visitors and residents.

Policy Document Guidelines

The following policy guidelines provide a basis for consideration and adoption by Council to guide and direct the development of tourism throughout the Council area, and to ensure a consistent approach to this development.

1. Council will liaise with the Western Australian Tourism Commission and other relevant Tourism and Government Departments and members of the public in all aspects of tourist development.
2. Council will establish an Advisory Committee which will address Tourism issues.
3. Council will endeavour to provide an adequate budget allocation for tourism expenditure.
4. Council will endeavor to assist (financially and by other means) tourist organizations or events which have the potential to develop tourism in the region.
5. Council will seek representation on local tourist associations.
6. In the formulation of its planning regulations and preparation of by-laws and other regulations, Council will have regard to the requirements of tourism development.
7. Council, in its review of planning instruments, ie Strategic Plans, Town Plans and Development Control Plans, will take into consideration policies on tourism and other leisure related issues.
8. In the preparation of by-laws and regulations, Council will have regard to their impact on tourism and the balanced development of the Council's area.
9. Council will encourage tourism product development and investment throughout the area and will facilitate the development application process.
10. Council will encourage a high standard of design and aesthetics in all forms of tourist development.
11. Council will ensure the welfare of the whole community when supporting tourism development and the provision of facilities.
12. When considering tourism developments, Council will consider the social, cultural, economic, and environmental impact of the proposal within the area.
13. Council will ensure that where sensitive environmental, historic or cultural areas exist, these areas will be adequately protected in relation to development or usage.
14. Council will initiate the provision of facilities sufficient to cater for destination and day trip visitors to appropriate areas within its boundaries.
15. Council will seek financial involvement from other sources wherever possible in the provision of tourist facilities.
16. Council will encourage the landscaping of residential and commercial centres within Council's area.
17. Council will, where practicable, support the establishment of National Parks, enhancement of specific natural features, conservation areas of outstanding beauty, and recognize items of heritage significance.

Related Policies

Tourist information services and distribution

Licensing of seasonal entertainment and attractions

Scenic routes and lookouts

Use of old buildings for tourism purposes

Proposals for specific areas of land

Traffic flows and generation

Levels of environmental impact

Protection of areas of outstanding scenic beauty

DESTINATION PLANNING MODEL

Reference again to the destination model illustrated in Figure 7-1 will help in identifying the key components that make up a tourism destination.

The engine that powers the destination for travelers is composed of the *attraction complexes*. These are geographic places, rooted in resources that have been developed to provide for visitor activities. These attractions serve two functions—drawing people to the places and fulfilling their expectations from a visit. The term *complex* is used to imply that there is value in clustering compatible attractions together, either physically or by tour. Attraction complexes may be within the focal city, nearby, or reasonably remote, such as a national park. (A national park is usually a complex unto itself because of the great number of compatible attractions it contains.)

Several other components of a destination zone function as facilitators. The *linkage* corridors between the key city and attraction complexes are important planning elements, requiring careful design consideration in order to provide a visual prelude to the attraction objective. For rural and remote attractions, self-guided and guided tours should provide the visitor with interesting explorations of the background and characteristics of the landscape being traversed. Key to planning these corridors are elements such as signage, maps, and other wayfinding information. Long linkages may require travel stops for rest rooms and food services, and interpretation of the travel corridor. Often, these are located along designated scenic highways. Again, the principle of adapting to the land resources and development as well as visitor desires and needs is paramount.

For all destination zones, one or more *cities* (communities) are essential. They provide several critical functions. All travel modes lead to terminals at cities. Terminals—train depots, airports, bus terminals, and highway exits—perform an entering function important to travelers. The quality of physical planning, development, and management can set the psychological setting for further visitor activities. Cities offer the preferred location for most travel services—hotels, restaurants, car services, travel agencies, tour companies, shops, and ancillary services such as post office, drug stores, health services, and communications. Cities are preferred settings because they offer greatest financial feasibility, catering to both resident and traveler markets. Cities contain a basic infrastructure that would be costly to develop at remote locations—water supply, waste disposal, police protection, fire protection, and power. Cities have an organized management structure providing public services and amenities important to tourism. Cities often contain existing and potential attraction complexes—

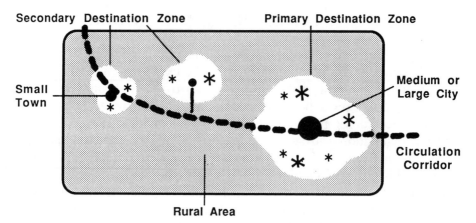

Figure 7-3. Rural-Urban Destination Zones. Relationship between primary and secondary destination zones can foster success in all provided they cooperate and integrate their planning (Gunn 1988a, 244).

entertainment, parks, exhibits, festivals, historic sites, sports arenas, convention centers, trade centers, industries, institutions (medical, religious, and organizational), and homes of friends and relatives.

Many destination zones will be served by a major city surrounded by several small towns in rural areas as illustrated in Figure 7-3. Many advantages to both small and larger cities can be derived through cooperation—tour efficiency, increased mass of attractions, and greater promotional impact.

Another important component of a destination zone is *access* from markets. Too often, communities internalize their tourism planning to the extent that cooperation and assistance are not provided to developers and managers of transportation systems. Many transportation agencies focus policies primarily on resident or nearby markets, thereby developing routes and signage not easily mastered by outside visitors. For example, the main places of transport route penetration of a destination zone and city deserve special planning attention for visitors. It is at these sites that directional information is critical. A major information center at the *gateway* that provides maps, brochures, and personal guidance is essential.

Although the actual configuration of destination zones will vary around the world, these same components and relationships will require planning and integration for best service to the traveler. All components must function in concert, each depending on the successful rendition by the other.

DESTINATION ZONE PLANNING PROCESS

As was recommended for regions, two approaches to destination planning are equally valid—*project planning* and *continuous planning*.

Destination Planning Project

A project should include the follow basic steps:

1. Identify sponsorship and leadership.
2. Set goals.
3. Investigate strengths and weaknesses.
4. Develop recommendations.
5. Identify objectives and strategies.
6. Assign priorities and responsibilities.
7. Monitor feedback.

1. Identify sponsorship and leadership. Because the focus of the destination zone will be on the principal community, it may provide the best organization and leadership. Although a chamber of commerce, convention and visitor bureau, or industrial development agency or organization may initiate destination tourism planning, a new ad hoc or permanent council or commission may be needed. The organization and leader should be drawn from a wide cross-section of the community and surrounding region. Again, it is important to have representation from the greatest diversity of constituencies possible, not only the primary tourism businesses. Commitment to tourism and the desire to collaborate on planning are more important than expertise in tourism.

2. Set goals. The same goals as were stated for regions apply to destination planning—enhanced visitor satisfactions, protected natural and cultural resources, improved economy, and integration into the life and economy of the entire destination area.

3. Investigate strengths and weaknesses. Local people, with perhaps input from a tourism specialist or consultant, should gain a good understanding of the area's strengths and weaknesses. Each destination will pose different problems but an objective study of the following in the entire zone would be useful:

- Natural resources: location, kinds, quantities, qualities, problems, issues, viability for attractions
- Cultural resources: location, kinds, quantities, qualities, problems, issues, viability for attractions
- Potential environmental impact
- Transportation and access: capacities, access, quality, deficiencies
- Service business: quality, suitability to all markets, problems, issues

- Information about area for tourists: quality of maps, guidebooks, descriptions, hospitality
- Promotion: effectiveness of advertising, publicity, public relations, incentives
- Organizations: sectors, organizations, agencies best suited to take leadership and implement development
- Present commitment by public and private sectors—resident attitude toward tourism growth

4. Develop recommendations. From the above investigation, those performing it will be able to conceive of how the positive factors can be enhanced and the negative issues can be ameliorated or corrected. Specific recommendations should be expressed on the same list of topics included in the investigation:

- Natural and cultural resource potential
- Transportation improvement
- Service business improvement
- Information improvement
- Promotion improvement
- Key organizations to take action
- How to improve commitment

5. Identify objectives and strategies. This step is a refinement and expansion of the last step. It should identify specific objectives and how to reach them for each of the recommendations above.

6. Assign priorities and responsibilities. The entire list of objectives and strategies should be reviewed for assignment of priorities. Short-range objectives are critical and deserve highest priority. They should be of small enough size and cost to demonstrate immediate improvement. But, long-range objectives need to be kept in mind so that each increment of shorter range accomplishment will build toward a well-planned overall destination zone. At this stage, it is important to assign responsibilities for action— who and what organizations are most logically the ones to get the job done?

7. Stimulate and guide development. With the identification of specific project development needed derived from steps 1 through 6, these opportunities should be publicized for action by business, nonprofit organizations, and governments. It is their responsibility to develop feasibilities, plan and design, build, and manage the needed development within the destination zone.

8. *Monitor feedback.* Regularly, all implementation of action should be monitored. Enthusiasm and commitment may wane if it appears that no one is concerned about whether the objectives and strategies are working. Each increment of development, whether it be a newly built project or a new program, will change overall relationships and demonstrate new market-supply experience. Part of this feedback is to check on the relationship between this and other destinations and regional plans. Especially for touring circuit markets who visit the destination en route, it is important to know about planning and action in the zones that come ahead and after in the touring sequence. Also, the relationship between zone and regional promotion should be understood. Related to this feedback step may be the need for new research and education—seminars, workshops, conferences, and hospitality training.

Organic/Rational Planning Process

The process outlined above for a Destination Planning Project, can be classified as a rationalist approach. It focuses on problemsolving, using a process that promises to implement specific objectives. However, this approach has its critics who claim that at a scale such as a tourism destination, the problems are too complex to resolve in such a direct manner. Within such an area there are too many factors—decisionmakers, influences, resource conditions, and trends in public opinion—to deal with in a strictly rational manner. Called for is a more organic approach.

Steiner (1991, 520) proposed a process that "reflects a middle ground approach to physical planning, somewhere between a purely organic and a truly rational one." Its basic premise is a flexible, iterative method that has the merits of a project as well as a continuing process that allows for contingencies. Again, it represents an integrated and interactive planning approach. The model sequence of steps is illustrated in Figure 7-4. The following summary paraphrases this process for a tourism destination zone.

Step 1. Problem and Opportunity Identification. By means of workshops and other public participation, concerns, opportunities, and issues within the destination area can be identified. For example, issues of growth, tax potential accompanying growth, quality of new development, and ability

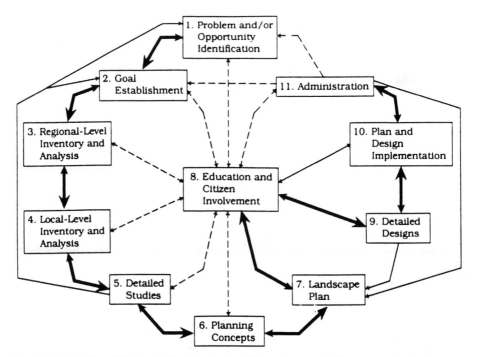

Figure 7-4. An Organic/Rational Planning Process. These steps provide for cooperative involvement in planning by professional designers, developers, and local citizens (Steiner 1991, 520).

of governments to respond with services may be major concerns in a destination zone.

Step 2. Goal Establishment. Local people and governments as well as outside investors develop a consensus on the kind of area they seek in the future. Based on the issues and concerns, goals are identified. These goals are long range and, for tourism, would involve a balance between growth and resource protection.

Step 3. Area Analysis. For a destination zone, analysis of factors is needed for the focal communities, surrounding area, and sites within. Key biophysical factors are examined, such as geology, physiography, climate, hydrology, soils, vegetation, and wildlife. Cultured factors, including historic settlement, economic development, land use patterns, demographics, and services, are identified. Documentation in narratives and maps represent this analysis step performed jointly by consultants and local people.

Step 4. Local Land Analysis. More detailed documentation is obtained for this step. Changes taking place and their environmental impacts are assessed. Population trends, relationship to physiographic features, and wildlife management issues are parts of this more specific descriptive analysis.

Step 5. Detailed Studies. These studies focus primarily on suitability analysis—how suitable portions of the destination are for projected development. Policies of public and private landholders are an important part of such studies. Although the focus may be on tourism, this step allows equal consideration of overall future growth such as housing, recreation, business and industrial expansion, and transportation.

Step 6. Planning Concepts and Options. Based on the foregoing steps, consultants can begin to conceive of planning concepts and options that these studies suggest could lead toward the desired goals. This step is based on logical and imaginative processes and suggests allocation of potential land uses. These concepts could include ideas for future tourism development projects, natural resource and cultural interpretation, transportation, and settlement appropriate to the interests of the public and resource base. Included could be appropriate themes for subareas.

Step 7. Guidelines. This step produces what may be described best as guidelines, rather than a plan, because they contain much flexibility. Local officials, property owners, investors, and consultants jointly identify options for growth and development. In some areas, such guidelines must be formalized into a master plan or comprehensive plan in order to meet legal mandates for planning.

Step 8. Education and Citizen Involvement. Although public input has characterized the entire process, this step assures that the plan concepts and guidelines are disseminated widely. Interaction between consultant planners and the many constituencies affected is essential. Use of the press and public meetings can stimulate open discussion on how well the concepts are directed toward all perceived goals.

Step 9. Detailed Designs. In some instances, the timing is appropriate for initiating project designs. Such design plans will require owner-developer initiative. Often, these are not possible until some later date until there are sufficient owner-developer interests and support for actually building these projects. These projects carry the destination planning guidelines to actual case development.

Step 10. Implementation. This step includes all policy and management implementation measures as well as specific projects. By means of close collaboration among local representatives, tourism businesses, and government agencies, initiation of land easements, zoning, and initiatives for purchase of private and public lands for development can be made.

Step 11. Administration and Evaluation. Public and private organizations and agencies that initiated the planning process now monitor progress of implementation. As projects are selected and begun, feedback may indicate changes needed in the overall plan. In cases where the city, county, or grouping of several legalized the plan, official administration and monitoring will take place.

Steiner (1991, 528) concludes that such a design and planning process at this scale must be dynamic and reflect newly gained incremental experience. Any land planning process must begin with understanding landscapes, and then making changes only in ways that protect and conserve these important foundations.

Destination Continuous Planning

Although a destination planning project for tourism development can stimulate specific action, accomplishment is likely to lag if a continuing planning function is not in place. The destination zone planning document can provide guidelines for development, but every change needs to be monitored for its impact. For example, the destination plan may have called for first creating new parks and historic sites but, because sponsorship for an interesting outdoor recreation park became available first, it was established first. In the recreation park's first year of operation, it demonstrated that there was a strong travel market interested in natural resource-based activities. Thus the potential was suggested for expanding existing parks, developing adventure travel, nature trails, camping, and natural resource interpretation.

However, unless there is a permanent body charged with tourism leadership and continuous planning, new opportunities may be missed. Such a body would represent a diversity of interests within the destination zone and also be capable of carrying out specific functions on a regular basis.

As was done in Alberta, a Tourism Action Committee may be the best organization for continuous planning at the destination level. This committee should have representation from all governing bodies within the destination area: major city, satellite towns, counties, and regional government. Committee members should also represent important constituencies, such as developers, businesses, nonprofit organizations, and residents.

Among the duties of such a committee would be the following:

- Foster the renewal of a Destination Zone Planning Project every five years.
- Monitor each increment of supply development to determine how well it is succeeding, resolve issues that impede its success, and examine its integration with other tourism development.
- Promote new and expanded attraction development based on the special natural and cultural resources of the area.
- Promote the establishment of needed service businesses to meet needs of travelers.
- Encourage resource protection, not only by tourism supply development, but other threats to the environment.
- Integrate tourism planning with city, county, and regional plans.
- Integrate all plans for information services and promotion.
- Monitor changes in market trends in order to determine new supply needs.
- Gain cooperation and integration of tourism development by all three sectors—governments, nonprofit organizations, commercial enterprise.
- Cooperate with regional tourism planners, managers, and policy-makers to assure a continuing viable role for the destination.

Evaluation

Planning actions at the destination level need regular evaluation. Communities and their surrounding regions are involved daily in a great many public and private actions other than tourism—services, education, sanitation, land use, and policing. Whatever is done to plan tourism will need to be evaluated frequently in context with all other planning and development. If the destination area has a tourism plan in place, it will need monitoring and frequent assessment. Go et al. (1992, 33) have developed a taxonomy (Table 7-2) for implementation of a community tourism action plan.

Integration with Community Planning

Because communities play such a critical tourism role in destinations, all plans and planning processes at this level need to be integrated.

Official community plans traditionally focus on physical public needs, especially for updating and enlarging public structures and systems. These

TABLE 7-2

TAXONOMY FOR IMPLEMENTATION OF COMMUNITY TOURISM ACTION PLAN

Level of Analysis	Activity and Questions			
	Interacting	Allocating	Monitoring	Organizing
Actions	How can community leaders and residents be encouraged to see their destinations through the eyes of a tourist?	How can communities best achieve their tourism action plan objectives?	How are community resource persons best evaluated by community tourism action members?	How can the local community become involved in the tourism action plan and get a feeling of ownership of the process?
Programs	How can the level of service and hospitality be developed to sustain and enhance the image of the community; specifically, the existing attractions, facilities, and infrastructure?	How should communities be selected for the funding of their tourism action plan?	How is research into present and potential tourism target markets best conducted by the tourism action committee?	How can sound local tourism strategies be built into a regional strategy?
Systems	How should the community promote attractions and facilities to travelers and tour operators?	How should a provincial government ensure that the local council is directly involved in plan development proceedings?	How is quality of a tourism action plan evaluated?	How should the community organize its own unique tourism strategy?
Policies	How should the tourism action plan be managed on the community level to coincide with existing master plans and economic development strategy on the provincial level?	How should dollar and manpower resources be allocated to ensure that a community covers all important steps toward plan preparation?	How does a community regularly check the effects of tourism on its social structure?	How should the industry be restructured so that it will have a broader base, making it more representative of and responsible to the community?

Source: Bonoma, Thomas V. 1984; Go et al. 1992. 33.

needs are often for resident transportation, water supply (potable and industrial), sewage disposal (solid and liquid waste), power (electrical and gas), fire protection, and police and public safety. Regulations for land use and structures, such as zoning ordinances and building codes, are included in most city plans. Also included are concerns over housing, education, trade, amenities (zoos, parks, and recreation areas), and industry.

Unfortunately, in most communities, these traditional plans do not include issues of tourism and visitors even though their decisions affect tourism and vice versa. Too often, planning for the five components of the supply side of tourism—attractions, services, transportation, information, and promotion—are not seen as responsibilities of city officials and city plans.

Dredge and Moore (1992, 8) examined this issue as found in Queensland, Australia. They cited several inhibitors to the integration of tourism planning into traditional community plans. Much of tourism involves private sector facilities and services, often outside the perceived role of local planning. Local understanding of the complicated multi-owner supply side of tourism is not helped much by their perception of industry involving only a few physical plants. The overlap between the needs of visitors and residents, as well as their differences, is not well understood. The dynamics and interdependencies of the components of the tourism functional system are foreign to their day-to-day decisions relating to residents. Finally, the training and education of planners and designers have not encompassed tourism as a curriculum topic.

The conclusion of Dredge and Moore (1992, 20), equally applicable elsewhere in the world, is that town planners have not only great opportunities but responsibilities to incorporate vision, guidelines, and specific plans for tourism into their traditional local roles.

SPECIAL DESTINATION NEEDS

Scenic Highways

Driving for pleasure, implying the use of scenic roadways, continues to be one of the top travel market activities. Although some scenic highways are major regional access routes, most lie within the context of a destination zone.

Many areas have designated scenic highway segments of travel routes. But, in creating such roads, their planners have discovered that what appeared to be a simple task became very complicated. Their dual function—transportation and scenic appreciation—poses a great challenge to policymakers and designers.

A report of the U.S. Department of Transportation (Federal Highway Administration 1991) pertaining to "scenic byways" identifies some of the key issues of design and designation for these special places:

Ambiguity of Definition. Although there may be common public opinion of what a scenic road is, the issue of defining it in order to plan, build, and protect its assets becomes very difficult. Generally accepted is the principle that it embraces both the visual countryside as well as the roadway. But there is no accepted definition of design standards—visual depth beyond the roadway, roadside maintenance, vertical and horizontal curvature, and vehicle speed and capacity. Each case needs its own definition and standards.

Corridor Protection. Because the entire highway corridor is involved, the protection of the natural and cultural resources that caused it to be identified becomes an issue. Owners of adjacent lands have property rights that sometimes conflict with the scenic highway concept. Special land use planning that is acceptable to adjacent owners must be employed.

Traffic Issues. When high-speed commuters and truckers are mixed with slower-speed, roadside-viewing tourists there may be increased conflict and accidents. Roadway design standards for these two types of users may need to be different, even requiring entirely new roadways.

Signing and Classifying. At present, there is considerable proliferation and diversity of policies on how scenic highways are to be classified and signed. Travelers are confused over the policy rules and identification of attractions and driving hazards. These need to be integrated and clarified.

Community Acceptance. Because many scenic highway designations have been put forward by others, local people may not agree that the rewards (tourist revenues) are worth the added traffic and land use restrictions.

Bicycle Conflict. Because both bicyclists and automobile tourists may enjoy the same qualities of scenic highways, their use is often in conflict. More automobile traffic creates hazards for the safety of slower bicyclists.

Funding and Management. Because scenic highways traverse many political jurisdictions and a multiplicity of adjacent properties with different owners, questions of who will fund and manage these special routes are not easily answered.

Even though the issues just described are widespread, the movement toward establishing more scenic road designation continues. For example, by 1990 there were 51,518 miles of designated and potential scenic byways in the United States, Virgin Islands, and Puerto Rico (Federal Highway Administration 1991, 8). All but seven states have some kind of scenic highway program. Germany has more than 70 scenic highways, including the Castle Route, Fairy Tale Route, and Route of Emperors and Kings. (Federal Highway Administration 1991, 36).

Although the criteria for designating scenic routes vary, most are similar to those adopted by the North Carolina Board of Transportation in 1990 (Federal Highway Administration 1991, 13):

They should be at least a mile long.

The development along the byway should not detract from the scenic character and visual quality.

There should be significant visible natural or cultural features along its borders. These include agricultural lands, historic sites, vistas of marshes, shorelines, forests with mature trees or other areas of significant vegetation, or notable geologic or other natural features.

There should be preference for roads that are protected by land use controls.

There should be provisions for de-designation should the character of the road change over time.

Smardon (1987) describes a survey process used in analysis of scenic highway potential for the 450-mile Seaway Trail, located along the Lake Ontario and St. Lawrence River waterfront in northern New York. Investigative panels of 50 college students and 45 area residents, guided by professional planners, documented and evaluated the entire corridor. Positive and negative attributes, listed by priority, included the following:

Negative Attributes	*Positive Attributes*
1. Utilities	1. Views/presence of water
2. Trailer parks	2. Vegetation
3. Screening development	3. Natural landscape
4. Signage	4. Rural image
5. Excessive vegetation	5. Water features
6. Flat topography	6. Views to opposite edge
7. General clutter	7. Unique landscapes
8. Boats, docks	8. Edge variety

9. Poor field maintenance	9. Superior view
10. Fences	10. Nearness of water
	11. Fences
	12. Dirt roads

In order to provide guidance for the designation and maintenance of scenic roads, the state of New York has developed a manual *Preserving New York State Scenic Roads* (n.d.). The manual recommended a five-step process.

1. Form a Nominating Group. A community nominates at least three members who then notify the Department of Environmental Conservation (DEC) of their intent. They are then given forms and further guidance.

2. Select Candidate Roads. The nominating committee tours roads for visual inspection needed to nominate potential scenic roads. The search should encompass the landscape characteristics that typify the scenery.

3. Prepare Narrative Description. Each candidate road is to be described in terms of topography, water, vegetation, sky, human or animal activities, structures, and patterns or rhythms. Cultural as well as natural resource features should be included in this description.

4. Evaluate Candidate Roads. The nominating committee, accompanied by special interests if needed, travel the roads again but with more detailed examination. This step usually eliminates some candidates and the team must describe its reasoning for the selections, noting the components that contribute most to its scenic quality. The list is then evaluated, using the form illustrated in Figure 7-5. This form serves two purposes—a checklist of uniform criteria and an organized cataloging for future reference. Both negative and positive characteristics must be identified. Designating team member roles will assist in the process. The driver identifies odometer readings as a front seat passenger appraises the scenery. Visual scanning should cover both sides of the highway. A recorder checks the characteristics as they are identified by the team. In order to expedite the process, a team of volunteers may be assigned to evaluate each candidate road.

5. Nominate Roads. The recommendations are then refined by team consensus. Further evaluation before nomination may include the length of the highway segment, relationship of road to other development, and implications for protection and future maintenance. The team's recommendations are submitted to the local government for approval. The evaluation forms and resolution of governmental support are then submitted to the DEC staff.

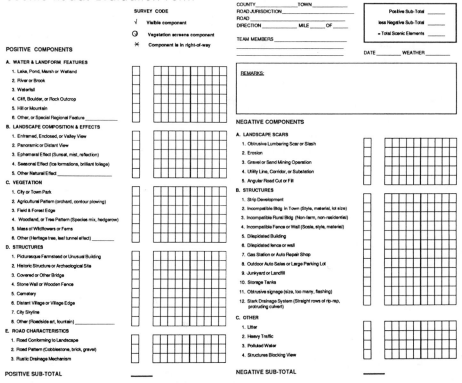

Scenic Roads Evaluation Form

SURVEY CODE

√   Visible component

◯   Vegetation screens component

✳   Component is in right-of-way

COUNTY_____ TOWN_____
ROAD JURISDICTION_____
ROAD_____
DIRECTION_____ MILE_____ OF_____

TEAM MEMBERS_____
_____
_____

Positive Sub-Total _____

less Negative Sub-Total _____

= Total Scenic Elements _____

DATE_____ WEATHER_____

POSITIVE COMPONENTS

A. WATER & LANDFORM FEATURES
1. Lake, Pond, Marsh or Wetland
2. River or Brook
3. Waterfall
4. Cliff, Boulder, or Rock Outcrop
5. Hill or Mountain
6. Other, or Special Regional Feature_____

B. LANDSCAPE COMPOSITION & EFFECTS
1. Enframed, Enclosed, or Valley View
2. Panoramic or Distant View
3. Ephemeral Effect (Sunset, mist, reflection)
4. Seasonal Effect (Ice formations, brilliant foliage)
5. Other Natural Effect_____

C. VEGETATION
1. City or Town Park
2. Agricultural Pattern (orchard, contour plowing)
3. Field & Forest Edge
4. Woodland, or Tree Pattern (Species mix, hedgerow)
5. Mass of Wildflowers or Ferns
6. Other (Heritage tree, leaf tunnel effect)_____

D. STRUCTURES
1. Picturesque Farmstead or Unusual Building
2. Historic Structure or Archeological Site
3. Covered or Other Bridge
4. Stone Wall or Wooden Fence
5. Cemetery
6. Distant Village or Village Edge
7. City Skyline
8. Other (Roadside art, fountain)_____

E. ROAD CHARACTERISTICS
1. Road Conforming to Landscape
2. Road Pattern (Cobblestone, brick, gravel)
3. Rustic Drainage Mechanism

POSITIVE SUB-TOTAL _____

REMARKS:

NEGATIVE COMPONENTS

A. LANDSCAPE SCARS
1. Obtrusive Lumbering Scar or Slash
2. Erosion
3. Gravel or Sand Mining Operation
4. Utility Line, Corridor, or Substation
5. Angular Road Cut or Fill

B. STRUCTURES
1. Strip Development
2. Incompatible Bldg in Town (Style, material, lot size)
3. Incompatible Rural Bldg (Non-farm, non-residential)
4. Incompatible Fence or Wall (Scale, style, material)
5. Dilapidated Building
6. Dilapidated fence or wall
7. Gas Station or Auto Repair Shop
8. Outdoor Auto Sales or Large Parking Lot
9. Junkyard or Landfill
10. Storage Tanks
11. Obtrusive signage (size, too many, flashing)
12. Stark Drainage System (Straight rows of rip-rap, protruding culvert)

C. OTHER
1. Litter
2. Heavy Traffic
3. Polluted Water
4. Structures Blocking View

NEGATIVE SUB-TOTAL _____

Figure 7-5. The Scenic Roads Evaluation Form used by the Department of Environmental Conservation of New York state for evaluating candidate scenic roads (Preserving New York n.d., 15).

Although not a specific requirement, a management plan is preferred. The plan may need professional guidance and preparation. It would include land uses, potential management issues, legal jurisdictions involved, and a schedule for meeting specific objectives of preservation and enhancement of the resources. Final approval for designation is then determined by the DEC. Such designation can assist in obtaining official zoning, grants for preservation, and general public assistance within the area.

Another example of a state program resulted from laws ARS 41-512 through ARS 41-518, enacted in Arizona in 1982, that provide for the establishment of parkways and historic and scenic roads (ADOT 1992). As of 1992, 17 roads have been so designated. The purpose is to provide a procedure that will ensure that future travelers will be able to enjoy important historical, cultural, and scenic resources along highways. Key to the process is evaluation and approval by the Parkways, Historic and Scenic Roads Advisory Committee (PHSRAC) for final approval and support by the Arizona Department of Transportation (ADOT). This advisory committee is made up of eleven members, including six citizen appointees by the governor, and one each from ADOT, Arizona State Parks Board, Arizona Historical Society, Arizona Office of Tourism, and Tourism Advisory Council.

The PHSRAC reviews, prioritizes, and evaluates the requests from individuals and organizations for designation. Figure 7-6 illustrates the flow chart for designation.

Documentation of an inventory process is included in each request and application for approval. Historic road applications emphasize cultural resources, and scenic road applications emphasize natural and visual resources. A list of the features for which information is to be determined and described follows.

Natural Resources
> Geology   Biota
> Hydrology   Topographic
> Climate

Cultural Resources
> Architectural   Archeological
> Historical   Cultural

Visual Resources
> Visual Quality Assessment Procedures
> - Landscape Classification Process
>   Identify on map proposed highway segments.
>   Identify biotic communities.
>   Identify transition zones.
>   Describe vegetative cover.
> - Landscape Inventory (a Visual Assessment Inventory and a Viewpoint Rating).

Criteria used by the PHSRAC for evaluating parkways and historic and scenic roads include the following:

Parkways
> One mile distance between access roads.
> Meet criteria for historic or scenic roads.
> Interpretive area space is available.
> Controlled access and property rights obtained.

Historic Roads
> Impact of route—importance within national, state, or local framework.

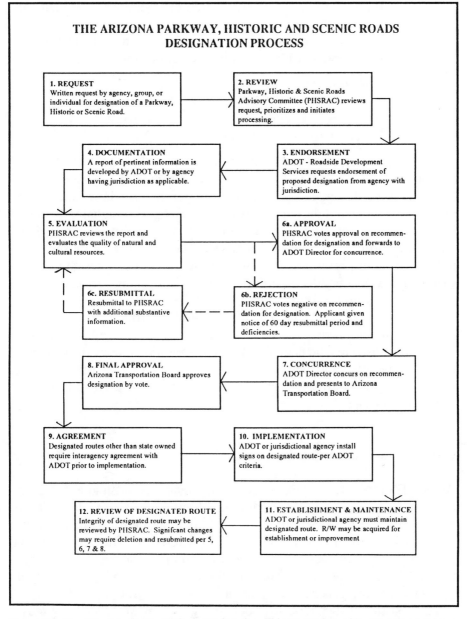

THE ARIZONA PARKWAY, HISTORIC AND SCENIC ROADS DESIGNATION PROCESS

1. REQUEST
Written request by agency, group, or individual for designation of a Parkway, Historic or Scenic Road.

2. REVIEW
Parkway, Historic & Scenic Roads Advisory Committee (PHSRAC) reviews request, prioritizes and initiates processing.

4. DOCUMENTATION
A report of pertinent information is developed by ADOT or by agency having jurisdiction as applicable.

3. ENDORSEMENT
ADOT - Roadside Development Services requests endorsement of proposed designation from agency with jurisdiction.

5. EVALUATION
PHSRAC reviews the report and evaluates the quality of natural and cultural resources.

6a. APPROVAL
PHSRAC votes approval on recommendation for designation and forwards to ADOT Director for concurrence.

6c. RESUBMITTAL
Resubmittal to PHSRAC with additional substantive information.

6b. REJECTION
PHSRAC votes negative on recommendation for designation. Applicant given notice of 60 day resubmittal period and deficiencies.

8. FINAL APPROVAL
Arizona Transportation Board approves designation by vote.

7. CONCURRENCE
ADOT Director concurs on recommendation and presents to Arizona Transportation Board.

9. AGREEMENT
Designated routes other than state owned require interagency agreement with ADOT prior to implementation.

10. IMPLEMENTATION
ADOT or jurisdictional agency install signs on designated route-per ADOT criteria.

12. REVIEW OF DESIGNATED ROUTE
Integrity of designated route may be reviewed by PHSRAC. Significant changes may require deletion and resubmitted per 5, 6, 7 & 8.

11. ESTABLISHMENT & MAINTENANCE
ADOT or jurisdictional agency must maintain designated route. R/W may be acquired for establishment or improvement

Figure 7-6. Flow Chart for Scenic Highway Designation. This process is used by the state of Arizona for designation of parkways and historic and scenic roads (ADOT 1992, 3).

Impact of area—contribution to exploration, settlement, or development.

Proximity—physical and/or visual access to historical place.

Uniqueness—relative scarcity or abundance.

Scenic Roads

Vividness—memorability of visual impression.

Intactness—integrity, freedom from encroachment.

Unity—harmonious composite.

Important criteria and standards of operation include protection of vegetation, freedom from negative impacts, and compatible development (if any) along all designated routes. Recommended are local and county protective zoning and design review overlay along all designated highways in order to protect, maintain, and enhance the quality of the highway corridor environment. Special emphasis is placed on the establishment of pullouts for interpretation. Normal highway standards of design and construction may be amended in order to protect and enhance special features or unique resources important to such designated highways. Final approval lies with the Arizona Transportation Board.

This examination of scenic highways, their importance, and planning issues, demonstrates the need for close collaboration among decisionmakers, local people, and designers/planners. It seems that the answer to better planning lies within each situation rather than a set of rigid standards and policies.

Historic Resource Inventory

Pollock-Ellwand (1991) developed a computer-aided technique for identifying and analyzing historic landscapes. Increased tourism development and use of historic areas requires several planning steps, the first of which is to know where they are and their characteristics. This technique has been tested in southwestern Ontario. It is unique in its approach, inventorying three modes of information: textual, audio, and images. Figure 7-7 illustrates the general sequence of steps in the process.

The first step is a generic scan of a study area by likely local sources—historical societies, garden clubs, environmental activists, and others. These individuals follow a questionnaire that asks for the historic event, historical activity, native and famous people, exemplary design, plants associated with history, and human and esthetic impressions.

The next step is performed by historic specialists and local representatives to narrow and deepen the analysis. All data is submitted to the

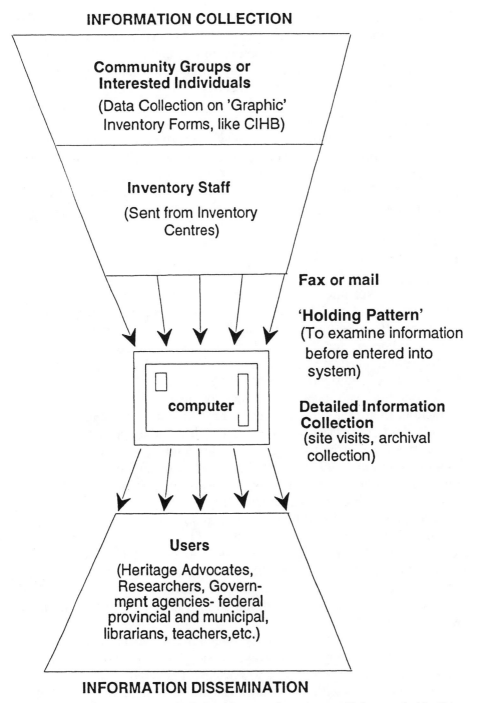

INFORMATION COLLECTION

Community Groups or Interested Individuals

(Data Collection on 'Graphic' Inventory Forms, like CIHB)

Inventory Staff

(Sent from Inventory Centres)

Fax or mail

'Holding Pattern'
(To examine information before entered into system)

computer

Detailed Information Collection
(site visits, archival collection)

Users

(Heritage Advocates, Researchers, Government agencies- federal provincial and municipal, librarians, teachers,etc.)

INFORMATION DISSEMINATION

Figure 7-7. Historic Inventory Process. Illustrated are steps in a computer-aided process for identifying and analyzing historic areas (Pollock-Ellwand 1991, 52).

Inventory Centre located at the University of Guelph where it is facsimilied directly into the computer system. Visual images, such as historic and contemporary photographs, context mapping, and original planning documents are scanned and stored directly with typed or handwritten descriptive data. Audio clips also can be received.

The final output can be accessed in several ways. Direct computer linkage and facsimile transmissions can be converted to hard copy printouts. Thousands of institutions are now on an Internet system that allows access to the process. However, the designer recommends an intervening step of clarifying relative significance. (The NeXT computer and software package, Media Station, was used for this Southwest Ontario Cultural Heritage Landscape Inventory. Many others may be equally suitable.)

Historic Cities

As travel market interest in historic background continues to increase, cities face special planning and design issues to cope with great volumes of visitors. Because historic sites and districts function as attractions for tourism, planning for their development may be aided by applying the spatial model illustrated in Figure 7-8 (Gunn 1965, 26). The diagram focuses planning/design issues on three zones.

Considering historic sites, buildings, or districts as the *nucleus* of the attraction, their planning requires more than restoration and protection. Too often, masses of visitors stimulate tasteless and inappropriate services within this zone. Adaptive use is more acceptable, whereby appropriate shops, restaurants, and other services are contained within structures that retain their architectural integrity. As visitor volumes increase, the zone may have to be closed to automobile traffic.

Of great planning importance is what could be called an *inviolate belt*—the area surrounding the historic district. This area serves as the psychological setting for introducing the visitor to history. Incompatible land uses, such as modern high-rise office buildings, encroach upon the nucleus and offer poor visual entrance to the main feature. Business and residential uses may be acceptable if designed in a manner that is in harmony with the historic district.

It is in the surrounding area, the *zone of closure*, that new structures and land uses including modern travel services would be most appropriate. Rather than locating them in the nucleus or inviolate belt where their design could clash with the historic theme, it is here that new hotels, restaurants, and other travel services should be located. Planning and managing these zones may require special legislation.

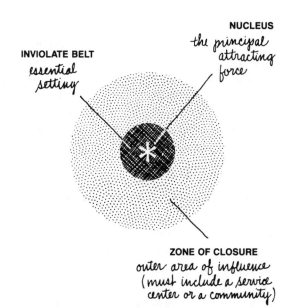

Figure 7-8. Model of Attraction. Planning of attraction development should consider the design of three parts: 1, nucleus; 2, inviolate belt; and 3, zone of closure, including a community service area (Gunn 1965, 26).

In the United States, the Main Street Program is a major planning aid to tourism development in destinations, particularly at the community level. It is a function of the National Trust for Historic Preservation, created in 1980, and by 1991 it was working in 630 communities and 38 states (Parrish 1991, 161). Although some public moneys are used, for every $1.00 of public funding over $11.00 of investment is generated because the emphasis is on local initiative and economic enhancement. Its focus is primarily on smaller communities; the present average is 16,000 residents.

The program is directed toward economic revitalization by means of local protection and restoration of existing assets. Emphasis is on business retention, preservation, and investment in the built environment rather than new shopping centers. "Main Street is a management approach, a structure, and a process for a community to use to discover its resources, take advantage of them, and build the kind of leadership capacity and vision needed" (Parrish 1991, 163).

A study of four successful historic cities in the United States (Said 1987)—St. Augustine, Savannah, Charleston, and Williamsburg—showed that even with distinctively different characteristics, several common contributing factors were identified. First, local citizen participation and commitment to historic protection was found to be critical. The community's financial support, efforts of volunteers, and donations of properties greatly fostered historic redevelopment. Second, the general economic viability of the city and surrounding area appeared to be an important factor. Private and public funding assisted these efforts greatly. Third, accessibility from travel market sources was found to contribute to success, even location within the city was important. Finally, a strong commitment by the local government was consistently essential. Planning of historic redevelopment requires processes that include inputs of professional planners and designers, governments, developers, and local citizens.

THE DESTINATION ZONE PLANNERS

Who plans tourism destinations? Increasingly, this is seen as a public-private cooperative venture. But, there are more guidelines and proposals than demonstrations of how destinations should be planned and by whom.

There is little question that this process must involve at least the following groups: tourism developers, public officials, resident groups, existing tourism businesses, organizations, and planners. They are all needed if decisions on a planned future are to be meaningful and have a good chance of being implemented. Such a process requires a great amount of leadership and coordination. Of the many planning groups, the following are cited for the promise they hold for effective destination zone planning.

Consultants

Increasingly, the design and planning professionals are taking on tourism planning assignments. Because of tourism's complexities, a team approach is often taken. Overall planning and integration with official planning is often assumed by professional planners, individuals with education and experience in urban and regional planning. Land use planning and site design, as well as detailed construction plans, are usually performed by professional landscape architects. They are individuals with training and experience in site planning. Specific structural design is usually handled by professional engineers with training and experience in structural design and specifications. For the design and specific planning of buildings, architects are engaged because they have the training and experience for this specialty.

Some firms have all or most of these specialties represented by staff members. Such firms are best capable of the larger scale planning projects for tourism—regional and destination. For tourism, often additional specialists are needed—golf course architect, museum design specialist, zoo designer, historical restoration specialist, archeologist, interpretive visitor center designer, and market researcher. The advantage of these firms is that they can perform a wide range of services, from general studies of tourism potential to complete working drawings and specifications for project construction.

Increasingly, other types of consultant firms are doing tourism planning work. Firms traditionally focused on accounting, finance, and feasibilities, such as Price Waterhouse and Pannell Kerr Forster, have now performed tourism planning projects. These firms usually are directed more toward policy and marketing than to physical planning. Sometimes marketing firms, such as Davidson-Peterson Associates and KPMG Peat Marwick become involved in tourism planning. Professors at universities are sometimes called upon to engage in tourism planning projects.

Task Forces

Task forces for tourism planning vary greatly in their makeup but provide an effective mechanism for a variety of needs. Some are made up entirely of planning professionals whereas others are composed of public and private representatives of groups interested in tourism.

For several years, the Pacific Asia Travel Association (PATA) has been co-sponsor of many tourism task force studies including planning. Generally, the request for outside overview assistance comes from the nation or city within the Pacific basin. Their needs are detailed and submitted to PATA. In response, PATA contacts four or five tourism specialists who have the competence and experience to address the issues of concern and requests their services. PATA then provides a leader. A rapporteur maintains close contact with the team and is responsible for the final manuscript of a written report. Travel expenses (but no professional fees) are provided by the host area. What ensues is an intensive on-site evaluation with a tightly scheduled agenda. The process includes site inspection, rapid review of documents, and interviews with individuals and representatives of public and private organizations. By the end of the week, consensus on recommendations is reached. Reports to the sponsor include an on-site oral report and a written report after the site visit. (See the example of Moorea in Chapter 8.) Compared to a major project by consultants, this technique is much less costly and provides immediate input. It is particularly effective in resolving a smaller number of issues and those requiring no long-term in-depth research.

The task force concept is also used in initial stages of planning to crystalize interest and organization. As an example, after several studies

by the U.S. National Park Service and Pennsylvania state agencies, the
state created a task force to develop coordination and guidelines for the
industrial heritage corridor in the southwestern part of the state (Plan for
Allegheny Ridge 1992). It was called the State Heritage Interagency Task
Force and was made up of 70 representatives of culture and heritage
groups, businesses, and public agencies having jurisdiction in the area.
These agencies included state departments of Community Affairs, Commerce, Environmental Resources, Education, and Transportation, and the
Pennsylvania Historical and Museum Commission, the Pennsylvania Heritage Affairs Commission, and the Pennsylvania Council on the Arts. This
task force studied reports, evaluated the resource base, reviewed several
alternatives, and selected a preferred approach. Allied with the task force
was a consulting team of planners. Together, they held meetings, open
houses, and workshops as planning concepts were developed. After two
years, a general conceptual plan emerged. (See the example of Allegheny
Ridge Heritage Park in Chapter 8.) The use of a task force demonstrates
an effective approach to integrate the ideas and policies of the many
constituencies that often are involved in destination and regional tourism
development.

Extension Tourism Planning

An effective method of public education about tourism and guidance for
planning has been adult educational programs sponsored by governments
and universities. In the United States, the Cooperative Extension Service
(CES) was created by Congress in 1914 (Smith-Lever Act) to carry educational information directly to farmers of the nation. An adaptation of
this first took place in Michigan in 1945 with the Tourist and Resort Service
Program, based at Michigan State University. The program was designed
to assist tourist and resort businesses with their technical problems. The
program had three themes: business management, building and grounds
planning, and food service. The methods used were preparation of technical bulletins, workshops, conferences, news releases, and personal on-
site consultation. Through this program, carried out by three Extension
Specialists (Robert W. McIntosh, Clare A. Gunn, and Gladys Knight),
thousands of motels, hotels, restaurants, campgrounds, marinas, and
parks benefited from better location, site, and building design, operational
management, accounting, financing, food production, and management
for over two decades.

Many states patterned new programs after this pioneering effort. Several states, such as Minnesota, have established university research and

extension centers to develop new information and disseminate it to those in need. Approximately 15 of these centers are located across the United States (Gitelson 1989, 9). Their main functions are: to foster multidisciplinary efforts, to provide on- and off-campus educational programs, and conduct applied research. In addition, adult education specialists in many states are providing tourism technical assistance, supported primarily by governments (federal, state, and local) with additional input from private organizations and businesses. Some 38 presentations have been published as *Using Tourism & Travel as a Community and Rural Revitalization Strategy*, proceedings of the national workshop of May 10–12, 1989. The USDA-CES now publishes *Update Tourism & Commercial Recreation*, as a newsletter of activity by CES in tourism.

Reviewing files of accomplishments by CES specialists also reveals much activity in tourism planning. The following illustrate some of these projects.

Boundary Waters Canoe Area

In the United States, wilderness areas are designated by Congress through the Wilderness Act of 1964 and managed by the U.S. Forest Service. Several regulations of use apply in order to fulfill the criteria demanded by the wilderness designation. Because of controversy over this change in one area, the Agricultural Extension Service, University of Minnesota, was requested to investigate the impact of these new administrative controls in the Boundary Waters Canoe Area, an area in northeastern Minnesota along the Canadian border (Blank et al. 1988). The economy, supporting the 13,000 residents, was based on timber production, iron mining, and tourism. In the Extension tradition, action to resolve issues is as important as identifying them. Following the federal legislation that designated the area as wilderness, there was much negative local reaction on two issues. Private holdings were to be eliminated and motorized vehicle access was to be prohibited. Over a period between September 1, 1979 to September 30, 1982, the Extension Service fulfilled a leadership and catalytic role to resolve issues and stimulate planning in the area. This effort included the following subprojects:

A Needs Assessment—determining needs of firms impacted by the area.
Educational and Technical Assistance to Tourism Related Firms—152 occurrences: physical plant, business management.
Educational and Technical Assistance in the Management of Community Grants—catalytic function.

Educational and Technical Assistance in Marketing Programs—
improved materials, strategies, and delivery.
Education and Technical Assistance in Special Project Management—
Canadian custom station closings, licensing outfitters, etc.
Applied Research Efforts—fostering data collection, management.
Building Communication Flows—integrating many agency and firm
plans and actions.

The Extension role has resulted in new understanding of public and
private roles, new cooperation, new investment in facilities and services,
much greater visitor use, greatly increased tourist business, and a significant increase in resource protection. One example was the marketing
assistance for the Lake Vermillion area, generating $360,000 in new busi-
ness. Another was the case of catalytic action between the U.S. Forest
Service and U.S. National Park Service for establishing the Cook Visitor
Center (Simonson 1992). The Extension program in Minnesota has greatly
enhanced tourism there for several decades.

Southern Kentucky

An example of constructive extension education was offered by Allan
Worms (1992), a recreation and tourism Extension specialist at the University of Kentucky. In 1986, a steering committee of representatives from
a 27-county area including members of a newly formed Southern Kentucky
Tourism Development Association was formed. Midwest Research Institute prepared a market study that included information on unfulfilled
potential, relationship to the I-75 highway corridor, natural and cultural
resources, and suggested project development. These results were then
disseminated by means of several extension techniques: meetings of key
leaders, presentations to civic clubs, press releases, and workshops. Study
tours were held to expose local participants to development opportunities.
   In a region of economic decline, these activities changed public attitudes, encouraged entrepreneurism, initiated new programs, and stimulated new interest in developing local resources into viable attractions.
New cooperation between communities was begun, resulting in awareness
of opportunities overlooked before. In addition to sociocultural improvements, following are some of the tangible results totaling over $72 million
from local and outside effort, coordinated by the Extension specialist as
a leader-catalyst.

   A major first project: $14.5 million Jamestown Resort & Marina on
   Lake Cumberland.

Renfro Valley Music Park & Museum ($7.5 million).

Five new motels in London, one each in Corbin, Somerset, Jamestown, and Russell Springs.

Sycamore Island boat sales business and several dry storage businesses.

Several new resort and/or retirement complexes.

In addition, an estimated $46.7 million in marinas and a great many other projects are in the planning stages—houseboat construction, new restaurants, and new festivals and events.

As a result of Extension guidance and technical information, the volume of visitors has increased greatly (one festival drew 200,000 in 1991) and is stimulating the local economy with jobs, incomes, and taxes paid.

Delaware Bays

Similar in function to CES but focused on coastal areas is the Sea Grant College Marine Advisory Service that includes tourism and recreation among its objectives. The service carried out a project in cooperation with the Delaware Department of Natural Resources and Environmental Control to determine carrying capacity issues and recommendations for management of the state's inland bays (Falk 1992).

The study included on-site interviews of recreational users, a mail questionnaire survey of shoreline residents, and reconnaissance of boating activity on Little Assawoman, Rehoboth and Indian River Bays.

Results indicated that:

- High boating density was creating safety hazards.
- Marine debris and litter were becoming a problem.
- Environmental degradation was taking place.

From the findings of the study several planning and management options were put forward and reviewed by the constituency groups. Main conclusions reached were:

- Discharges of pollutants into the bays should be stopped.
- Boat speed and jet ski use should be controlled for safety.
- Number of marinas should be limited.
- Fishing management should be improved.
- Water use should be zoned.
- Boat users should accept funding support for bay improvement.
- Monitoring and enforcement need improvement.
- Boat use and safety education programs are needed.

In many coastal locations throughout the United States, the Sea Grant Program has provided educational and technical guidance for better planning of tourism.

CONCLUSIONS ON INTEGRATED DESTINATION PLANNING

Several very important conclusions regarding destination tourism planning can be drawn from past approaches and examples of development. As communities look toward the field of tourism for greater economic support, they need to be aware of the issues that accompany the opportunities. Following are some of the key conclusions that may be of assistance to communities and their surrounding areas as they plan for destination tourism development.

Integration into Regional Plans

Communities and their surrounding areas must plan their tourism expansion within the context of regional plans. If regional tourism planning is not in place, lobbying for such planning may be the first item on the community's agenda. Destinations are dependent upon regional (federal, state, and provincial) policies and action on such matters as transportation network, national parks and protected resource areas, incentives for community tourism development, and cooperative marketing and promotion.

Placeness as a Fundamental

In today's competitive travel market, excessive replication of the same theme of tourism development dampens rather than fosters economic success. Travelers seek destinations because of the special qualities of place. Otherwise, why travel? Every destination has a different set of geographical factors, traditions, relationship to markets, and host characteristics. Analysis of these factors can lay the foundation for building upon the uniqueness of place.

Community-Area Potential

Because a destination includes cities and their surrounding areas, the planning for future tourism must include the entire geographic area—not just the city. Tourism's attraction potential lies within the nearby rural area, as well as the cities, within a destination zone. It is likely that the abundance of cultural resources will be found within communities, whereas most natural resource assets are located in the surrounding area. The logical location for most travel service businesses is within communities where they can benefit from public services and both the residential as well as the travel market. However, the reason travelers will come to the destination will depend on the quantity and quality of attractions in the surrounding area as well as within the city.

Public-Private Cooperation

At issue in many potential destinations is the lack of cooperation between the public and private sectors. City and county governments are preoccupied with public services, such as water supply, waste disposal, police, education, and related functions. Essential as these are for the residents, they are of equal concern in tourism planning and development. Too often city councils believe tourism is the prerogative of business only. Even though the business sector does play an important role in tourism development, a successful destination is one in which policies and actions of both public and private sectors are complementary, rather than competitive or divisive. In addition to the need for government-business cooperation on tourism planning is the equal need for them to cooperate with nonprofit organizations as they plan and make decisions on historic restoration, parks and preserves, and festivals and events.

Destination Leadership/Organization

It is becoming clear that for effective tourism planning at the destination scale the traditional functions of a chamber of commerce or tourism department may be too narrow. These organizations usually focus only on tourism promotion. Their scope is usually restricted to within the city limits. They also lack representation from needed constituency groups.

Instead, a special tourism council is usually required. Such a council needs the official support from the jurisdictions encompassed within the zone—cities and counties. Its membership must include representatives of government, tourist businesses, civic groups, nonprofit organizations, planners, and environmentalists. Planning guidelines have a much greater chance of implementation if these influencers and decisionmakers are represented.

Destination Planning

Destination areas will be less successful, less fulfilling to visitors, and less sensitive to environmental stress if not planned in an orderly step-by-step sequence. A combination of both approaches—planning project and continuous planning—is likely to produce the best results.

Although planning processes vary, all have similar basic elements: setting goals and objectives; analyzing the present situation; identifying issues, constraints, and opportunities; creating alternative concepts for development; and identifying action strategies. Destination planning can identify project ideas and recommend action in order to stimulate development by those best able to create and manage a new supply side.

Environmental Degradation

Because most pollution of air and water and erosion of land resources occurs within and around cities, the challenge for tourism planners is to foster environmental improvement and continued protection.

This responsibility at the destination scale must address all sources of environmental degradation, not only from tourism. Municipal sewage and industrial waste must be brought under control if tourism is to thrive. Land use regulations are necessary to avoid overdevelopment, excessive congestion, and incompatible development. They are necessary to protect the environmental resources that are so critical to tourism's success.

Special Cultural and Natural Resources

Because of geographic differences, opportunities exist for destination areas to capitalize on their unique cultural and natural resources. Two major categories of potential should be considered in planning processes. First, within the surrounding areas of cities, and even connecting corridors between destinations, there may be great opportunities for designating, planning, and maintaining scenic and historic routes. Second, because most history was developed at cities, most have the potential for identification, restoration, protection, and interpretation of historic sites within communities.

REFERENCES

Alberta Tourism (1988). *Community Tourism Action Plan Manual.* Edmonton: Alberta Tourism.

Arizona Department of Transportation (ADOT) (1992). *Application Procedures for Department of Parkways, Historic and Scenic Roads in Arizona,* T.D. Walker (ed.). Phoenix: ADOT.

Blank, Uel et al. (1988). "Contributing to Tourism Industry Vitality of a Natural Resource Based Region Through Educational/Technical Assistance." *Staff Papers Series,* 83-20. St. Paul: University of Minnesota.

Blank, Uel (1989). *The Community Tourism Industry Imperative: The Necessity, the Opportunities, Its Potential.* State College, PA: Venture.

Cheek, Neil H. Jr., and William R. Burch, Jr. (1976). *The Social Organization of Leisure in Human Society.* New York: Harper & Row.

Dredge, Dianne, and Stewart Moore (1992). "A Methodology for the Integration of Tourism in Town Planning." *Journal of Tourism Studies,* 3(1), 8–21.

Durrell, Lawrence (1969). "Landscape and Character." In *Spirit of Place,* A.G. Thomas (ed.). New York: E. P. Dutton.

Economics Research Associates (1989). *The National Policy Study on Rural Tourism and Small Business Development.* Prepared for the United States Travel and Tourism Administration. Vienna, VA: Economics Research Associates.

Edgell, David (1990). *Charting a Course for International Tourism in the Nineties.* Washington, DC: U.S. Travel and Tourism Administration.

Falk, James et al. (1992). "Recreational Boating on Delaware's Inland Bays: Implications for Social and Environmental Carrying Capacity." Prepared for Inland Bays Estuary Program, Delaware Department of Natural Resources and Environmental Control, Division of Water Resources. Lewes, DE: University of Delaware Sea Grant College Program.

Federal Highway Administration (1991). *National Scenic Byways Study,* Pub. PD-91-010. Washington, DC: U.S. Department of Transportation.

Ferrario, Franco F. (1979). "The Evaluation of Tourist Resources." *Annals of Tourism Research,* 17(3), 18–22, 24–30.

Gitelson, Richard (1989). "What's Happening with Centers in the U.S.A.?" In *Using Tourism & Travel as a Community and Rural Revitalization Strategy.* Proceedings, National Extension Workshop, May 10–12, Minneapolis: University of Minnesota.

Go, Frank et al. (1992). "Communities as Destinations: A Marketing Taxonomy for the Effective Implementation of the Tourism Action Plan." *Journal of Travel Research,* 30(4), 31–37.

Gradus, Yehuda, and Eliahu Stern (1980). "Changing Strategies of Development: Toward a Regopolis in the Negev Desert." *APA Journal,* 46(4), 410–423.

Gunn, Clare A. (1965). *A Concept for the Design of a Tourism-Recreation Region.* Mason, MI: B J Press.

Gunn, Clare A. (1982). "Destination Zone Fallacies and Half-Truths." Presentation at International Conference on Trends in Tourism Planning and Development, Surrey, U.K.: University of Surrey.

Gunn, Clare A. (1988a). "Small Town and Rural Tourism Planning." In *Integrated Rural Planning and Development,* Floyd Dykeman (ed.), Rural and Small Town Research and Studies Programme. Sackville, New Brunswick: Mount Allison University.

Gunn, Clare A. (1988b) *Vacationscape: Designing Tourist Regions,* 2nd ed. New York: Van Nostrand Reinhold.

Koth, Barbara et al. (eds.) (1991). *Rural Tourism Development Training Guide.* St. Paul: Tourism Center, University of Minnesota.

Morris, Philip (1990). *Southern Places.* Birmingham, AL: Oxmoor House.

Motloch, John L. (1991). *Introduction to Landscape Design.* New York: Van Nostrand Reinhold.

Pannel Kerr Forster (1985). *Calgary-Canmore Tourism Destination Area Study, Vols. 1 and 2.* Edmonton: Travel Alberta.

Parrish, Bill (1991). "The Main Street Program." In *Enhancing Rural Economies Through Amenity Resources,* Joanne F. Zeigler (ed.). Proceedings, a national policy symposium, pp. 161–163. State College, PA: Pennsylvania State University.

Plan for the Allegheny Ridge (1992). Prepared by the Allegheny Ridge Industrial Heritage Corridor Task Force, Hollidaysburg, PA.

Pollock-Ellwand, Nancy (1991). "Discovering the Hidden Resource: Historic Landscapes." In *Tourism-Environment-Sustainable Development: An Agenda for Research,* L. Reid, (ed.). Proceedings, Travel and Tourism Research Association Canada, Hull, pp. 43–54.

Preserving New York State Scenic Roads (n.d.) New York: Department of Environmental Conservation (DEC).

Ruest, Gilles (1979). *The Tourism Destination Concept.* Ottawa: Canadian Government Office of Tourism.

Said, Asad Abdelkarim (1987). *Historic Preservation and Restoration: Case Studies of the Factors Contributing to the Success in Four Historic American Cities.* Dissertation, Urban and Regional Science, College Station, Texas: Texas A&M University.

Shepard, Paul (1967). *Man in the Landscape.* New York: Alfred A. Knopf.

Simonson, Lawrence (1992). Personal correspondence, August 10, former Extension Specialist of Tourism, Grand Rapids, MN.

Smardon, Richard C. (1987). "Visual Access to 1,000 Lakes". *Landscape Architecture,* 77(3), 86–91.

Steiner, Frederick (1991). "Landscape Planning: A Method Applied to a Growth Management Example." *Environmental Management,* 15(4), 519–529.

Stewart, George R. (1967). *Names on the Land.* Boston: Houghton Mifflin.

Using Tourism & Travel as a Community and Rural Revitalization Strategy. (1989). John Sem, ed. Proceedings of National Extension Workshop, Minneapolis, MN, May 10–12.

Weaver, Glenn D. (1991). *Tourism USA.* Washington DC: U.S. Travel and Tourism Administration.

Western Australian Tourism Commission (n.d.). *Draft Local Government Tourism Policy.* Perth, WA: WATC.

Wight, Pamela (1992). "Tourism-Recreation EIAS in Alberta: A Need for an Integrated Approach in Legislation, Environmental Assessment, and Development Planning." Presentation, 12th International Seminar on Environmental Assessment and Management, July, University of Aberdeen, Scotland, U.K.

Worms, Allan J. (1992). "The Southern Kentucky Tourism Development Project." Presentation, Partners in Rural Development 1992 conference, Washington, DC.

Zimmerman, Erich (1933). *World Resources and Industries.* New York: Harper.

Chapter 8

Destination Planning Cases

Introduction

Although the term *destination* is used with several meanings, from a nation to a relatively small area, it is interpreted here to mean a community (or cluster of several) and surrounding attractions. Examples of discovery of potential destination zones were presented in Chapter 6.

The attractions within a destination zone are located in the surrounding area as well as within the community. Although destination type markets sometimes engage in their total activities in situ, such as at beach resorts or casinos, they often take trips to surrounding attractions as well. Conversely, remote attractions, such as national parks, depend on the nearest community for basic lodging, diversity of food services, travel services, communications, health services, and shopping.

The following examples show how several destination zones became involved in planning for an improved tourism future.

MOOREA, FRENCH POLYNESIA

For many years the Pacific Asia Travel Association (PATA) has acted as catalyst in organizing study task forces to respond to requests for tourism projects in the Pacific region. In 1990, a request to PATA was made by the French Polynesian government to analyze tourism issues and potential for the destination island of Moorea, located in the South Pacific, near Tahiti (see Figure 8-1). Under the leadership of Ian Kennedy, vice president of PATA, Pacific Division, a task force of four specialists (Clare Gunn, Kenneth Chamberlain, George Lipp, and Stephen LePage) was organized. The typical pattern of projects like these is to make intensive reconnaissance and study for one week to produce findings and recommendations. The project was reported in *Moorea and Tourism* (Kennedy et al. 1991). A summary of the project follows.

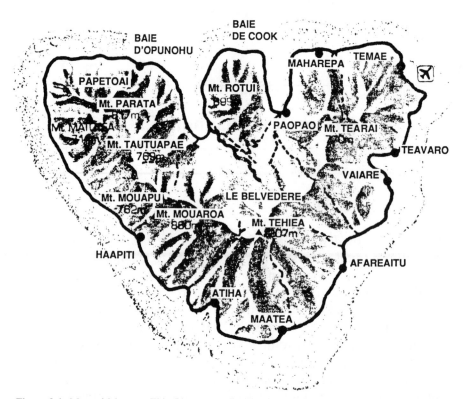

Figure 8-1. Map of Moorea. This 54-square-mile island, 11 miles from Tahiti, was studied for its tourism issues and potential by a task force sponsored by the Pacific Asia Travel Association and government of French Polynesia (Kennedy et al. 1991).

Objectives

Identify options for tourist development in Moorea maintaining balance between industry growth, the needs and desires of the local population, and protection of the environment.

Advise on future hotel capacity, including the maximum capacity that can be sustained or should be permitted.

Advise on an effective marketing strategy in relation to Moorea's competitive position, its image, and its characteristics.

Advise on criteria for tourist zoning, including hotels, activities, and parks and reserves zones.

Secondary Objectives

Comment on planned golf course developments.

Assess options for the development and expansion of tourist ground transport.

Advise on the harmonious integration of future hotel development into the local economy, especially in relation to agriculture and fishing industries.

Study Process

Familiarization tour of the island.
Aerial survey of the island.
Visits to hotels, restaurants, tourism facilities.
Meetings with government officials, private sector operators, and community representatives.
"Verbal" report of the team's initial findings in which the Task Force received feedback and comment from public and private sector industry representatives. (Kennedy et al. 1991, 7)

Key Findings

The task force was impressed by two major observations. The physical appearance of the island of Moorea coincides with the traditional image of a South Sea Island paradise. The small (54 square miles) island is dominated by a mountain range in the center and circled by a narrow coastal edge adjacent to quiet lagoons protected from the sea by a coral reef. Second, the statistics of tourism revealed stagnation—hotel occupancy at about 50 percent and a generally low morale of local attitude toward tourism. These observations supported the need to address the stated objectives. A travel market survey revealed that the top preferences for visiting the island were scenery, the sea, and unspoiled setting.

However, a review of strengths and weaknesses revealed that in spite of these expressed market preferences, the resource foundations for related activities were neither protected nor managed for visitors. Development on fragile mountain slopes was causing erosion. Wildlife habitat was being diminished. Some hotels were polluting the sea with sewage. Rare Polynesian archeological sites had no protection. Neither the indigenous natural or cultural resources were in park management control for protection as well as public use with trails, tours, and interpretive centers.

Recommendations

Based on the short-term but intensive study of the island's tourism, the task force identified 14 specific conclusions and recommendations.

1. Major upgrading is needed to meet competition.
2. Not more advertising but major improvement of supply is needed.
3. Decisions must be made on scale, nature, and control of tourism.
4. Gradual and small scale development is preferred.

5. Transportation problems must be remedied.
6. Sameness of resort offerings must be replaced by diversity.
7. Foreign Independent Travel, not package sales, provides greatest market opportunity.
8. Finite resources demand growth control.
9. Greater commitment and cooperation are needed.
10. Increased environmental attractions are needed.
11. Environmental protection is needed: sewage treatment plant, mountain national park, and beach parks.
12. Cultural attractions offer abundant opportunity
13. A major culture center is needed.
14. Moorea should take a stronger position in the marketing of French Polynesia. (Kennedy et al. 1991, 10, 11)

Related to these specific recommendations were some supplementary ones. For example, increased local resident training is needed for tourism jobs. An island-wide tourism organization should be established to address the issues and changes needed. Greater emphasis on ecotourism marketing is needed but only after the natural and cultural resources are protected, developed, and managed for this market. The task force recommended that the proposal to build a major resort with a golf course along Opunohu Bay be denied not only because of its detrimental environmental impact but also because more rooms are not needed when occupancy already is low. The existing attractiveness and recommended new attractions offer great opportunity to meet market needs, enhance tourism's economic impact, and improve local quality of life.

This is a case example of a different kind of tourism planning, characterized by short-term, local involvement in workshop meetings, and intensive study input from a panel of tourism specialists. Implementation of these recommendations may not be visible for several years but the reaction of the local people and government appeared to be favorable. In less than one year, for example, the local people voted against the establishment of the large resort and golf course at Opunohu Bay. It would appear that this short-term and relatively inexpensive planning approach is effective.

KOSRAE

Another island destination area in the Pacific basin that has been studied and planned for tourism is Kosrae State, Federated States of Micronesia (FSM) (Figure 8-2). About 42 square miles in size, the island is dominated

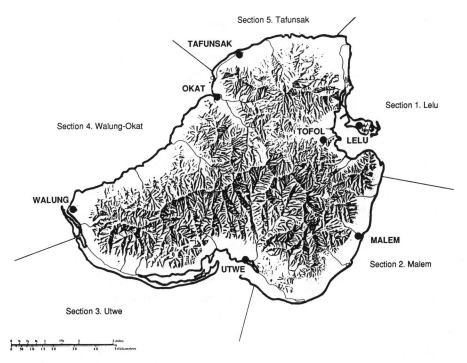

Section 5. Tafunsak

TAFUNSAK

OKAT

Section 1. Lelu

Section 4. Walung-Okat

TOFOL

LELU

WALUNG

MALEM

Section 2. Malem

UTWE

Section 3. Utwe

Figure 8-2. Map of Kosrae. Kosrae State, an island 42 square miles in size located in the Federated States of Micronesia, was examined for its tourism potential, especially for ecotourism. Illustrated are the five coastal sections given special study. (Auyong 1990, 2).

by lush tropical forests in the central mountainous area, with peaks at about 2,000 feet, and is surrounded by coral reef. It is in the outermost eastern limit of the Caroline Island chain. The following discussion is paraphrased from several reports (Auyong 1990; Wilson and Hamilton 1992).

In 1986 the U.S. Army Corps of Engineers, at the request of the Governor of Kosrae, Yosiwo George, performed the first resource inventory surveys. The purpose of this work was to increase the awareness of the need for sustainable development and it involved Kosrae government as well as several local natives. In 1988, the governor requested the University of Hawaii Sea Grant Program and East-West Center specialists to engage in resource analysis and evaluation for future development.

Purpose

The intent of this resource project was to identify opportunities and constraints for ecotourism development. Long-term conservation as well as economic enhancement were primary goals. More specifically, the study was directed toward questions about natural and cultural resource foundations, and how they can be protected as tourism grows. A secondary goal was to develop local agency philosophy and framework as well as provide technical skills in support of sustainable development.

Process

Documents, maps, and reports were reviewed but most of the study was based on physical reconnaissance by a multidisciplinary team of eighteen persons (eleven from Kosrae and seven off-island). Represented were specialists in coral reefs, fisheries, mangroves, tourism, historic and cultural preservation, and small business development. Collaborating institutions included the East-West Center, University of Hawaii, Kosrae State government agencies, FSM National Historic Preservation Office, Pohnpei State Division of Forestry, University of Hawaii Sea Grant Program, U.S. Forest Service, U.S. Peace Corps, and the University of Guam.

The eight days of island visit included meetings with government and village leaders as well as inspection of existing conditions. This visit was preceded by extensive study of island background, including many telephone and satellite conferences as well as review of inventories and atlases. Critical was the role of local counterparts of the visiting team of specialists. This important step in the process fulfilled two functions—providing local technical input and adding to the knowledge transfer and training of local specialists. These valuable preparations enabled the off-island specialists to create initial work plans, plan site visits, identify critical elements for review, and develop cooperative working relationships with local interests. The task force was divided into resource-specific teams for more efficient study: marine resources, forest resources, historical resources, tourism aspects, and community interviews. Surface and underwater inspections were included. Each night the entire task force convened to report on findings.

Findings

The findings can be described in two main categories—land characteristics and current activities and services.

1. Land Characteristics. For descriptive purposes the island was divided into five segments radiating from the center. Lelu, a northeastern segment has a deep harbor, shore road, and forested mountain backdrop. The area is known for several wrecks (ship and airplane) that may have scuba diving potential. A southeastern segment is dominated by mangrove growth, and ocean access is difficult except at the village of Malem. Coastal erosion is evident. The district is known for Japanese artifacts from World War II and the community depends on some local agriculture. A southwestern section is partially open to the sea but most shoreline areas are protected by coral reef. Utwe village, located at the water's edge is sometimes inundated. The embayment at Utwe is biologically very productive. Mangrove islets house several species of seabirds that add to the scenic interest. The entire western shore is characterized by a rural, peaceful atmosphere against the forested mountain backdrop. Two picturesque villages are located there—Walung and Okat. Although some overland trails exist, access is primarily by water. Walung is fronted by a sizeable reef, has extensive fine-grained beaches, and features a beautiful waterfall. Between Walung and Okat, the coast contains reef holes, passes, mangroves, and some of the tallest Sonneratia in Micronesia. The Okat River basin is a spectacular scenic resource. A portion of the Okat Reef has been modified for the airport and harbor facilities. The area is not far from the governmental/commercial centers of Tofol and Lelu. The northern segment is the most windswept and contains the village of Tafunsak. Its location near major transportation facilities favors the development of light industry.

Marine resources consist primarily of sand beaches, scuba diving areas, birdlife, marine animals (e.g., green sea turtles and porpoises), varied fishlife, and coral reefs. The rich and healthy coral reef, seagrass, mangrove and swamp forests may be among the best in Micronesia.

Approximately 63 percent of Kosrea's land area is in forest, once heavily harvested but now generally reforested. These forests add much to the natural beauty, and provide habitat for a variety of wildlife, especially birds. They are important in preventing erosion and improving watershed quality. High rainfall precludes fires. *Agroforests* (cultivated or grazed land within forest and fruit trees) are located in the coastal lowlands.

Kosrae is rich in historic and archeological resources. Ruins of dwellings of the king, high chiefs, burial compounds, and spirit houses are among the most important archeological wonders of the Pacific. The missionary culture of the late 1800s virtually eliminated native customs including dress, dancing, rituals, crafts, and foods.

Each village has its own character but the population demonstrates a strong unified society. Respect for the church, strong allegiance to place, and a sense of finite and fragile homeland resources dominate this society.

There is a general lack of understanding of outside societies and characteristics of tourism except for strong opposition to a Japanese proposal for a large hotel and golf course.

2. Current Activities and Services. In 1990 there were 6 hotels on the island with a total of 34 guest rooms. Only two had food service. There are no international class accommodations. The circumferential road is being paved, but in places the alignment may preclude development. Public island transportation is not available. Air access is costly and infrequent.

Outdoor recreational activities are virtually unavailable, although the potential is great. Visitors must provide their own beach and water use equipment, but there are a few charter boat and dive shops.

Solid waste and sewage disposal are primitive and even now create unsightly pollution problems, especially from the many piggeries and roadside landfills.

Management Concerns

Management of resources is beginning to evolve but the transition from a traditional to a tourism culture faces many obstacles that require critical decisions by the local population. Liaisons are being developed between the Division of Tourism (in the Department of Conservation and Development) and divisions responsible for marine resources, agriculture, forestry, history, and culture.

However, there is no clear mandate to guide tourism development and protect resources. No plan is available that identifies where and how new tourism development should take place. Even the establishment of parks and preserves and their public use are foreign concepts and looked upon with suspicion by the locals.

Recommendations

Needed are new organizational and action plans and processes to deal with all future cultural and economic change, including tourism. Recommended is a districting policy (comparable to zoning) adapted from the International Union of Nature and Natural Resources criteria for protected areas as related to development. It is recommended that five types of districts be used to guide tourism and recreational development in Kosrae (Auyong 1990, 32).

Reserve or Sanctuary. These areas would be managed by policies of resource protection and enhancement but with use restricted to scientific and educational purposes.

Marine Recreational Park. These areas would allow continued subsistence gathering uses and planned recreation, tourism, and educational development. Outstanding, largely unmodified, and highly scenic features are especially important for resource protection measures.

Traditional Use. Local landowners and communities would designate districts important for conservation of specific resources important for living.

Historical/Archeological. These areas would be managed for protection and educational objectives based on thorough investigation of sites and removal of key artifacts to museums.

Commercial/Tourism. Zones would be identified for commercial exploitation of local scenic and recreational resources, maximizing recreational opportunities.

Final recommendations put forward by Auyong (1990, 51) include the following:

1. Kosreans should retain local control over the land itself or its resources.
2. Development should keep pace sustainable by the local people without resort to substantial amounts of external capital, since external capital usually involves some degree of external control.
3. Take positive steps towards visitor-host relations including: retaining friendly relations; providing the type of facilities which guests desire, with an emphasis on quality rather than quantity, and keeping prices as low as possible in order for tourists to feel that they are obtaining value for their expenditures; desirability of having some distinctive community attractions to serve as an identifying characteristic and special attraction.
4. Consider tourism, recreational and scientific activities for protected areas which will generate revenues to offset the removal of consumptive activities.
5. Develop mechanisms by which a portion of the revenues generated by recreational or tourism use of protected areas are returned to the participating landowner and possibly to the management agency.
6. Create buffer zones between major resource use districts such as recreation and forestry, industrial and protected.
7. Develop interagency coordination procedures.

This project demonstrates the many planning issues that local populations of relatively undeveloped islands face in the future. Although the residents here seek economic opportunities for a growing population, they wish to retain the traditional values that are important to them as a society. Interdisciplinary task force investigations such as this can provide an objective perspective and overview that can stimulate local awareness.

Folowing these investigative studies, plans for the future were recommended jointly by the University of Hawaii Sea Grant Program and the Pacific Island Network. These plans became the foundation for local discussion and approval by the governor in 1990. After several drafts, new land use legislation was passed on April 13, 1992 (Katter 1992, 13). The new legislation establishes a Development Review Commission which will prepare a land use plan and permitting process. Provisions also establish a technical advisory committee. The plan will be comprehensive and identify potential sites for conservation as well as development.

As with the study of Moorea, small and fragile resource islands cannot withstand mega-resort development more appropriate elsewhere, but can gradually adapt to markets seeking ecotourism experiences. Future action will depend on the extent that the local leadership and populace make plans and establish firm guidelines for their future, the short and long range.

LOWER RIO GRANDE

A well-studied first phase for a tourism destination plan was prepared for the 200-mile Lower Rio Grande Heritage Corridor (Figure 8-3). The project was developed jointly by public and nonprofit agencies of the United States and Mexico (Sanchez 1989). This phase resulted in the report, *A Shared Experience,* published by the Texas Historical Commission (Sanchez 1991, 5).

The purpose of the project was defined to:

Enhance the existing visitor experience,
Broaden the visitor market to encompass the cultural and heritage tourist,
Contribute to the economic development of the area, and
Enhance regional community pride.

The Historical Commission staff collaborated with business, heritage, and civic organizations on the U.S. side and the Secretariat of Tourism and local community leaders on the Mexican side. The primary focus of this phase was to inventory history, historic sites, and designations, regional architecture, and crafts. It emphasized the cultural continuity between the U.S. and Mexico along the lower Rio Grande from Laredo to Brownsville, Texas.

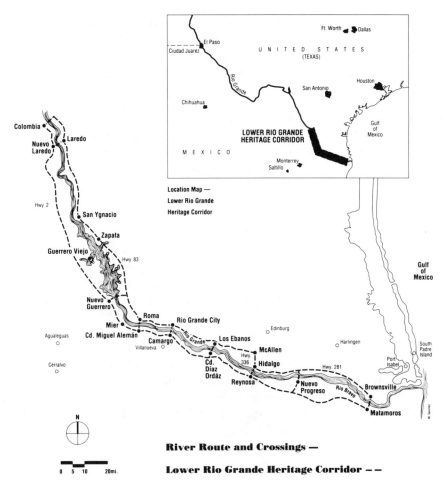

Figure 8-3. Lower Rio Grande Heritage Corridor. This 200-mile corridor along the Mexico-Texas border was analyzed for historic site protection and tourism development potential (Sanchez 1991, 2).

Themes

A major result of this study, forming the foundation for later tourism plans, was the defining of themes. The following summary of these themes illustrate heritage threads common to both sides of the river (Sanchez 1991, 6–8).

Colonial River Settlements. Several archeological remains, structures, and sites have potential for interpretation of the Spanish Colonial enterprise theme. Among these are the San Agustín Historic District of 1767, Old Dolores, Dolores Nuevo, ruins of Guerrero Viejo, Camargo, and the first Escandón settlement.

Ranching. In Zapata county, early ranches were fortified against attack from Apache and Comanche tribes. Several ranch sites could be restored and adapted to visitors, including the Jesús Treviño Fort in San Ygnacio, Rancho San Francisco, and other demonstration ranches.

The River Trade Route Theme. In the mid-19th century, great expectations for navigation focused on the Rio Grande. The riverport Roma and several townsites hold potential for restoration and interpretation. The towns of Camargo and Rio Grande City could be linked with historic river excursions.

Agriculture. An agricultural land boom, especially in citrus production, occurred in the early years of this century. Artifacts of this period could be restored and interpreted to describe this very important time in the river valley's life. An example would be restoration of the Old River Pumphouse at Hidalgo and adjacent land and intake channel.

Military. The Mexican-American War and the U.S. Civil War left their mark on this river corridor. Fort Ringgold in Rio Grande City that features the house where Robert E. Lee resided, could serve as a showcase of the military theme. Other forts include Fort Brown, Fort McIntosh, and Casa Mata Fort. The Palo Alto Battlefield of 1846, Palmito Hill Battlefield of 1865, and the Battlefield of Santa Gertrudis hold promise of further military interpretation for visitor enrichment.

Coordination

Throughout this project and for future phases, nonprofit organizations, permanent project staffs, and technical assistance in both countries are fundamental to its success. The concept of a two-nation visitor destination and heritage corridor dominates all policies and actions.

Closely related are the many recreational opportunities that remain for further development. Birdwatching, visiting native preserves, beach activities, and shopping are yet to be fully developed on both sides of the river. An integral part is the river itself that requires stronger protection and redevelopment controls to assure its quality, especially as a scenic river corridor. Educational opportunities and the stimulation of craft revival also hold promise.

Recommendations

The members of the investigative team derived conclusions and recommendations important to the future accomplishment of the main objectives.

1. Planning. Needed is a master plan for the corridor. This is not only a physical plan but also a plan of techniques and facilities to best interpret the area. The principal desciplines needed to prepare plans include landscape architecture, community and land-use planning, tourism, preservation, historic site management, and transportation.

2. Preservation. Architectural drawings and photographs are needed to document historic protection measures. Endangered landmarks need immediate protection. Oral histories should be documented.

3. Promotion. To foster greater interest and support of the project, a touring bilingual exhibit should be prepared and displayed at museums on both sides of the border.

4. Designations. A program nominating key historic sites and structures should be initiated. Support should be obtained from interested organizations such as the U.S. National Park Service and local historic organizations.

5. International Coordination. All project phases and actions should be coordinated between the two countries, especially to develop a dual-project organization and to explore heritage preservation scenarios.

6. Intergovernmental Coordination. It is recommended that a State/Federal Inter-Agency Task Force be created, paralleling the present Texas State Inter-Agency Task Force. Endorsement by the U.S. Congress would complement the resolution passed by the 72nd Texas Legislature.

This 245-page document by Sanchez with hundreds of photographs and plans is an excellent illustration of the importance of the first step in destination tourism planning—documenting an area's characteristics. This step is not mere tabulation, it is also inspiration because the process of documentation can stimulate ideas and concepts for new development and resource protection.

THE MINERAL WELLS AREA

In 1984, the Mineral Wells (Texas) Chamber of Commerce Tourism Committee wished to discover if it had opportunities for tourism development. The city has an approximate population of 20,000. It is located in Palo Pinto county (with an area of 948 square miles) in north Texas, about 50 miles west of Fort Worth. The Texas Agricultural Extension Service, Recreation and Parks Program, responded by sponsoring a project to study the potential (Gunn et al. 1985). Specialists from Texas A&M University and graduate students performed the study in collaboration with a local liaison committee representing a diversity of local citizenry.

The project process was as follows:

1. Setting goals.
2. Identification of existing markets and resources.
3. Identification of key obstacles to tourism development.
4. Concepts for problem-solving.
5. Recommendations:
   a. Development: downtown, environs, countryside.
   b. Program: activities, information, promotion, research.
   c. Organization and development strategy.

Goals

The goals agreed upon by the planning team and liaison committee were:

1. Increasing economic inpact (jobs, incomes, and taxes paid).
2. Enhancing visitor satisfactions (more things to see and do, and better orientation to visitors).
3. Protecting the basic cultural and natural resources of the city and surrounding area.

Identification of Markets and Resources

Travel *markets* were identified as primarily those coming for business, personal reasons, recreation in area, and passing through. (The study scope did not provide for new market surveys but interviews with motel operators and other business people provided some insight into travel markets.) The area is within 100 miles of 4 million people, and over 15 million live within a day's drive.

Natural resources, such as the wooded hills in and around the city of Mineral Wells, offer an attractive scenic contrast to the dominantly flat ranch land in the surrounding area. The setting provides good wildlife habitat—whitetail deer, turkey, dove, quail, rabbit, and squirrel. The climate is subtropical and subhumid, supporting outdoor recreational activities nearly year round. The area receives about 70 percent of available sunshine. The Brazos River winds through the entire area, providing recreational opportunity as well as landscape beauty.

The *cultural resources* are dominated by historic assets. Several Indian tribes, including Ioni and Comanche, inhabited this area at one time. The settlement era left many scars of Indian conflict and frontier hardship. Hardy and vigilant ranchers and trail drivers, such as Goodnight and Loving, molded here a significant chapter of Texas history. Mineral Wells experienced two growth booms. In the early 1900s, the city became one of the most prominent health spas in the Southwest. Many artifacts of this era remain. The second boom came with establishment of Fort Wolters, that provided the majority of U.S. trained helicopter pilots for three decades. The human resources show initiative, business ability, and an increasing motivation to enhance the economy and quality of life.

Identification of Obstacles

Through several workshop meetings, the liaison committee and planning team identified the following as the key restraints to tourism development:

> Insufficient attractions
> Low level of attractiveness/image
> Low level of public sector involvement
> Insufficient information
> Insufficient promotion
> Lack of research data
> Insufficient organization (Gunn et al. 1985, 15)

Concepts for Problemsolving

Illustrated in Figure 8-4 is a conceptual diagram of six types of development changes needed in and around the city of Mineral Wells. Improvements needed are shown on the diagram for downtown, parks, retirement village, recreation, airport, and highways. Emphasis is placed on new attractions as well as a new parking plaza, new Crystal Canal Park, new miniparks downtown, and new East Mountain Park. Concepts for Palo

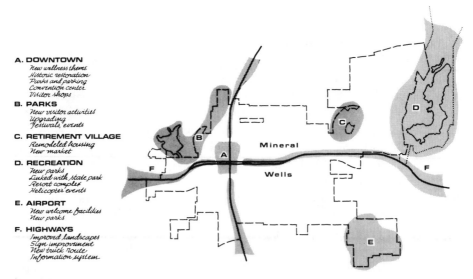

A. **DOWNTOWN**
   New wellness theme
   Historic restoration
   Parks and parking
   Convention center
   Visitor shops

B. **PARKS**
   New visitor activities
   Upgrading
   Festivals, events

C. **RETIREMENT VILLAGE**
   Remodeled housing
   New market

D. **RECREATION**
   New parks
   Linked with state park
   Resort complex
   Helicopter events

E. **AIRPORT**
   New welcome facilities
   New parks

F. **HIGHWAYS**
   Improved landscapes
   Sign improvement
   New truck route
   Information system

Figure 8-4. Tourism Concept Plan, Mineral Wells. Illustrated are six major kinds of new development needed in order to improve tourism potential for the city of Mineral Wells, Texas (Gunn et al. 1985, 25).

Pinto County are illustrated in Figure 8-5. These encompass recommendations for historic, scenic, and recreational attractions.

Together, the planning team and the liaison committee concluded that all seven issues can be solved, allowing considerable expansion of tourism in the destination. The first step recommended was review of all project ideas for their feasibility. This would require study by all three action sectors: commercial enterprise, nonprofit organizations, and government agencies involved in development. The next step would require actual building and managing of specific projects, primarily new and expanded attractions. After these projects are in place, increased visitor demand will stimulate the need for new services—lodging, food service, and travel services. This step, in turn, would increase expenditures in the local area, providing greater tax input, more employment, and greater social as well as economic impact. The increase in amenities will also enhance the local quality of life for residents.

A major concept derived from the study is adoption of the *theme*, Wellness Capital of Texas. The great increase in market demand for health, fitness, outdoor recreation, and personal enrichment could be matched with supply development to support this theme. There are ample foundations for this locally because of its one-time prominence as a health spa. The natural resources of the surrounding area as well, such as the Brazos River, hills, wooded areas, and wildlife, provide abundant support for developing this theme.

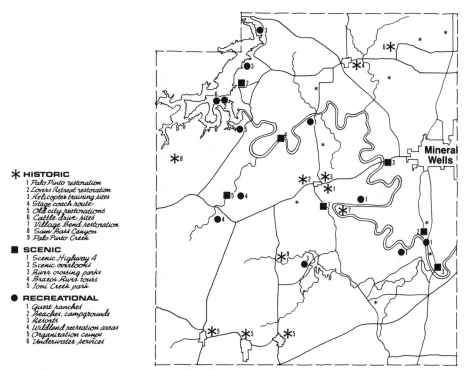

HISTORIC
1 Palo Pinto restoration
2 Lovers Retreat restoration
3 Helicopter training sites
4 Stage coach route
5 Old city restorations
6 Cattle drive sites
7 Village Bend restoration
8 Sam Bass Canyon
9 Palo Pinto Creek

SCENIC
1 Scenic Highway 4
2 Scenic overlooks
3 River crossing parks
4 Brazos River tours
5 Joni Creek park

RECREATIONAL
1 Guest ranches
2 Beaches, campgrounds
3 Resorts
4 Wildland recreation areas
5 Organization camps
6 Underwater services

Figure 8-5. Tourism Concepts for Palo Pinto County. Mineral Wells is the principal city in Palo Pinto County. Illustrated are the kinds and locations of new attraction opportunities in the county and in three categories: historic, scenic, and recreational (Gunn 1985, 28).

Downtown redevelopment is needed to overcome the stark, bland, and uninteresting appearance. Restoration of old bathhouses, reorienting downtown businesses to travel trade, and addition of sidewalk cafes and arts and crafts shops would enhance the downtown for tourism. Equally important is the creation of miniparks and addition of landscape materials in all open spaces downtown. An improved and landscaped parking area to the rear of downtown shops could multiply parking availability and increase attractiveness. Proposed redevelopment is shown in Figure 8-6.

The remainder of the *city environs* require removal of the sign clutter along main streets, new tree planting, conversion of Fort Wolters into a retirement village, and renovation and improved maintenance of parks. Plant tours, festivals, and outdoor theater productions should be considered.

Surrounding area improvements are needed. Outdoor recreation services radiating from Mineral Wells as well as land and water based activities should be added: camping, fishing, hunting, boating, hiking, canoeing, and passive outdoor recreation. Restoration of rural small towns, such as Palo Pinto, could stimulate historic tours. Highway scenic

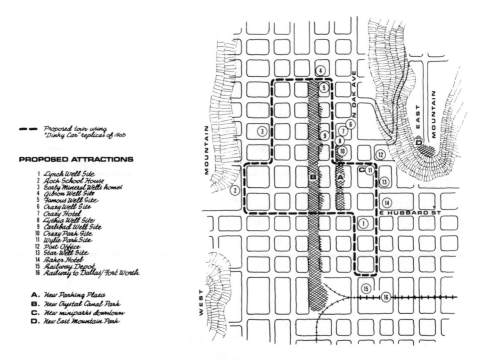

— — Proposed tour using
      "Dinky Car" replicas of 1905

PROPOSED ATTRACTIONS

1 Lynch Well Site
2 Rock School House
3 Early Mineral Wells homes
4 Gibson Well Site
5 Famous Well Site
6 Crazy Well Site
7 Crazy Hotel
8 Lythia Well Site
9 Carlsbad Well Site
10 Crazy Park Site
11 Wylie Park Site
12 Post Office
13 Star Well Site
14 Baker Hotel
15 Railway Depot
16 Railway to Dallas/Fort Worth

A. New Parking Plaza
B. New Crystal Canal Park
C. New miniparks downtown
D. New East Mountain Park

Figure 8-6. Potential Development, Mineral Wells. Shown are 16 recommended attractions and four new park areas for the downtown area of the city. A replica of a minibus of 1905 could provide a tour of all major historic sites (Gunn et al. 1985, 26).

easements are needed. Ranch resorts and expanded development of Possum Kingdom Lake and Lake Mineral Wells could aid tourism.

Several concepts for *program development* resulted from the study. New entertainment, reunions of former helicopter pilots, horse shows, and historic tours could be added. Lack of local awareness of tourism needs to be countered with informational clinics. The quality and quantity of informational literature for visitor use should be improved. Increased promotion should be emphasized only after all other improvements have been made. A research program to regularly monitor economic impact and provide statistics in tourism should be established.

Recommendations

Three major categories of recommendations were derived from the study: development, program, and organization. Emphasis was placed on the responsibility of the local community through its politicians, sector developers, and tourism leaders to make the changes needed for increased tourism.

For *development*, thirty-six recommendations were made:

1. Establish theme of Wellness Capital of Texas.
2. Provide greater landscaped parking space downtown.
3. Restore original historic Lynch Well site.
4. Restore historic buildings: Baker Hotel, Crazy Water Hotel, depot, post office, bath houses, Fannin School, Rock School.
5. Establish new truck routes around downtown.
6. Add miniparks downtown.
7. Add visitor-oriented shops downtown.
8. Add new wellness craft and art shops.
9. Convert Fort Wolters to retirement village.
10. Add recreational complex in Fort Wolters.
11. Increase quality of park maintenance.
12. Revitalize the clean-up, paint-up programs.
13. Establish sign control.
14. Landscape entrance highways.
15. Establish tree and shrub planting program.
16. Promote film production in this locale.
17. Add new convention center.
18. Improve hospitality services at airport.
19. Add outdoor theaters and dramas.
20. Establish wellness theme throughout area.
21. Establish new guest ranches.
22. Develop and control Highway 4 as scenic route.
23. Establish new beaches, campgrounds at Possum Kingdom Lake.
24. Provide public scenic lookouts on highways.
25. Protect and develop Brazos River for recreation.
26. Restore Palo Pinto.
27. Establish year-round resorts.
28. Redevelop "Lover's Retreat" into public park.
29. Establish esthetic easements along highways.
30. Redevelop Indian, settlement, stagecoach sites for tours.
31. Develop natural resource parks for visitors.
32. Establish new youth organization camps.
33. Add new marinas and tourism facilities at Possum Kingdom Lake.
34. Establish scuba diving, and dive shops.
35. Redevelop old towns—Mingus, Strawn, Gordon, Thurber, Brazos—for historic tours.
36. Develop creek valleys for nature tours.

For *program activities*, the following 13 items were recommended:

1. Establish new festivals based on the wellness theme.
2. Expand and improve the Crazy Water festival.
3. Use the Texas Sesquecentennial as focus for new activities.
4. Add new rodeos, horse shows, racing events.
5. Package and promote historic tours.
6. Add evening entertainment—wellness theme.
7. Add new water tours, cruises on the Brazos River.
8. Hold reunions of former helicopter pilots.
9. Establish new health spa pageants and plays.
10. Open industries to plant tours.
11. Develop loop scenic tours from Mineral Wells.
12. Package historic rural town tours.
13. Package nature tours.

For *program information*, these recommendations were offered:

1. New attraction and tour maps be prepared.
2. New brochures, videos, guidebooks be prepared.
3. Hold public educational seminars on tourism.
4. Introduce tourism talks to school system.
5. Prepare literature on destination zone basis.
6. Hold hospitality training program.
7. Place new electronic information equipment.
8. Offer novels and writings about area for sale.

For *program promotion*, the following seven recommendations were made:

1. Establish a Mineral Wells Area Tourism Council.
2. Create a new promotional plan to include advertising, publicity, public relations and incentives.
3. Increase the budget for promotion.
4. Identify specific target markets for promotion.
5. Create special promotion for each segment.
6. Emphasize unique qualities of destination in all promotion.
7. Promote new attractions as they are added.

For *program research*, the following six recommendations were offered:

1. Annual inventories of supply side be made.
2. Study market sources for interests.

3. Study results of hospitality program.
4. Investigate need for revision of laws and regulations pertaining to tourism.
5. Study and report economic impact of tourism.
6. Make conversion studies of promotion.

In addition, the following recommendations for *organizations* and *strategy* were made. It is recommended that a Mineral Wells Area Tourism Council, under the aegis of the Mineral Wells Convention and Visitors Bureau be established with these three main functions: (1) development, (2) program, (3) operations.

The strategy would include:

Visit comparable destinations elsewhere.
Review of pertinent literature.
Participate in state professional tourism conferences.
Engage professional assistance when needed.
Assist in removing obstacles to tourism development.
Contact potential developers.
Develop feasibility studies with developers.
Foster implementation of recommendations.
Maintain close cooperation among all stakeholders.

Because all recommendations could not be implemented at once, priority was given to key projects in the first phase:

Wellness theme	Recreation complex
Parking space	Improved park upkeep
Lynch Well Park	Cleanup program
Historic building restoration	New guest ranches
Retirement Village feasibility	Scenic highway plans
	Possum Kingdom beaches, parks, marinas

Later phases would address the remaining balance of recommendations.

This project was begun with the creation of a local liaison committee charged with the responsibility of assisting in study of the area, making input as the project progressed, reacting to concepts and recommendations of the consultant team, and implementing action. It was emphasized at the start that the project report would provide the local people with vision of their potential but that all action was their responsibility.

Seven years after issuing the report, a review of the extent of implementation to date was made by means of interview (Cunningham 1992).

Progress had taken place but had been hampered by several leadership and organizational events. Just as the report was completed, the key local leader, director of the chamber of commerce, resigned his post and left. In the interim, several changes in city administration have occurred. The breach between city and county officials has widened, further limiting cooperation and joint development between the city and surrounding area. The city was accepted as a Main Street city within the state program of Texas but faltered after four years, suggesting that the economy and political support had weakened. For the first time in many years, a major civic improvement bond issue was passed, eventually helping tourism but diverting public attention for a time.

In spite of these obstacles, several improvements have been started or completed over the seven years since the plan was initiated (Cunningham 1992 and Midkiff 1992).

> The Palo Pinto Historical Foundation has been formed and has taken an active role in restoration of the Famous Water Company, the Depot, public use of the Crazy Water Hotel, some progress on historic highways, renovation and tours of Lover's Retreat.
> New Visitor Center has been built.
> Keep Mineral Wells Beautiful organization has become active; fostered a new park downtown; new plantings; new sign ordinance; enhanced the entrance highway right-of-way and median; landscaped a downtown canal; developed new recreational complex near the high school; and fostered a county science tour.
> A marker has been placed at Lynch Well site.
> Fort Wolter Recreation Building now houses many conferences.
> Clean-up, paint-up program has expanded—now semi-annual.
> Mineral Wells State Park has expanded its recreational activities and programs.
> An ostrich farm has been established—open to public.
> Scuba diving in Possom Kingdom Lake has increased.
> A new rodeo arena has opened.
> Reunions of members of the Vietnam Helicopter Association are held regularly.
> New maps and informative literature have been prepared and distributed.

This destination project demonstrates the value of planning collaboration between university tourism specialists and local people. Within a year's time and at comparatively low cost, many worthwhile recommendations evolved from joint study and analysis. This project also shows how political changes and economic slowdown can delay implementation of needed strategies and projects. Even so, the project provided local enlightenment on tourism development and stimulated new interest in planning for tourism.

GONZALES

The Gonzales Area Development Corporation requested a study of the tourism potential of the community of Gonzales, Texas, and surrounding area in 1982. The city of Gonzales has a population of approximately 7,000, is the county seat of Gonzales County in south central Texas, and is 1,056 square miles in size. The study was completed by tourism specialists of Texas A&M University and reported in *Gonzales Tourism-Park Opportunities, Part I and II* (Gunn et al. 1983). A local liaison team worked with the specialists in setting objectives and carrying out the project. It was agreed that the project would examine the factors for potential and make recommendations for action. However, it was understood that it was the responsibility of all tourism sectors to make their own feasibility analysis and to follow up with development.

The study steps included:

1. Research
2. Synthesis of Research/Themes
3. Tourism Potential/Concepts
4. Staging of Implementation
5. Final Recommendations

Research

Several factors of the existing situation were studied by means of review of literature and maps, reconnaissance of the area, and workshop meetings with the liaison team.

Present Attractions. Several attractions were already developed: a partially restored jail, county museum, self-guided tour of 40 historic homes, festivals, Texas Revolution sites, state park, a major community park, and a dog racetrack.

Markets. Commercial travelers dominated visitor trade with a smaller number of pleasure travelers coming for festivals, mainly from Texas cities within 200 miles.

Physical Factors. The Guadalupe and San Marcos Rivers and a few small reservoirs make up the water resources. Many wooded areas follow creek and river bottoms and an unusual ecological mixture of plants is located in Palmetto State Park. Wildflowers are especially attractive in spring. Game and nongame wildlife can be found in the surrounding area. The climate is well suited to year-round outdoor recreation. The topography is generally flat to rolling. An abundant and rich resource is the historic background, especially the significance the area played in early Texas history: the first battle of the Texas Revolution; patriot sites; Chisholm Trail; Confederate fort; and Spanish layout of the city plan. Indian tribes (Comanche, Karankaway, Tonkaway, Waco, Keechi, and Towakawa) once occupied the area. The ranch landscape is attractive and fitting. Economic development is dominantly based on petroleum production, agriculture, ranching, a few small manufacturing plants, and a rehabilitation hospital. Services included one hotel, three motels, camping area, 30 restaurants, service stations, and shops. Transportation access is by highway.

Program Factors. Most travel promotion is carried on by the Gonzales Chamber of Commerce from motel tax funds. A few pieces of literature are available. Directional signage on highways assist the traveler. The community generally is apathetic regarding tourism.

Synthesis of Research/Themes

Study of these findings resulted in the conclusion that tourism development should be carried out within three main themes. *History* is a dominant theme centered on the area's role in the Texas Revolution. Victorian mansions, the Spanish imprint, ethnic heritage, and Civil War events add to this historic background. *Recreation/Resort* potential is a second theme based on the natural resource base for outdoor recreation. *Trade* will continue to be a strong theme because of agribusiness, health services, business center, and industrial park.

Tourism Potential/Concepts

From the research and synthesis steps, several opportunities for future development were identified. First, these were grouped according to the three themes—history, recreation/resorts, and trade. Opportunities were identified for the city of Gonzales and throughout the surrounding area to complete the concept of destination.

Key elements of potential in the *area* are illustrated in Figure 8-7. Along main routes, entrance signage and vernacular landscape treatment would give the visitor a desirable introduction to the destination. Historic auto

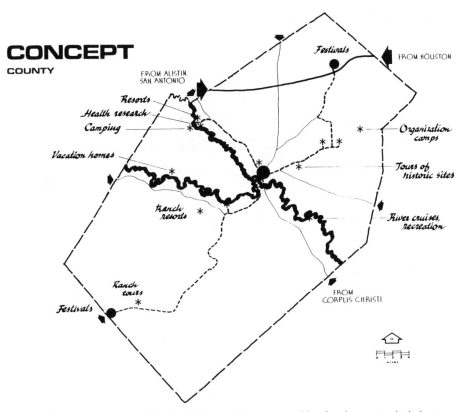

Figure 8-7. Gonzales County Tourism Concept. Key opportunities for the county include tours, festivals, vacation homes, organization camps, trails, waterways, and ranch tours. The Guadalupe and San Marcos Rivers offer interesting outdoor recreation and historic redevelopment opportunities (Gunn et al. 1983, 18).

and motor coach tours would be suitable after the historic sites were developed and managed for visitors. New festivals could be established based on the rural foundations of agriculture, ethnicity, and history of settlement. Ranch resorts are in demand and would be highly appropriate in this area. These could range in type from working ranches to completely contrived ranchlike settings offering appropriate foods, lodging, and entertainment. Vacation home projects should be investigated for their feasibility. Organization camps (Scout, church, and adult) are well suited to the setting and resources. Campground development for both transient and longer-stay guests has potential here. The area is well suited to the establishment of rural resource trails for hiking, bicycling, and horseback riding. Waterway trails, capturing not only the scenic beauty of the valleys but also the important roles in early history, could offer rewarding experiences for visitors. Ranch tours that offer interpretation of the diversity

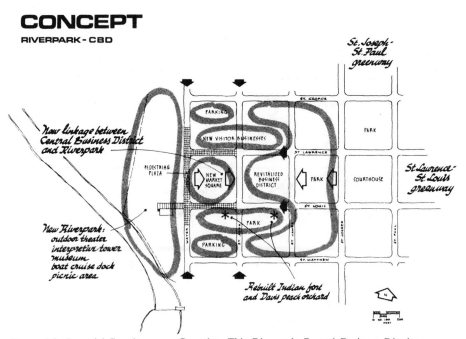

Figure 8-8. Potential Development, Gonzales. This Riverpark Central Business District concept focuses on new pedestrian and park linkage between downtown and the Guadalupe River. It also features revitalizing downtown business for travel markets (Gunn et al. 1983, 28).

of land use and management practices have potential here. The health theme, springing from the rehabilitation hospital, has great potential.

For the *city* of Gonzales, a great amount of potential became evident. Before adequate visitor use could be made the traffic issue, especially for major trucking, would need to be resolved. Recommended is a new truck route around the city, encouraging new facilities and services along this bypass. This would avoid the noise and accident potential downtown, provide needed new services for visitors, and preserve the theme and esthetics of the historic district.

Figure 8-8 illustrates a concept for redevelopment of the city that would stimulate visitor use and demand for shops, as well as add to the quality of amenities for local residents. Key elements are an expanded central business district, and new visitor-oriented businesses, market square, park-historic development, greenways, and river park.

The centerpiece of this concept is a Riverpark Central Business District development. It would be approached from the east and north by the two greenways. Much of the redevelopment west of the courthouse would be based on the original Spanish city layout including a new market square on the original site. Perimeter parking would allow conversion of this core to a pedestrian mall leading to a park between the Guadalupe River and

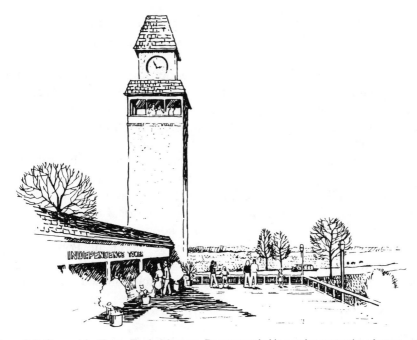

Figure 8-9. Concept for Tower, Deck, Museum. Recommended is a major centerpiece feature—tower, deck, and museum—to enhance historic and scenic linkage between the existing downtown center and the Guadalupe River (Gunn et al. 1983, 31).

the CBD. Features of the park would include an outdoor theater, museum, boat cruise dock, picnic areas, and an interpretive tower as a major feature. This tower (Figure 8-9), deck and interpretive museum would offer a visual and functional expression of the important role of Gonzales in history.

Staging of Implementation

Meetings and discussions identified priorities to the several recommended improvements in tourism. The first step should:

> Stimulate local and area-wide interest in tourism,
> Protect special heritage and resource assets,
> Arouse curiosity and interest among travel markets, and
> Stimulate activity and interest in renovating downtown. (Gunn et al. 1983, viii)

Actions were recommended for six stages of development. Actions involving larger capital investment are scheduled later, and the immediate action would stress getting ready with proper leadership and organization.

The next phase would offer great visibility at relatively low cost. Following these, the remaining phases should have greater support and guidance for accomplishment.

Although this project was developed cooperatively between university specialists and a local liaison team, implementation has faltered. The university input terminated upon completion of the report and final presentation. The liason team disbanded at the same time, removing local leadership and commitment for the recommended program of action. The study, however, will remain valid for several years and may be utilized by future groups as they assume new leadership for tourism development.

Follow-up in 1992 (Hand) identified both constraints and progress. A general oil production recession has slowed the local economy and the ability to finance projects. Highway officials continue to support expansion of a route that is incompatible with tourism development. Political cooperation on tourism between the city and county has not taken place. However, the following have been implemented following the project report:

- Historic and wildflower tours have been improved.
- A viable and representative Tourism Committee has been formed and is active.
- Hotel/motel tax has been raised from 2 percent to 5 percent, providing some additional funds for tourism.
- The city has been established as a "Main Street City" and is taking action on their recommendations.
- Major improvements have been made to the Independence Park, including a new RV park.
- Pioneer Village now includes 11 historic buildings and attracts thousands of visitors.
- Many downtown shops have been refurbished and now cater to visitors as well as local needs.
- Festivals and events have been expanded.

CHUN-CHEON RESORT AREA

An example of destination planning is the case of the Chun-Cheon resort area, located 100 kilometers northeast of Seoul, Korea. At the request of the Korean Transportation Institute (KOTI), a consultant team was formed at Texas A&M University to evaluate existing plans and develop a revised plan concept. The team was led by Turgut Var, Texas Tourism

Research and Information Program, and reported in *Chun-Cheon Plan 2001* (Var et al. 1991).

Evaluation of Existing Plan

KOTI had prepared a rough tourism development plan. Review indicated that it was superior to previous plans, identified new attraction clusters on the islands including a natural history museum, an aquaplanting garden, youth camping, a folk village, and recreational facilities. However, the plan included building high-density resorts on the islands, requiring costly new infrastructure (water supply, waste disposal, police, and fire protection) difficult to provide and maintain on the islands. These resorts would likely produce sewage pollution, present difficult access problems, erode esthetic appeal, and would not be economically feasible.

Recommended Plans

The consultant team visited the area, interviewed key parties, and studied pertinent documents. From this, several recommendations were made based on the assets of the area (Figure 8-10). Their plan illustrates the concept of considering not only the islands but the entire Chun-Cheon area as a destination zone. Such a concept incorporates the surrounding mountain region as well.

The plan concept puts island development into the context of overall destination. Instead of placing high density resort development on the islands where it would be difficult to develop and service, it is recommended that it be established on the mainland adjacent to the city. The islands would be developed with day-use activities at developed attractions that are indigenous to the area. The opposite mountainside should be placed into national park status with properly designed public access appropriate to the resources.

A summary of the recommendations for seven site areas within this overall destination zone follows.

1. Sangjundo Islands. These two islands, separated by a canal, are well adapted to a park area, fishing sites, reception village (vernacular architecture, shops, and food services), craft center, and small scale tourist services.

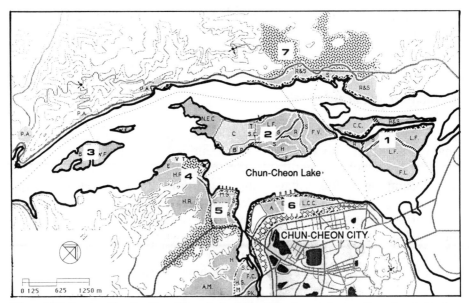

Figure 8-10. Tourism Plan for Chun-Cheon Lake Area. This plan emphasizes the entire destination zone including seven major attraction clusters: 1, Sangjundo Islands; 2, Hajungdo Area; 3, Bangeseom Area; 4, Samcheondong Area; 5, Toegye-Dong/Onui-Dong Area; 6, Train Station Attraction Cluster; and 7, West Shore Development Area (Var 1991, 15).

2. Hajungdo Area. Tourist activities on this major island could be expanded beyond the existing campground. Several attractions could be linked together by walkways, trains, bicycle trails, and horse-drawn carriages. Included would be a nature center complex (aquaplanting garden, nature preserve, interpretive center, trails, observation tower, and museum), outdoor theater, living farm museum, folk village (vernacular architecture, cultural foods, and crafts), historic museums, fishing village museum, fishing village restoration, boating clubhouse, specialty stores, and natatorium recreation center.

3. Bangeseom Area. Because of its low elevation and special natural resources, this island would be maintained as a nature interpretive area. Included would be a botanical garden, major nature interpretive center, boardwalk trails, observation tower, new food shops, and a ferry landing.

4. Samcheondong Area. This area southwest of Chun-Cheon city already contains the Velodrome, riding track, Memorial Hall, Children's Hall, and some resort development. Recommended attractions are a hillside resort complex, equestrian center, vista overlook parks, resort village complex, harbor, and shoreline promenade with walks and rest stops.

5. *Toegye-Dong/Onui-Dong Area*. Just east of the Samcheondong area, there is potential for an amusement theme park, new hotel cluster, new health spa and fitness center, and easy access by rail and highway.

6. *Train Station Attraction Cluster*. Located near the central business district and adjacent to rail and highway access is a site with the following potential: new gateway train station, lakeside convention center, exhibition conference center, educational conference center, fitness and aquarium area, shopping and entertainment, food services, and new marina and yacht service area.

7. *West Shore Development Area*. A dominant scenic resource is the mountainside across the lake from the city. This natural feature should be incorporated into the overall destination zone complex. Probably the best design and management policy would be to place it under national park status. Recommended are mountain scenic drives, overlook and rest stops, major nature interpretive center, children's play areas at service centers, boardwalks along the lakeshore, service business expansion at connection points with scenic drives, and ferry landings.

Planning Principles

In order to be of greatest assistance to KOTI, some basic principles were recommended to be applied to the physical concepts. These included:

Accommodations should be suited to the travel market mix.
All waterside development should be integrated into the natural landscape setting.
A "village square" concept can foster host-guest relations.
Parking should not intrude upon lakefront; multi-level structures may be needed.
Landscape attractiveness must be protected and enhanced at all water and land entrance points.
Pedestrian circulation must be properly planned.
All development must protect the water quality of the lake.
Public-private cooperation and collaboration holds promise of best support for development.
Properly planned, this area has potential of becoming a major tourism destination area for both domestic and international travel markets.

When the public and private developers begin action, they have a blueprint for directions that their tourism development might take in order to attract and satisfy more domestic and international travelers.

ALLEGHENY RIDGE HERITAGE PARK

An example of a planned tourism destination based on historical foundations is the Allegheny Ridge Heritage Park, an area of nine counties in southwestern Pennsylvania. It includes two major service communities, Altoona and Johnstown. This complex project involves many jurisdictions, businesses, and varied populations within a 50-mile broad corridor. Nearly 200 years of transportation and development have laid down a special set of cultural characteristics now deemed worthy of redevelopment as a tourism destination.

Background

In 1985 (Reconnaissance Survey) the U.S. National Park Service (NPS), as part of its historic preservation mission, performed a study along the Allegheny Ridge with these objectives:

> Identification of areas of national and/or state significance;
> Evaluation of the significance and feasibility of recognizing possible sites, scenic trails, or parkways;
> Presentation of alternatives to preserve and interpret significant resources in the most effective manner;
> Preparation of preliminary cost estimates for any necessary development, preservation, and interpretation of resources to fulfill the congressional mandate. (Reconnaissance Survey 1985, 3)

The area includes portions of two physiographic provinces of the United States—the Valley and Ridge province and the Appalachian Plateaus province with the area between, the Allegheny Front. It is characterized by low, open, sandstone-quartzite mountains. Over half of the land is vacant, with the remainder in recreation, residential, transportation, mining, industrial, and manufacturing land uses. The principal cities of Altoona and Johnstown have a total population of approximately 92,000, with the remaining portion of the region dominantly rural and small towns. A main highway threads through the center of the region in a northeasterly-southwesterly direction, connecting with the Pennsylvania Turnpike to the south.

Resources

The NPS study documented both natural and cultural resources.

Natural resources are abundant. Although the area was originally heavily forested, much timber was cleared for agriculture and charcoal for use in iron furnaces. Major rivers were once used to complete transportation between Philadelphia and Pittsburgh. Iron and coal underlie most of the area.

Cultural resources span several eras from original native populations to modern times. The area is laced with many Indian trails and early roads resulting from armed conflict between French and British claims. Many fortifications were constructed along these routes. In the early 1800s the demand for cheaper transportation fostered the creation of several canals. The Pennsylvania Railroad concentrated its manufacturing in Altoona. With better transportation, a major iron industry developed. Heavy industry, including the Bethlehem Steel Corporation of Johnstown, flourished for several decades.

Already, these natural and cultural resources, even though only partially developed, attract many visitors to the region who are seeking active outdoor recreation as well as observation of the interesting historical past.

Planning Progress

Based on the 1985 survey and initiative of preservation and tourism promoters, Congressional action in 1988 authorized the U.S. Department of Interior to establish a Southwestern Heritage Preservation Commission (Public Law 100-698). The main charge given the commission was to coordinate public and private sector action to foster historic preservation, education, public appreciation, and enjoyment. A result of the commission's action was the creation of the *Action Plan—America's Industrial Heritage Project* (1987).

The Commission was organized into four committees: Cultural Resources Committee, Tourism and Marketing Committee, Economic Development Committee, and Transportation Committee. Each committee developed action and implementation strategies. In addition, specific projects having potential in the area were identified. An important part of the Commission's mandate was the charge to

> . . . devise creative ways to protect, interpret, and manage those resources through a *cooperative partnership*. This partnership . . . requires the efforts and resources of local, regional, state, and federal agencies, the private sector, and, most important, the residents of the region to combine promotion and preservation of the region's cultural and natural resources. (Comprehensive Management Plan 1992, 14)

This charge then was translated into a vision statement:

> To celebrate and conserve the cultural heritage of the region, vigorously promote high-quality visitor experiences, and provide regional economic revitalization and opportunities to maintain the quality of life for residents by telling the story of America's industrial heritage and the people who have lived and are living in it. (Comprehensive Management Plan 1992, 17)

Further refinement came in 1989–1990 when the State Legislature of Pennsylvania established the Pennsylvania State Heritage Parks Program. This program, administered by the Department of Community Affairs, has the primary goals of encouraging economic development, intergovernmental cooperation, cultural conservation, recreation, and education (Plan for Allegheny Ridge 1992). An Allegheny Ridge Industrial Heritage Corridor Task Force was created, and with combined support and planning cooperation between the commission and the State Heritage Parks Program, produced a *Plan for the Allegheny Ridge* (1992). The plan contains four major parts: the vision, the park, implementation, and recommendations. Paralleling this effort was the production of a marketing plan (Davidson-Peterson Associates 1992) and a visitor behavior profile (Gitelson et al. 1992).

The Planning Process

The Task Force identified five goals as their overall aims (Plan for Allegheny Ridge 1992, 15): cultural conservation, education and interpretation, recreation, economic development, and intergovernmental and interagency cooperation.

The decision was made to create a nonprofit entity, the Allegheny Ridge Corporation (ARCORP) to manage the project. It was established to secure, organize, and market the cultural resources; develop the natural assets; work with local citizens; establish the infrastructure needed; and become financially independent.

From the beginning of the task force in 1990, the process of planning has been interactive, involving citizens, public agencies, cultural institutions, and business interests. Several subcommittees were formed to hold workshops, open houses, and planning meetings.

Early in the process, it was determined that the park should include representation of the key cultural and natural resource stories. By 1991, alternative approaches were considered:

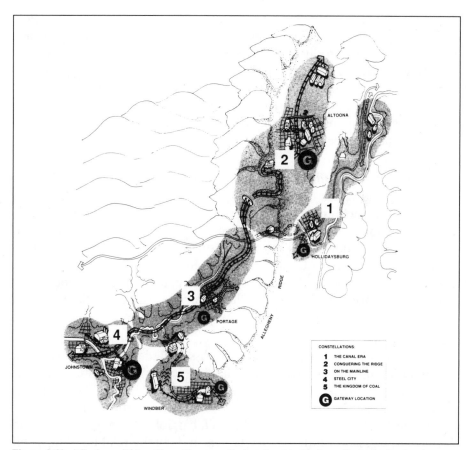

Figure 8-11. Allegheny Ridge Plan. The overall plan for this Heritage Park destination between Altoona and Johnstown includes five constellations: 1, The Canal Era; 2, Conquering the Ridge; 3, Along the Main Line; 4, Steel City; and 5, The Kingdom of Coal. Also shown are gateway locations (Plan 1992, 25).

The cultural axis approach—focus on major communities.
Dispersed sites approach—small scale interpretive locations.
A constellation approach—thematic units.

(Plan for Allegheny Ridge 1992, 15, 16)

The Plan

The final decision was to use the constellation approach which identified five constellations, each representing a different cultural landscape shaped by different forces and circumstances. The five constellations are illustrated in Figure 8-11.

1. The Canal Era (1810s onward). Anticipated is a cluster of attractions focused on the Historic Canal Theme with Hollidaysburg functioning as a gateway offering introduction by means of an interpretive visitor center. Planning would include early trails and settlements; rejuvenation of historic places in downtown Hollidaysburg; preservation of the basin area; retention of tow path along the canal; restoration of the canal town of Williamsburg; expansion of Canoe Creek State Park; and restoration of the Mt. Etna furnace site.

2. Conquering the Ridge (1830s onward). This natural barrier 1,200 feet above the headwaters of the Juniata River played an important part in heroic railroad technology, civil engineering, and urban development. Featured attraction development would include former Pennsylvania Railroad shop complexes; downtown Altoona historic form; old town restoration; Railroaders Memorial Museum; Baker mansion and nearby furnace; the Ridge landscape and landform; engineering features of Horseshoe Curve/National Historic Landmark/Allegheny Portage Railroad National Historic Site; and Gallitzin Tunnels.

3. Along the Mainline (1850s onward). Associated with the Pennsylvania Railroad Main Line and its cultural landscape, this theme would feature several attractions: Portage Railroad and route; Mineral Point (recreational potential); Portage restoration; St. Michael National Historic District (South Fork hunting and fishing club); Johnstown Flood National Memorial; Cresson (20th century homes and commercial buildings); hill towns of South Fork, Wilmore, Ehrenfeld, Cassandra, Summerhill, and Lilly; and small hotels of the period.

4. Steel City (1870s onward). This attraction cluster encompasses Johnstown and the nearby communities of Westmont, Franklin, and East Conemaugh. Planned attractions include downtown Johnstown, as a planned community; restoration and interpretation of Cambria City/Minersville; Cambria Iron Lower Works (a national historic site); Conemaugh Basin and Gautier plant; East Conemaugh/Franklin and Franklin Plant; Westmont/Incline; Johnstown Flood Museum; riverfronts and bridges.

5. The Kingdom of Coal (1890s onward). This theme would be expressed by organizing a cluster of attractions including Windber Center/Miners Park; Windber/Graham Avenue; Paint Center; Scalp Level/Mine 40; Scalp Level/Miners Housing; Boney Piles (residue of decades of subsurface extraction); and rail lines that shaped the pattern of development.

Other Guidelines

Included in the plan are several guideline recommendations. *Site development* guidelines include concepts for functional and developmental features of constellation gateways, heritage discovery centers, and satellite sites. *Linkage* recommendations include design and planning to foster visitor access and interrelationships among the attraction clusters of the entire destination. Included in this are concepts for regional linkages, constellation linkages, and setting linkages. *Interpretation and education*, as important functions throughout, are described. These guidelines cover education at all levels, vocational training, research and documentation, exhibits, interpretive programs, excursions and tours, and special events.

Allegheny Ridge Corporation

A very important aspect of this destination plan was recognition of the need for a central management body because of the great number of jurisdictions and constituencies involved in the entire area. Its stated mission includes (Plan for Allegheny Ridge 1992, 74, 75):

> Ensure successful development of the Park and its principal features as specified in the Allegheny Ridge Plan; to undertake further planning and design as necessary to achieve this objective.
>
> Ensure the preservation of the region's historical and cultural resources.
>
> Manage and operate park facilities, where appropriate.
>
> Coordinate and support the activities of the Corporation Partners and the operation of industrial heritage and cultural tourism attractions in the region so as to create a unified project.
>
> Market the Heritage Park and its component constellations and resources as a destination for international, national, and regional visitors.
>
> Provide standards and technical assistance for the design and development of physical sites and educational and interpretive programs associated with the regional cultural heritage efforts.
>
> Lead the efforts to educate the public, including visitors to the region as well as local residents, about the significance of these resources and the heritage of the Ridge.
>
> Promote local and regional development of recreational opportunities, linkages, and facilities.
>
> Seek funding from local, state, and federal agencies and private foundations and corporations.
>
> Create public/private funding packages to finance projects and initiatives
>
> Accomplish the above in a way which will promote economic development of the region and its cities and towns.
>
> Ensure intergovernmental and interagency cooperation in the achievement of these objectives.

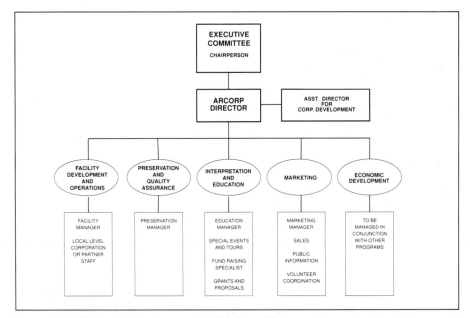

Figure 8-12. Allegheny Ridge Corporation. This figure illustrates the organization of the nonprofit governing body, the Allegheny Ridge Corporation, for managing this destination complex (Plan for Allegheny Ridge 1992, 77).

Organization of ARCORP is illustrated in Figure 8-12 (Plan for Allegheny Ridge 1992, 78).

Because of the recent nature of these plans, implementation of new development remains in the future. But, the strength of this destination approach lies in the high degree of participation among the many jurisdictions and constituency groups. The evolution of this project demonstrates the value of a lead group—here, the U.S. National Park Service—initiating action and interest with an analysis of the resource base and then serving as catalyst for further action. Typical of most destinations, it was necessary to integrate existing development and future plans of many decisionmakers into a common goal.

ST. MARIES, IDAHO

An example of planning guidance for a rural/small town destination zone was prepared under the leadership of university specialists (Harris et al. 1989). The process used was one of collaboration between representatives of the local economic development corporation with those interested in tourism and three members of the staff of the Department of Wildland Recreation Management, University of Idaho.

This destination consists of an area adjacent to the well-established Coeur d'Alene resort area. It includes the town of St. Maries (population 5,000), a small logging and mill town located at the south end of Lake Coeur d'Alene and surrounding outdoor recreation areas of Heyburn State Park, nearby national forest lands, and the St. Joe River.

The first step in the planning process was to give the local people the *Idaho Rural Tourism Primer: A Tourism Assessment Workbook* (Rundell et al. 1989). The second step was a workshop meeting with the local economic development corporation and others interested in tourism. Participants were supplied a profile of existing travel markets and asked what role they would want tourism to play in the next decade. They were to focus on servicing the through and day use travelers, overnight needs, and major and minor attractions. This workshop resulted in a description of the existing tourism situation, a desired future tourism scenario and a list of projects necessary to accomplish the future scenario.

Following is a description of specific projects developed at the workshop, Desired Future Scenario—1999.

> Clean up town.
> Restore town as a river city through building renovation and uniformity in architecture, especially Kootenai River Inn (historic preservation district).
> Interpret and promote the St. Joe River's uniqueness and its role in the town and area.
> Develop a tram for backwoods skiing up Mount Bald.
> Develop a system of groomed snowmobiling trails (tied into Shoshone system) and cross-country ski facilities that could perhaps be used for horseback riding in summer.
> Develop and promote recreation opportunities at nearby natural-history sites (e.g., Fossil Bowl, Emerald Creek Garnet Mine).
> Develop, interpret, and promote the logging/agricultural heritage of town (including wild rice).
> Develop river-front park and marina (with ships and boat rentals) with system of biking/walking paths.
> Develop biking opportunities: bike lanes on roads, bike paths.
> Promote networking of community events that minimizes fluctuation in visitation and extends visitor stays (e.g., develop community calendar); increase communication and networking among organizations.
> Provide old-home tours.
> Encourage expansion of outfitting and guiding (hunting, fishing, horseback riding, etc.).
> Develop a dude ranch.
> Develop more lodging.
> Develop additional RV parks.

Develop more tourist restaurants and nightlife.

Develop self-guided sightseeing tours (e.g., wild rice, logging, scenery).

Develop an information/visitor center and museum that capitalizes on local history, culture, and attractions.

Develop a cultural center (art gallery, workshop space, storage, and 200-seat theater).

Hire a person for a tourism answering service. (Harris et al. 1989, 9–10)

The next step was review and assessment of this information by the university consultants. It resulted in three major sets of conclusions and recommendations: regional fit, a five-year achievable scenario, and a matrix for evaluating proposed projects.

Regional Fit

It was concluded that because St. Maries is a small town located some distance from main highways (19 miles from U.S. 95 and 33 miles from I-90), it is unlikely it will be more than a satellite destination to the larger Coeur d'Alene area. Even so, it has potential.

A major need is to coordinate its relation with Sandpoint, Coeur d'Alene, and Wallace. Shared planning and development of an information center, loop travel routes, and historic sites are opportunities. Expanded development of water resources, community clean-up, and improved outdoor recreation facilities are needed. Greater coordination of festivals and events would benefit all.

The people of the community and surrounding area need to decide the extent to which they wish to ally themselves with the larger and more established area around them. In any case, such development must be compatible with the resource base and the surrounding tourism offerings. Careful planning and new capital investment will be required.

Five-Year Scenario

This scenario is based on the assumptions that:

Travel to northern Idaho will continue to grow.

Family and retiree travel will increase.

Rediscovering culture is an increasing motivation.

The trend toward shorter trips will continue.

Outside capital will move into Idaho.

Vision by local people is key to future tourism success.

The scenario for tourism development in this subzone includes the following:

Improved quantity and quality of services.
Focused attention on scenic values of area and river.
Increased camping and RV services.
Local capital is available and can be leveraged.
Tourism is needed to supplement the timber industry.
Networking related attractions in area is needed.
Access and development of resources into attractions is needed.

To the list of projects created at the workshop, the consultants, based on their observation and study, added the following;

Develop a signage plan.
Develop railroad logging interpretive center.
Develop a loop motorcoach tour/boat trip.
Continue participatory planning, including new mapping of attractions, identify infrastructure needs, seeking potential investors, and gaining implementation support from populace.

Matrix of Project Proposals

All twenty-four of the project proposals were evaluated and resulted in the matrix in Table 8-1. Ten criteria, as illustrated in the table, were used to evaluate the projects.

Key conclusions included emphasis on need for local commitment and leadership. It was believed that hiring of a tourism planning consultant was essential if implementation was to occur. Sufficient activities and attractions need to be provided before lodging demand can be generated. Additional factors requiring consideration include seasonality, sequencing, and packaging. Promotional efforts will have a minimal impact if there are few products/services to promote.

This destination project demonstrates effective planning of tourism for a rural and small town setting. The process used was interactive between local constituencies and university specialists. Education and communication were essential elements of this process. Throughout, the vision and action strategies were in scale with the setting and the local ability to develop.

TABLE 8-1
EVALUATION MATRIX FOR ST. MARIES, IDAHO

Projects	Dominant Type	Time	Investment Level	Investment Control	Community Support	Enhancement	Diversification	Human Resources	Market Potential	Project/Site Availability
Achievable scenario (for next 5 years)	Servicing	Medium	Moderate	Inside/Shared	Moderate	Moderate low	Moderate low 1, 2	Trainable employed trained volunteers	Very high 1, 2, 3, 5, 7, 8, 10	Available underutilized other uses
Town clean-up	All	Short	Small	Inside	High	Moderate low	Not applicable	Trained volunteers	Not applicable	Available underutilized
Building renovation in historic district	Day use	Long	Large	Inside/Shared	High	Moderate low	Moderate low 1, 2	Trainable employed	Low 1, 2	Available undeveloped
Interpret/promote river	Day use	Short	Moderate	Inside/Shared	Moderate	Low	Moderate high 1, 2, 3	Trainable employed	High 1, 2, 3, 5, 7, 8	Available undeveloped
Develop team for backwoods skiing up Mt. Bald	Day use	Long	Large	Shared/Outside	Moderate	High	Moderate low 1, 2	Limited	High 1, 2, 3, 5, 7, 8	Available undeveloped
Develop trail system and ski facilities	Day use	Long	Large	Shared	High	Moderate low	Low 1	Limited	Moderate 1, 2, 3, 8	Available undeveloped

326

Develop/promote Star Garnet and Fossil Bowl	Day use	Short	Moderate	Inside	Moderate	Moderate low	Moderate high 1, 2, 3	Limited	High 2, 3, 5, 7, 8	Available underutilized
Develop, interpret and promote logging and wild rice operation	Day use	Medium	Moderate	Shared/Inside	Moderate	Moderate low	Moderate high 1, 2, 3	Limited	High 2, 3, 5, 7, 8, 10	Available undeveloped
Develop riverfront park	Day use	Long	Large	Shared/Inside	High	Moderate low	Not unique	Limited	High 1, 2, 5, 7, 8	Available other uses
Develop biking opportunities	Day use	Medium	Large	Shared	High	Moderate low	Low 1	Limited	Moderate 1, 2, 7, 8	Available undeveloped
Networking of events	Day use	Short	Small	Inside	High	Moderate low	Moderate low 1, 2	Trained volunteers	Not applicable	Available undeveloped
Provide old home tours	Day use	Short	Small	Inside	Moderate	Moderate low	Low 1	Trained volunteers	Low 1, 2	Available undeveloped
Encourage expanded outfitting and guiding	Day use/ Overnight	Medium	Moderate	Inside	Moderate	Low	Low 1	Trained volunteers	Not applicable	Not applicable
Develop dude ranch	Overnight	Long	Large	Outside	Moderate	Low	Low 1	Limited	Very high all but 10, 11	Available undeveloped

327

MANCHESTER, SALFORD, AND TRAFFORD

The English Tourist Board (ETB), as part of a five-year program to develop tourism, sponsored a limited number of Strategic Development Initiatives (SDI). One was the case of creating the area of Manchester, Salford, and Trafford as a destination. The plan for this area has been developed jointly by the English Tourist Board and LDR International, a design-planning firm. The project was coordinated by ETB Area Development Group in partnership with the Councils of Manchester, Salford, and Trafford, Trafford Park Development Corporation, Central Manchester Development Corporation, and the North West Tourist Board. The following description is paraphrased from the report *Manchester, Salford and Trafford Strategic Development Initiative: A Framework for Tourism Development* (English Tourist Board 1989).

Purpose

The purpose of this project was to consider the potential of this area as a whole and encourage economic generation and employment by means of creating a tourist destination of international dimensions and enhance the local quality of life. More specifically, the goals were identified as:

1. Preserving and building upon the great industrial heritage of the region.
2. Introducing strong, permanent residential components into an improved environment.
3. Providing for significant enhancement of the river and canal systems as major public amenities.
4. Providing a more desirable environment for the museums, visitor attractions, GMEX, conference facilities, and business areas.
5. Providing expanded and improved green space, park lands, and pedestrian systems throughout the study area.
6. Providing major new business and job opportunities both during and after construction. (English Tourist Board 1989, 8)

Market and Area Analysis

The study revealed a strong *market demand* for the kinds of tourism development the area could support. More than 7 million people live within an hour's drive, and more than double this number within two hours away. There were indications of demand for new specialty and craft shopping; visits to historic sites, restaurants, and pubs; concerts; family recreation; and housing.

Study of the *area* identified several important factors that support its value for further development and redevelopment. It has good access linkage and is served by the United Kingdom's third largest airport. There are ample financial resources available. The area possesses a strong historical and cultural background. Already a number of facilities are available for sports, exhibitions, and conventions. The river and canal systems provide a major asset, lending special place character to the area. Some constraints and weaknesses were identified: derelict buildings, unsightly portions of waterways, limited activities and attractions beyond working hours, and limited choice of housing.

Concept Plans

Based on this information, concept plans were developed for seven districts within the destination zone (Figure 8-13).

Cathedral-Exchange Station District. In one of the oldest and most historic parts of the area, several new and exciting projects have potential along the River Irwell. Linkage between the several attractions can be accomplished by means of well-landscaped parks and pedestrian ways. Features include the Cathedral, the Corn Exchange, and the medieval Chetham's School and Conservatory. Needed is new automobile access and parking. The plan would enhance sites for new hotels, a central city athletic club and leisure facility, and new business offices.

Granada/Irwell-Sanford/Regent Road District. This corridor contains the River Irwell, major rail and road arteries, and museums. Figures 8-14, and 8-15 illustrate the sketch plan and designer's view of a planned continuous promenade along the River Irwell. The river's edge offers opportunity for development of new visitor-oriented development such as hotels, restaurants, public house, and public park plazas. Commercial leisure shopping would be appropriate. Exploration of the riverside by foot is designed into the plan.

Liverpool Road District. Proposed are new pedestrian linkages between the central business district and the river. The historic block of Deansgate and the area south of Liverpool Road would be preserved, restored, and

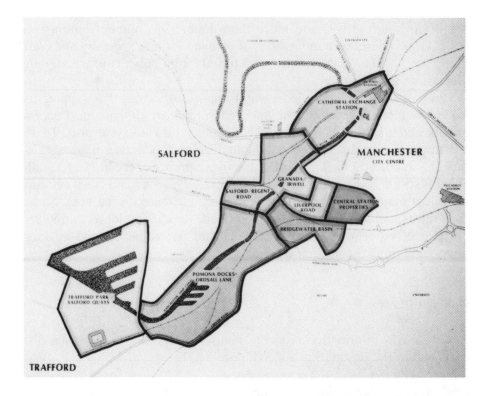

Figure 8-13. Plan for Manchester-Salford-Trafford Destination. Proposed development plan includes seven districts. This concept resulted from analysis of resources and market potential. Planning emphasis is on restoration, protection and environmental enhancement (English Tourist Board 1989, 9).

appropriately infilled with small shops, services, pubs, and other complementary uses. The Roman fort would be enhanced by creating a continuous enclosed space which would serve to unify the two existing historic sites. Outdoor exhibits, fairs, and events would be planned into this district.

Central Station Properties District. GMEX and existing historic buildings provide the foundation for new retail/entertainment and cultural facilities. A landscaped pedestrian linkage across Deansgate to Liverpool Road is critical. An inviting open-space entry, with recreation/leisure/entertainment elements as well as specialty shopping would be important attractions for visitors. A conference center, a concert hall, and specialty retail and hotel uses are planned for the GMEX area.

Bridgewater/Basin District. The large site along the south side of the canal is planned for mixed use development including office, commercial, retail, and residential uses. These would be compatible with the nearby

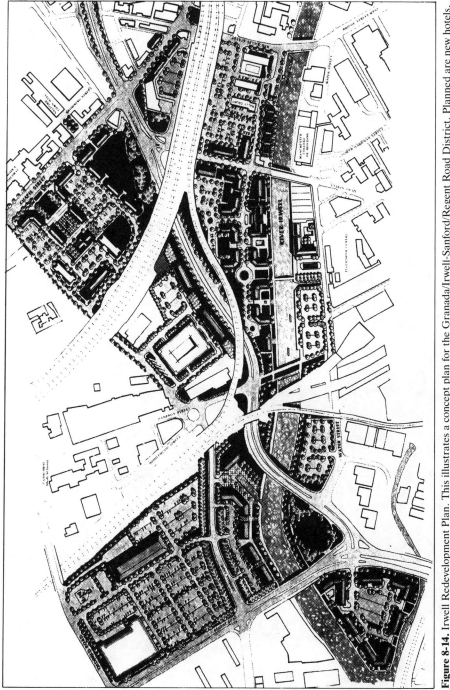

Figure 8-14. Irwell Redevelopment Plan. This illustrates a concept plan for the Granada/Irwell-Sanford/Regent Road District. Planned are new hotels, restaurants, public house, and park areas for visitors and residents (English Tourist Board 1989, 14).

Figure 8-15. River Irwell Promenade. Concept includes redevelopment of the waterfront to provide enriching experiences for visitors (English Tourist Board 1989, 15).

historic buildings of interest to visitors. Featured would be small shops selling crafts, artwork, and antiques, and a pub and eating house. Continuous towpath improvements combined with pedestrian bridges across the canals would greatly improve access and create a visitor destination as well as a local amenity area.

Pamona Docks—Ordsall Lane District. This area has been dominantly industrial, but two factors now influence its future plan for tourism. This 30-acre district is virtually an island and it is negatively impacted by older industrial and warehouse buildings. Properly redesigned with new uses, these could be turned into assets by creating an entirely new identity for the area. Development of a central urban park and themed attractions over a period of time would completely transform this area. The designers emphasize that new images, such as beautiful landscaping, lighting, fountains, gardens, small boats, wild waterfowl, playing fields, bandshells, carousels, fairs, games, and places of refreshment would raise this area to the level of an international attraction.

Trafford Park/Salford Quays District. New transportation access and waterfront amenities would provide the central focus for redevelopment of this district. A great waterfront park would be the centerpiece. A sports and leisure theme could enhance the area greatly. The addition of businesses, hotels, theaters, residential, restaurant, and commercial activities should achieve a truly dynamic environment.

Implementation

Recommended for implementing these concepts and proposals is close cooperation between the ETB, SDI, local authority partners, the Urban Development Corporations, and the private sector. However, in the majority of cases, it is up to the local authorities with the Urban Development Corporations to take the lead. They would need to accept the overall concept for the destination, develop private sector interest and set priorities for infrastructure investment. In order to implement this plan, two major recommendations are made.

1. Feasibility Studies. In the beginning specific projects will be selected for the development of feasibilities. In this phase, they are likely to be the Exchange Station, Pomona Docks/Ordsall Lane, Conference Center, and several heritage and tourism service projects.

2. Management. Emphasis is placed on the need for a common management strategy for both the public and private sectors in order to: oversee overall design, maintain design and maintenance standards, franchise and monitor special transportation, and plan and run visitor events.

Still in its planning stage, this project demonstrates the destination concept of incorporating several attraction sites, community centers, services, transportation, and pedestrian use into an overall plan of development and management. The handsome and well-illustrated document including many details of the proposals and their justification, provides a lucid, descriptive argument in support of the plan. Throughout, the local citizen concerns have been addressed alongside worthwhile development for tourism.

CONCLUSIONS

The nine destination zone cases described here represent a diversity of situations but also some common planning principles. All represent the newer planning sensitivity to the natural and cultural resource foundations. They show how these resources can be protected as well as designed for enriching visitor use. Although several planner types—government, profession, specialist task force, university—are represented, all cases have been planned cooperatively with local people. The emphasis on public involvement is also a comparatively recent innovation for professional planners and designers. The issue of implementation remains unresolved because of the diversity of local organization, leadership, and commitment. However, the greater local involvement throughout the planning process promises better fruition of plans in the future. As with regional tourism plans, there are so many unknown variables at this scale that feasibility of individual projects must wait until the next phase of planning—the site scale. The accomplishment of creative recommendations that capitalize on carefully planned use of resources to meet market needs is sufficient for destination planning. Because communities are an integral part of destination zones, planning for tourism provides amenities applicable to residents as well as travelers. Even though these cases include a variety of settings and vary in scope, the characteristics common to all suggest basic principles of value to planning all destinations.

REFERENCES

Action Plan, America's Industrial Heritage Project (1987). Washington, DC: National Park Service.

Auyong, Jan (1990). "Coastal and Marine Tourism and Recreation Opportunities in Kosrae State, Federated States of Micronesia." In *Kosrae Island Resource Management Plan,* Vol. II. University of Hawaii: Honolulu-Sea Grant Program.

Comprehensive Management Plan (1992). Comprehensive Management Plan for the Southwestern Pennsylvania Heritage Preservation Commission. Washington, DC: U.S. National Park Service.

Cunningham, Melissa. (Interview on May 29, 1992, now director of Main Street Program, Denison, TX; formerly director at Mineral Wells.)

Davidson-Peterson Associates (1992). *A Marketing Plan for Increasing Visitation to America's Industrial Heritage Project (AIHP).* York, ME: Davidson-Peterson Associates.

English Tourist Board/LDR International (1989). *Manchester, Salford and Trafford: Strategic Development Initiative.* London: English Tourist Board/LDR.

Gitelson, Richard et al. (1992). *Part II A Socio-demographic and Behavioral Profile of Visitors at Five Sites Included in the America's Industrial Heritage Project.* University Park, PA: Penn State Center for Travel and Tourism Research.

Gunn, Clare A. et al. (1983). *Gonzales Tourism-Park Opportunities, Part I and II.* College Station, TX: Texas Agricultural Extension Service.

Gunn, Clare A. et al. (1985). *Mineral Wells: Opportunities for Tourism Development.* College Station, TX: Texas Agricultural Extension service.

Hand, Barbara. (Interview on December 28, 1992, director of tourism, Gonzales Chamber of Commerce.)

Harris, Charles C. et al. (1989). "An Assessment of Tourism Development Potential in St. Maries, Idaho—1090 to 1995." In *An Approach to Assessing Community Tourism Potential,* pp. 7–18. Moscow, ID: University of Idaho.

Katter, Jill L. (ed.) (1992). "From Inventory to Legislation." *Malama Kai,* 1(1), 11–15.

Kennedy, Ian et al. (1991). *Moorea and Tourism.* Sydney, Australia: Pacific Asia Travel Association.

Midkiff, Sandra. (Interview on June 5, 1992, now director, Keep Mineral Wells Beautiful program, Mineral Wells, TX).

Plan for the Allegheny Ridge (1992). Prepared by the Allegheny Ridge Industrial Heritage Corridor Task Force, Hollidaysburg, PA.

Public Law 100-698 (1988). "Southwestern Pennsylvania Heritage Preservation Commission, Establishment." Washington, DC: 100th Congress of the United States.

Reconnaissance Survey of Western Pennsylvania Roads and Sites (1985). Washington, DC: U.S. National Park Service.

Rundell, John B. et al. (1989). *Idaho Rural Tourism Primer; A Tourism Assessment Workbook.* Moscow, ID: University of Idaho.

Sanchez, Mario L. (1989). "Establishing an Historic Corridor from Laredo to Brownsville— An Approach for the Development of Cultural Tourism Along the Texas-Mexico Border." Presentation, Third Regional Conference, U.S./Mexico Border States on Parks and Wildlife, McAllen, TX.

Sanchez, Mario L. (ed.) (1991). *A Shared Experience: The History, Architecture and Historic Designations of the Lower Rio Grande Heritage Corridor.* Austin, TX: The Texas Historical Commission.

Var, Turgut et al. (1991). *Chun-Cheon Plan 2001.* A Comprehensive Resort Development Plan for the Chun-Cheon Lake Area. Prepared for the Korean Transportation Institute by the Texas Travel Research and Information Program, Texas A&M University.

Wilson, A. Meriwether, and Lawrence A. Hamilton (eds.) (1992). *Kosrae Island Integrated Coastal Resources Assessment for Biodiversity/Cultural Conservation and Nature-Based Tourism.* Honolulu: East-West Center.

Chapter 9

Site Planning Concepts

Introduction

The most commonly practiced scale of tourism planning is the site—here defined as a land area within a destination zone usually controlled by one individual, firm, or governmental agency. In other words, the focus of this chapter is on the planning of attractions, facilities, and services for tourists. This level of planning is the final implementation of physical development guided by regional and destination plans. It is at this stage that ideas and recommendations become real tangible development of the supply side of tourism.

PLANNING-DESIGN INTEGRATION

Planning-Design Professionals

In many countries, the professions engaged in planning land areas and structures are divided into urban and regional planners, landscape architects, architects, interior designers, and engineers. These distinctions are often carried out in training, education, and licensing. Although definitions are not precise, the focus for each of these planners/designers is different. For example, urban and regional planners focus primarily on official government functions related to zoning, transportation, and other physical development at the city and county scales. Landscape architects are site designers. Their practice is defined as "the profession which applies artistic and scientific principles to the research, planning, design and management of both natural and built environments" (ASLA 1992, 2). Architects usually focus on the design of buildings, utilizing "associated design disciplines that deal with the man-made, or built, environment in reciprocal, interrelated ways" (Antoniades 1986, 1). For the creation of environments inside buildings, the profession of interior design has been created. Engineers focus on many of the technical aspects of design, such as for structures, electricity, plumbing, irrigation, and drainage.

In practice, especially in recent years, professional firms often maintain representatives of all these professions on their staffs. Even though each profession has its own focus and need for basic knowledge and skills, there is great compatibility and complementarity. At the site scale, landscape architects and architects dominate the planning field and are more commonly called designers who deal with design rather than planning. But, even though they may take the lead in tourism projects, they often incorporate other specialists depending on the need—golf course architects, historic restorers, interpretive exhibit designers, museum designers, park designers, and environmentalists. It is clear that most tourism projects require the talent and training of several kinds of designers. Integration of design activity is essential.

Other Influentials

Although professional designers play a major role in finalizing plans so that they can be built, a final plan is not under their exclusive control. Several other groups can exercise direct and indirect control of a design, even to the extent that a good design may never be built. The following discussion identifies several groups that have critical roles in influencing design beyond that of professional designers.

Owners/Developers

No tourism development takes place unless landowners/developers want to do it. And, they want to do it their way. No matter whether recommendations are made at the regional or destination scales, the final decisions are played out at the site scale. As has been stated before, these decision-makers for tourism are of three sectors: government, nonprofit organizations, and the private sector.

In many countries, governments have delegated development of certain aspects of tourism to their agencies—parks, recreation, streets, highways, air travel, and historic preservation. This delegation is bound by certain legal mandates that define the powers and activities of each agency. Generally, however, most of these agencies were established for purposes other than tourism. For future planning of tourism at any scale, government agencies will need greater understanding of tourism and input from other sectors involved.

Nonprofit organizations, by definition, are not engaged in activities to accumulate wealth but to fulfill other purposes of value to each organization and to society. But, for each development activity related to tourism, the decision on what to develop will be based primarily on their goals. For example, restoration of a historic building may be a prime objective of a historic society. The tourism implications, however, such as parking, toileting, and interpreting, would be secondary. So, final action hinges more on how well each project fits the aims of the organization.

Private sector commercial owners usually make land use decisions primarily on economic feasibility. But, experience demonstrates that for small business, there may be many other factors that influence final decisions. Continuing family ownership, interests of heirs, love of location, security, and other external factors often have more bearing on development than profitmaking. Certainly, entrepreneurship in other cultures may not be as strong as in industrialized nations, tending to inhibit development of tourism. Final plans and implementation of development vary greatly no matter how designers may have conceived of plans.

Moneylenders

Critical to all implementation are the decisions of the financial sector. Financial institutions have their own policies and practices regarding funding. Both public and private organizations have precise criteria for financing projects. Many excellent plans have never reached fruition because either judgment or regulations prevented financing. On publicly-supported projects, such as parks, arenas, and recreation complexes, critical to implementation will be the public vote to issue bonds or increase taxes. Often, plans for projects are modified following first estimates; they are usually downscaled. Financing has a major influence by limiting or fostering what is designed and built.

Construction Industry

All projects that require land modification and construction require bids from construction firms. Often, the designer's estimates do not reflect true building costs, causing major modification of plans. Labor strikes, supplier business failures, shortages of supplies, bad weather, and many other contingencies can often delay or even deny completion of projects. Until costs are known, plans are only ideas, excellent as they may be. Construction costs can either halt or permit the implementation of plans.

Managers

Unfortunately, future managers are seldom brought into planning negotiations until after projects have been approved. Especially important for hotels, restaurants, marinas, entertainment centers, and resorts is the input of managers' experience. Details of functional operation are much more easily changed at the planning stage than after construction. Often owners and developers do not have sufficient experience and knowledge of these details to make sure problems are avoided.

Publics

Several public groups can influence greatly whether a plan is executed. For any governmental expenditure, the voting public would have supported the agency's budget with taxes. In a democracy, if this public is dissatisfied with an agency's management, change can come via the next vote for officials. Or, as American politicians are learning, the electronic age allows direct feedback via radio and television without waiting for the next election.

Increasingly, public organizations are voicing advocacy on many issues relating to tourism. Hotel associations, tourism associations, tour organizations, and airline associations are more active than in the past. Many environmental organizations are bringing political pressure to bear on public and private tourism developers. Health and safety organizations often foster new regulations that tourist businesses must comply with. In areas where planning is becoming more active, nearly all plans require several stages of public input and approval.

On the market side, there is an increased influence from membership travel groups, particularly those for older citizens. By their travel decisions toward destinations, they have a vital influence on the fulfillment of tourism plans. Finally, communities, by their public support of building codes and zoning ordinances, often have direct influence on what is built and where, especially for new motels, restaurants, and shopping areas. All tourism plans are influenced greatly by a wide range of public input.

Place Meanings

As has been described, regions and destinations of tourist development are collections of individual sites. In a democratic society, these sites are owned, developed, and managed by individuals, governments, organizations, and firms. But, even in a democracy, social values are ascribed to sites, such as health, safety, and general welfare. All the attributes of places, as described Chapter 7, are equally important for site and building design. Relevance to place is a basic principle of all tourism design.

Places have a variety of meanings, important to all who now own or wish to develop sites. Perhaps a better descriptor is the landscape—land with all its collective attributes. Over time, and in all cultures, landscapes have accumulated characteristics that must be dealt with for any development, including tourism. Motloch (1991) has paraphrased Meinig's (1979) classification of how landscapes are perceived:

As nature—unspoiled, deserving of conservation.
As habitat—supportive of man, animals, vegetation.
As artifact—to be subdued, conquered by man.
As system—holistic, human-nature as one.
As problem—all is in disarray, needs solving.
As wealth—a commodity to be owned, sold, used.
As ideology—holds ideals, cultural meaning.
As history—cumulative record of man's use.
As place—visual and spatial geography.
As esthetic—intrinsic beauty, visual value.(Motloch 1991, 10–21)

In the design of hotels, restaurants, museums, parks, and other tourist attractions and services, the decisionmaker and designer must recognize these many perceptions of place. It is not enough to design the basic functions solely for the tourist service or activity. All attributes of the site and surrounding area must be taken into consideration.

Many times efforts toward increased economic development of communities are so misdirected that qualities of place are eroded and even destroyed. For manufacturing plants and other industries these qualities are not as important as for tourism. Essential to most tourism products are the unique place characteristics that set a community and a site apart from others. Designers of tourist attractions and businesses have the obligation to maintain major qualities of place in their land and building plans. Garnham (1985, 9) has identified several items that give a site special sense of place:

Architectural style.
Climate, particularly the quality and quantity of light, amount of rainfall, and variations in temperature.
Unique natural setting.
Memory and metaphor, what the place means to people who experience it.
The use of local materials.
Craftsmanship.

Sensitivity in the siting of important buildings and bridges.
Cultural diversity and history.
People's values.
High quality public environments which are visible and accessible.
Townwide activities, daily and seasonal.

New Paradigms

As observed by Motloch (1991, 251), important changes are taking place
in how sites and buildings are designed. The traditional approach has been
oversimplified and narrowly focused. As a consequence, both sites and
their surroundings suffer from lack of understanding interrelationships.
The former mindset of designer-client agreement on project objectives is
giving way to the reality that sites are integral parts of a larger whole. For
tourism, the context of destination and region must be incorporated into
every site design decision.

As has been discussed earlier, sustainable development is more than a
catchword and slogan. It is a principle of significance to every site design.
Environments surrounding sites impact upon them, as well as sites impacting on the external environment. Even though sites and buildings will
continue to require working drawings in order for them to be built, every
internal feature and specification must have been influenced by many
externalities.

An essential part of this issue arises from the traditional "great-man"
and "creative genius" philosophies held by designers in the past. When
designers are carried away with their own egos and argue that they know
best what good design really is, the finished built project is likely to be no
more than a monument to the designer's ego.

Designer Scarfo (1992, 3) admonishes his professional colleagues to be
more concerned about the quality of the eventual users of projects than
winning awards from peers. He states:

> Do we have the scientific knowledge to understand the dynamics of a site within its
> larger ecosystem, or do we simply apply technical formulas within limited site
> boundaries? Do we stop to identify the political, economic, and spiritual dynamics
> that will sustain our project? Do we outline management strategies that contribute
> to its maintenence? Do we really know how to identify the expressive appreciations
> of a user group, and transform indigenous aesthetics and historical character into
> new landscapes?

This is the paradox of design. It is essential that the special talent,
insight, and creative intuition of the designer be unleashed as driving

forces for every design project. But, good design is more than this. The final and enduring test will be its value not only to the designer and the new investor but to all people who will view and use the site as an integral part of human experience in the environment.

This new design paradigm requires a new kind of designer. It requires architects, landscape architects, and engineers with new sensitivity to human behavior and the science of the environment. For tourism, it is essential that designers cooperate with clients to focus more on the characteristics and interests of the travelers than only on the financial bottom line of the project's feasibility. It is equally essential that designers and clients turn more attention than in the past to the causes of environmental degradation now being proved not by sensational journalism but by scientific fact.

An increasing number of designers today are proving the value of implementing this new paradigm by accepting the new role as catalyst or facilitator. Marshall (1983, 88) states that the designer is

> . . . one whose role is to bring participants and processes into sync and insure progression toward common quality-of-life goals. The design facilitator would be a prime mover, a mediator, a conciliator, and a communicator of ideas, concepts, and viable alternative solutions to design issues.

Instead of being only a "plan-maker", this new designer is also one who brings needed forces to bear upon the creation of a design. Motloch (1991, 264) calls for a new design "landscape management hierarchy" as illustrated in Figure 9-1. The "metasystems" designer exercises a much broader role than the traditional design role. A further narrowing to place level context is the role of the "systems" designer. With these as prerequisites, the "project designer" has a clear understanding of parameters and design objectives.

What is called for today in design for tourism is a shift from the traditional architectural and landscape project emphasis to *placemaking*. Placemaking is not merely the manipulation of materials of architecture and the landscape. Rather, it is the creative adaptation of given site characteristics to new uses, such as for visitors. This adaptation is in sharp contrast to the bulldozer-scalping mindset that destroys the meaning of place that a site once possessed. Placemaking is the retention of the essence of place while giving it new physical and psychological meaning.

For tourism, new placemaking is being exemplified in renewal of deteriorated urban waterfronts. Owners, designers, local citizens, and developers are now incorporating new project designs into a larger context of human use and enjoyment. For coastal planning and design, this larger

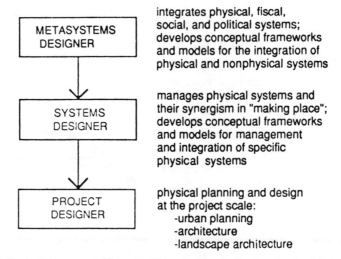

integrates physical, fiscal, social, and political systems; develops conceptual frameworks and models for the integration of physical and nonphysical systems

manages physical systems and their synergism in "making place"; develops conceptual frameworks and models for management and integration of specific physical systems

physical planning and design at the project scale:
-urban planning
-architecture
-landscape architecture

Figure 9-1. A Design/Management Hierarchy. This concept calls for three levels of design, from the ecological/cultural landscape to the project level (Motloch 1991, 264).

whole encompasses retention of historic values, retention of viable economic uses (shipping and fishing), adaptation of historic structures, retention and restoration of land-water interface values, as well as linkage with land uses surrounding the waterfront site. While new uses for visitors—boardwalks, marinas, shops, restaurants, and entertainment—are incorporated into projects, the overriding essence of place is retained. Such is placemaking for tourism.

Public Involvement

Several techniques are being utilized to obtain collective public opinion on tourism projects. The Nominal Group Technique has been applied effectively in many instances. Ritchie (1987) used this technique in Alberta with the public and private sector groups—Tourism Alberta (the provincial public agency) and the Tourism Industry Association of Alberta (the provincial private sector). This study was carried through in three phases: definition of priority issues, identification of needed initiatives and action, and monitoring of recommendations. The study identified 15 themes of highest priority and 22 themes of second level priority. This technique was also used in Fredericksburg, Texas, to determine information needed for more effective operation of tourism (Watt et al. 1991). Workshops with a broad cross-section of community residents yielded needs of market profile, advertising effectiveness, and economic impact. These have led to new plans for development and promotion.

Another technique for obtaining public input has been devised in Canada, called the Co-Design Approach (Callaway et al. 1990). This was applied to harborfront planning for tourism development in British Columbia. Through a focus-group session, waterfront images and themes were identified. The design features derived from this process included:

- Use of natural landscaping with indigenous species;
- A marine architectural theme for all commercial buildings, and whenever possible, street furniture;
- Uniform structural theme of round posts and square or rectangular beam pedestrian features;
- Water theme areas—fountains, children's play area;
- All "urban-native" walkways, to connect the downtown to the wharf via Harbourfront Village's commercial core. (Callaway et al. 1990, 109)

This technique utilizes a seven-step process of public participation and features artists who capture the themes with graphics. This technique is credited with helping to implement the waterfront plan into reality.

There is little question about the power of public involvement in all tourism planning. Although the use of these techniques is no substitute for utilizing the talent and experience of professional designers and planners, there is strong symbiotic value in combining public input with that of professionals.

A classic example is one of the most popular tourist attractions in the United States—the San Antonio River Walk (Gunn et al. 1972) (see Chapter 10). Over its history, a great many different individuals and groups have been involved. Perhaps this diversity is responsible for the resulting amalgam of characteristics that make it so dynamic and popular. Following a flood in 1921, a bypass canal was built, providing a stabilized water level for the horseshoe bend. A local architect, Robert H. Hugman, developed a plan for a major visitor attraction. But only after 1938, when a local bond issue provided some funding supplemented by the Works Progress Administration of the federal government, was major work begun—rock retaining walls, picturesque foot bridges, rock-surfaced walks, and landscape enhancement of river edges. In 1961, a chamber of commerce plan for converting it to an amusement area was rejected. Since then, under the umbrella supervision of a River Walk Commission, the parks department has continued landscape beautification of the river edges; private owners have developed night clubs, restaurants, and shops; the San Antonio River Authority has controlled water volume and quality; and the Conservation Society has protected historic structures and plants. No one individual or group has been fully responsible for this outstanding, enriching, and popular travel and local attraction.

On the other hand, a different but comprehensive waterfront redevelopment plan for the Baltimore harbor has met with equal success. It is now one of the most popular gathering places on the U.S. east coast. Redevelopment of the derelict waterfront was sparked by a local water resource engineer upon returning from a visit to the impressive harborfront of Stockholm (Billing 1987). The challenge was picked up by Mayor Theodore R. McKeldin who then authorized the City Planning Commission, the Greater Baltimore Committee, and the Committee for Downtown to work with planners Wallace, McHarg & Associates. Representatives of many publics were involved throughout the process. A quasi-governmental agency, the Neighborhood Progress Administration, formed in 1984, manages 283 acres that include the Center, Inner Harbor, Inner Harbor East, and Inner Harbor West. Since then, new parks, marinas, 90 major new buildings (restaurants, shops, museums, and aquarium) valued at over $2 billion have been established. As a result, not only has a major tourist attraction been created but also the surrounding area has been stimulated into complete renovation. This example demonstrates that there is no single and most effective category of planner type to do tourism planning and design.

The Western Australian Tourism Commission (n.d.) has produced the guide, *Public Involvement in Tourism Development: What Does It Mean for the Developer?* The publication firmly recommends that all tourism developers have the obligation of letting the public know about plans, because it can be in their best interest. Local people have the right to know how a project will affect them. Several mechanisms can be utilized before and after sketch plans have been prepared: personal contact, open houses, workshops, community liaison group, and media releases. As the involvement progresses, suggested is monitoring, for the following obectives:

To determine public preferences.
To identify outstanding issues of concern.
To incorporate public input into the planning process.
To determine if the public is receiving and understanding the
    information.
To identify areas which may not have been covered by the program.
    (WATC n.d., 20)

Even though public involvement will entail some cost and perhaps delay, it can avoid the need for weathering protest too late and often provides constructive recommendations for improving the project. Public involvement today is an essential element of tourism planning and design.

DESIGN CRITERIA

Functional Criteria

Although no one would deny that all tourism plans and designs should produce development that functions, it is not always clear just how it should function. Certainly, one can readily document many monuments to plans that didn't work—many communities still have relics of bad urban renewal plans of the 1960s.

Tourism leaders of site plans could benefit by testing their plans against the following four criteria.

First of all, plans must demonstrate that they will create development that will function *as a system*. This means simply that the several parts will meet the needs of the traveler, the only one to see and use tourism development as a whole. How well can the traveler reach desired attractions considering transportation routes and guidance information? How well have service businesses (lodging, car service, food, and souvenirs) been located in relation to attractions? Have time and distance been considered in relation to attraction access and significance? Necessary as these requirements may be, the coordination of all parts of development becomes very complicated because of the many decisionmakers of development. But, it is essential to mentally pose as a traveler and move through the planned development to see how well the individual site fits into an overall system.

Designed and built development must also meet the very critical criterion of *structural stability*. With the availability of today's engineering technology, there should be little excuse for structures that are weak and, possibly even dangerous, for people to use. Yet, sometimes standards are overlooked and incompetent builders take shortcuts. Most cities have building codes that require adequate standards that must be demonstrated on all plans and specifications. Most business managers of amusement and theme parks enforce their own rigid standards of inspection and maintenance for public safety. Buildings, drives, walks, drainage systems, and all other development of the land must be designed and maintained to withstand use as well as weather conditions that could shorten the life of the structure or threaten the safety of users.

A third criterion is the *use* function—how planned development will be used. This function depends completely on the estimated volume and other characteristics of use by people and vehicles. Decisions must be made on the estimated capacity of roads, walks, decks, and building spaces. These decisions usually cannot be based on peak use because of overdesign and excessive costs for all other times of use. For natural resource-based attractions, esthetics and limits of environmental stress may dictate that management control use, setting arbitrary standards of capacity. People-use also involves highway directional and informative signage that is legible and not misleading. Functional building design requires cooling and heating that is easily manipulated, interior design that provides for proper reaching, walking, and seating, especially for children and tall or short adults. Special needs of the physically impaired travelers must be considered in all design. Consideration for parking involves proper planning for buses as well as compact cars and other vehicles, such as motorcycles and bicycles. Planning for service vehicles— supplies, waste removal, and repair—is important. Owners and developers must insist always upon plans that provide for physical use functions by management as well as visitors.

Equally difficult but necessary is function that is *esthetically pleasing and appropriate*. Here, standards are not as easily defined as for engineering standards of structures. And, the traveling market includes people of a great variety of tastes. But, with greater sophistication of travelers, they no longer will patronize ugly and inappropriate landscape and structural planning and design. Some cities and some attraction complexes have provided for legal permitting of the appearance of landscapes and buildings based on opinion of a panel of specialists of planning and design. Some developments are opened to planning and design competitions. The choice of a winner may be made by government officials, a panel of planners/designers, or public opinion workshops. It should be emphasized that for all planning and design, there must be adequate allowance for creativity and innovation in order to avoid repetition and stagnation.

Integration with Other Plans

All tourism planning must be *integrated with other plans*. New tourism plans may run counter to official city plans. City plans may not allow for the traffic expansion, increased demands on water and other utilities, and the extra burden on police and fire protection. Rural and extensive area development planning for tourism must be integrated with plans and policies of major resource managers, such as for forests, hunting and fishing areas, or historic and archeological sites. Again, because many jurisdictions are involved, the task of fulfilling this criterion is not easy but is necessary.

Such integration begins with the first designer-client contact. When an entrepreneur, investor, or developer first contacts a professional design firm, the first item on the agenda is communication. Designers will need to obtain information about the proposed project. But equally important for successful tourism is the need to raise questions about the relevance to all other factors that will influence success of the project.

The Visitor Experience

A problem at the site scale is understanding the "real" client. Although a decisionmaker has identified *his* project requirements for tourism, considerable discussion must take place with the designer regarding characteristics of the visitor, who eventually is the true client when the project is completed. Often this represents a gray area where both client and designer expect the other to have complete information, and often neither does.

Today, travel market research is providing better descriptions of visitor characteristics. Generalized categories of travelers are no longer sufficient. Now, for good design it is essential to predict as much as possible about potential users, such as their demographic characteristics (age, sex, income, education, and occupation), activities preferred, extent of group interest as compared to independence, and travel experience and degree of sophistication. Even though no decisionmaker or designer can guarantee satisfaction, a plan has a much greater chance of realization if the prospective guest can be visualized in advance. Because visitor satisfaction is the true tourism product, it translates into business success.

Individuality

In the past there has been a tendency of financial institutions to favor support of new projects that are similar to existing establishments. Apparently this policy suggests less financial risk. Perhaps this has some merit regarding some types of development. Franchise lodging and food services standardize their designs on the basis that the traveling public becomes brand conscious and are assured of the same services and quality wherever they go.

However, when attractions (and some services) are being designed, there is merit in strong design creativity. Creative design is sensitive to the unique characteristics of sites and travelers and produces new and different solutions. The seeming risk of being different is offset by a better match between market and supply, a basic principle of tourism development. Design professionals are not mere technicians, although technical accuracy is essential. They possess the mental capacity and special talent to be creative. Their intuitive powers must be allowed to flourish in order to avoid the sameness that is encroaching upon the landscape. Creativity is essential if the visitor is to be enriched by the travel experience.

Authenticity

To strive for authenticity is a desirable design goal. Travelers resent being promised attractions, services, and facilities only to be disappointed upon arrival. If ethnic dances are promoted, for example, they must be delivered by the site attraction. If historic architecture is promised, it should be genuinely available upon reaching the destination site. These qualities of authenticity again require close communication between the decision-maker, promoter, and designer.

However, increased volumes of visitors and their subsequent wear and tear on sites sometimes demand a modified design policy. For a historic building, for example, five or ten thousand visitors a day could damage rare carpeting and historic artifacts if the restoration design allowed close visitor contact. Channeling visitors over durable walkways and controlling access so that views can be obtained without close contact are often design requirements. Other design modifications, such as air conditioning, new electrical systems for lighting and exhibits, and installation of public toilet facilities, can be tastefully accomplished in historic buildings with care in design.

Authenticity, as a principle, again endorses the need for sensitivity to place and special environmental characteristics. The more that a designer can emulate the special place attributes, the more competitive will be the business establishment.

Esthetically Satisfying

For the business person and developer, the concept of beauty may seem remote from success factors. For tourism, it is essential to success. Although principles and standards of beauty are less scientific or technically precise, experience has demonstrated its value. Even though travelers may not realize the details of why some establishments are more satisfying than others, they can discriminate between ugly and pleasing. It is the responsibility of designers to incorporate principles of esthetic expression into even the smallest detail of tourism development. Professional designers generally have the talent, training, and experience to create esthetically satisfying development.

Among the several principles of beauty in tourism design, a designer should seek *order*. The positioning of buildings on the site and the order in architecture make all development easier for the visitor to grasp. Disorganized sites and building interiors cause confusion and disorientation. Orderly development need not be rigidly oriented but should make the flow of walking, viewing, and experiencing places a pleasurable and unobstructed event.

Especially important in the design of tourist sites and structures is *continuity*. By design, each part of the landscape and buildings logically flows from another. Too often, especially in places that have been modified over the years, tourist masses block movement. In other instances, the detailing of architecture and landscape features is so mixed up that the visitor sees a jumble of disconnected parts. Good design would engage repetition of style and theme to provide continuity throughout the site.

An aspect of continuity is the balance between *harmony* and *contrast*. Too much repetition of the same design can be monotonous. Some resorts are monotonous because all bungalows were designed exactly alike. However, a high degree of repetition can create harmony in both settings and buildings. The same sign format and style, light fixtures, benches, and walk materials throughout a landscape can produce harmony. One way of relieving monotony is to introduce a contrasting element. In an otherwise flat and repetitious landscape, the introduction of a tower or tree cluster can provide interest and focus.

Visitor interest and feelings of beauty can be created by a designer's tasteful use of *color, texture,* and *ornamentation*. In both architecture and landscapes, visitors are increasingly weary of bland and sterile settings for their activities. How these elements are expressed in the design of tourist sites varies from urban to rural settings. Generally, more formal and engineered styling is most appropriate for urban sites. But, for outlying areas, natural resource settings are dominant and site and building design should be compatible with these settings. In all cases, building and site design need to be in harmony, requiring close collaboration between developers, landscape architects, and architects.

These are just a few of the design tools for creating beauty available to building and landscape designers. They have become an integral part of their training and creative talent. But, fundamental to all design is first to recognize the intrinsic beauty of a place. The given beauty of a piece of property—trees, slopes, and distant vistas—are too often destroyed with a slash-bulldoze policy. Landscapes already have character, and it is the designer's duty to retain as much of the natural beauty as possible.

Marketability

Although the artistic and creative talents of designers are essential for attractive tourism development, the finished project must be marketable. Tourism facilities and development must meet the test of matching traveler demand. In order to meet this objective, close collaboration between designer and developer is required. Innovation may gain favorable response from a new or untapped market segment but cannot be so extreme that no one would wish to visit and use the finished project. As stated in *Successful Tourism Design* (WATC 1990, 10), "Ultimately, developments which have a strong, unique sense of place become quality marketable products."

SUSTAINABILITY

The concept of sustainable development, introduced in Chapter 4, has greatest application at the site scale. It is here that the specific issue of balancing resource protection with development changes from policy to action. As stated in a guide to tourism developers, "In tourism, perhaps more than in most industrial developments, there is an opportunity to blend conservation and development in a continuing, lasting and sustainable marriage" (WATC 1989, 5).

Implicit in every design for a tourism project must be a clear identification of potential negative environmental impacts. Developers need not consider this action a constraint but rather a necessity for doing business. The more that harmony can be struck between the natural setting and new development, the more appealing a project can be for visitors. If the scale and intensity of a project is so massive that all the original site conditions are drastically modified, one may question why travelers would go there. Following are some concepts directed toward achieving sustainable tourism development.

Eco-Design Ethics

If tourism developers and designers were to adhere to a set of eco-design ethics, environmental protection could become an integral part of project success, either public or private. The following is a capsule of some important eco-design fundamentals.

1. Resort design shall be in scale with the setting and not dominate the natural resources. All waste shall be disposed of without polluting air, water, or soil.
2. Waterfront development design shall not be separated from the water's edge by a road. Access shall be provided back of the development.
3. The location of tourist facilities shall be separated from major cultural and natural resources. Access to these resources shall be planned and controlled so as to not exceed the capacity without environmental damage.
4. Public agency-held parks and preserves shall zone these lands to identify those locations deserving protection as well as locations of "hardened sites" suited to commercial development.
5. All project design shall be acceptable to nearby community residents.
6. Attraction development dependent upon natural resources shall be designed with overlook towers, boardwalks, trails, and other features in accord with protecting wildlife habitat and the native flora.
7. Cultural attraction development (historic and archeological sites) shall be planned ethically so that visitors are given a rich experience without eroding cultural values.
8. Major resort and tourist projects should not be developed in remote areas where the infrastructure (water supply, waste disposal, police and fire protection, and road access) are unavailable.
9. The immediate area within and surrounding important cultural or natural resource attractions must not be developed with incompatible uses that diminish a quality visitor's experiences.
10. All shoreline development, such as for marinas, residences, hotels, and shops, shall respect the natural erosive forces of waves, storms, and flooding and be placed far enough back from the water's edge so that development will not be damaged.
11. Major land use projects, such as golf courses, shall not be developed in pristine natural areas but rather at locations where minimum stress upon the environment will be made.
12. In the siting of buildings as much of the natural topography, trees, and other plant materials shall be retained as possible in order to provide maximum visitor enjoyment and also protect the resources.

Adoption of these basic environmental ethics by all designers and developers can help build and protect the very resource foundations so important for tourism to succeed—for visitor satisfaction and for business. *The Eco Ethics of Tourism Development*, produced by the Western Australian Tourism Commission (1989, 17), states, "environmental correction is more expensive than environmental protection . . ."

Cultural Sites

The increased travel demand places much greater responsibility on planners and designers to create attractions that protect cultural resources and yet open them for visitor enrichment. Regarding the designer's new role Antoniades (1986, 398) states, "We could say that 'this discipline' is a most refined one regarding civilizations; it concerns itself with the continuity of civilization, the values and physical testimonials of the past."

The first responsibility of the designer, but not easily accomplished, is cultural preservation. Today, the field encompasses prehistoric sites, historic districts, cultural landscapes, ethnic centers, and places of significant historic events. Prevention from demolition is a first step. But, many structures will need restoration and even complete replication. The designer must work closely with owners and cultural specialists to maintain the patina of an earlier era without creating an artificial appearance. Addition of heat, air conditioning, fire control, new utilities, and toilet facilities must be done with great design care.

Equally important is the role of designers for integrating the site into the community. Too often, citizens view restoration as an unnecessary and noneconomic act. For tourism, cultural development is a part of attraction development, an essential part of new economic and social input to a community. Stokvis (1984, 180) has identified several key steps for cultural adaptation to tourism:

> Establish a responsible organization;
> Establish public-private input for decisionmaking;
> Coordinate site and regional cultural planning;
> Return a portion of tourism revenues for cultural development; and
> Design sites as integral parts of the community.

Stokvis emphasized the need to coordinate the local groups involved in the arts, economic development, design, and planning, as well as tourism. McNulty (1984, 187) further emphasized the need in cultural tourism to relate site design to public policy, educate for public understanding of cultural tourism, design facilities and restoration with environmental care, and manage sites with regular monitoring of visitor impact.

Another important aspect of cultural tourism design is the creation of plans for festivals and events related to culture. Museums, exhibition halls, and outdoor exhibit areas require specialized design for display, interpretation, and especially, the physical handling of masses of visitors. The relationship of these designed places to support tourism facilities is particularly important. These cultural attractions not only stimulate local interest and pride but provide strong economic impact. For example, the Rameses The Great exhibition featuring seventy-four Egyptian antiquities, including a 47-ton, 25-foot statue, required special design for housing and interpreting this important exhibit in the city of Memphis, Tennessee (Kyle 1992). It attracted over 675,000 visitors, including 110,000 school-children. The economic impact is estimated at $85 million.

In addition to historians, archeologists increasingly play an important role in tourism planning. To protect rare artifacts and also offer worthwhile visitor interpretation requires close collaboration between designers and archeologists, both terrestrial and nautical. Some time ago, King et al. (1977, 193) admonished archeologists to "serve as critics, advisors, and watchdogs over both statewide survey and planning and over the execution of particular projects."

Cultural site design promises to take a major place in all tourism planning and development in the future.

Interpretive Centers

An excellent design and development solution to many of the environmental concerns at the site scale is the establishment of visitor interpretive centers. As defined here, *a visitor interpretive center* is a facility and program designed to provide a rich, accurate and entertaining visitor understanding of natural and cultural resources. These installations are proving to be successful in providing a fascinating and memorable visitor experience and preventing degradation of the resources. The keys to success for visitor interpretive centers are as follows.

The purpose should be clearly defined as:

- to interpret the area's natural and cultural resources;
- to provide an enjoyable and stimulating visitor experience;
- to provide a setting for environmental education;
- to provide a design alternative to mass erosion of natural and cultural resources; and

- to add an important tourist attraction complex to others within a destination.

They should be located on "hardened" sites, away from rare and fragile resources that would be damaged from excessive human intrusion.

These locations should be accessible by automobile and tour bus. Adequate parking around the facility would allow for volume use.

The interpretive center would include a lobby, receptionist, rest rooms, exhibits, demonstrations, and video room. Optional features would include food service, souvenir and gift sales, and lecture room. Exhibits and dioramas, as used in museums, would provide resource information in themes for best enrichment, education, and enjoyment by visitors. The facility would often have outdoor exhibits of features important to the resource setting. These exhibits would have descriptive signs and/or video presentations for visitor understanding. Appropriate would be a living museum nearby that would mix cultural with natural resource interpretation.

The landscape and building design styling should not be extreme but rather should be a timeless expression of purpose as well as a themed adaptation to the site. All structures should be designed in harmony and provide the visitor with a sense of place. The visitor should be more aware of the content and purpose of structures than of the architectural styling of the interior.

The center could also serve as a staging area for guided or self-guided tours to nearby natural or cultural resource features. Such tour walkways would be designed with proper surfacing, stairways, and sizes to accommodate a maximum capacity of visitor use.

Management and service facilities should be located off-site where their appearance and functions will not intrude upon the esthetics and dominant theme of the center. Only sufficient office space for minimum operational activities should be included in the main interpretive center.

When properly located, designed, and managed, such visitor interpretive centers can function as a surrogate attraction. In other words, instead of allowing visitors to wander over the resource base promiscuously, threatening the resource elements and learning little about them, visitors gain great insight and leave without damaging the environment. For the purists who wish a more intimate natural resource experience, a quota system by management can provide a limited number of properly trained individuals to penetrate the resource to a greater depth. (See Figure 9-2 for proposed visitor interpretive sequence.)

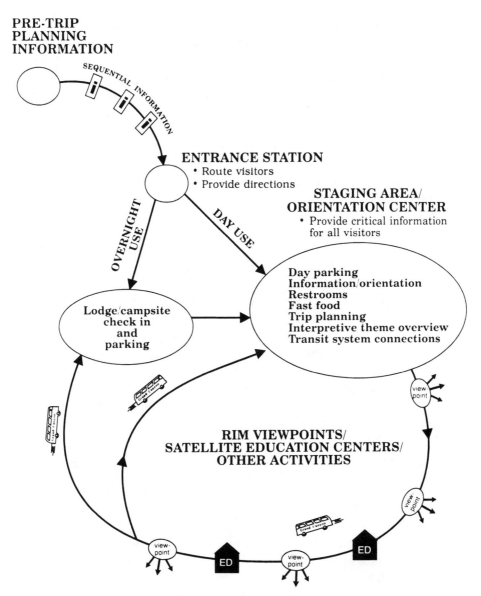

**PRE-TRIP
PLANNING
INFORMATION**

SEQUENTIAL INFORMATION

ENTRANCE STATION
• Route visitors
• Provide directions

**STAGING AREA/
ORIENTATION CENTER**
• Provide critical information
for all visitors

OVERNIGHT USE

DAY USE

Lodge/campsite
check in
and
parking

Day parking
Information/orientation
Restrooms
Fast food
Trip planning
Interpretive theme overview
Transit system connections

**RIM VIEWPOINTS/
SATELLITE EDUCATION CENTERS/
OTHER ACTIVITIES**

view-point

view-point

ED

view-point

ED

view-point

Figure 9-2. Proposed Park Visitor Sequence. A concept for protecting the Grand Canyon National Park environment and also enhancing visitor experience (USNPS 1992, 12).

For example the results of a public-private workshop sponsored by the U.S. National Park Service (NPS) included "the absolute need for adequate funding for state-of-the art, high quality interpretation" (NPS 1992, 19) to meet the present visitor needs of the Grand Canyon National Park and other areas managed by NPS. Among the recommendations was the redesign of the park orientation into a visitor center that would provide introduction to the several themes of the park. Existing historic structures should be studied in terms of what they represent regarding the area, natural or cultural history, specific resources, and what the structure represents in terms of park development or design style. These structures should be converted into museums. Where shops are appropriate, sale items should relate to the exhibits and theme of the site. The workshop results included also an expansion of park interpreter responsibility and function, such as initiating impromptu comments, presenting brief programs at noon in restaurants, and relating factual information in an entertaining manner. The intent is to give visitors not only an enriching experience but greater pride and respect for the resources and facilities provided by NPS. Volunteers and employees of concessions should also be trained as park interpreters. Especially important are programs in other languages to assist visitors from other countries.

When located at the edge of protected resource areas, such as parks and preserves, visitor interpretive centers could be augmented by other supplementary services, such as an outdoor theater for appropriate drama production, a specialty restaurant featuring foods of the area, a base for motorcoach tours, and possible car service. The private sector could provide valuable input to government for establishment and operation of these facilities.

Modern-day aquariums, museums, and zoos, often located in urban settings, are proving extremely popular. Similarly, visitor interpretive centers for natural and cultural resource enjoyment and education are becoming equally popular tourism design features.

The design and management of cultural centers need to be directed toward desired objectives for both visitors and local people. Six objectives were identified by those sponsoring the design and development of a model center in New Mexico—Pueblo of Pojoaque (Warren 1991, 4):

1. Involve 800 local artisans—dance, pottery, crafts.
2. House headquarters of the Eight Northern Indian Pueblos Art Council.
3. Retrieve significant local artifacts from the Smithsonian Institution, Washington, D.C.
4. Expand the visitor center—greater interpretation, cultural exhibits, crafts, shops, traveler services.
5. Create fifty jobs locally.
6. Distribute report on this model to other Indian tribes.

This project is partially sponsored by the Administration for Native Americans, U.S. Department of Health and Human Services. The overall goal is to increase Native American self-sufficiency as well as educate the public on this interesting cultural era, ethnic group, and locale.

There is little question about the greatly increased demand worldwide for traveler visits to cultural sites. Critical then is the increased application of creativity, skill, and cultural sensitivity by designers and developers of these sites in order to enhance visitor satisfactions and perpetuate cultural qualities that are being threatened.

Again referring to Figure 7-7, this model of attraction design suggests a planning concept whereby new and contrasting development does not completely smother its cultural sense of place. However, historic small towns often face great controversy in their plans to preserve or become modern. The case of the historic mining town of Central City, Colorado, provides a typical example.

From the perspective of today's visitor, two images of the community are projected. New gambling establishments within and beside historic structures of this small town (population 335) have engulfed the community. Raw land grading, a cacophony of gaudy signs and voluble hucksters at high-priced parking lots dominate the landscape. For the gaming travel market segment, this new image is an ideal match. For the cultural tourist segment, however, it is a shock. It is extremely difficult for this traveler to imagine the character of this important jewel of Americana as it appeared in the 1870s. Even as late as 1964, it was such an excellent example that the entire canyon was designated a National Historic Landmark.

This dichotomy of tourism planning is symptomatic of long standing community divisiveness. Stokowski's study (1992, 37) of Central City concludes that planning has not yet resolved the stress between the preservation of an historic spirit of place and externally imposed gambling. Her challenge to planners is expressed as follows:

> Tourism development should be concerned with producing and creating sustainable futures, not only in economic terms, but also in terms that are human, and on very personal and collective scales.

Xeriscape

A major issue of sustainable site development is the large quantities of irrigation water needed to maintain the landscape improvements that have been popular in the last few decades. In many regions, water availability has been reduced greatly, humidity levels have escalated, and costs have risen.

The preferred solution is to design landscape changes at tourist developments so that a minimum of new irrigation is required. In many instances, large lawn and ornamental plant beds can be avoided with studied design. Designers, owners, and maintenance staffs need to collaborate on design in the early stages to minimize the demand for water. Today, recycling of waste water from the facilities is becoming a practical solution in many locations. Many resort golf courses are now irrigated with such waters, reducing the demand on local aquifers.

These trends have given rise also to the concept of "Xeriscape", the selection of plant materials requiring much less water and yet offering desirable esthetic functions. Landscape architect Ueker (1992) has summarized this concept with the following seven principles.

Planning and Design. Plan and zone areas according to water needs and microclimatic conditions.

Soil Analysis. Results can assist in reshaping land form for greater water retention.

Plant Selection. Select plants adapted to area and require minimum amounts of supplemental irrigation.

Practical Turf. Place turf in areas to be irrigated separately and only where absolutely necessary for effect.

Efficient Irrigation. Select system that can provide irrigation only when and were needed.

Use of Mulches. Mulched planting beds can retain moisture, reduce weeds, and prevent erosion.

Appropriate Maintenance. If these recommendations are followed, less fertilizer and less water and chemicals will be needed, reducing maintenance costs.

Resource Protection Controls

Many developers, especially business interests, resent the concept of controls. There is no doubt that in many instances, governmental controls have become excessive, conflicting, and obsolete. Even accepting a degree of truth to this connotation, there is another, and very constructive, side to controls. In a modern society, rules and regulations are necessary in order to accomplish objectives and pursue goals.

The major focus of this book is the absolute necessity of resource protection for tourism's survival. Owners, developers, and designers can *enhance* success of establishments by utilizing the land use tools available to them. For example, the Planning Department of New Castle County, Delaware, (1989) has identified several strategies for resource protection available in the United States that could be utilized to the betterment of tourism land development. They are paraphrased as follows.

Government Regulation

County zoning and land use controls may be of value. These can place limits on disturbance of identified resource areas. A delay-of-demolition process can foster the preservation of historic sites. Flood plains, steep slopes, and certain resource/open space areas could be given resource protection.

Controls exercised by government agencies at the state and federal level could be effective in protecting important resources.

Some other strategies that have potential are prohibition of demolition of selected historic structures, performance zoning, mandatory clustering, scenic road overlays, improved flood and drainage controls, density transfer, conservation easements, acceptance of donated lands for protection, tax abatement, and recreation dedication of subdivision lands.

Site Planning Techniques

Increased dialogue between land developers and government planners early in the planning of projects can increase understanding of the benefit of resource protection. The maps and reports prepared by professional planners can help explain the rationale of balancing resource protection with development. Site design processes that include resource analysis can heighten awareness of protecting fragile sites rather than using them for development. A site plan review process between developer and government planner can foster mutual agreement on common goals of development and resource protection.

Private Land Stewardship Actions

Where land is owned primarily by a few large landholders, cooperation on resource protection issues is more readily obtained than among a great number of owners. A smaller constituency can more readily reach consensus on principles of land development and protection. When put into practice it can be used to leverage owners of smaller properties. Donation of tracts of special resource assets can often be to the advantage of land-owners, such as, gifts of land with retained life estates; bargain sales of land in which part of the value of the land is given and the remainder is purchased by an organization or government; and donation of conserva-tion easements which allow some uses but restrict others. The publishing of planning documents can serve as a stimulus to private landowners to initiate conservation easements. Because this is interpreted as a legal donation, there may be tax reduction advantages.

Historic Resource Protection

Official state and national designation of historic sites, following inventory recommendations, assists greatly in resource protection. Tax abatement, revolving fund, and general public education can aid in the application of this strategy. Important as a foundation is the cultural resource inventory that must be extensive and regularly updated. Efforts need to be increased to encourage owners of potentially worthy historic redevelopment to nom-inate them to federal and state historic protection authorities. For exam-ple, owners of income-producing National Register properties, rehabilitated to U.S. National Park Service standards, can receive a 20 percent tax credit on the project cost. It may be necessary to revise historic zoning regulations to allow a greater number of properties to obtain his-toric protection status and to exercise more realistic controls. For example, legislation may be needed to increase fines for unauthorized demolition of historic sites. There needs to be a program of increased incentives for adaptive reuse of historic resources. New zoning stipulations could increase identification of historic resources during all land planning processes.

Highway Planning

A major need as related to tourism is to encourage and assist highway authorities to consider the needed changes in standards required for scenic highway planning development. A *scenic road* could be defined as one having a high degree of natural beauty and historic or cultural value. The criteria of the Federal Highway Administration were modified slightly for this area. The results of scenic landscape inventory were also used. Posi-tive and negative attributes of roads were identified leading to designation of highway segments with scenic potential. Highway planning policies may need revision to favor less scenic routes for expansion as traffic increases. Especially important will be collaborative planning between highway offi-cials and landowners adjacent to scenic routes. County officials, responding to their constituencies, may be the best catalysts for accomplishing scenic highway protection.

Public Agency Coordination

A major need identified in this study was increased cooperation among all governmental agencies if better resource protection is to be accomplished. For some issues, such as water, interstate cooperation is needed. Intergovernmental cooperation will not come about without better communication of environmental issues. Perhaps a joint advisory group is needed.

This example demonstrates some of the environmental control problems and techniques for solution that are applicable to tourism planning and development. Without clean water, abundant wildlife, attractive vegetation, reduction of soil erosion, reduction of air pollution, and protected cultural resources, tourism cannot thrive. Resource protection is an essential part of doing business.

PROCESSES

Even though the design steps for tourism sites are similar in principle to other applications, there are many special needs of tourism that must be recognized by planners and designers. For example, for virtually all other site and building design, the user of the finished project is more readily visible. Second, a great amount of tourism design is for rural and small community settings, often outside the normal professional work load of designers. Finally, no other site design demands resource protection to the extent required by tourism.

Generally, the sequence in the design of a site for a tourism project would follow the steps as listed in Figure 9-3.

Market Analysis

Generally outside the designers realm of training and experience is the field of tourism markets—the people who do and might travel. This is a specialized topic and designers should not be expected to have expertise in it. However, for every tourism project at the site scale, understanding the potential travel user is absolutely essential.

Designers, in collaboration with the owner-developers, will need to engage the services of a market analyst. Today, the total travel market is

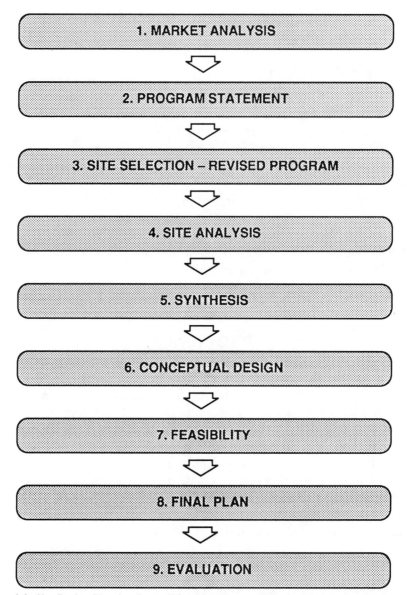

Figure 9-3. Site Design Planning Steps. When these steps are performed by a combined team of designers, developers, and local publics, site plans for tourism attractions, facilities, services, and transportation can result in effective sustainable development of tourism.

segmented into several specialized groups. Few attractions, services, and facilities can satisfy all. Forbes and Forbes (1992, 143) recommended the following points for evaluating special interest travelers:

> Identify and articulate specific, significant profiles of potential customer groups that contain detailed characteristics, purchasing behavior, needs, and expectations.

Develop clear management goals as a foundation to conceive, organize and execute the various roles required to serve the customer.

Determine the existing competencies available to serve these customer needs and expectations.

Carefully assess new market opportunities—areas of significant potential.

Assess modification of current products and services and determine the new supply side development needed.

Although the responsibility for assessing the market potential for the proposed project to be designed is that of the owner-developer, such information must be in the hands of the designer in order to create the proper project design. Consideration should be given to both potential domestic as well as international travelers. Sources of help in assessing market demand include government agencies, nonprofit organizations, and private consultants.

Program Statement

The program statement is a listing and description of what is to be designed. Although it would appear obvious that this statement is important, experience reveals that many weaknesses of projects can be traced to incomplete or incorrect problem statements.

This statement of work to be done is primarily the responsibility of the owner-developer. However, the best statement—one clearly understood by both designers and client—is one that is cooperatively prepared. The owner should have a clear estimate of the size of project, the number, type, function, and quality level of structures, and general configuration of layout. If a site has been selected, designers can advise on its suitability and make recommendations for a revised program.

Site Selection/Revised Program

The ideal process brings designers into the site selection process. Landscape and building architects are experienced in qualities of suitability of land for project development. Often, a preliminary study is made comparing the suitability of three or four prospective sites for the project. Even without detailed analysis and estimating, rough feasibility can be determined for each, resulting in one being selected as superior to all others. Many factors need to be considered such as access, extent of land preparation, size, location, cost, availability of land, land use regulation, and relationship to competition. Often, property that may appear relatively costly may be favored because it has a better feasibility for financial success.

After narrowing the choice to one site, cooperative discussions between designers and owners may result in modifying the program. For example, because of the environment the program for a resort hotel may have to be changed from the original highrise to a series of separate lowrise units.

Site Analysis

Detailed analysis of the piece of land selected for the proposed project is a two-part investigation. Very important is a detailed description of the several internal characteristics of the site. But, equally valuable in the design process is assessment of external characteristics. Molnar and Rutledge (1986, 93) has identified several factors needed in the analysis of a site for the design of parks. The following is an adaptation for tourism site design and development.

On-Site Factors:

1. Constructed elements:
   - Legal and physical boundaries, public easements.
   - Existing buildings, bridges, and other structures including those of historical and archeological interest.
   - Roads, walks, and other transportation ways.
   - Electric lines, gas mains, and other utilities.
   - Existing land uses.
   - Applicable ordinances, such as zoning regulations and health codes.

2. Natural resources:
   - Topography, including high and low points, gradients and drainage patterns.
   - Soil types, for clues regarding permeability, stability, and fertility.
   - Water bodies, including permanence, fluctuations, and other habits.
   - Subsurface matter: geology and functionally valuable material such as sand, gravel, and water.
   - Vegetation types—trees and other plant materials and individual specimens of design importance.
   - Wildlife habitat and species of importance.
   - Climate and weather: temperature, days of sunshine per year, sun exposure, precipitation, wind and storm frequency, and directions.

3. Perceptual characteristics:
   - Esthetic characteristics including views and features.
   - Smells and sounds within the site.
   - Spatial patterns, such as distribution of wooded areas, open spaces, and water features.
   - Design character as derived from lines, forms, textures, colors, and size relationship.
   - Overall impressions derived by the designers.

Off-Site Factors:

1. Surrounding land uses and their characteristics, especially compatibility with intended site program, trends in land use change, shading from high rise development.
2. Stream and drainage sources and their characteristics such as stability, flooding, and potential pollution.
3. Negative influences of sounds and smells generated nearby, such as from agriculture, industry, and entertainment.
4. Esthetic influences, such as views from site outward. If landscape factors are beautiful in surrounding area, are protective measures in place?
5. External utilities—their accessibility and capacities.
6. Transportation and access, new and future trends.

It must be emphasized that these qualities are identified only for one reason—to assist in design decisions. Every factor may have a bearing on what is to be placed where and how the layout will function best. Sometimes designers become so caught up in details of analysis they fail to relate these facts to their design objectives. Close communication between designers and clients can avert this problem.

The documentation and presentation of results from this analysis process often utilize maps, descriptive narratives, and verbal presentations. Computer Geographic Information System overlays and other graphic programs can be utilized to simplify complicated analysis tasks, make rapid visual images, and reduce costs.

Synthesis

Although intuitively, thus far in the process the owner-developers and designers have been considering how well the proposed site and its development will meet the needs of visitors, there must be a time for double-checking these factors. Too often, designers are tempted to skip the checking step and go directly into the preparation of plans.

This step of synthesis is intended to derive meaning from the great amount of facts that have been gathered. Throughout the study of market trends, the designers and owners should have been getting ideas for appropriate development. Perhaps the earliest concept of a high density resort has now been modified to serve a different market segment. Perhaps this modification has completely changed the potential sponsorship from a purely commercial operation to a joint venture with a nonprofit organization. Perhaps the site analysis revealed new opportunities to develop facilities for a market segment not considered possible in earlier stages.

An important part of synthesis is experimenting with functional relationships between the several elements of the project. Illustrated in Figure 9-4 are bubble diagrams showing rough relationships between the program elements required by a park agency (Molnar and Rutledge 1986, 99). Although this effort is roughly related to the site, it is primarily for the purpose of establishing plan policies. Such experimentation by the designer can raise many questions of the owner. The owner can react by visualizing how well different arrangements will suit visitor needs, fit the general site conditions, meet feasibility requirements, and provide for efficient management and maintenance.

Conceptual Design

If all the preceding steps have been taken and considered thoroughly by the owners and designers, the design team can now engage in the creative thinking and conceptualizing to give form to a plan. This results in what is often called a sketch plan or a preliminary plan. It is at this stage that the value of the first five steps becomes clear. The many hours of discussion between designer and client concerning the research data, analysis, and synthesis now begin to pay off.

Recommended are two or three alternative sketch plans. Several alternatives allow discussion and debate upon the relative merits of each. These are based on facts but incorporate the imaginative thinking and artistic creativity of the designers.

This sketch plan of both site and structures for the first time give form to the project. The site plan shows protected areas, all program use areas, circulation systems (drives, walks, and parking), and entrances—all logically and creatively related to program and site conditions. Building sketch plans reveal the bulk, character, and functional spaces of all structures.

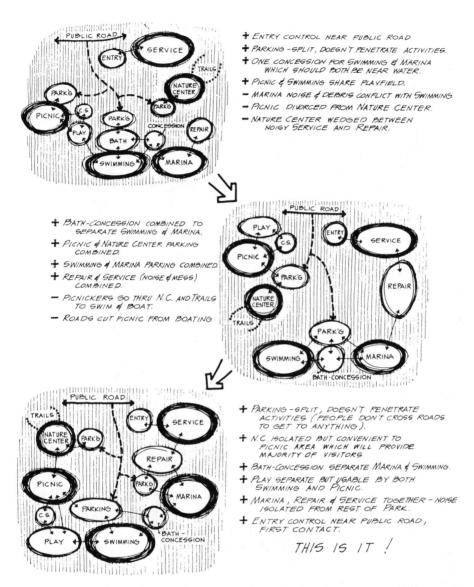

Figure 9-4. Relationship Diagrams. These diagrams help focus developers and designers on important functional relationships among all elements of a plan. From consensus, final plans are assured implementation (Molnar and Rutledge 1986, 99).

Feasibility

With a clearer vision of what is to be developed and where, it is now possible to come to conclusions on feasibility. In the past, feasibility has meant primarily *financial feasibility*. Today equally important are *physical and social environmental feasibility*.

The first step in preparation of financial feasibility is an estimate of total capital costs—site, site development, and architectural development. Designers, in collaboration with landscape and building contractors can make estimates of total costs of construction for each of the alternative sketch plan solutions.

A physical environmental feasibility refers to the negative and positive environmental impact of each of the designs. Even if environmental impact statements are not a legal requirement, an accurate assessment of how the project will influence all existing natural resource factors is needed.

Social environmental feasibility is an increasingly important step. All new tourism projects will exert some impact on the social, economic, and lifestyle factors of an area. Too often, in the past these considerations were not made early in the planning process resulting in strong local opposition. The local people of an area have the right to pass upon changes that will affect their lives. Social feasibility includes also meeting all legal requirements of land use and buildings.

Taking all these feasibility factors into consideration, the owner can now develop revenue return estimates for each of the alternative plans. Perhaps one shows a favorable profit conclusion but will cause great social and physical stress in the area. That alternative should be passed over in favor of the alternative that places the least stress on the area and also shows profitability.

Final Plan

After the most feasible alternative sketch plan has been selected, final plans for development can be prepared. The sketch plan generalities now need detailed refinement so that the landscape and building contractors will have clear instructions on exactly what is to be built and how. These final plans include three main documents: *construction drawings* (working plans), *specifications,* and *contract.*

Construction drawings show precise dimensions for every aspect of development. On layout plans, all drives, walks, and structures are located. Often, separate drawings with details are made for grading, drainage, plumbing, heating, air conditioning, and plantings. It is at this stage that earlier steps prove their worth. Changes at this stage are confusing and costly. These drawings are prepared by licensed specialists in all related fields of design in order to meet requirements of health and safety.

Specifications provide detailed descriptions of materials and how they are to be used. Again, these details are exacting and must meet all the needs of the designed development. Specifications make sure that no matter the final contracting firm, the same standards are maintained.

The contract is the final agreement between contractors and owners/designers. Contracts define the complete and itemized costs of construction as well as schedule of work to be performed. Methods of payment, insurance, bonding, and other legal requirements are included.

With the completion of these documents the project is advertised for construction bids. Implementing the policies of the owner (public or private), selection of the best firm is made.

The project is then developed and ready for staffing and management so that visitors can be received.

Evaluation

Often in the past, no mechanism was put in place for evaluation of the success of the designed project. Needed is an assessment by both owners and designers of how well the design met its objectives. Because the entire project was based on *estimates* of market interest and quality of management, there may be need for modified design after the experience of a year or two. Tourism is extremely dynamic, making it difficult to make precise forecasts of success no matter how well designed a project may be. Feedback from visitors, managers, and local residents can provide needed enlightenment.

CONCLUSIONS ON INTEGRATED PLANNING/DESIGN: SITE SCALE

Site Scale Design Is the Culmination of All Tourism Planning.

It is at the site scale that regional and destination planning yield concrete results. Regional and destination tourism planning lay the foundation for the best general areas and types of development that have potential. But, it is only when the three sectors of decisionmakers—governments, non-profit organizations, and commercial enterprise—actually create the supply side development that all planning efforts bear fruit. This fact endorses the need for great care in all site scale design for tourism.

Today's Site Development Success Demands Professional Design.

Although decisionmakers and others contribute greatly to site development, land and building design requires input from professional designers.
Today, most projects require team collaboration among several professionals—architects, landscape architects, engineers, and often several
other specialists. They translate concepts of decisionmakers into buildable
and manageable development for visitor fulfillment.

Tourism Design Is Greatly Influenced by Groups Other than Designers.

Often overlooked is the great influence imposed by moneylenders, owners,
the construction industry, managers, and several publics. The final design
of hotels, resorts, restaurants, shops, travel ways, and other facilities and
services is the result of their input as well as that of professional designers.
This fact requires close collaboration among all for best design results.

The New Design Paradigm Requires New Kinds of Designers.

No longer can design professionals operate as narrowly as in the past.
Their role includes several new dimensions, especially for tourism design.
Today, they need greater insight into social, behavioral, economic, and
environmental aspects of every project. Integration of the many constituencies and influences on tourism design problems requires a new catalytic and facilitating role and new ethics of design.

Placemaking Is Essentially The Creative Process of Tourism Design.

Although resource characteristics are critical foundation factors, they are
not truly available to visitors unless so designed, built, and managed.
Natural and cultural resources are not attractions until decisionmakers,
designers, and others develop these resources for visitor use. A major
responsibility is maintaining the integrity of places, especially their social,
environmental, and economic uniqueness.

**Public Involvement Is Essential Throughout the Process of All Tourism
Design.**

Unlike other economic development, tourism has impact upon many public groups who have the right to know about a tourism project planned for

their area. Their input can provide constructive recommendations and raise issues that will need to be resolved for best public acceptance. For all sectors of developers, public involvement is an essential part of tourism design and development.

Tourism Project Design Must Meet Several Criteria.

Although most designers practice their profession to meet these criteria, they are especially important for tourism projects. Criteria such as functionality, visitor needs, integration with other plans, individuality, authenticity, esthetics, and marketability are critical to tourism project success. Best results are derived from designer-developer collaboration toward meeting these criteria.

Tourism Project Design Is the Final Expression of Sustainability.

Theories and philosophies of sustainability remain as postulates until given substance in actual project development. Sensitivity to environmental factors is a basic rule of all planning and design today, but it has special meaning for tourism. Tourism depends heavily on the perpetuation of resource qualities. All techniques should be employed, such as interpretive centers, land design details, xeriscape, and protection controls so that every design for tourism can provide maximum visitor satisfaction and environmental enrichment.

Tourism Project Design Requires a Special Process.

In addition to traditional design process steps, tourism projects have some especially important steps. Information on travel markets, clarity of program statement, care in site selection, special understanding of on-site and off-site characteristics, and feasibility are important for tourism. Follow-up evaluation is especially needed to determine how valid were all of the design decisions.

REFERENCES

American Society of Landscape Architects (1992). *1992 Members Handbook.* Washington, DC: ASLA.

Antoniades, Anthony C. (1986). *Architecture and Allied Design,* 2nd ed. Dubuque, IA: Kendall/Hunt.

Billing, John C. (1987). "Baltimore's Past Harbors Its Future." *Landscape Architecture,* 77(5), 68–73.

Callaway, Clive et al. (1990). "The Salmon Arm Waterfront—A Win-Win Project." Proceedings, Planning for Special Places Conference, Banff, Alberta, May 13–16, pp. 107–110.

Forbes, Robert J. and Maree S. Forbes (1992). "Special Interest Travel," pp. 141–144. In *World Travel and Tourism Review,* Ritchie and Hawkins, eds. Oxon, U.K.: C.A.B. International.

Garnham, Harry L. (1985). *Maintaining the Spirit of Place.* Mesa, AZ: PDA Pub.

Gunn, Clare A. et al. (1972). *Cultural Benefits from Metropolitan River Recreation—San Antonio Prototype,* TP-43. College Station, TX: Texas Water Resources Institute, Texas A&M University.

King, Thomas F. et al. (1977). *Anthropology in Historic Preservation.* New York: Academic Press.

Kyle, Jack (1992). Personal correspondence from Manager Communications & Public Relations, for Wonders: The Memphis International Cultural Series, letter October 22, 1992.

Marshall, Lane L. (1983). *Action by Design.* Washington, DC: American Society of Landscape Architects.

McNulty, Robert H. (1984). "Tourism Development and Cultural Conservation: Ways to Coordinate Heritage with Economic Development." In *International Perspectives on Cultural Parks.* Proceedings, First World Conference, Colorado, pp. 183–187.

Molnar, Donald J., and Albert J. Rutledge (1986). *Anatomy of a Park,* 2nd ed. New York: McGraw-Hill.

Motloch, John L. (1991). *Introduction to Landscape Design.* New York: Van Nostrand Reinhold.

New Castle County Department of Planning (1989). *The Red Clay Valley Scenic River and Highway Study.* Newark, DE: NCCDP.

Ritchie, J.R. Brent (1987). "The Nominal Group Technique—Application in Tourism Research," Chapter 37, pp. 439–448. In *Travel, Tourism and Hospitality Research,* J. Ritchie and C. Goeldner (eds.). New York: John Wiley & Sons.

Scarfo, Bob (1992). "Ethics: What We Say and What We Do." *L.A. Letter,* 3(3),pp. 2–3.

Stokowski, Patricia A. (1992). "Place, Meaning and Structure in Community Tourism Development: A Case Study from Central City, Colorado." In *Mountain Resort Development.* Proceedings, conference in Vail, Colorado, April 18–21, Alison Gill and Rudi Hartmann (eds.). Burnaby, British Columbia: Centre for Tourism Policy and Research, Simon Fraser University.

Stokvis, Jack R. (1984). "Utilizing Tourism, Both as an Economic Stimulus for Community Development and to Improve the Quality of Life for Residents." In *International Perspectives on Cultural Parks.* Proceedings, First World Conference, Colorado, pp. 179–182.

Ueker, Raymond L., Jr. (1992). "Water Conserving Landscapes: Focus on Xeriscape." *Landscape Design,* 5(7), 22–24.

U.S. National Park Service (1992). *Visitor Use Management Workshop Findings and Recommendations: Grand Canyon National Park*. Washingon, DC: USNPS.

Warren, Winonah (1991). "A Model Cultural Center at Pejoaque Pueblo." *Cultural Resources Management*, 14(5), 4–6.

Watt, Carson et al.(1991). "Rural Tourism Development Case Study: Fredricksburg, Texas." College Station, TX: Texas Tourism and Recreation Information Program, Texas A&M University.

Western Australian Tourism Commission (n.d.). *Public Involvement in Tourism Development: What Does It Mean for the Developer?* Perth: WATC.

Western Australian Tourism Commission (1989). *The Eco Ethics of Tourism Development*. Perth: WATC.

Western Australian Tourism Commission (1990). *Successful Tourism Design*. Perth: WATC.

Chapter 10

Site Planning Cases

Introduction

In all of tourism development, the real brick-and-mortar action takes place on sites. Although regional and destination planning provide important policies, guidelines, and stimulation for development, it is at the site scale that development materializes. Tangible development occurs within all five functioning components of the tourism system—attractions, transportation, services, information, and promotion.

Traditionally, site development results from collaboration between two groups—owners and designers. Although this is basically true for tourism development, the interdependent nature of tourism requires a much broader scope of planning and design. For example, attraction design must consider plans and development of transportation and services as well as plans for the attraction site. The design of services, such as for hotels, and food and automobile service, must include study of plans and development of attractions and transportation. Very critical for all tourism design at the site scale is relevancy to anticipated travel market segments.

Worldwide, casebooks and files of tourist-oriented site planning and design are much more plentiful than destination or regional plans. It is more commonly accepted and often a legal requirement that the design and planning professions are engaged by owners to develop properties at this scale, such as for attractions, hotels, resorts, and restaurants. And, in recent years, with the shopping mall concept, more tourism site clusters, such as theme parks, have appeared.

It is at the site scale that the many characteristics of the land area become very important. The physical elements of topography, soils, drainage, wind flow, and plant materials provide both opportunities and limitations for design. External factors of adjacent land use and access are also important in guiding design solutions. A major challenge to the designer is to balance protection of resource assets and fulfillment of the owner's and user's objectives.

Included here are a few cases of planning and design at the site (and site cluster) scale that demonstrate a variety of approaches used to meet varying needs and circumstances. (More cases of well-planned tourist site design are presented in *Vacationscape: Designing Tourist Regions*, 2nd ed., 1988, by C. A. Gunn.)

SAN ANTONIO RIVER WALK

This case is described in three phases. First is a research study made in 1970–1972; the second is the result of an investigation in 1986; and the third is special development study performed in 1987. These studies concern the planning and management issues associated with a major travel attraction site complex, the San Antonio River Walk, Texas.

A 1972 STUDY

Description

The San Antonio River Walk encompasses a relatively small area, about four by six city blocks, in the older central part of the city (Figure 10-1). The river is mostly a horseshoe bend natural cut of about 35 feet deep in the surrounding land. It is criss-crossed by many bridges of city streets.

A serious flood in 1921 caused several civic leaders to consider covering the river valley with concrete and using the interior as a sewer. Instead, conservation interests prevailed and flood control measures were prepared and installed, stabilizing the horseshoe bend. Several plans have been offered over three decades but the major impetus came with a 1938 bond issue for planning and enhancement. This bond issue was matched by the Federal Works Progress Administration to build rock retaining walls, picturesque foot bridges, and rock-surfaced walks. Establishing the River Walk Commission in 1962 provided a mechanism for guiding and controlling development. Ever since 1924, the San Antonio Conservation Society has been a strong force for historic and plant protection. A world fair—Hemisfair—of 1968 gave further stimulus for beautifying and adding ranger patrol for the River Walk in order to create a major local amenity and a vital attraction for visitors.

Because of major redevelopment and increased popularity of the San Antonio River Walk by 1970, it became the focus of research study to

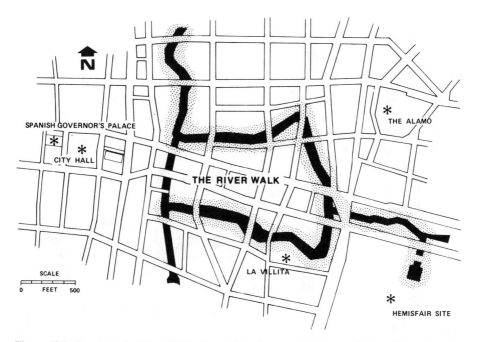

Figure 10-1. San Antonio River Walk. Located in the central business district of San Antonio, development for residents and visitors along the San Antonio River has become a major attraction. The private sector and several public agencies have cooperated on design, development, and management. Nearby attractions include the Alamo, Spanish Governor's Palace, LaVillita, and Hemisfair site (Gunn et al. 1972, 11).

determine how and why it had developed and became such a major tourism force in San Antonio and the state of Texas. This study was supported by the Texas Water Resources Institute, the Texas Agricultural Experiment Station, the Texas Agricultural Extension Service, and the Recreation and Parks Department of Texas A&M University. It resulted in the report *Cultural Benefits from Metropolitan Recreation—San Antonio Prototype* (Gunn et al. 1972).

The objectives of the study were to sketch the present trends in river development in U.S. cities, analyze the landscape character of the River Walk, and obtain opinions and attitudes toward the use and characteristics of the River Walk.

General Urban River Development

By means of a survey of the fifty largest U.S. cities, review of literature, and reconnaissance visits to ten cities with urban water development, the following information was obtained:

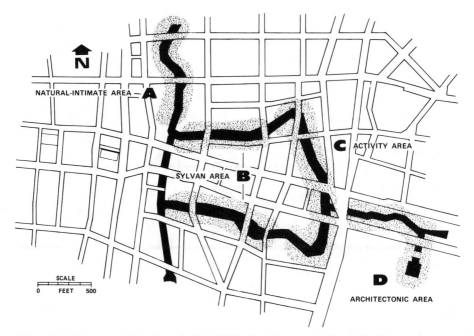

Figure 10-2. Subzones of San Antonio River Walk. Landscape analysis revealed four environmental and development subzones that have resulted from periodic planning and organic growth. A, Natural-Intimate Area; B, Sylvan Area; C, Activity Area; and D, Architectonic Area (Gunn et al. 1972, 53).

- An increasing concern over the deterioration of urban centers.
- Pressure from conservationists, preservationists, and historic restorers to redevelop urban corridors.
- Continued concern over flooding problems of urban areas.
- New and inappropriate development in urban areas along waterfronts that ignores the aesthetic and visual amenities of the water.
- Some new, low-quality downtown river development that perpetuates an already serious problem because land is low-priced.
- Little acceptance by business that waterfront has value in an urban setting.

Landscape Analysis

As illustrated in Figure 10-2, the consultants were able to identify four distinct environmental subzones of the River Walk.

Zone "A," "Natural-Intimate Area," is characterized by a parklike setting along both sides of the river. The river banks along the walkways are attractively flanked by plant masses maintained by the Park and Recreation Department.

Zone "B," "Sylvan Area," includes two legs of the horseshoe riverbend and were the first portions to be given conservation protection as early as the 1930s. It contains large cypress and cottonwood trees, and forms a pleasant area for reading, relaxing, and visiting. It is relatively free from building construction. Walks, bridges, and retaining walls were designed in harmony with the setting by the Works Progress Administration.

Zone "C," "Activity Area," has an attractive landscape setting but is dominated by restaurants, night clubs, gift shops, an amphitheater, and downtown shops. Night lighting of trees allows intensive night and day use of the zone.

Zone "D," "Architectonic Area," consists of an extension of the river created for the Hemisfair of 1968. It connects the newly built arena, exhibition hall, and theater with the remainder of the river.

Visitor Survey

Interview surveys of a sampling of over a million visitors during all four seasons of 1971 provided the following major findings:

- A wide diversity of age, business, and professionals.
- A high number of repeat visitors (82.6% visited the year before).
- Primary activities included sightseeing by foot, shopping, relaxing, followed by a variety of other passive recreation activities.
- About 34% made the boat trip of the river.
- The majority (70.3%) came from outside San Antonio.

Voter Survey

By means of a cross-section sampling of all resident voters of San Antonio, the following opinions were obtained:

- 96.6 percent believed it was an attraction for the city.
- 80.7 percent believed it was of economic benefit to the city.
- 74.9 percent believed it was of value to them.
- 63.9 percent would support a bond issue for further improvement even if it would raise taxes.

Landowner, Controller Survey

Both contiguous landowners and the primary controlling agencies were interviewed for their opinions and assessment of the River Walk. The interviews revealed that at that time 70 percent of the contiguous property owners still oriented their business activity to the streets rather than the River Walk. Over 93 percent had no plans to develop a business oriented to the river level visitors.

At the time of this study, six agencies and organizations managed and controlled the River Walk: San Antonio River Authority, San Antonio Chamber of Commerce, San Antonio Conservation Society, Paseo del Rio Association, and River Walk Commission. Collectively, their opinions regarding the value of the River Walk paralleled those of the visitors. There was consensus that the importance of this site would grow and become an ever increasing focal point for the city, not only for tourism but for local lifestyle and economy as well.

Conclusions and Inferences

From this study the following fifteen conclusions and inferences were derived:

1. The River Walk is a special place and therefore deserves special planning and care.
2. The River Walk, in spite of diverse organic growth over many years, has emerged as a unified whole.
3. The River Walk, in spite of such unity is made up of a great diversity of activity opportunities for visitors provided by a diversity of owners-managers.
4. A delicate but very critical balance exists between a natural and cultural resource setting and business enterprise.
5. The River Walk already has proven to be of great social and economic value.
6. A dynamic future is promised. Many changes in attitude, land use, and visitor use are possible, requiring constant monitoring to protect valuable assets.
7. The River Walk setting is not typical of most other urban settings; it is a relatively small valley with a stabilized water level, very important to its planning and operation.
8. The River Walk is counteracting the universal trend toward urban heart decay.
9. Success does not require a large amount of water surface. Both sides of this river interact to provide strong internal unity.

10. The River Walk demonstrates that it is not necessary to wait for a superagency to control development. Here, six agencies and organizations are cooperating toward similar goals.
11. A business-park mix can succeed. The River Walk is neither pure park nor commerce but rather is a new amalgam, demonstrating strong complementarity.
12. Diversity of activity in a small area is possible.
13. Future internal and adjacent land uses must continue to be compatible or the important values—social, economic, environmental—can be destroyed.
14. Citizens and tourists can enjoy and become enriched by the same amenity.
15. The River Walk is demonstrating that indigenous tourist attraction development is important to the state and nation.

Because the River Walk is not owned or legally controlled by any one individual, corporation, or governmental agency, reaching desired planning and design objectives required cooperation and agreement on rules for development. By ordinance of the City Council, the River Walk Commission was charged with this responsibility. As a result, the *River Walk Policy Manual* was approved by the Commission on January 4, 1977. Following is a summary of its regulations and conclusions.

Permitting. The issuance of permits for construction, remodeling, or signs must be preceded by preparation of preliminary plans that illustrate these project developments and how they are to be done. Approvals by the Commission are required for a permit to be issued by the Director of Building and Zoning; denial may be appealed.

The River Walk Commission. It consists of nine members appointed by the City Council—three of whom are practicing professionals in architecture, design, landscape architecture, or a related profession. It advises the Director of Building and Zoning, the City Manager, and the City Council.

Policies. By ordinance, the City Council created and adopted a special overlay zoning district to identify, plan, and control the area in order to retain its special natural and historic place qualities. It encompassed three parts: the River Walk Area, River Walk easements, and LaVillita (historic Mexican village). Provisions provide for several planning and design directions:

Minimum audio usage
No billboards
Prohibition of nudity   Controlled sign design, use

No solicitation	Permitted visitor services
No visible waste	Single tour boat concession
Well-maintained walks, stairs	Well-maintained plants
Adequate, safe lighting	

FOLLOW-UP OF 1979

A brief review of changes in the River Walk was prepared by Gunn (1979). Interviews with key knowledgeables and reconnaissance of the area led to the following observations.

Cities elsewhere were stimulated to plan their urban water resources, revealed by a demand for several reprintings of the report.

Over 100 historic buildings in the River Walk area have been restored and are in adaptive use.

Many new structures are being designed, built, and oriented to the River Walk theme.

Many millions of dollars are being invested in new hotels adjacent to the River Walk.

The Housing and Urban Development Department has awarded $450,000 to redevelop all electrical work under River Walk bridges for increased esthetics and safety.

A $6.4 million urban development grant has been made to extend the river toward the historic Alamo and a new Hyatt Hotel.

A new bus system for visitors has been established.

The adjacent King William historic district has been stimulated to make major redevelopment of homes.

Older hotels along the river are being converted into new apartments and condominiums.

The River Walk has stimulated new office and hotel development in the vicinity.

Testimony from officials indicate that the original research study stimulated greater awareness of tourism, greater cooperation among agencies and organizations, stronger design theme for new development, and an important catalyst for downtown revitalization.

A 1987 STUDY

The overwhelming popularity and success of the San Antonio River Walk development had precipitated some issues of concern. Texas A&M University was approached to study these concerns and apply specialized expertise for resolution. The issues were identified as follows (Roessler 1987, 9):

> The need for the San Antonio River Walk Area Commission (SARWAC) to expand its jurisdiction over newly developing river environments.
>
> The visual impact of adjacent high rise development was threatening to create "canyonization," or a "tunnel effect."
>
> The ecological impact of such shading on flora and fauna was critical to its value and reputation as an enjoyable attraction.
>
> The need for greater coordination of development criteria by governmental departments.
>
> The need for a review process for evaluation of new projects.

These concerns were placed before the university and an interdisciplinary team of faculty and students was created by Wolfgang Roessler of the Urban and Regional Planning Department. Beginning in 1985, the study of the issues resulted in a *San Antonio Development Guidelines System* (Roessler 1987), and the *SARWAC Development Guidelines System Notebook* (six modules for use by commissions, staff, and developers; computerized procedures; computerized data bases; regulatory guidelines; and general information).

The results of this investigation had many implications for tourism even though the study was focused on specific design and development issues. It resulted in two bodies of recommendations. The first dealt with development guidelines and preparation of a manual. The second conceptualized building envelope standards and recommended regulations. Each is summarized as follows.

Development Guidelines

For prospective developers of properties adjacent to the River Walk a guidelines manual was prepared containing five basic categories of requirements.

1. Data Base. Each prospective developer would be required to provide basic information about the applicant, description of the land parcel, and the proposed development project. Proposed improvements to existing buildings as well as any new structures are to be included. Land use characteristics, such as location, historical significance, and needed action, are to be described.

2. *Infrastructure Check List.* Pertinent infrastructural requirements are to be described. The project must meet the city's requirements for all utilities including water and sewer service. Evidence that traffic and access needs are met must be presented. Site proposals must be coordinated with the city's traffic and transit authorities. Impact on other community services, such as fire, police, schools, and parks, must be documented. The design must be such that other public use of these facilities is not impaired. Finally, detailed design plans would be required for all drainage structures and patterns. Flood threats are of particular importance.

3. *Locational Considerations.* Four important locational criteria were identified. Special technical solar gradient criteria are to be met. Locational relationship to historic sites is to be documented according to design criteria. Encroachment and visual gradients are to be assessed. Compatibility with existing landscape settings is to be evaluated by SARWAC.

4. *SARWAC Criteria.* Development criteria used by SARWAC would include historic value, street level linkages, view corridor, land use compatibility, pedestrian/handicap access, and site planning/landscape considerations. Design criteria include such items as height/bulk proportions, setbacks, rhythm, materials, colors, textures, and amenities (signage and lighting). Functional criteria include the provision and quality of waste handling, parking, drainage, and delivery service.

5. *Disposition and Recommendations.* When SARWAC receives from a project developer the total evaluation of all criteria listed in the required guidelines, it can approve, deny, or request a resubmittal. Detailed procedures and forms were prepared by the consultant team to provide SARWAC with the needed formalities. A point system of evaluation assists in judging the merit of each application for permit.

Concepts and Conclusions

Included in the recommendations of the consultant team was a computerized building envelope system, offered and detailed as a technique for identifying visual and shadow impacts of proposed structures.

The study again reinforced the basic principles discovered earlier regarding the significance of this special place and the need for care in its planning. This philosophy was expressed in the report as follows:

> The River Walk area is the principal economic asset of central San Antonio. If the integrity of this delicate environment is severely damaged, the loss of that asset will

turn into a devastating liability. The aesthetic values created through careful recognition of the man-made subtropical environment and of architectural achievement of San Antonio's rich past can be lost by unwise shortsighted decisions of development or redevelopment. (Roessler 1987, 3.14)

Although the breadth of this project went beyond tourism, many traveler development implications were included. Tourism was seen as integral to the life or death of the central business district. The recommended new policies, procedures, and coordinating mechanisms, when implemented, would enhance tourism at the same time that it improved the amenities and quality of life for local residents.

These studies of a major tourist attraction prove that planning is a dynamic and continuing process. The different studies have assisted local authorities and businesses greatly in their planning and design decisions. Evaluating planned development and regularly monitoring change are essential steps in all tourism planning and design at the site scale.

MAHO BAY CAMPS

An ecotourism resort, Maho Bay Camps, U.S. Virgin Islands, is an award-winning development designed for maximum resource protection and visitor satisfaction. This example also proves that meeting such an objective can be profitable. In 1991, after paying the U.S. National Park Service $217,000 for the land lease, profits exceeded 20 percent (Leccese 1992, 54). After 16 years of operation, occupancy has averaged 85 percent, rare for resorts anywhere.

This development is a 114-unit hillside resort of spacious tent-cottages nestled in the treetops in an unspoiled natural resource setting. The layout is illustrated in Figure 10-3. The furnished cottages are connected by wooden walkways and stairs rather than paved drives or walks. Pipes and electrical systems are hidden under these walkways. Recycled wastewater contributes toward rehabilitation of vegetation and wildlife. Each cottage contains a sleeping area, a living room (with sleeping sofa), a screened cooking and dining area, and an open porch. Several centrally located bathhouses are equipped with modern toilets, sinks, and showers. A self-service outdoor restaurant features healthful foods. The kitchen uses biodegradable cleaning products, composts waste foods, and uses water saving devices. A commissary is stocked with dairy products, frozen meats and fish, vegetables, canned goods, and staples (Selengut 1992).

Maho Bay grew from a New York developer's belief that the traditional mega-resort was inappropriate for sensitive natural resource sites. It took

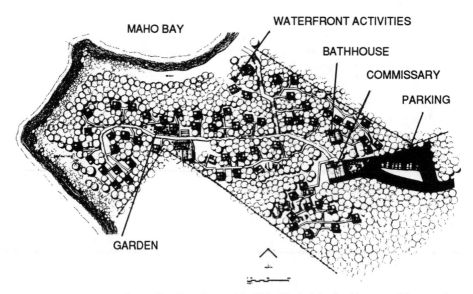

Figure 10-3. Maho Bay Camps Site Plan. Located in U.S. Virgin Islands, this successful ecotourism development demonstrates compatibility between resource protection and business success. All cottage units are built on posts and all access is by elevated walkways to protect resource assets (Stubbs 1991, 37).

him a year to convince local residents that an entirely new ecotourism resort was scheduled for the area. Developer Stanley Selengut and architect James Hadley collaborated on setting rigid environmental policies for all design and management. Among these are the following recommendations to landscape architects, architects, and planners (Leccese 1992, 54):

> It should be site-adaptive, meaning you work with existing grades, leave existing vegetation, minimize the use of heavy equipment.
> It should be sustainable. You should use local plants, control feral species.
> It should be recyclable—not just the building materials but the walkways. If you build stone walls, they should be dry stone [laid without mortar], so the stones can be used over again.
> It should support wildlife.
> It should be non-polluting. You have to watch for erosion and avoid pesticides and fertilizers.
> It should involve cultural restoration and ecological restoration.
> Conservation is the last principle: use solar power, wind, pumps, etc.

Selengut's advice to others who plan resorts includes the following (Stubbs 1991, 9):

> Inventory natural assets and heritage.
> Identify local values and opportunities. These include historic preservation and public parks.

Design compensation measures to protect species; for example, how much site draining will make the land too dry for a particular native plant.

Describe and designate development and construction practices that mitigate damage.

Design with natural logic over geometry on the design of lot lines.

Write protective covenants that are understandable, acceptable, and legally enforceable.

Selegut concludes that (1992):

It is more profitable to work with nature than against it.

That environmental restoration can be a marketing tool, and that working with government and private agencies is better than working against them. In fact, many conservation groups such as the Audubon Society with large travel programs might even become your customers. (Leccese 1992, 55)

This is an excellent demonstration of an ecotourism resort designed and managed to exacting environmental standards that accomplishes three objectives: protects fragile resources, provides enriching and enjoyable visitor satisfactions, and makes a profit.

BLUE RIDGE PARKWAY

One of the most outstanding and popular attractions of the world is the Blue Ridge Parkway, nearly 500 miles of uninterrupted scenic drive in eastern United States, linking Shenandoah National Park on the north with Great Smoky Mountain National Park on the south. Although its size might suggest a more appropriate classification as regional or destination, its scope and planning process are more closely those at the site scale. The following description is paraphrased from *Blue Ridge Parkway: The First 50 Years* (Jolley 1985).

Political/Economic Origin

What today is a preeminent example of landscape design and resource protection grew primarily from an economic need. In the 1930s the United States experienced unprecedented hard times with mass unemployment. One solution, led by President Franklin D. Roosevelt, was the National Industrial Recovery Act of 1933, including a Public Works Administration (PWA) with a $3.3 billion budget to provide relief employment.

Several political leaders are credited with proposing to the president that the building of a scenic highway was an appropriate project for this federal program. Senator Harry F. Byrd (formerly governor of Virginia) had for some time recommended the extension southward of the Skyline Drive of Shenandoah National Park and he proposed this to PWA. Theodore E. Strauss, then advisor for District 10 of PWA, claims his suggestion initiated the parkway concept. On September 23, 1933, Governor John G. Pollard of Virginia appointed Byrd chairman of a Virginia Committee to seek federal aid for such a project. A meeting on October 17, 1933, brought together representatives of the Bureau of Public Roads, the U.S. National Park Service and PWA, resulting in the following basic policies that have guided development ever since:

1. The project would be totally funded with Public Works Administration money, thereby eliminating tolls.
2. The scenic highway was officially designated a *parkway*.
3. It would be a unit in the National Park System.
4. The states would acquire and donate the required right-of-way. In return, the federal government would design, construct and maintain the Parkway.
5. $16,000,000 would be requested to finance a projected 414 miles of road and provide employment of four thousand men. (Jolley 1985, 12)

But, even as the first $4,000,000 was appropriated from PWA, considerable controversy surrounded siting of the project. Public hearings generated much acrimonious wrangling regarding the location and states involved. Although Tennessee's representatives fought for a route in their state, they lost on the basis that they were already benefiting from federal funding of the Tennessee Valley Authority development. The final routing decision, giving the Blue Ridge Parkway its present route, was made by the then Secretary of the Interior, Harold L. Ickes.

Design Concept

Because the U.S. National Park Service had no staff available to design such an unprecedented project, it turned to the private landscape architectural firm of Gilmore D. Clark. Clark's staff member, Stanley W. Abbott, was appointed Resident Landscape Architect on December 26, 1933, and director of all design and construction of the Parkway.

The first step was landscape analysis, but it was handicapped by "unfamiliarity of the region, rural isolation, lack of roads, sparse food and lodging accommodations, a rugged terrain, and pathetic map resources" (Jolley 1985, 16). Even so, Abbott worked with state engineers to reconnoiter and locate the route, determine the right-of-way, donate the land to the federal government, design a plan to fit the terrain, and put the designed project up for bids by construction contractors.

By 1934, Abbott had been assigned two assistants—Edward H. Abbuehl and Hendrik E. Van Gelder. Together they conceived of their mission as *preservation, reclamation, and vistas.* For their design policies, they agreed upon the following:

> Utilize that which exists.
> Carve and save, not cut and gut.
> Preserve the lived-in look.
> Keep a managed landscape in mind.
> Preserve nature and history.
> Marry beauty with utility.
> Emphasize simplicity and naturalistic.
> The horizon is the boundary-line. (Jolley 1985, 23)

These policies dominated all design decisions on routing, varieties of elevation, frequent parking overlooks, short hiking trails, wayside museums, and roadside parks. Funds from another federal program, the Resettlement Administration, were used to acquire adjacent worn out submarginal lands and resettle the owners.

In order to facilitate planning and design, Abbott divided the route into segments. Borrowing from railroad practices, the decision was made to set mileposts throughout. A logo, representing open sky, mountain peaks, a wind-swept white pine tree, and a swath of the road, was designed and is still in use today. A major innovation for its time was Abbott's policy of communication. He established a regularly issued bulletin, the *Blue Ridge Parkway News,* that published information on work as it progressed, and why the several design decisions were being made. This became a dynamic public relations piece, establishing community support.

Two years after the Parkway was initiated, sufficient right-of-way and design plans had been completed to invite bids for the first stage of construction. Today's travelers are not aware of the thousands of legal transactions that accompanied the process from design through construction of the Blue Ridge Parkway. Most of the construction labor came from members of the Civilian Conservation Corps, another federal employment program involved in final adaptation of the project to the original landscape, such as, grading and planting slopes, constructing native rail fences, clearing and erosion control, salvaging and rehabilitating historic buildings, constructing utility lines and substations, and constructing park facilities.

A major setback came with the advent of World War II. After two-thirds of the project had been developed, funding and support came to a halt. The major sponsor, the U.S. National Park Service, found itself with many new responsibilities nationwide but with much reduced moneys and staff. However, following public outcry regarding the status of parks, by 1956, U.S. National Park Service Director Conrad L. Wirth, was able to initiate a new program of development labeled Mission 66. This program gained enough support from Congress to renew Parkway development, especially for more construction, new visitor centers, campground facilities, campfire and outdoor amphitheaters, historic restoration, and establishment of the Museum of North Carolina Minerals. A unique part of the mission was retraining of neighboring farmers in skills of land conservation to enhance the beauty of the Parkway and protect resources.

A Public/Private Conflict

In spite of its many successes, the issue of service facilities along the Parkway became critical. Abbott had envisioned the need for some lodging and food services directly along the Parkway, sensing a market demand from the millions of visitors who began to use this attraction. However, he was confronted by strong protest of these concession proposals, especially from older resort areas around Blowing Rock, North Carolina. The argument was that the federal government had no right to use taxpayer's money to establish competition. A balance has been struck over the years since, allowing only a few concession operations in the most remote locations of the Parkway and supporting private sector businesses in communities nearby.

Another major conflict occurred with the Parkway section around Grandfather Mountain, North Carolina, toward the southern end of the project. Right-of-way had already been purchased from Hugh Morton, landowner. But, the U.S. National Park Service had new plans for a route at a higher elevation, based on environmental reviews. Morton refused to accept the new plan and a stalemate ensued. A final compromise included a new alignment between the high and low road, Morton's exchanging right-of-way for other state land, and implementation of environmental impact assessment not available in the 1930s. An innovative solution for an especially sensitive one-fifth mile segment was the building of the Linn Cove Viaduct at a cost of $12 million in 1983. It is structurally supported independently alongside the mountain to avoid environmental damage to the slope.

Planning Success

Today, the Parkway regularly receives worldwide acclaim as an environmentally sound natural and cultural resource visitor attraction. In 1991 there were approximately 16 million visits to the Parkway (Statistical Abstract, 1991). The outstanding scenery, natural resources, and many cultural sites now are protected for the future. At the same time, adjacent communities have received a substantial economic boost from tourism and millions of visitors are educated, enriched, and fulfilled by their experience. Current Superintendent of the Parkway, Gary Everhardt, former U.S. National Park Service Director, is now engaged in expanded liaison with nearby communities and political jurisdictions. Testimony to its success is a prayer uttered by the Reverend Arsene Thompson, a full-blooded Cherokee Indian:

> Where once there was only a buffalo trail, where Indian campfires once blazed . . . where once the red man and the white man fought . . . there is a road of peace and we are thankful. (Jolley 1985, 44)

This planned natural resource feature is proof of the long term value of perpetuating environmental values at the same time visitors are given an enriching experience. Conceived many years ago, the design is as valid today as when it was first built.

FRANCONIA NOTCH

The Challenge

An unusual travel way has now been established in New Hampshire as the result of design and planning effort combined with cooperation from agencies and organizations. Completed in 1988, the project resolved conflicts of opinion that had held up action for many years (Figure 10-4) (Rigterink 1992).

Environmental groups had resisted standard Interstate highway specifications that, in their opinion, would damage the environmental character of the landscape. The project involved an eleven-mile segment of Interstate 93, which also traverses several miles of Franconia Notch State Park. Already the park attracts over two million visitors a year and at all seasons. A natural rock profile, The Old Man of the Mountain, is a special visual landmark, the state symbol of New Hampshire since 1945.

Process

Of special significance for resolving conflict and planning a solution was a three-part catalytic and review process. Even though the designers were

Figure 10-4. Franconia Notch Scenic Freeway. After much controversy designers and developers agreed on special design standards for Interstate Highway 93 at this important environmental location. Sensitive design and construction were needed to protect the dramatic beauty of the site (Green 1986).

free to develop a creative and esthetic design solution, an important public input process was established at the outset.

1. Design Team. Because of the diversity of needed site development, four design and planning firms made up the Design Team: DeLeuw, Cather & Company, responsible for project management, planning and engineering; Roy Mann Associates, Inc., responsible for park master planning; Johnson, Johnson & Roy Inc., responsible for landscape and site design concepts and details; and Gruen Associates, responsible for architecture. The Design Team met monthly with the principal environmental group, the White Mountain Environmental Committee (WMEC) for the following purposes: to monitor progress, schedule upcoming work, present and critique alternatives, and identify problems, coordination, and data requirements. No work was to be taken to the main client, the New Hampshire Department of Public Works and Highways or Division of Parks and Recreation without having first been reviewed by the Design Team.

2. Staff Review. After work proposals had undergone interdisciplinary review of the Design Team, they were submitted to the official staffs of the two key state agencies. Comments and recommendations were made concerning the acceptability of the sometimes innovative design solutions. Especially important were the esthetic and environmental characteristics of the concepts.

3. Technical Review. Senior technical staff members of the Department of Public Works and Highways and the Division of Parks and Recreation then made more critical review of each step in the planning process. Each month, the Design Team's proposals and modifications were examined to determine how they had been changed based on comments of the month before. At each month's meeting, the following were discussed: progress from the month before; work schedule for the next month; planning and design alternatives; and recommendations requiring policy review and comment.

In addition to these three elements of the review process, all planning recommendations were reviewed once a month by an Overview Committee. This committee included representatives of WMEC, the Department of Public Works and Highways, the Division of Parks and Recreation, and the Federal Highway Administration. The purpose was to regularly monitor planning progress in terms of a WMEC agreement.

Chronology

Because of the unusual circumstances surrounding this special site problem, the project had an equally unusual chronology of development. This aspect is related here to demonstrate the need for the planning process to include the diversity of opinion of both proponents and critics.

For many years, a single highway had provided north-south transportation through Franconia Notch, a pass in the White Mountains. When the original system of Interstate and Defense Highways was planned in the 1940s, this stretch of highway was scheduled to become part of this system. The rigid high-speed nationwide standards immediately became the core of controversy over future plans. At the center of the controversy were environmental and social issues that delayed construction for over three decades. A major delay was caused by the U.S. Congressional passage of the National Environmental Protection Act of 1970, which required greater public involvement.

A breakthrough came in 1973 with a congressional amendment to the Federal Highway Act providing for a parkway-type highway through Franconia Notch. This allowed specifications less than normal interstate standards. Soon thereafter, several setbacks occurred, including an injunction against construction. In all, seven different alternative routes were proposed but none was acceptable to all parties. Several major environmental groups allied themselves to form the White Mountain Environmental Committee. It seemed the only solution was to create a compromise acceptable to both the state agencies and WMEC. In order to work toward this objective a memorandum of agreement was signed in 1977.

In 1981, a Design Team was assembled and charged with close cooperative planning among the several state and federal agencies and the WMEC.

Design Issues and Analysis

Because there was no precedent for this special highway plan and its unusual corridor, many environmental issues had to be studied throughout the process. Following are some of the highlights of these concerns.

The Notch posed unusual landscape problems because of high winds and intense cold. A twelve-year-old spruce tree is typically only two feet tall. Modifying the land forced the decision to obtain new specially adaptable plantings. Interstate standards prohibited bicycle paths, and also demanded divided highway construction that would have destroyed much of the setting. Road shoulder widths were excessive for the conditions. Concerns over the state park landscape and features required special design considerations. Water runoff was a major issue that had to be resolved.

A great amount of time and effort went into studies of all the physical and esthetic resources. Because it was a special case, common practices, familiar to designers and highway builders, had to be modified, one item at a time.

Solution

Today, a pleasing and innovative highway corridor provides for multiple functions in a manner now acceptable to travelers, environmentalists, and traffic engineers. The solution was not a divided highway but rather a four-lane design with granite rumble strip three feet wide, separating opposing traffic. In order to blend the highway color with the surroundings a special asphalt mix was used producing a permanently dark surface. Native rock was often used on severe cuts. But, workers had to avoid using traditional techniques of orderly stone courses. Landscape architect Richard Rigterink stated "We wanted stones and boulders to look as if they fell down from the mountain. In fact, we spent more time with boulders than with trees" (Green 1986). Because bicycles are prohibited from Interstate highways and their use is popular in the adjacent state park, an entirely new bike path was created. Specially designed shoulders and right-of-way widths were used to adapt construction to the setting.

Park and recreation facilities were relocated and redesigned. Newly developed features included a visitor center and park interpretation facility, park headquarters building, special interpretive and observation facilities and trails, walk-in and drive-in camping areas, boat launch maintenance complex, and trailhead facilities. A special nine-mile bikeway through the Notch was designed. The route parallels the parkway through the forest and meadows of the corridor, crossing from side to side through underpasses and over bridges, connecting various park facilities along the valley.

Conclusions

This special site planning project is proof that with the right goals, adequate mechanism for cooperation among affected parties, and application of professional design/planning talent, environmental assets can be protected at the same time tourism is developed. It also proves that seemingly unsurmountable conflict can be resolved. In the words of one member of the Design Team, ". . . My reaction was one of respect and amazement that these folks who had talked to one another primarily through attorneys for so many years could calmly discuss pros and cons of various alternatives. . . . I think one of the strengths of the consultant team was that each of us could establish a relationship with our counterparts within the client group and appreciate their perspective and work to convince them the proposed alternatives were responsive to their project objectives" (Rigterink 1992). The results are obvious to the travelers. Response from all sides has been positive and the design has received widespread recognition and awards—from the federal highway agency, the American Society of Landscape Architects, and a regional engineering organization.

WHITEMAN PARK

Following a request from the Western Australian Tourism Commission, the Pacific Asia Travel Association (PATA) formed a task force of professional tourism consultants to study the tourism potential of the 5,000-acre Whiteman Park, Perth. The task force included Ian L. Kennedy of PATA, Terence W. Beckett, Robertson E. Collins, Robert M. Priest, and Clare A. Gunn. The format for this project was a one-week intensive investigation followed by an on-site oral report, and a written document at a later date (Whiteman Park, 1989).

Objectives

The purposes of this study, as specified by the client were to:

- Prepare an "action plan" to facilitate the development of "a clear management plan for all aspects of the park's operations and future growth."
- Comment on the Maunsell Report (1978).
- Review and comment on the park's present operations.
- Comment on the park's tourism potential.
- Prepare a long-term "vision" for Whiteman Park.
- Prepare concepts for future tourism development having regard for events, accommodation, legislative options, and management structure.
- Examine financial considerations. (Whiteman Park 1989, 6)

Process

The method used included: inspection of site, reconnaissance of area context, extensive interviews with agencies, organizations, review of documents, interviews with park users, and study of cultural and natural resources.

Results

1. Assessment of the Maunsell Report. The task force determined that this report addressed recreational issues but not plans for tourism adaptation. The technical description was helpful as a reference. The plan concepts did not apply to travel markets.

2. Present Operation. The task force concluded that existing operational management had no stated policies to guide it. There appeared to be safety hazards, lack of an interpretive program, little or no formal tourism planning or marketing, inadequate sewage disposal, erratic land use pattern, and absence of natural and cultural resource management. At issue was the random acceptance of several land use claims and developments within the park—a hobby railroad organization, a hobby trolley car organization, a firing range, an equestrian park, and a youth camp.

3. Natural Resource Protection. There appeared to be complete lack of protection of wildlife and plant materials. All development and management are contrary to principles set forth in *An Administrative Guide to*

Environmental Requirements for Tourism Developments in Western Australia (Porter 1989).

Recommendations

1. Goals. Recommended by the task force were the following goals for adapting the park to tourism development:

Protect the natural/cultural resource base.
Provide visitor satisfactions for domestic and international travel markets.
Promote economic development.
Integrate Whiteman Park into the Swan Valley tourism plan.

2. Tourism Potential. It was the consensus of the task force that the park did have potential for becoming a major tourist attraction, but only with significant change in policies, plans, organization, and management. The cultural/natural resource assets could provide the dominant theme to meet travel market interests. New policies should call a halt to more nonconforming use areas and support stronger resource protection and interpretation.

3. Physical Plan. Using a new theme of natural/cultural heritage park, several physical plan recommendations were made. The railroad and trolley operations could continue if adapted to visitor use. An outstanding interpretive visitor center, located on the south of the property, would enrich the visitor experience without damage to the environment. It should contain indoor and outdoor exhibits, a museum of agriculture, crafts, auditorium, classrooms, a heritage and natural resource library, and a heritage food center. Demolition or readaptation of existing structures should be considered. This new visitor interpretation complex should also serve as an educational and research center for study of the important natural and cultural history of the area.

Several other basic recommendations were made. Safety hazards of the rail line must be eliminated. Well-designed on-site commercial facilities could include a restaurant, souvenir shop, photo shop, bike hire, theater, and an aviary and reptile house. The proposed golf course should be denied on the grounds of noncompatible use and poor feasibility because another is being established nearby. All design should be esthetically

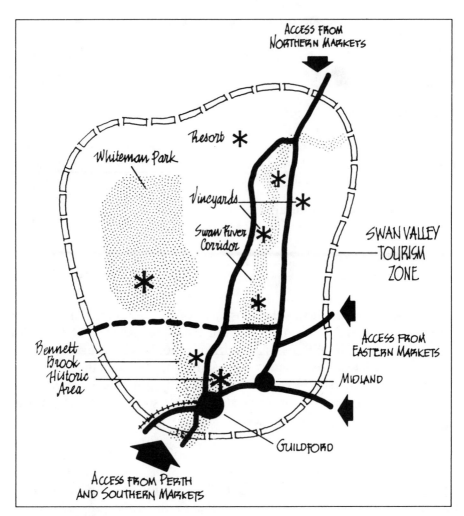

Figure 10-5. Whiteman Park Related to Zone. Diagram illustrates relationship between proposed redevelopment of the park for tourism and the surrounding attractions. Guildford would be focal point for travel service businesses (Whiteman Park 1989, 19).

appropriate to the natural/cultural heritage theme. No accommodations are recommended on site but rather in the nearby community of Guildford. A new sewage treatment plant must be established. New plans for visitor access and transportation need to be created and implemented. Adaptation of the park to tourism should include integration into an overall Swan Valley Tourism plan as shown in Figure 10-5.

4. Financial Considerations. Recommended is strong public-private cooperative leadership and investment. Resource protection requires governmental support. Economic impact can come from two sources: reve-

in new restaurants, hotels, and shops in Guildford after the park is reno-vated for tourism. The Interim Board of Management should be abolished and a new organizational structure created—one dedicated to the goals of tourism and resource protection. The park should be developed only in context of the area and its tourism development.

This project illustrated a form of planning that involves several experts, local input, and a brief but intensive investigation. Because the experts volunteered their time and the time frame was only one week, the cost is relatively low. Yet, the process allows a full grasp of the existing situation and major issues. Pertinent recommendations were published and widely distributed for greater understanding of the potential and stimulation of action.

UNDERGROUND ATLANTA

An example of how new planning and management have revived a failed tourist site is Underground Atlanta (Kent and Chesnutt 1991, 36). The new area was opened in June 15, 1989, replacing the original that was begun in 1968.

The Original

By 1973 following the establishment of an entertainment attraction in a rundown area of central Atlanta, 65 businesses were thriving and attract-ing local residents as well as tourists. It had already won international fame as a special place.

But, it began a rapid decline in 1975. Many causes have been cited, among which were six damaging fires. Other factors included an economic recession, fewer convention visitors, undercapitalization, unscrupulous merchants, but mostly the fear of crime and lack of safety. It seemed that the area accepted any and all kinds of developers without any plan coor-dination. Still, a favorable image continued to remain in the minds of many visitors.

The New Underground Atlanta

The Mayor of Atlanta, Andrew Young, is credited with being the catalyst for the revival of this site, in a planned way. In 1982 he authorized a study for a new underground attraction. This proposal enlarged the area to include five more city blocks.

Private enterprise formed Underground Festival Development, Inc., and the city floated an $85 million bond issue. A former nightclub operator showed faith by opening again which stimulated others to follow. The area now features historical attractions, specialty retailing, and public areas.

Safety was a dominant design policy for all new development, especially for rest rooms, lighting, walkways, ingress and egress. A security force of 30 guards were put in place to control not only the site itself but also the surrounding area for safe access to nearby hotels and shops.

This attraction was designed to entertain as well as to stimulate shopping. Nightclubs, restaurants, and bars are plentiful. Folk-country music and jazz abounds. Mimes, clowns, magicians, and (approved) street performers give the visitors a fun experience in a special place. Coca Cola has opened a visitor center illustrating the history of the drink and its acceptance around the world. Especially important to the success of this area is competent management by the Rouse Company.

The new Underground is not only financially successful, it has attracted more visitors than anticipated—7.8 million local and 5.2 million tourists in the first year of operation. It is demonstrating the value of good planning and experienced operational management. The site provides visitors with a strong attraction complement to the other local tourism factors of meeting facilities, world class airport, modern hotels, and a historic city. It ranks fourth as a U.S. convention city with 1.8 million delegates in 1989 (Kent and Chesnutt 1991, 38).

GREAT LAKES CROSSROADS MUSEUM AND WELCOME CENTER

Included in the concept for tourism development of the Upper Peninsula of Michigan in 1966 (Blank et al.) was the recommendation for a special "gateway" at the highway entrance to the region from the south and across the Mackinac Bridge. An example of the long-term nature of regional planning is the fact that it took over twenty years for detailed initiative and project plans for such a gateway center to be completed (Bridging the Straits 1988). Following is a sketch of this example of planning for an interpretive visitor center.

In 1986, Governor Blanchard appointed a task force to analyze the potential for more effectively developing the northern Mackinac Bridge base for the benefit of local citizens and visitors. The administrative agency for much of this land (as well as Mackinac Island and Fort Michilimackinac at Mackinaw City) was the Mackinac Island State Park Commission. The task force engaged consultants in marketing, planning, landscape architecture, and architecture to produce feasibility and sketch plans for a specially designed facility at this important entrance to the Upper Peninsula from its largest travel market source.

Market Research

A first step in the planning of this interpretive museum and visitor center was a travel market survey, performed by Market Opinion Research. A representative sample of 1987 travelers through the Straits of Mackinac area revealed that 53 percent believed they would visit such a site and pay $2.50 for the museum visit—a total of 950,000 to 1,300,000 visitors a year. The market researchers, however, based this on past experience of respondents promising more than they would actually do, and revised this estimate to approximately 300,000 a year. Even so, this was strong evidence that a significant travel segment was interested in visiting a museum and interpretive center at this important gateway location.

Site and Building Program

The firms of Quinn/Evans, architects, and landscape architects Johnson, Johnson & Roy/Inc., collaborated on site and building concepts and designs in response to the development program articulated by the Mackinac Island State Park Commission. This program included a Michigan Department of Transportation (MDOT) Welcome Center and a transportation museum focusing on the Mackinac Bridge and the Straits of Mackinac. The Welcome Center and museum were to be contained in one structure and the parking, service, and other site development were to be shared. The building program included preliminary space allocations and space descriptions. The interpretive concept was refined with the assistance of a museum consultant and was named "Bridging the Straits." Two major themes were defined: "The Bridge" and "Straits Maritime History," with subthemes of "Transportation" and "Tourism."

Site Design Concept

Review of market findings, the planning program, and the proposed site revealed conclusions pertinent to site design. Figures 10-6, 10-7, and 10-8 illustrate the site context plan, the site plan, and a conceptual aerial view.

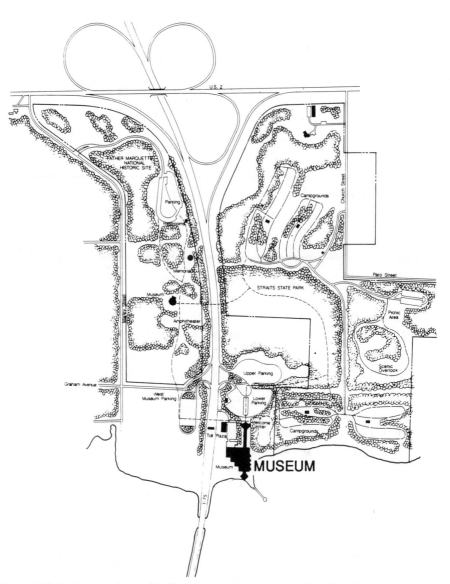

Figure 10-6. Bridging the Straits Site Plan. Site plan shows relationship of new interpretive museum to highway access and other features at north end of Mackinac Bridge, Michigan. The plan offers easy access and views of the bridge and Straits of Mackinac (Bridging the Straits 1988, 21).

Because the majority of travelers come from the south and arrive at the Upper Peninsula via the Mackinac Bridge, one of the largest suspension bridges in the world, the vista toward the land-water edge is particularly important. It is here that the center/museum is to be established, offering a visual welcome, as well as easy access from the highway immediately adjacent to the toll plaza. The site context plan shows relationship to

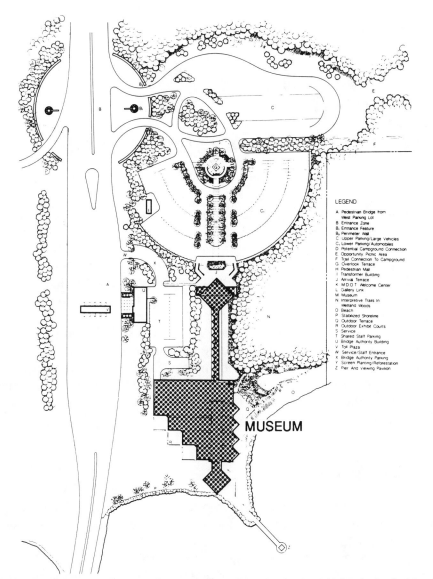

LEGEND

A Pedestrian Bridge from
  West Parking Lot
B Entrance Zone
B₁ Entrance Feature
B₂ Perimeter Wall
C Upper Parking/Large Vehicles
C₁ Lower Parking/Automobiles
D Potential Campground Connection
E Opportunity Picnic Area
F Trail Connection To Campground
G Overlook Terrace
H Pedestrian Mall
I Transformer Building
J Arrival Terrace
K M D O T Welcome Center
L Gallery Link
M Museum
N Interpretive Trails In
  Wetland Woods
O Beach
P Stabilized Shoreline
Q Outdoor Terrace
R Outdoor Exhibit Courts
S Service
T Shared Staff Parking
U Bridge Authority Building
V Toll Plaza
W Service/Staff Entrance
X Bridge Authority Parking
Y Screen Planting/Reforestation
Z Pier And Viewing Pavilion

MUSEUM

Figure 10-7. Bridging Museum Site Plan. An enlarged site plan for the Bridging the Straits Museum shows locations for museum, parking, and access (Bridging the Straits 1988, 20).

Highway 2; the trunk line to western Upper Peninsula; the Father Marquette National Historic Site; Straits State Park, Memorial, and Museum; and the main north-south highway, Interstate 75. For southbound traffic, a parking area on the west side of the highway and a pedestrian bridge would provide access to the center and museum.

One goal of the site plan was maximum preservation of the native landscape vista including existing vegetation. The upper and lower parking

Figure 10-8. Bridging the Straits Aerial View. A perspective aerial view of the museum and Welcome Center of the Bridging the Straits project. This illustrates care in adapting architecture and site design to the existing landscape (Bridging the Straits 1988, 19).

lots are adjusted to existing wooded edges. New planting would use the same kinds of plants found locally and be placed in a naturalistic form. The plan is simple and strongly ordered. First, it presents the arriving visitor with a clear sequence of experiences. Second, it makes efficient use of a compact site, preserving Bridge Authority functions, fragile woods and wetlands, as well as a considerable amount of existing mature landscape vegetation. And, finally, Bridging the Straits placement provides maximum opportunities for fine views of the Mackinac Bridge and the panorama of the Straits of Mackinac and Mackinac Island, an important historic and resort area.

Building Design Concept

The site concept with its north-south orientation strongly influenced the building design, providing the visitor with a smooth transition from site to building functions.

Upon entering the building, one continues to sense the axis moving southward toward views of the bridge and water. A skylit orientation area offers a dramatic introduction to the museum and its setting. Upper and lower exhibits carry out the several historic themes and subthemes. The visitor may also continue on to an observation deck that offers a panoramic view of the straits and access to a multimedia theater. Special services within the structure include tourist information and guidance, gift shop, food service, and lounge areas.

The guiding concept is the creation of a strong relationship between major interior spaces and the unique setting. The design thereby heightens the visitor's experience of both the museum and the surrounding natural features. Drama and anticipation are created by this special interaction between building and site. External to the building are outdoor exhibits as well as dining and viewing areas. Movement from inside to outside within the exhibit and public spaces of the museum is encouraged. The overall facility is proposed as an exciting and informative attraction and one that complements the quality of its dramatic surroundings. Its purpose goes way beyond the site, providing an introduction to the many features of the Upper Peninsula, close relationship to the tourist services of nearby St. Ignace community, and linkage with the Lower Peninsula and dominant market access.

This tourism plan illustrates a basic planning principle—implementation often takes many years. Regional and destination plans may provide recommendations for strategies and specific projects. But, action must wait until a mixture of needed factors is just right—a willing investor, commitment to design and build, feasibility of success, and competent management for operation.

ORANGE VALLEY RESORT

On October 12, 1990, Lester Bird, Deputy Prime Minister and Minister of Tourism and Economic Development for the island of Antigua, signed an agreement with planners to develop concepts for a new national park and resort (Figure 10-9) (Orange Valley 1991). The objectives were to create:

> A National park which will cater to the needs of islanders and the desires of the visitors;
> A destination resort which will support the Government's future economic plans for tourism in the 1990s;
> A development to be constructed in "Caribbean style" which respects and complements the vernacular architectural style of St. Johns, the island's capital; and
> An improved landscape through the introduction of new plants and trees to enhance the existing setting. (Orange Valley 1991, 1)

The consultant team included developers, development managers, landscape architects, golf course architect, environmental analyst, and cable car firm. This team was guided by two basic principles: "(1) to ensure the permanent preservation of the wonderful natural beauty of Orange Valley, Ffryes Mill and Beach, and (2) to make that beauty accessible without spoiling the natural scenery in the process" (Orange Valley 1991, 1).

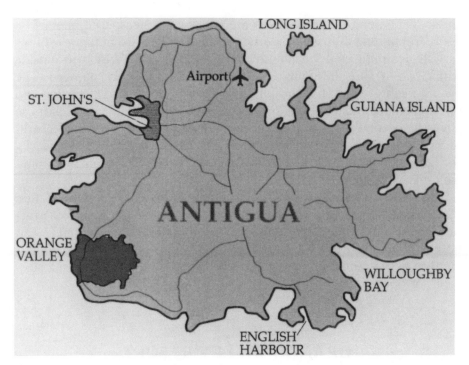

Figure 10-9. Orange Valley Project, Antigua. Map shows location of Orange Valley Resort project with reference to St. Johns and airport. The plan includes a park and resort complex (Orange Valley 1991, 1).

Existing Conditions

The analysis of existing conditions (Figure 10-10) and master plan (Figure 10-11) encompass both the proposed national park and Orange Valley Resort. Following are summary descriptions of elements of the entire project.

Orange Valley, a portion of land on the southwestern coast of Antigua, offers tourism opportunities year-round. The valley floor is quite spacious and views toward the sea are spectacular. It provides wildlife habitat, especially in the salt marsh and lagoon. Waterfront is dominated by Darkwood Beach.

Dark Valley, a watershed of 785 acres, lies to the northeast of Orange Valley. It is an upland area with limited views to the sea. The pristine beauty of this valley suggests a dominant policy of resource protection rather than intensive development. Some public use could be allowed, such as for trails, picnic areas, and campgrounds.

Boggy peak is the highest point on the island—1,319 foot elevation—and is located toward the east of Orange Valley. It has opportunity for 360-degree vistas if made accessible by cable car.

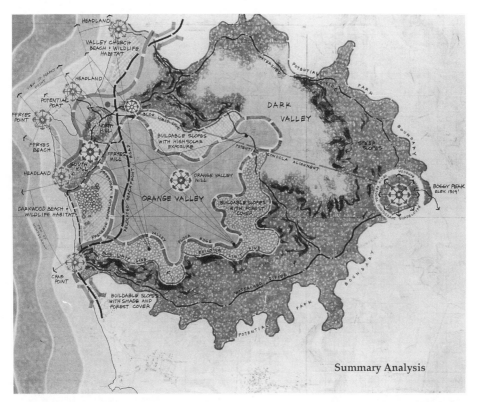

Figure 10-10. Orange Valley Resource Analysis. Study revealed slopes, forests, beach areas, and buildable areas. Such site analysis is critical for the development of a master plan (Orange Valley 1991, 4).

Valley Church offers an idyllic approach to the national park but the beach requires restoration.

Ffryes Bay. Ffryes Mill and Beach with its magnificent beach are premier natural settings for the entire project. With salt pond enhancement, small shore habitat can be improved. Ffryes Point should remain undeveloped. The remains of a windmill punctuate the northern portion of the hill.

Environmental Considerations. Each of the four watersheds is unique. Managing the levels and quality of water of Orange Valley presents a challenge. New wetlands and mangrove swamps have potential but are contingent on use of safe and biodegradable fertilizers and pesticides. Present grazing and agricultural uses of Dark Valley should continue. Constructing a port and village at Ffryes Bay will demand great care to minimize disturbance of natural assets. Proposed separation of wetlands from intense park use includes the establishment of botanical gardens. Development of this area is an ecologically sensitive challenge.

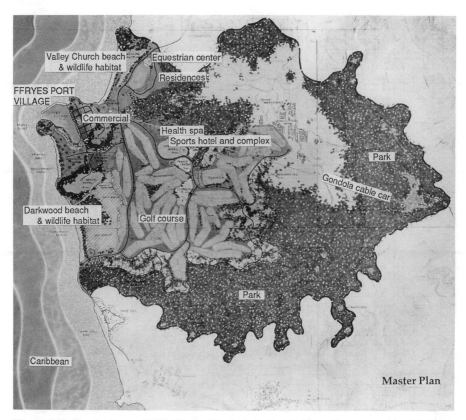

Figure 10-11. Plan for Orange Valley Resort. Plan includes location for golf course, residential villages, national park, relocated road, and beaches. All recommended uses are adapted to the environmental characteristics of the site (Orange Valley 1991, 7).

National Park Zones

Proposed is dividing the area into three major zones.

Natural Reserve Zones total 1,565 acres (70 percent of the park). These are typified by steep slopes, quality vegetative cover, scenic resources, aquatic and terrestrial wildlife habitats, and historical sites.

Recreation zones total 413 acres (18 percent of the park). Because resource protection is critical here, these areas require special planning care. The golf courses must follow principles of adaptation, enhancement, and resource protection.

Development Zones include 272 acres (12 percent of total) and offer the setting for most intensive visitor use. Economic and cultural benefits generated from this area would support scenic and other resource protection.

Master Plan

The dominant theme is to capture the beauty and ecological integrity of the seascape and landscape. The intent is to demonstrate that with proper design the public and private sectors can coexist as resource protection becomes a paramount policy.

Four characteristics of *Natural Reserve Zones* are emphasized in the plan. Limited Access Zones would allow only swimming, sunning, hiking, equestrian trails, picnicking, camping, wildlife observation, photography, and similar activities. Environmental tours, educational, and invitational use will be encouraged. Minimum facilities will be provided. The landscape concept includes not only resource protection but rehabilitation for improved wildlife habitat, stimulation of native landscape character, and enhanced esthetics. Beach use will be improved by removal of the beach road, providing access at either end. Replenishment of Valley Church Beach is needed. Plans include reintroduction of commercial citrus fruit agriculture. This will not only help supply local markets but also allow export and reinforcement of the Orange Valley theme.

Orange Valley plans call for both intensive and extensive development and recreational use. A new sports hotel, health spa, sports complex, and residences would be placed on the foothills of surrounding mountains, affording views of magnificent scenery toward the sea. Golf course design policy is to retain natural assets and make *least change* to the landscape. It is planned to blend into the natural setting and conserve water use. A gondola cable car system, from Valley Church to Boggy Peak, will provide ecologically sound access and 360-degree vistas of the surrounding Caribbean destination. Trails will provide alternate access.

Ffryes Bay plans include forest protection, a museum and park orientation center, a botanical garden, and Ffryes Port and Village. The port is planned to be a functioning fish landing area, marina, and new village designed to emulate vernacular architecture and provide many visitor services. New housing and hotels are planned.

For *Valley Church Bay*, several functional areas are planned. An equestrian center, multifamily dwellings, and preservation of open space are key themes for this area.

Conclusion

The planners, designers, and developers stated the following as their plan conclusion:

> Our objective is to create a world-class tourist resort, fully integrated into Antigua and its way of life. The resort will be promoted world-wide to attract a growing number of visitors, contributing to the islands tourist economy and providing long-term employment for present and future generations of Antiguans. (Orange Valley 1991, 10)

This plan illustrates a national park-public use concept proposed many years ago but seldom implemented. The fundamental land use policy of this concept is to concentrate public use facilities and services, thereby protecting the remaining extensive resource qualities. It accepts volume public use in specific zones that can be designed and managed for capacity functions. At the same time, rare and fragile resource zones are prohibited from degradation. It demonstrates that environmentalism and development are compatible, rather than antagonistic, ideologies if properly planned, designed, and managed.

THE IRONBRIDGE GORGE MUSEUM

Description

Declared a World Heritage Site by United Nations Educational, Scientific, and Cultural Organization (UNESCO) in 1986, the Ironbridge Gorge Museum, has been organized, planned, and developed as a major attraction site, attracting 690,000 visitors in 1991 (Ironbridge Gorge 1991). The museum is made up of seven major features covering six square miles at Telford, Shropshire, England (Figures 10-12 and 10-13). The Ironbridge Museum Trust was established in 1967, and the first site opened in 1973. The theme, The Birthplace of Industry commemorates the source of the world's first iron rails, wheels, boats, cast-iron bridge, and over two centuries of industrial development. The key features of the museum complex include the following.

Museum of Iron and the Darby Furnace. Visitors can view many displays, models, and exhibits and experience the sound, light, and smoke display of the original Coalbrookdale Smelter established by Abraham Darby in 1709. The museum's main collection is housed in an 1818 warehouse nearby. Original Coalbrookdale products—iron rails, boilers, and saddle tank locomotive—are on display.

Museum of the River and Visitor Centre. In the Severn Warehouse, built in the 1840s, is contained an interpretive introduction to the early history of the Industrial Revolution. The significance of the River Severn is

Figure 10-12. Ironbridge Gorge Museum. View of 1779 Ironbridge and the several historic museum structures along the River Severn, located at Telford, Shropshire, England (Ironbridge Gorge 1991, 1).

explained by means of a 40-foot model of the gorge as it was in 1796. Changes in management of the river over two centuries are described.

Rosehill House. Approximately 100 yards from the Darby Furnace are Dale house and Rosehill House. Dale House, originally commissioned by Abraham Darby I who did not live to see it completed, is now being restored. Rosehill House was built for a son-in-law and now displays artifacts of the way of life of a Quaker ironmaster in the early 19th century.

Iron Bridge and Toll House. This centerpiece of the museum complex was designed by Shrewsbury architect, Thomas Pritchard, in 1775, and work

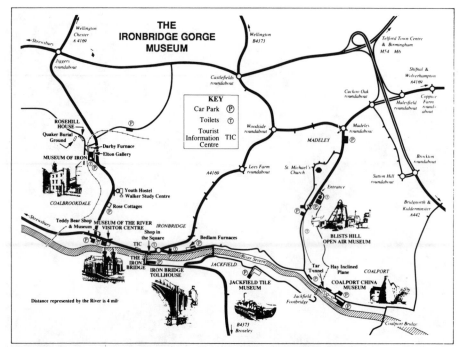

Figure 10-13. Plan of Ironbridge Gorge Complex. This six-square-mile museum complex includes Blists Hill Museum, Museum of Iron, the Iron Bridge, Coalport China Museum, Jackfield Tile Museum, Rosehill House, and Museum of the River (Ironbridge Gorge 1992, 3).

began in 1777. It was the first such cast-iron bridge in the world with single span of 100 feet, six inches. It became the prototype for stimulating similar construction elsewhere. It was in constant use until the 1930s, when vehicular traffic was prohibited. Inside the Toll House is an exhibition about the bridge. In the 1780s the town of Ironbridge developed on the north bank.

The Tar Tunnel. Visitors are able to go underground to observe natural bitumen that has been oozing from the walls since it was discovered in 1785.

Blists Hill Open Air Museum. On a 50-acre site, a turn-of-the-century living community has been redeveloped and opened to visitors. Travelers can walk along gas-lit streets of this Victorian town, past railway sidings, yards and pigsties, shops and offices. The sounds of machinery in action add to the realism. A candle factory, pub, and butcher shop add to the atmosphere. Skilled tradesmen in costume assist in interpretation.

Coalport China Museum. An old china works producing Coalport ware has been restored as a museum of china. Techniques of manufacture are demonstrated and products are displayed.

Jackfield Tile Museum. Two of the largest decorative tile works in the world—Maws and Craven Dunhill—were thriving in nearby Jackfield in the 1880s. Today, the original Craven Dunhill works has been restored and the manufacturing process can be observed. On display is an abundance of decorative wall and floor tiles produced from the 1850s to the 1960s.

Planning and Development

What is now an attraction of world-class stature nearly missed this opportunity as the Shropshire Coalfield and the area was in rapid decline (Smith 1989). In 1950, an ironfounder firm made the first excavation to reveal the Old Furnace at Coalbrookdale. By chance, the area became the locale for the development of the New Town of Telford, based on the New Towns Act of 1946, stimulating interest in restoration. A solicitor in the New Town encouraged the establishment of a Museum Trust in 1967. Meanwhile, architects from Birmingham had been commissioned to prepare a feasibility study for the museum. Basic development principles included that the museum would be a charitable trust, that operations would be funded from entrance fees, development funds would be solicited; a community support group would be established, and the museum would include a complex of related structures and sites.

Restoration and redevelopment have been accomplished by a variety of planners and designers over a period of several years. Although much of this work is now done by staff, outside professional designers, such as landscape architects, architects, engineers, exhibit designers, archeologists, and historians are engaged as consultants from time to time.

Organization and Management

This nonprofit operation is under the control of the Ironbridge Gorge Museum Trust with its Board of Trustees Executive Board, an Academic and Curatorial Committee, and the Rosehill Trust. All retailing, wholesaling, manufacturing, catering, and accommodation services are managed by a Trading Company, also under the control of the Trust.

A Monuments Management Team has been established to supervise all physical maintenance and is setting high level standards for this work. It is responsible for maintaining a large collection of archeological material, once handled by a contractor. A senior archeologist assisted by two other archeologists and an illustrator have been appointed on contract to record major monuments, monitor excavations, and repair works and produce reports for English Heritage.

The Ironbridge Institute has programs of postgraduate courses, short courses, research and consultancies, and maintains close liaison with the University of Birmingham. Special emphasis recently has been placed on training for museum practice, heritage tourism, and international relations. Many foreign students have enrolled in these programs. The Institute has sponsored special studies and plans for evaluating archeological importance, surveys of buildings, and recommendations for interpretive exhibits and programs. (Ironbridge Gorge 1992).

Close linkage between visitors and exhibit demonstrators is a basic planning and management policy. Although a limited number of explanatory panels are used, the managers depend greatly on staff input to explain and interpret the specific objects as well as the fascinating story of this site's role in the beginning of the Industrial Revolution.

The museum maintains a library that provides service to the staff, students of the Ironbridge Institute, and the general public. It derives its operating and capital improvement revenues from several sources: admission fees, a capital endowment fund, commissions from retail sales, grants and donations.

A Tourist Information Centre provides tourist guidance and information about the museum and surrounding area. It is part of the overall information network of the English Tourist Board.

Future plans include restoration and redevelopment of several sites within the area such as a Museum of Industrialization, Social History Gallery, a PipeWorks Museum, and a Geology Gallery.

A major merit of this attraction is the exponential value to visitors as a result of creating an overall complex, linking several related historic sites together. This integration principle is carried out not only by well-designed and -managed physical development but also by attractive, readable, and informative literature, such as *The Visitor's Guide 1992* (Wrekin Council 1992). This planning vision of the responsible developers enhances all tourism goals—greater economic impact, expanded visitor satisfactions, protection of significant resources, and integration with local and area economic and social life.

VICTORIA & ALFRED WATERFRONT

An outstanding example of planning for redevelopment of an historic waterfront complex is the Victoria & Alfred Waterfront (V&AW), Cape Town, South Africa (Victoria & Alfred 1991, 1992). It is making effective reuse of historic structures for resident and visitor enrichment and enjoyment. The mission statement follows.

> V&AW manages and develops Cape Town's historic docklands to maximize the long term benefit to its shareholders, Capetonians and visitors.
>
> V&AW is committed to enhancing its maritime image and retaining working harbour activities; [and] creating a quality environment; a desirable place to work, live and play; preferred location to trade and invest; and satisfying the aspirations of Capetonians and visitors. (Victoria & Alfred 1991, 2)

The prime investor-developer is the private firm of Transnet with the subsidiary of the Victoria & Alfred Waterfront. However, planning and development have been the result of close cooperation and specific agreements with the City Council since the beginning of the project in 1988. The concept has benefited from site visits to and review of several other waterfront developments in Baltimore, San Francisco, Vancouver, Toronto, and Boston. Many planners/designers have collaborated on the overall concept as well as individual projects. Core planners/designers have included Gallagher Prinsloo & Associates, MLH Architects & Planners, and Waterfront Landscape Architects, as well as specialized inputs from designers of signs, transportation, hotels, hydrology, maintenance, and security.

The location of the site is the harbor edge of Cape Town, just below the Central Business District, as illustrated in Figures 10-14 and 10-15. It is accessible by regional freeways and an airport. Nearly one-half million people live within fifteen minutes from the waterfront and the region's population is about three million. The project encompasses five major development sites with refurbished and new construction of wharfs, aquarium, hotels, conference center, offices, residences, marinas, restaurants, and shopping areas. These five sites and the planned completion dates are:

Pierhead	1995	
Portswood Ridge	1996	
Alfred Marina	2000	
Amsterdam Battery	1997	
Granger Bay	2003	(Victoria & Alfred 1992, 5)

Of the total spent on the first phase of development (R63 million) R35 million was spent on infrastructure—roads, water, stormwater and sewage reticulation, hard and soft landscaping, street furniture, and relocation of existing services. Although still under construction, Pierhead (a planned complex of Victoria Wharf & Market Square, an aquarium and a hotel and conference center) attracted 1.4 million visitors in its first four months after opening.

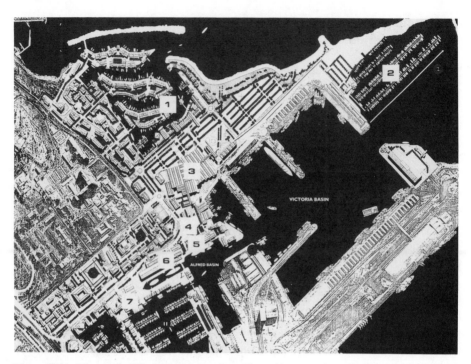

Figure 10-14. Victoria & Alfred Waterfront, Cape Town. New waterfront development includes: 1, residential; 2, marina; 3, specialty marketplace; 4, center and services; 5, hotel; 6, maritime museum; and 7, aquarium (Victoria & Alfred 1992, 7).

Special agreements with the City Council have expedited progress of planning and construction. For example, the waterfront land use control is under a new Legal Succession to the South Africa Transport Services Act of 1990 rather than the former Land Use Planning Ordinance. Negotiations were complicated by the fact that the municipal boundary runs through the site. Because of this and in order to resolve the tax issue, V&AW are paying contributions in lieu of rates for the area outside the boundary.

Throughout the planning and design process, the management organization, the City Council, and the consultants have worked closely together. From initial concepts through sketch plans and final design, these group sessions were often demanding, lively, and sometimes tense. The success of the resulting development is endorsed by the many awards such as Cape Institute of Architects Conservation Award, Cape Times Centenary Medal for Conservation and Building Rehabilitation, South African Institute of Civil Engineers Regional Award, Institute of South African Landscape Architects Merit Award, South African Institute of Town & Regional Planners Biennial Merit Award, Architecture SA Project Award, Mayor's

Figure 10-15. Victoria & Alfred Waterfront, Cape Town. View of new harborfront development with scenic Table Rock Mountain in background (Victoria & Alfred 1991, 2).

awards for greening the city and tourism, Lions International Award to the Information Centre, and an audio-visual award from New York Film & TV Festival.

WILPENA STATION RESORT

A continuing planning challenge is integrating tourism with national parks. Although national parks around the world vary greatly in size and administrative policy, resource protection is a dominant theme. But, increasingly there is recognition of the important visitor function in national parks. New planning policies permit only a minimum of visitor services—lodging and food—within the park, encouraging major traveler service development in nearby communities. Because most of these services are provided by the private sector, new cooperation and collabora-

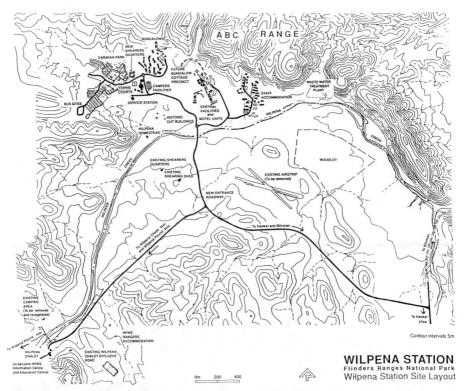

Figure 10-16. Wilpena Station Resort Site Plan. Located within Flinders Ranges National Park, north of Adelaide, Australia, this commercial resort is designed in harmony with the national park (Williams & Associates 1988).

tion are required between national park officials and commercial enterprise developers.

A special design case within a national park as a private concession is the proposed Wilpena Station Resort within Flinders National Park, 430 km north of Adelaide, South Australia (Williams and Blake 1990). Figure 10-16 illustrates the general site layout of this project. Figure 10-17 illustrates the relationship between the major feature of the park, Wilpena Pound, a giant oval shaped basin within great serrated walls, and the proposed resort. This is a plan *for* use, but in a managed manner.

Objectives

Required was an Environmental Impact Statement (Williams & Associates 1988, 2). This report stated project objectives as follows:

- Facilities that will expand opportunities for visitors to Flinders National Park to use and enjoy the park.

Existing Wilpena Chalet Resort

Majority of buildings to be removed. One building to be re-
used as NPWS Information Centre and Department of
Education Outdoor Education Centre.

Wilpena Station Site

Lake Torrens

To Hawker 40 km

To Blinman 50 km

Figure 10-17. Wilpena Pound, Flinders Ranges National Park. This view illustrates the relationship between the main feature of the park and the proposed Wilpena Station Resort site (Williams & Associates 1988).

- Facilities that will increase opportunities for visitors to recognize and understand the natural and cultural features of the Park.
- Facilities in a manner that offers alternatives, and minimizes the impact that existing numbers of visitors are having, and that predicted numbers of visitors may have on the Park.
- A site specific framework through municipal services and other lessee obligations (sewerage, water, power, wood supply) to manage the consequences of visitors staying in the Park.
- A variety of facilities that satisfies almost all of the accommodation needs of the range of visitors that visit the Park.
- Facilities that enable the Flinders Ranges to realize its potential to attract state, national, and international visitors, thereby adding to the value of the tourist industry's contribution to South Australian economy.

- And for the development of a site that the South Australian government has identified as being the most appropriate site in the region for the development of a large-scale integrated resort.

Solution

As occurs in many similar situations, controversy began to surround this proposal, based primarily on the generalized assumption that environmental degradation is a foregone conclusion from increased volumes of visitors. Part of the objection arose from the proposed hotel that would accommodate a travel segment contrary to more traditional camping and recreation travelers. However, the proposed design and management plan demonstrate that both of these assumptions are false. In fact, the state encourages a diversity of visitor types, endorsing the variety of accommodations. Those who visit will leave with new information about environmental values, producing a public constituency with a strong resource protection ethic. By recognizing several visitor segments rather than just one, there is less likelihood of the design and management being as exclusionary as in the past.

This is an example of a well-designed visitor center within a national park that promises to satisfy criteria of resource protection and tourism. The plan encompasses issues of visitor behavior control, interpretation, use of hardened site for major services and facilities, tour guide training, zoning of uses to avoid conflict, marketing linkage with resource capabilities, and esthetically appropriate design of all structures.

AUSABLE FORKS, ADIRONDACK PARK

Related to the Adirondack Park Regional Plan described in Chapter 5 is the design recommendation for the gateway hamlet of Ausable Forks (Trancik 1985, 98, 99) illustrated in Figures 10-18 and 10-19.

This community of 1,500 population is located on Route 9 at the confluence of the East and West Branches of the Ausable River. This river is one of the most important fishing streams in New York. Protecting the flood plain and increasing the esthetics of the river became essential parts of the design program. Participants in local workshops stressed the need for attracting environmentally appropriate industries as well as expanding tourism.

Figure 10-18. Hamlet of Ausable Forks. This perspective illustrates planned improvement of visual quality of the bridge and entrance area. The visitor information center and landscape enhancement are intended to provide incentives for renovation and reuse of buildings (Trancik 1985, 98).

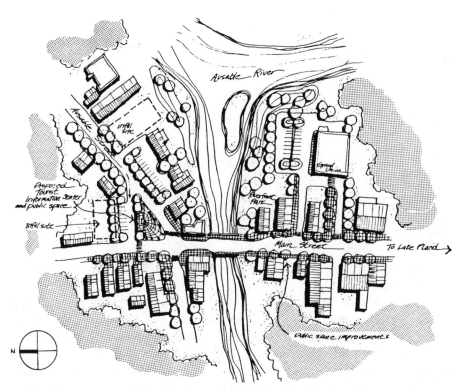

Figure 10-19. Plan for Ausable Forks. Features of the plan include improved visitor functions as well as enhanced landscape character. Relationships between visitor use areas are improved (Trancik 1985, 99).

A Self-Help Area Revitalization Program is stimulating improvements, such as a circulation and parking plan. This program brought public and private planners and developers together for both short- and long-range plans. Recommended is a central sewage treatment system.

The hamlet revitalization plan recognizes the dominant physical asset of the riverfront. Analysis revealed recreational opportunities as well as need for concern over potential flooding and pollution. Because this is a major gateway to the region, entrance functions became important elements of the design. An information center was placed on an easily accessible traffic island in an attractive public park setting. Included are tree plantings, decorative paving, and curb cuts for access to surrounding buildings.

A very important element of the design, so frequently overlooked, is separation of vehicle from pedestrian circulation. Although vehicular access and ample traffic flow is maintained, provision is made for dominant visitor experience and enrichment on foot. In this design, the decorative walk paving provides a visible code for pedestrian flow and access to all key elements of the community such as the central shopping area and riverfront park.

Recommended is major renovation of older buildings for adaptive tourist use. This restoration together with easier access and improved landscape quality should stimulate greater commercial activity within the hamlet.

This local plan demonstrates valuable planning and design linkage between overall regional and site plans.

CONCLUSIONS

The twelve cases of site scale planning and development described in this chapter offer a wide range of challenges and solutions. Even with their great diversity, some characteristics of planning and design are common to all. For example, virtually all show special sensitivity to the indigenous natural or cultural resources. This principle is epitomized by the ecotourism resort plan for Maho Bay Camps. This tourism planning axiom represents a new understanding of the importance of protecting resources at the same time as developing them for tourism. Most of these cases broke away from the traditional professional-only design process. Instead, several publics—local, environmental, and governmental—were involved at several steps in the process. Nearly all demonstrated that political involvement in tourism design and development is necessary—initiation, commitment, leadership, and approval. High volume visitor use dominates all cases (except the ecotourism resort). This proves that with good planning and design a great many visitors can be accommodated without damage to resources. These site plan examples show that setting specific objectives at the very start is an essential step in the design process.

The differences among these cases need to be cited. The ecotourism resort demonstrates great care in designing for a specific market segment, and for not only environmental protection, but also enhancement. The final study of the San Antonio River Walk shows how unusual local situations, such as urban canyonization, need special architectural and site controls. This site example also illustrates the influence of organic planning over many years and the value of multiple agency coordination and management.

All of the cases emphasize the need for adaptive, integrative, and creative design for tourism site development.

REFERENCES

Blank, Uel, Clare A. Gunn, and Johnson, Johnson & Roy (1966). *Guidelines for Tourism- Recreation in Michigan's Upper Peninsula.* East Lansing, MI: Cooperative Extension Service, Michigan State University.

Bridging the Straits (1988). A summary report concerning the feasibility of a proposed Upper Peninsula Welcome Center/Straits of Mackinac Transportation Museum. Presented by the Mackinac Island State Park Commission, St. Ignace, MI.

Green, Peter (1986). "New Hampshire Adapts Interstate." *Engineering-News Record*, Nov. 20, p. ?.

Gunn, Clare A. (1979). "Aesthetic Improvement of Metropolitan Rivers," a presentation, conference of the Universities Council on Water Resources, Rutgers University, NJ, July 30.

Gunn, Clare A. (1988). *Vacationscape: Designing Tourist Regions,* 2nd ed. New York: Van Nostrand Reinhold.

Gunn, Clare A., David J. Reed, and Robert E. Couch (1972). *Cultural Benefits from Metropolitan River Recreation—San Antonio Prototype.* Technical Report No. 43, Texas Water Resources Institute. College Station, TX: Texas A&M University.

Ironbridge Gorge Museum Trust (1991). *Annual Report.* Telford Shropshire, England: IGMT.

Ironbridge Gorge Museum Trust (1992). *Education at Ironbridge: Preliminary Information for Teachers.* Shropshire, England: Education Department, Ironbridge Gorge Museum Trust.

Jolley, Harley E. (1985). *Blue Ridge Parkway: The First 50 Years.* Mars Hill, NC: Appalachian Consortium Press.

Kent, William, and J. Thomas Chesnutt (1991). "Underground Atlanta: Resurrected and Revised." *Journal of Travel Research,* 29(4) Spring, 36–39.

Leccese, Michael (1992). "Can Sightseeing Save the Planet?" *Landscape Architecture*, 82(8), 53–56.

Orange Valley, Antigua (1991). A Proposal for a Major Resort within the Antiguan and Barbudian National Park. Prepared by a development team of architects, landscape architects, golf course architect, and other specialists. Columbia, MD: LDR International, Inc.

Porter, Colin (1989). *An Administrative Guide to Environmental Requirements in Western Australia*. Prepared for the Western Australian Tourism Commission and Environmental Protection Authority. Perth: WATC.

Rigterink, Richard (1992). Correspondence, May 20, Johnson, Johnson & Roy, Ann Arbor, MI.

River Walk Commission (1977). *River Walk Policy Manual*. San Antonio, TX: River Walk Advisory Commission.

Roessler, Wolfgang G. (ed.) (1987). *San Antonio Riverwalk Development Guidance System*. College Station, TX: Center for Urban Affairs, Texas A&M University

Selengut, Stanley (1992). "Building Partnerships Between Protected Areas and the Tourism Industry." Presentation, IVth World Congress on National Parks and Protected Areas, Caracas, Venezuela, February 10–21.

Smith, Stuart B. (1989). "The Next Thirty Years." In *Dynasty of Iron Founders*, Arthur Raistrick (ed.). York, England: Ebor Press.

Statistical Abstract (1991). Washington, DC: U.S. National Park Service.

Stubbs, Stephanie (1991) ."Good Things Happen at Maho Bay." *Memo*, April, American Institute of Architects, p. 9.

Trancik, Roger T. (1983). *Hamlets of the Adirondacks: History, Preservation and Investment*. Ithaca, NY: Author.

Trancik, Roger T. (1985). *Hamlets of the Adirondacks: A Manual of Development Strategies*. Ithaca, NY: Author.

Victoria & Alfred Waterfront (1991). *1991 Review*. Cape Town, South Africa: The Victoria & Alfred Waterfront (Pty) Ltd.

Victoria & Alfred Waterfront (1992). *1992 Review*. Cape Town, South Africa: The Victoria & Alfred Waterfront (Pty) Ltd.

Williams, Michael, & Associates (1988). *Proposed Wilpena Station Resort-Flinders Ranges National Park. Draft Ammendment to the Flinders Ranges National Park Management Plan and Draft Environmental Impact Statement*. Prepared for the SA National Parks and Wildlife Service, Adelaide, South Australia.

Williams, Michael, and Lynn Blake (1990). "Wilpena Station, Flinders Ranges National Park: Planning for Cultural Tourism." *Historic Environment*, 3(4), 61–71.

Whiteman Park (1989). An assessment of present and future tourism appeal. Perth, Australia: Western Australian Tourism Commission.

Wrekin Council (1992). *The Visitor's Guide 1992*. Shropshire, England: Wrekin Tourism Association, Wrekin Council.

Chapter 11

Conclusions and Principles

Throughout this book many conclusions regarding tourism planning have been offered. Reflecting on the entire concept of planning supply side development at the three levels—regional, destination, and site—an overall summary of conclusions and principles seems appropriate. Grouped into five categories for easier understanding and application are basic principles, processes, the environment, policies and goals, and challenges of the future.

BASIC PRINCIPLES

Tourism Planning Must Encompass All Travel—Business and Pleasure.

Even though definitions of tourism vary, from a planning perspective all travel (except commuting) should be included. This principle is based on the fact that all the components of the supply side actually cater to all travelers, not just vacation or pleasure travelers. Although plans and designs for the business market segment may be slightly different from those catering to pleasure travelers, the basic functions are generic to both. For example, hotel guests may have quite different travel objectives but accept lodging in the same hotel. If plans for tourism development are to be comprehensive and meet the needs of both travelers and hosts, virtually all markets should be included in the scope of planning.

Planning Objectives, Processes and Outcomes Vary from Macro- to Microscales.

Because the term planning has so many popular meanings, it is necessary to consider what is meant when planning for tourism is proposed. Suggested here are three levels. At the *regional* (federal, state, and provincial) level, the outcome of planning is primarily guidelines, not project construction. At this level, planning can provide policies, guide destination identification, foster integration of destinations, coordinate action, and resolve issues for the region. *Destination* planning, however, has a narrower scope, including focal communities and their surrounding rural areas. Much stronger local participation in planning is required at this level. Destination planning involves new cooperation among governmental jurisdictions—city, county, surrounding municipalities. The outcome may include identification of many site project opportunities. Finally, *site* scale planning is also called design and utilizes principles and processes that guide actual construction of supply side development. It is helpful to discriminate between these three levels in order to meet desired objectives for the best tourism.

Integration of Planning at All Scales Is Essential.

Although there are differences in sponsors and techniques at the three scales—regional, destination, and site—the overall success of tourism depends on how well these three are integrated. Regional planning provides guidance for destination and site locations as well as for the region. This principle of integration requires constant communication among the tourism leaders of regions, destinations, and sites. National, state, and provincial tourism organizations and agencies (public and private) can play a major role in integration of plans and planning at all levels.

Planning of the Supply Side Should Meet
the Needs of Market Demand.

Because tourism is driven by supply side development as well as market demand, both should be in balance. As plans are laid for tourism development, there should be clear understanding of travel market trends. This understanding is required of planners, designers, owners, developers, and local citizen groups affected by tourism. Knowledge of potential market origins and the interests, habits, and other travel characteristics of the population is needed in order to plan the several components of the supply side. For example, there is no need to plan attractions and services for youth activities if market analysis shows market origins are dominated by older people. Because both the market and the supply side are dynamic and change over time, plans for the supply side must be flexible enough to adapt to market changes.

Supply Side Planning Must Be Directed Toward the Three Developer Sectors.

There is a prevailing misconception that supply side development is performed exclusively by the business sector. Although the commercial enterprise sector usually produces the greatest economic impact, tourism also is developed by nonprofit organizations and governments. Tourism planning cannot be effective unless the nonprofit and government developers are included alongside business. Nonprofit organizations own, plan, and manage many natural and cultural resource areas. They are prime actors in future establishment of historic sites, nature preserves, museums, and places for cultural events such as festivals and performing arts. Government agencies have a large stake in future planning, such as for parks, highways, campgrounds, wildlife preserves, interpretive centers, and infrastructure (water supply, waste disposal, fire and police protection, and health and safety). Planning only for the business sector—lodging, food service, travel service, and shopping—omits other equally vital input from the nonprofit and governmental sectors.

Planning Must Integrate All Components of the Supply Side.

The five components of the supply side—attractions, transportation, services, information, and promotion—need to be planned in concert. For example, plans for new lodging can be more meaningful if plans for new attractions and transportation are known. The success of lodging depends greatly on decisions made by developers and managers of the other four components. In fact, all developments within all components are influenced greatly by one another's plans and decisions. They are in a very dynamic relationship that requires new communication, cooperation, and even collaboration. All plans for tourism must be directed toward integration of development in all components if owners are to be successful and market needs are to be met.

Urban-Rural Planning Must Be Integrated.

The dominant mode of tourism development today is focused on two separate geographic areas—cities and rural areas. The planning and development of parks, hunting and fishing areas, resorts, wildlife areas, and small town historic sites take place primarily in rural areas. The creation of new convention centers, sports arenas, historic architecture attractions, theme parks, and festivals is primarily a city function. Both cities and rural areas are essential to tourism. But, new lodging, food services, transportation, information systems, and promotion depend on the decisions made in both urban and rural areas. In order to meet desired tourism objectives, plans and decisions in the surrounding rural areas must be integrated with city tourism plans. This new interrelationship may require new kinds of organization and programs.

Traffic and Pedestrian Functions Need Integration.

Preoccupation with expanding traffic ways and automobile parking by transportation officials has tended to divert needed planning attention away from pedestrians. Virtually all visitor activities take place after the train, bus, or automobile has been abandoned. Even driving for pleasure produces its greatest rewards at turnout overlooks where people can get out of their automobiles to walk and view the scenery. Although it is essential that new and better traffic handling is accomplished, equally important is planning for people on foot. Urban scenes, natural resource access, and culturally significant areas must retain their identity without intrusion from massive traffic ways. Vehicle movement is necessary for access, but its planning must be integrated with pedestrian movement, so essential to all visitor activities.

Clustering Is Basic Principle of Planning and Design.

Clustering—grouping together rather than dispersing—has many advantages as a planning principle. All transportation systems bring travelers to focal points. Expressways lead travelers to exit locations where clustering of services best satisfies demand. When travelers become interested in food service, they prefer a variety of restaurant choices, favored by clustering. The same principle applies to lodging. Generally, resource protection is more easily accomplished when traveler facilities and services are not dispersed throughout parks. Clustering favors better visitor control, better management, and more efficient engineering of infrastructure. National parks, for example, can best manage visitor use of resources when major services of accommodations, food service, shopping areas, and traveler services are concentrated in a well-planned community nearby. When high quality urban design principles are applied to such communities, they complement rather than detract from the value of the adjacent park.

ENVIRONMENT AND RESOURCES

Global Environmental Deterioration Demands Tourism's Attention.

The deterioration of environmental conditions worldwide is of major significance to all tourism planning and development. Certainly, all tourist development must not be detrimental to natural and cultural resources. Successful tourism must have clean air, abundant wildlife, unpolluted water, and freedom from resource erosion. The establishment of resorts, hotels, restaurants, and roads must not destroy basic resources. Especially fragile are archeological and historic resources, demanding extreme care in design and management for tourism. Of even greater concern to tourism are the many causes of environmental degradation by others, such as poor practices by industries, municipalities, forestry, mining, and agriculture— leading to water and air pollution, toxic waste, soil erosion, loss of animal habitat, and acid rain. If tourism is to succeed, its advocates must become more proactive in all environmental protection issues.

Park Protection and Tourism Can Be Compatible.

The ideological premise that tourism is destructive of parks is false. National and state parks would not exist if a vocal public, made up largely of visitors, were not strong advocates of their establishment and support. Instances cited of destruction of park resources by visitors are largely due to poor planning and poor management. Better planning involves zoning the park area so that major masses of visitors, primarily at service centers, do not disturb fragile and rare resources. New cooperation between the three developer sectors—nonprofit organizations, commercial enterprise, and government resource agencies—can result in plans that provide visitor rewards as well as resource protection.

Sustainable Development Is a Planning Principle for Tourism.

The planning of tourism, from the macro- to microscales, must include consideration of its potential impact on the social, economic, and environmental qualities of host areas. Local area leaders, government officials and general citizenry have the prerogative to make their own planning decisions on how much tourism should be allowed and how it should be developed. The short-range mindset of some developers, such as for resorts, must be tempered by long-range planning and development that can sustain environmental, social, and economic values. It is primarily at the site scale that sustainable development is carried out.

Planning and Design Can Resolve Visitor Impact Management Issues.

Some recommendations have been made for numerically setting visitor limits not to exceed environmental capacity. However, because of the number of variables, visitor impact issues have not been resolved. Instead, planning and management techniques are proving more effective. For example, visitor interpretive centers can be designed for mass tourist use, leaving fragile resource areas untouched. Motorcoach and tram systems are less threatening to environments than private automobile use. For some specific uses, such as forest and wilderness trails, quotas may be necessary. Perhaps the best environmental management comes with regular monitoring of how the planned and developed visitor use is affecting the environment. As soon as negative effects are observed, new planning and management policies and practices can be implemented.

Appropriateness Is a Planning and Design Fundamental.

Much of the objection by environmentalists to tourism development stems from issues of esthetics. When new attractions, facilities, and services are designed, they can be created and located in ways that respect the quality and dominant characteristics of resources. For example, the architectural qualities of historic buildings would be damaged visually if modern hotels and restaurants were built too close or with incompatible design. Professional designers are especially adept at creating designs appropriate to natural and cultural resource settings. But, owners and investors must be amenable to this fundamental for the best tourism development to occur.

Ecotourism Requires Special Site, Area, and Regional Planning and Design.

The surge in travel market interest in natural and cultural resources can be met with carefully designed destinations and places. Low-scale, modest, and slow-paced development that is planned in concert with local residents can be good business as well as environmentally sensitive. Especially important are parks and preserves that are managed with both visitor interest and resource protection principles. For example, in coastal areas, trained guides can help visitors understand underwater life as well as guide activities in ways that perpetuate coral and other sea life. The planning and design of ecotourism requires the very best of owner-manager principles as well as design creativity.

Ecotourism Can Foster Conservation.

Ecotourism businesses that depend on government resource protected areas have the opportunity to return revenues to the managers of these public areas. Frequently, the major attractions bringing visitors to ecotourism settings are not profitmaking, depending mostly on contributions and support from nonprofit organizations or government agencies. Because of the interdependency between developers of ecotourism and these resource areas, reciprocal agreements should include funding for the privilege of visitor use. Recently many ecotourism areas have been planned and managed to provide for this mutual support.

Economic Success of Tourism Depends on Resource Protection.

Preoccupation with promotion in most tourism agencies tends to give low priority to resource protective measures. A planning objective must be the demonstration of how a tourism economy depends on resource protection. Proper planning procedures can bring the environmentalists together with developers to create resource protective projects. Roads, vacation homes, resorts, marinas, and other services can be planned with minimum intrusion of valuable resources. Central sewage treatment plants and other technical solutions, such as water recycling, can eliminate resource damage. Essential is early recognition of the role of resources in creating plans for tourism development. The economic impact of jobs, incomes, and tax returns is dependent upon how well resources are protected.

Placeness Is a Tourism Planning Fundamental.

Because of the success of some attractions, there is a tendency among developers to replicate them whether or not they fit local settings. Excessive duplication reduces chances of success and denies more competitive development based on uniqueness of place. Every destination has a different set of geographical factors, traditions, relationship to markets, and host characteristics. It is essential, then, for a host area to plan, design, and develop its own special personality based on its special qualities of place.

POLICIES AND GOALS

Economic Development Cannot Be an Exclusive Goal.

Although economic benefits from tourism are valuable and are a valid goal for tourism planning, there are several other goals of equal importance. Certainly, many communities and regions derive substantial numbers of jobs, greater incomes, and worthwhile tax returns from tourism. For many areas, tourism is replacing dwindling former economies. But planning also must be directed toward three other goals. Planning must enhance visitor satisfactions if economic improvement is to accrue. Planning must integrate tourism into the social and economic life of communities and destinations. Tourism, if properly planned, can not only protect but can even improve the quality of fundamental environmental resources.

Tourism Planning Policies Should Be Directed Toward Quality as well as Growth.

In today's competitive tourism world, an increase in numbers of visitors does not always equate with the four desirable goals. It is quite likely, considering today's more discriminating travel markets, that better quality of all development has a much better chance of fostering desired goals. Planning should reveal the need for upgrading the supply side development and the potential for attracting higher quality trade. Better quality trade implies greater sensitivity to more satisfying visitor experiences as well as high grade physical plant.

Tourism Policy Must Be More than Promotion.

Although most nations, states, provinces, and cities spend the majority of their tourism budgets on promotion, newer and more comprehensive policies are needed. Certainly, promotion continues to be needed, but it should be balanced with policies on other very important topics. For example, health and and safety policies should be in place in order to protect travelers from poor sanitation and other travel hazards. As travel becomes more universal in scope, international agreements on travel regulations need to become essential policies at all levels. Government and private sector tourism policies need to ensure greater support of research, training, and education in tourism. Increasingly, universities are showing interest in adding tourism programs but lack adequate support from business and government. Establishing broader policies is essential in today's dynamic tourism field.

Tourism Planning Policy Requires Greater Public-Private Cooperation.

As more and more nations turn to the private sector for the provision of services and production of products, new cooperation with government is needed. Tourism development is not created exclusively by private commercial enterprise. But an adversarial attitude often inhibits tourism progress. In order for the tourism system to run more smoothly, greater understanding of the roles of both sectors is needed. All private sector actors in the supply side components of tourism—attractions, services, transportation, information, and promotion—depend greatly on investment, planning, and management policies of government. Conversely, governments can reduce budgets by diverting many tourism responsibilities to the private sector. New cooperation between the public and private sectors is essential.

Regional Tourism Policies Can Strengthen All Planning.

At the national, state, or provincial level, planning policies can foster better development at not only that level but also the destination level. For example, policies for transportation can influence greatly the access from markets and between other destinations. National and destination promotion can be integrated. National policies on uniform visitor information and directional systems can foster the traveler's understanding of attractions at destinations and how to find them. These advantages can accrue from greater cooperation between planners and decisionmakers at both national and destination levels.

Regional Policies for Development Incentives Can Stimulate Business.

Government incentives at the regional level can assist tourist business planning and establishment. These incentives could include tax abatement or direct grants contingent upon factors of destination plans and feasibility documentation. Within many government agencies, such aids are available for other businesses but not for tourism. New legislative mandates may be needed in order for these agencies to broaden their policies to include tourism. Such incentives can stimulate destinations to create their own plans.

Policy Should Link Business with Government and Nonprofit Attractions.

New business planning policy is required to provide financial aid to attractions that support business but are not profitable within themselves. Parks, museums, festivals, pageants, and many other natural and cultural attractions provide much of the travel pull to an area. Most of these attractions do not produce enough revenue to support themselves. It is incumbent upon tourist businesses (lodging, food service, and transportation) that depend on these attractions for their livelihood to provide a portion of their profit revenues to ensure financial success of these attractions.

PROCESSES

Processes for Plans and Continuous Planning Need Integration.

Essential at regional and destination levels is the integration of two forms of tourism planning: plan projects and a continuous planning process. From time to time, an in-depth project is needed that involves essential process steps: setting objectives; researching markets, resources, and programs; synthesizing research; developing concepts for development; and preparing recommendations. Such a planning process not only provides guidelines for development but also (when done properly) stimulates involvement by key developers and decisionmakers. However, such projects are limited by the research information and forecasting abilities at a specific time period. These projects should be updated, probably every five years. But, in order to be most effective, plans should be accompanied by a continuous planning process that is carried out regularly and cooperatively by the public and private sectors.

Geographic Heterogeneity Requires Destination Identification.

Although areas are not all alike, there is a dominant development tendency toward sameness of development. Universal design styles tend to make all places look alike, reducing greatly the competitive edge of each destination.

Destinations vary greatly in their geographic content and location. Natural resources are not evenly distributed nor of the same characteristics. Even beaches and waterfronts at different locations that seem similar have different physical characteristics of sand composition, wave action, shoreline topography, vegetative cover, climatic conditions, and development. Nor are cultural resources evenly distributed. Some locations were important to national or world events—others are of little cultural consequence for future tourism development. Place differences are critical to planning for tourism's best future.

Process Techniques Can Assist Identification of Potential Destinations.

Analysis of physical factors can reveal geographic differences within a region that are important to future tourism development. By researching and mapping an overlay map series, computer Geographic Information System programs can produce composite maps showing areas of strongest and weakest resource foundations. These foundations can be generalized into two main categories—natural and cultural resources. Common to both are the location and significance of cities and transportation systems. Planning processes that identify potential destination zones and their special characteristics can provide: a new perspective for policymakers, a foundation for local tourism planning and development, clues for future opportunities, and the basis for project feasibilities.

Destination Planning Processes Encompass Cities and Surrounding Areas.

A planning process for destinations cannot stop at the city limits. Research analysis, synthesis, and concepts for tourism planning of destinations must encompass surrounding areas as well as focal cities. This conclusion is based on the principle that lands with attraction potential for visitors are located in suburban and rural areas as well as within cities. However, the dominant location for travel services—lodging, food, shopping, and entertainment—is within the city. Steps for planning destinations must include analysis of development factors surrounding cities as well as within them. New jurisdictional cooperation will be required.

Destination Cooperation of Leadership and Organization Is Essential.

Tourism, in contrast to a manufacturing plant, cannot be managed by a single director. It can be guided, stimulated, and led, but not managed, by a central authority. Especially important at the destination scale is leadership, not dictation.

Leadership implies both guidance and organization. Organization is needed in order to bring together the many entities that develop and are affected by tourism. This approach means more than the organization offered by the typical chamber of commerce or tourism agency. It means the enlistment of representatives of the many facets of community and surrounding life because all are involved in tourism.

Leaders can come from many sources—government, business, planners, environmentalists, and educators—but their role for tourism will be the same. Their role is not managing in the sense of forced control but rather guiding, stimulating, and regularly reaching toward desired goals. When leadership cooperates with a comprehensive organization, plans and planning can be most productive.

Placemaking Is Essential to Destination Planning Processes.

Planners and designers have rich opportunities to create attractions and services that reveal the uniqueness of place, especially for destinations. Planning processes that build upon the special natural and cultural resource qualities can counter the present trend toward homogenizing the tourism landscape. This planning policy is especially critical for business and economic success. Duplicating functional features of design may support brand continuity but architecture and site design have much greater visitor appeal when adapted to the special qualities of place. The incentive to travel is much diminished if every destination begins to look alike and offer the same amenities. Planning policies and processes should accentuate indigenous qualities of place.

Site Scale Design Is Interrelated to All Tourism Planning.

Although the design of parks, hotels, resorts, transportation, and other elements of the supply side must meet requirements of owner-clients, designers must consider interrelationships as well. The traveler perceives and uses such site development only in context with a larger whole. Design for a hotel, for example, must meet all functional needs of lodging but will be inadequate if external factors are not considered. Adjacent land uses, accessibility, relationship to attractions, and adaptation to the destination are among key factors that need to be incorporated into site design concepts for a hotel. Processes for site scale design fall short of their full purpose if they fail to include external as well as internal factors.

Design Professionals Do Not Have Exclusive Control of Design.

Certainly development for tourism can be much more successful when designed by professionals, such as architects, landscape architects, and urban designers. But it is false to assume that they have exclusive control of design. Land owners-developers have their own agendas for tourist attractions, facilities, and services. Parks, dominated by governmental agencies, have their own mandates, traditions, and regulations for design of their places. Investors in theme parks, hotels, and resorts have their own opinions of design based on their experience and observation. Money-lenders have the power of acceptance or denial of design by virtue of their policies and practices. The construction industry can make or break the acceptance of a design because of cost estimates of construction. Managers can, when involved, exercise constructive control of design through their experience of site and building functions. Professional designers have the opportunity to work together with these forces to meld design into a whole that meets the criteria of all design influences.

New Design Paradigms Require New Kinds of Designers.

Traditional design education and practice fall short of meeting today's design needs. Reliance only upon intuition and skill is an incomplete agenda for a design process in modern tourism. To these desirable factors must be added a greater understanding of facts resulting from research of two important subject matter areas. First, designers must become cognizant of studies of traveler characteristics, preferences, and behavior. Assumptions based only on the designer's experience can provide a false and misleading foundation for design. Second, today the many scientific characteristics and environmental factors of the land are equally important foundations for design. Mere casual inspection of a site and shallow discussions with clients are inadequate in today's planning and design processes for tourism development.

Site Design Must Meet Several Design Criteria.

In addition to meeting the requested program of owners-developers, designers are bound to several other criteria for their design concepts. (1) All designs must function as a system with structural stability to satisfy all use functions, and to provide esthetically satisfying development. (2) Tourism plans must be integrated into all other plans and planning processes. (3) All tourism designs must meet the needs of the true clients— the visitors. (4) Individuality of design can provide the greatest adaptation to settings and the best competitive edge. (5) Authenticity is an important criterion. (6) All designs should incorporate esthetically satisfying appeal rather than seem sterile, drab, and ordinary to visitors. (7) All design processes must provide designs that are marketable. Satisfying the interests and needs of the several travel markets is an important design criterion.

Site Design Requires Special Design Processes.

Although planning and design processes for tourism may be similar for all scales—regional, destination, and site—those for sites require special emphasis. Key steps include market analysis, program statement, site selection/revised program, site analysis, synthesis, conceptual design, feasibility, final plan, and postconstruction evaluation. It must be emphasized that these process steps are not the exclusive prerogative of designers. The best designs will result from close collaboration not only with owners-developers but also marketers, specialists in natural and cultural resources, local residents, and others who can offer constructive assistance.

FUTURE CHALLENGES

Entrepreneurship Is Essential to Future Tourism Plans.

Because tourism contains a large component of service businesses, special programs to stimulate entrepreneurship are needed in all nations. There is no substitute for the establishment of new businesses by individuals with initiative. Entrepreneurship is a product of a culture, and where absent, a nation may have great difficulty in providing the services needed by travelers.

Several qualities are required of an entrepreneur. The ability to visualize a marketable service is essential. An entrepreneur must understand the field of travel well enough to sense an opportunity to fulfill some new or improved traveler need. Essential also is commitment. Full and enthusiastic belief in a business fires the development process from concept through construction and management. Although rewards from profits may be a major incentive, personal satisfaction from achievement may be equally important. Tourism plans must include strong incentives for entrepreneurship.

Plans Should Foster Low-Impact Development.

The past trend toward environmentally insensitive mega-resort development appears to be giving way to smaller-scale and more adaptable tourism expansion. Although the market for major tourist complexes continues, interest in low-key attractions and services has increased. This trend is a reflection of a more sophisticated travel market segment as well as stronger worldwide sensitivity to the environment. Local residents are recognizing that low-impact tourism development places much less stress on the community. This stronger local role provides closer scrutiny of new projects. There is increasing questioning of major outside investments as compared to local sponsorship of indigenous tourism. In the future, plans for tourism expansion will include closer examination of local impact upon the environment and society.

Much Greater Intersector Cooperation Is Needed.

In the future, the go-it-alone policy of all development sectors will be modified by greater intersectoral cooperation. This will result not from altruism but from self-interest. Governmental land development projects, such as parks and recreation areas, will meet their objectives more fully when created in concert with commercial enterprise. Policies of mutual support will supplant adversarial roles of the past. Tourist businesses will increasingly recognize the need to support environmentally sensitive attractions that create markets for their services. Nonprofit organizations will understand the need for new cooperation with governments and commercial enterprise. Future planning for tourism at all levels, macro to micro, will include policies and processes that foster intersector communication and decisionmaking because of the mutual benefits that they can produce.

**Greater Support for Research, Education, and Training
Will Become Evident.**

Recognition of the great complexity of tourism, more than any other form
of economic development, will demand greater study and information.
The need for better skills and understanding of tourism will stimulate the
establishment of more and better training programs. College and university curricula will be expanded to include better educational programs
directed toward planning, development, and management of tourism projects. Especially important will be new multidisciplinary university programs for tourism. Mere experience and conventional wisdom about
tourism will no longer be sufficient for success in all sectors. Scholarly and
scientific research is needed for better planning of supply side development
that meets market needs and adaptability of resources. Greater policy and
financial support for tourism research, education, and training will be
required from all three sectors—governments, nonprofit organizations,
and commercial enterprise.

A New Proactive Environmental Protection Planning Policy Is Needed.

In the past, tourism business focus has been primarily internal. Resorts,
hotels, restaurants, and other travel service businesses have directed their
attention toward internal site development and management. As a result,
an apathetic and even adversarial role has developed between business
and environmentalists.

   In the future, the tourist business sector will gain by revising this attitude and taking a proactive stand toward resource protection. Most travel
attractions—entities that create markets for travel businesses—depend
upon quality natural and cultural resources. As this fundamental is recognized by business, its self-interest will be fostered by support of policies
and planning processes that improve resource quality. Instead of being
reactive to environmental controls, business will gain from a proactive
role in support of environmental protection.

A New Catalytic Professional Planning Role Is Needed.

Planning and design professionalism will continue to be needed for better
tourism development. But, this will be accompanied increasingly by a new
role of practice—a catalytic role. The complexity of tourism cannot be
planned by the singular roles of the past. Urban and regional planners,

architects, urban and environmental designers, and landscape architects are now spending much of their consultative time and effort on gaining consensus on development objectives. Conflict resolution, integrative planning, public involvement, and sustainable development are becoming functions as important to planners and designers as specific project creation. These new roles are proving that client objectives, visitor functions, and environmental protection are compatible goals. When planning/design professionals take on this new role, everyone gains.

Creativity and Innovation Characterize Future Tourism Planning and Design.

Review of tourism development over several decades shows the importance of breaking away from repetition of the past. Markets change, demanding inventive solutions to new visitor needs. Equally challenging to the resourceful and imaginative design abilities are the requirements of environmentalism. No longer can designers create tourism projects for only the developer's objectives. Ingenuity and originality must be directed toward all major goals of tourism planning—economic improvement, better visitor satisfaction, resource protection, and integration into the local economic and social setting. This new philosophy places heavier professional demands upon all education and practice of planners and designers. But the results will be far more rewarding than in the past.

A New Planning and Design Principle of Land Use Stewardship Is Needed.

Even though owners of land in a democracy have rights of land use, their short-range objectives must be tempered by long-range stewardship of resource use. Owners and developers will come and go, but land continues forever. Mankind has a custodial responsibility that reaches beyond today. But, all three tourism development sectors tend to believe such long-range planning limits today's potential. Actually, the opposite is true, as is being demonstrated by other resource exploitation such as forestry and agriculture. Wasted and abused resources diminish opportunities, often even in the short range. It is incumbent upon future tourism planning and design professionals to promote protracted as well as immediate goals and objectives. The highest and most noble objectives of society at large must always take priority over occluded self-interest.

Federal to Local Government Roles Need To Be Clarified.

Tourism plans of the future can ensure better functioning of the system if
they clarify roles at all scales, macro to micro. The present overlapping
and confusing roles of all sectors waste funds and misdirect effort. For
example, the potential traveler is now confused by proliferation of promotional literature produced by federal, state, provincial, and city agencies as well as businesses and destinations. Nationwide and regional plans
should be integrated with destination and site plans if all tourism objectives are to be met. New policies, revisions in regulations, and new incentives for the private sector should have high priority at all governmental
levels if tourism is to thrive.

Societal Objectives Pose a Major Challenge to Planners.

No matter whether tourism increases the economy and provides jobs, it
will have failed if its planning and development have not provided enrichment, enlightenment, cultural exchange, and other life-fulfilling rewards.
No matter the models, concepts, processes, and techniques, planning for
tourism must utilize whatever steps are necessary in order to reach the
highest societal objectives. Every investor, developer, planner, designer,
policymaker, regulator, and local citizen shares in the responsibility for
accomplishing these virtuous objectives.

Tourism Must Not Be Overplanned.

To say that tourism must not be overplanned is to place constraint upon
excessive manipulation of tourism development. There is much to be said
for planning that is open-ended enough to allow spontaneous and innovative growth. The tendency today toward contrived tourism development
must be curbed, rather than fostered, by new planning concepts and
processes.

Paramount is the freedom of travelers to seek out their own rewards
from travel experiences. So much of modern life denies this opportunity,
only available through travel. Work, duty, law, social responsibility, and
personal obligation continue to remain but travel offers the one remaining
opportunity for emancipation.

Tourism must be planned at all scales with such restraint that travelers
can be free to obtain the enriching rewards of discovery, adventure, and
achievement. Planned physical settings, programs, political action, man-

agement decisions, and promotion can and should foster, not inhibit, the individual originality and personal satisfaction that can be derived only from travel. If domestic travel is to break down the barriers of parochialism, and if international travel is to stimulate world understanding and peace, all policies and practices of planning must be so dynamic and flexible that these objectives are assured. Planning policies, concepts, and processes are merely tools, not ends.

Index

Abbott, Stanley, 390
Abruzzo, Italy, 58
Action Plan—America's Industrial Heritage Project, 317
Adams, Robert McC., 71
Adirondack Park, 194
Adirondack Forest Preserve, 194
Adirondack Park Agency (APA), 194
Adirondacks, 193–200
An Administrative Guide to Environmental Requirements for Tourism Developments in Western Australia, 399
Africa, 46
Alamo, 8
Alaska, 81
Alberta Environmental Protection and Enhancement Act (AEPEA), 238
Alberta tourism opportunities, 239–244
Allegheny Ridge, 274
  Heritage Park, 316
Allegheny Ridge Corporation (ARCORP), 318, 321–322
Allegheny River, 92
Allen, John W., 65
Altoona, 316
America's Cup Match, 8
American Society of Landscape Architects (ASLA), 337
Anasazi, 71
Annals of Tourism Research, 34
Antoniades, Anthony, 337, 354
Appalachian foothills, 186
Appropriateness, 91, 432
ARC-INFO, 188
Archer, Brian, 35
Arizona, 71, 265–268
Arkansas River, 228
Arts, museums, 48, 50
Ashman, R. 63
Aspen, Colorado, 50
Association of Independent Tour Operators (AITO), 98

Attractions, 41, 57–61
  by length of stay, 60
  classifications, 58–60
  clustering of, 60
  complexes, 251
  functions, 57–58
  linkage with services, 61
  management of, 59
  ownership, 59
  planning of, 59
  and resources, 8, 59
  rural and urban, 61
  scope, 58
  spatial model, 270–271
Attractivity index, 114
Ausable Forks, Adirondack Park, New York, 422–424
Australia, 16, 23, 26, 39, 216–219, 231
Auyong, Jan, 289, 292, 293
Avon, California, 83
Ayers Rock (Australia), 91

Baker, P., 74, 84
Baltimore Harbor, 346
Baud-Bovy, Manuel, 115
Bechyal (Yap), 89
Becker, R., 84
Bed-and-Breakfast, 81
Bekker, Pieter, 138
Berlin Wall, 113
Bermuda, 88
Best Western, 63
Bevins, M., 63
Big Thicket, 46
Billboards, 74
Billing, John, 346
Birdwatching, 95, 296
Blake, Lynn, 420
Blank, Uel, 42, 162, 165, 168–173, 232, 248–249, 275, 402
Blue Ridge Parkway: the First Fifty Years, 389

Blue Ridge Parkway, 389–393
Bok Tower Gardens, 44
Boniface, Brian, 41
Boo, L., 95
Boundary Waters Canoe Area, 275–276
Brake, L., 89
Branch, Melville, 17, 18, 20
Brazilia, 228
Brazos River, 229, 299
Brenham, Texas, 81
Bridging Museum Site Plan, 405
Bridging the Straits Site Plan, 404, 406
British Columbia, 135, 138, 345
Brittain, Robert, 45, 119
Brown, L., 82
Brown, D.R.C., 15
Burch, William, 230
Business. *See also* Services
   concession, 64–65
   franchise, 63
   independent, 63
   nonprofit, 65
   type, 62

Calgary-Canmore destination zone, 238
Calgary Stampede, 8
California, 82
Callaway, Clive, 345
Camelback Mountain resort, 58
Canada, 23, 37, 39, 46, 49, 67, 81, 84, 90,
   117, 119, 149, 231, 232, 345
Canadian Government Office of Tourism
   (CGOT), 117
Canadian Museum of Civilization, 71
Canadian National and Historic Parks
   Branch, 96
Canberra, 228
Canyon de Chelly, 71
Capacity, 80, 81, 86, 88
Caroline Island, 289
Carribean, 46
Catholicism, 229
Cayman, 88
Central City, Colorado, 359
Chadwick, Robin, 34
Chamberlain, Kenneth, 285
Charleston, South Carolina, 271
Cheek, Neil, 230
Cherry, Gordon, 19
Chesnutt, J. Thomas, 401
China, 82, 112
Chincoteague National Wildlife Refuge, 58
Chun-Cheon Plan 2001, 313
Cineplus, 71

Clemson University
   Department of Parks, Recreation and
      Tourism Management, 186
   Regional Resource Development
      Institute, 186
Climate and weather, 45, 46–47
Clustering, 60, 68, 430
*Coastal Tourism Resource Inventory
   Project* (CTRIP), 135–138
Code of Conduct, 80, 81
Collins, Charles, 119
Collins, M., 98
Colvin, J., 93
Commercialism, ugly, 3, 92
Communication, 111
Communities and services, 97, 251
Community, 44, 51, 225
   planning steps, 237
Community integration as a goal, 16–18
Community rejuvenation, 81
*Community Tourism Action Plan Manual,
   Alberta*, 235–238
*The Community Tourism Industry
   Imperative: The Necessity, The
   Opportunities, Its Potential*, 248–249
Compass computer program, 182
Competition, 44, 51
Competitive markets, 4, 67
Comprehensive Management Plan
   (Allegheny), 317
Computer composite map, 177, 178, 182,
   188
Computer mapping. *See* Geographic
   Information System
*A Concept for the Design of a Tourism
   Recreation Region*, 121
Concessions, 64–65
Concord, Massachusetts, 83
Conservation, and ecotourism, 95–99
Cooper, Christopher, 41
Cooperation and collaboration, 114, 233,
   435, 441
Corpus Christi, Texas, 229
Costa Rica, 94
Cote des Blancs, France, 58
Creativity, 443
Crompton, John, 35, 125
Cuba, 113
*Cultural Benefits from Metropolitan
   Recreation—San Antonio Prototype*,
   352
Cultural resources, 3, 15, 47–50
Cultural sites, 354–355
Cunningham, D., 71

Cunningham, Melissa, 305

Davidson-Peterson, 273
Daytona, 58
Decisionmaking model, 22
Delaware, 361
Delaware Bays, 277–278
Delaware Department of Natural
    Resources and Environmental
    Control, 276
Demars, Stanford, 119
Denali National Park, Alaska, 58
Denmark, 17, 23–25
    Tourism Declaration of 1986, 23
    Viborg county, 17
Department of Tourism and Recreation of
    Oklahoma, 185
Dephi, Mount Parnassus, 228
Des Moines, Iowa, 229
Design
    co-design approach, 345
    criteria, 347–352
    management heirarchy, 343–344
    new paradigms, 342–344
    placemaking, 343–344
    public involvement, 344–347
Designers, influences on, 338–340, 439
Destination plans
    Allegheny Ridge Heritage Park
        (Pennsylvania), 316–322
    Chun-Cheon Resort Area (Korea), 312–
        316
    Gonzales (Texas), 307–312; Kosrae
        (Micronesia), 288–294
    Lower Rio Grande (Texas, Mexico),
        294–297
    Manchester, Salford, and Trafford
        (England), 328–334
    Mineral Wells (Texas), 298–306
    Moorea (French Polynesia), 285–288
    St. Maries, Idaho, 322–328
Destination scale, 27–28, 428
    planning conclusions, 278–281
    planning process, 236–237, 245–250,
        252–261
Destination zone, 27, 117–118, 120, 125,
        285
    community, 225
    concept, 225–226
    discovery of potential, 138–141
    elements, 27–28, 226
    misunderstandings of, 232–235
    planners, 272–278
    planning, 118

planning model, 231, 251–252
planning needs, 261–272
rural-urban, 252, 429
spatial patterns, 118–120
Destinations, 5
    organization, 438
    planning guides, 231–250
    planning issues, 231, 235, 437
Developer sectors, 4, 9, 43
Development council, 21
Development impacts, 3–4
    cultural and social costs, 112
Development Review Commission
    (Micronesia), 294
Dickert, T., 92
Dilbeck, Eugene, 185
Discover Upcountry Carolina Association,
    186
Division of Tourism (Micronesia), 292
Dredge, Dianne, 261
Drucker, Peter, 62, 63
Dudnik, Elliott, 172
Durrell, Lawrence, 229
Dykeman, F., 85

Eagles, P., 93, 94
Earth Day, 82
Easements, 362
East-West Center, University of Hawaii,
    290
Eco-design ethics, 352–354
The Eco Ethics of Tourism Development,
    354
Economic
    balance, 68
    development, 434
    diversity, 18
    freedom, 66
    growth, 78–81, 83
    incentives, 66
    success and resources, 433
Economic Research Associates, 245
Ecosystem, 60, 82, 82, 94
Ecotourism, 71, 92–99, 432–433
    defined, 92, 93
    principles, 98
Edgell, David, 151, 245
Education, 442
Egypt, 44, 113
Engineering, 70
England, 80, 147
    planning in, 19
English Tourist Board (ETB), 328, 416
Entertainment, 48, 50

Entrepreneurship, 44, 50, 68, 120, 440
Environment, 4, 68, 70, 71, 79, 80, 82–85,
    442
  awareness, 79
  degradation, 80, 82–85, 112, 431
Environmental controls, 99
Environmental Systems Research
    Institute, Inc., 188
Environmentalism, 15
Ethic, land, 90
Ethics, 112
Ethnicity, 36, 48, 49
Europe, 43
Everhardt, Gary, 393

Fagence, Michael, 119
Falconer, B., 81
Falk, James, 277
Fennell, D., 93, 94
Ferrario, Franco, 233
Ferrell, O., 36
Fesenmaier, Daniel, 125
Festivals, 355
Finance, 44, 50
Finger Lakes Association, 200
Finger Lakes Region, 200–209
*Finger Lakes Region Tourism—
    Development Opportunities*, 203
Finlandia Hall, Helsinki, 58
First Nations Tourism Association,
    Canada, 49
Flavin, C., 82
Flinders Ranges National Park, Australia,
    89, 402, 420
Floriade, Netherlands, 58
Florida Audubon Society Center for Birds
    of Prey, 44
Forbes, Maree, 39, 364
Forbes, Robert, 39, 364
Forecasting of travel, 35, 36
Forster, R., 96, 97
Fort Wolters, 299
Franconia Notch, New Hampshire, 393–
    397
Franconia Notch Scenic Freeway, 394
Franconia Notch State Park, 393, 396
Frechtling, Douglas, 14, 34, 35
Fredericksburg, Texas, 344
Free enterprise, 65–67; fundamentals of,
    65–67
French Polynesia Government, 83, 285,
    286, 288
French Quarter, New Orleans, 228

FSM National Historic Preservation
    Office, 290

Galopagos, 88
Galveston Bay, 82
Gambling, 359
Gap analysis, 39
Garnham, Harry, 341
Geographers, 119–120
Geographic content, 121, 123, 437
Geographic Information System (GIS),
    (computer mapping), 137, 139, 140
Geographic position, 121–122
George, Yosiwo, 289
Georgia, 186
Germany, 117, 263
  scenic highways, 263
Getz, D., 87
Gill, A., 86, 87
Gitelson, Richard, 275
Go, Frank, 232, 237, 259, 260
Gonzales Area Development Corporation,
    307
Gonzales County, 176
Gonzales, Texas, 307, 309
*Gonzales Tourism-Park Opportunities, Part
    I and II,* 307
Government, 8–9, 19
  limited role of, 67
  regulation, 361
  role clarified, 444
Governmental policies, 44, 52
Gradus, Yehuda, 225
Grand Canyon National Park, 357
Great Britain, 119
Great Lakes Crossroads Museum and
    Welcome Center (Michigan), 402–407
Great Smoky Mountains National Park,
    58, 389
Greeks, 13, 19
Green Flag International, 98
Green, Peter, 394, 396
Grey Advertising, 178
Griffiths, Alan, 216, 219
Groom, M., 95
Guam, 89
Gulf of Mexico, 47
Gulf of St. Lawrence, 58
Gummerson, Ray, 167
Gunn, Clare, 41, 61, 92, 113, 120, 121,
    122, 123, 125, 139, 149, 162, 164, 169,
    171, 172, 176, 178, 179, 181, 186, 187–
    190, 226, 232, 233, 270–271, 274, 285,

298, 299, 300, 307, 310, 311, 345, 378, 379, 380
Gustke, Larry, 119
Gwaii Hannas/South Moresley, British Columbia, 80

Haleakala Crater, Hawaii, 58
Hall, C., 47
Hall, Peter, 147
Hamed, S., 85
Hamilton, Lawrence, 289
Hamlets of the Adirondacks: Development Strategies, 194
Hamlets of the Adirondacks, 194
Hand, Barbara, 312
Harris, Charles, 322, 324
Hawaii, 46, 93
Helleiner, Frederick, 119
Helsinki Accord of 1975, 113
Henry Dooly Zoo, Omaha, 71
Himalaya, 229
Historic cities, 270–272
Historic resources, 48
    inventory, 268–270
    protection, 362
Historic Roads, 266–267
Historic sites, 88
Holdsworth, D., 81
Holiday Inn, 63
Hosts, 73
Hoteliers, 57
Hugman, Robert 345
Hull, Quebec, 71
Hungary, 113
Hunt, John, 5
Hyma, B., 119

ICOMOS, 47
Idaho Rural Tourism Primer: A Tourism Assessment Workbook, 323
Implementation, 20, 22, 110–111, 118, 168
Improved economy as a goal, 13–15
India, planning, 18
Indians, 49, 72
Industry, 5–6, 48
Information (traveler), 41, 70–74
    planning, 72–74
    scope, 70
    system, national, 73
Infrastructure, 9, 61, 68, 80
The Inn Business, 67
International Azalea Festival in Norfolk, 8
International Union for Conservation of Nature and Natural Resources, 96

Interpretation, 71, 95, 99
Interpretive centers, 71, 73, 194, 355–359, 403
Inventory, 135–137
Investment, 57, 161
Ireland, 229
Ironbridge Gorge Complex Plan, 414
Ironbridge Gorge Museum, England, 412–416
Italy, 229

Jafari, Jafar, 42
Japan National Tourist Organization (JNTO), 209, 212–216
Japan, 209–216
    New Sites of Discovery, 214–215
Johnson, Johnson & Roy, 162
Johnstown, 316
Joliet, Louis, 229
Jolley, Harley, 390
Journal of Travel Research, 34

Kansas, 229
Kaplan, Atid, 63
Katter, Jill, 294
Kennedy, Ian, 285–286, 397
Kennedy Space Center, 58
Kent, William, 401
Kentucky, 121, 164, 276–277
Kiemstedt, H., 114
King, Thomas, 355
Kirtland warbler, 46
Knechtel, Karl, 7
Knight, Gladys, 274
Korean Transportation Institute (KOTI), 312, 315
Kosrae State, Federated States of Micronesia (FSM), 288, 289
Koth, Barbara, 245
Krippendorff, Jost, 5
Kyle, Jack, 355

Labor, 44, 51
Lackawana River Corridor Association (LRCA), 92
Lake Eola, 44
Lake Ontario, 263
Lancashire, D., 71
Landscape architecture, defined, 337
Landscape expression 121, 124
Land use, 361, 443
Lang, Reg, 20, 21, 148
Larsen, Terry, 139, 181
Lawson, F., 115

Layne, Donlynne, 5
Leccese, Michael, 388, 389
Leid Jungle, 71
Leiper, N., 41
LePage, Stephen, 285
Leu Botanical Gardens, 44
Lipp, George, 285
Location, 68
Long, D., 88
Los Angeles Olympic Arts Festival, 50
Lower Rio Grande Heritage Corridor, 294
Low-impact development, 441
Lue, Chi-Chuan, 125
Lundberg, Donald, 67

Maaq (Yap), 89
Machlis, G., 84
Mackinac Bridge, 402
Mackinac Island State Park Commission, 403
Madrid, 113, 229
Maho Bay Camps, U.S. Virgin Islands, 387
Mahoney, Edward, 37
Main Street, 81, 271, 306
Manchester, Salford and Trafford, 328
Manchester, Salford and Trafford Strategic Development Initiative: A Framework for Tourism Development, 328
Manila, 113
Manila Declaration on World Tourism, 12
Manning, Edward, 90
Mansperger, M., 89
Manta Ray Bay Hotel (Yap), 89
Manu Biosphere Reserve, Peru, 94
Mapping methodology, 135–138, 188
Mardi Gras, New Orleans, 8
Markets, 128–131
  ability to travel, 129
  friends and relatives, 131
  governmental constraint, 130
  image, 130
  mobility, 130, priority, 130
  proximity, 131
  social constraint, 130
  volume, 131
Market (demand)-supply match, 39, 40, 117–118, 428
  model, 40
Market segmentation, 36–39
  by activities, 39
  of Canada, 37
  by demographics, 36
  by expenditures, 37
  seven categories of, 38

Marquette, Jacques, 229
Marshall, Lane, 21, 22, 343
Mathieson, Alister, 5
McDonald's, 91
McIntosh, Robert, 274
McMillen, J.Ben, 172, 176, 178–180
McNulty, Robert, 354
Memphis, Tennessee, 355
Menominee, Michigan, 170, 171
Mexico, 113, 294
Michigan, 37, 46, 228
Michigan State University, 125, 274
Michigan's Upper Peninsula, 37, 121, 123, 124, 125, 138, 144, 161–171, 402
Middle Ages, 230
Midkiff, Sandra, 306
Midwest Research Institute, 276
Mill, Robert, 42
Mills, R., 49
Mineral Wells Chamber of Commerce Tourism Committee, 298
Mineral Wells, Texas, 298, 300, 301, 304
Minister of Supply and Services, Canada, 67
Ministry of Tourism (Peru), 95
Minnesota, 274, 275
Mississippi River, 194
Missouri, 229
Molnar, Donald, 366, 368
Molotch, H., 80
Montreal, 231
Moore, Stewart, 261
Moorea, 83, 285
Moorea and Tourism, 285
Morocco, 113
Morris, Philip, 228
Morrison, Alistair, 42
Motloch, John, 227, 230, 341–344
Mount Everest, 229
Mount Vernon, 8
Munk, Inger, 17
Murphy, Peter, 42, 80, 119
Museums, 355

National Park Act (U.S.), 92
National parks, 8, 26, 60, 70, 84, 89, 95–97
National Parks and Conservation Association (U.S.), 92
National park-tourism model, 96
National park zones, 96, 97
The National Policy Study on Rural Tourism and Small Business Development, (U.S.), 245

National Tourism Policy Study (U.S.), 65
National Trust for Historic Preservation, 271
Natural resources, 3, 15, 43–47
Natural Resources Conservation Board (NRCB), Alberta, 238
Navajo, 71
Nelson, J., 80, 89
New Brunswick, Canada, 85
New Mexico, 358
New South Wales, 220–222
New South Wales Tourism Development Strategy: A Plan for the Future, 220
New York, 43, 200, 231
Nolan, Mary Lee, 37
Nolan, Sid, 37
Nominal Group Technique, 344
North Carolina, 186, 263
North Carolina Board of Transportation, 263
Norvell, H., 37

Oklahoma, 177–186
Okrant, M., 80
Olga Mountains (Australia), 91
Olympic games, 50
Omaha, Nebraska, 229
Ontario, 268
Orange Valley Resort, Antigua, 407–412
Orange Valley Resort Plan, 410
Organization, 44, 52
Organization of American States (OAS), 113
Organization of Economic Cooperation and Development (OECD), 113
Orlando, Florida, 44, 80
Outdoor recreation, 44, 63, 114
Overlay maps, 115
Overplanning, 444

Pacific, 285, 288
Pacific Asia Travel Association (PATA), 83, 273, 285, 397
Packard, J., 92
Palo Pinto County, Texas, 301
Pannell Kerr Forster, 238, 273
Parc Guell, Barcelona, 58
Paris, 58, 113, 234
Parker, Barry, 49
Parks and tourism, 431 *See also* National parks
Parkways, 266
Parkways, Historic and Scenic Roads Advisory Committee (PHRAC), Arizona, 265–266

Parrish, Bill, 271
Pearce, Douglas, 118–119
Peat Marwick, 273
Pedestrians, 69
  integration with traffic, 430
Pendleton District Historical and Recreational Commission, 186
Pennsylvania State Heritage Park's Program, 318
Pennsylvania, 92, 274, 316
  Turnpike, 316
Peoria, 229
Peterson, K., 47
Philippines, 113
Piazza San Marco, Venice, 58
Piedmont, 186
Pilgrimages, 37, 39
Place, 227–231
  age of, 228
  characteristics of, 227–229
  defined, 227
  human attribution of, 229–231
  meanings, 340–342
  name of, 228
  qualities, 229
  social aspects of, 230
  spacial distribution of, 228
  temporal aspects of, 227
Placemaking, 230, 343–344, 438
Plan for the Allegheny Ridge, 318, 319
Planners, 19, 21, 23
  consultants, 272–273
  task forces, 273–274
  extension, 274–278
Planning
  antecedents, 110–114
  background, 18–20
  coastal project, 135–138
  concepts, 123–126, 168
  constraints, 118
  continuous, 115, 146–150, 258
  conventional vs. interactive, 21
  destination, 27–28
  discovery of potential zones, 138–141
  discursive/intuition, 109
  goals, 11–18
  governmental, 19, 21, 23
  integration, 428
  lack of, 4, 11
  new approach for, 18–25
  processes, 115, 121, 141–150
  regional factors for, 120
  for resource protection, 92
  responsibility, 21

role, 442
scales, 25–29
site, 25–27, 361
for sustainable development, 86–88
synthesis stage, 122
*Planning Better Vacation
    Accommodations*, 121
Planning Department of New Castle
    County, Delaware, 361
Planning-design professionals, 337–339
Planning processes (techniques)
    continuous and plans, 142, 436
    destination, 236–237, 245–250, 252–261
    historic resources, 268–272
    organic-rational, 255–258
    regional, 114, 121–125, 135–150
    scenic highway, 263–268
    site, 363–371, 440
    supply side plan project, 142–146, 253
Poland, 113
Policy, 61, 64, 83, 112–113, 120, 249–250,
    434–436
    Finger Lakes Region, 207
    Japan, 211
    protection, 89, 95
    for regional development, 145
    for sustainable development, 88
Policy, planning, 12, 17, 23, 25
Pollock-Ellwand, Nancy, 268–269
Port Authority of New York-New Jersey, 50
Porter, Colin, 399
Postel, S., 82
Prehistory, 47, 48, 72
Price Waterhouse, 177, 180, 185, 200, 273
Pride, W., 36
Private property, 66
Process of planning/design, 22
Products, 6, 33, 138
Product's Analysis, Sequence for Outdoor
    Leisure Planning (PASOLP), 115
    model, 116
Profits, 62, 64, 67
Project proposal matrix, 326–327
Promotion, 4, 41, 74
    defined, 74
    and policy, 434
*Proposed Master Plan for Travel Marketing
    and Development for the State of
    Oklahoma*, 178
Public involvement, 20, 22, 111, 162, 435
*Public Involvement in Tourism
    Development: What Does it Mean for
    the Developer*, 346
Public sectors, 20, 22

Pueblo of Pojoaque, 358
Puerto Rico, 263

Queen Charlotte Islands, 81
Queensland, Australia, 261

Rails-to-Trails Conservancy (RTC), 92
Rameses The Great exhibition, 355
Read, A., 81
Rees, W., 85
Regional development heirarchy, 128–134
    diagram, 129
Regional plans
    Adirondacks, 193–200
    Australia, 216–219
    Finger Lakes, New York, 200–209
    Japan, 209–216
    Michigan's Upper Peninsula, 166–168
    New South Wales, 220–222
    Oklahoma, 177–186
    South Carolina, 186–193
    South Central Texas, 171–180
Regional scale, 28–29, 429
    planning concept, 125–126
    planning conclusions, 29–31, 150–157
    planning processes, 114, 121–125, 135–
        140
Regiopolis, 227
*Report of Progress Toward a Sustainable
    Society*, 82
Research, 442
Resource degradation, 16
Resource development, 131–134
    available entrepreneurs, managers, 134
    available finance, 134
    available labor, 134
    available land, 133
    cultural resources, 132
    easy access, 132
    existing development, 133
    favorable development image, 133
    favorable governmental controls, 133
    local acceptance of tourism, 133
    natural resources, 132
    viable service communities, 132
Resource foundation factors (Michigan's
    Upper Peninsula), 165
Resource protection, 95, 433
    controls, 360–363
    as a goal, 13–16
Resource tour, 93–95
Resources
    natural, 3, 15, 43, 47, 121
    cultural, 89, 95

Revolving fund, 362
Rigterink, Richard, 393
Ritchie, J.R.Brent, 344
River Walk Policy Manual, 383
Roessler, Wolfgang, 385, 387
Romans, 13, 19
Romsa, Gerald, 114
Rose, Edgar, 19
Ross, Glenn, 16
Rotes Rathaus, Berlin, 58
Rothman, R., 80
Ruest, Gilles, 233
Rundell, John, 323
Rural attractions, activities, 61, 231–232
Russia, 113
Rutledge, Albert, 366, 368
Ryan, Chris, 37

Said, Asad, 271
San Antonio, 229
San Antonio Conservation Society, 378
San Antonio Development Guidelines System, 385
San Antonio River Walk, 345, 378–387
  Conservation Society, 345
  1979 study, 384
  1987 study, 384–387
  River Walk Commission, 345, 385
  San Antonio River Authority, 345
San Jacinto, Texas, 229
San Saba, Texas, 229
Sanchez, Mario, 294, 295
Santa Catalina, 82
Sargent, F., 82
SARWAC Development Guidelines System Notebook, 385
Sauer, Carl, 45
Savannah, 271
Scales, 25–29, 427–428
Scarfo, Bob, 342
Scenery, 230
Scenic roads, 61, 261–268
  designation, 267
  evaluation form, 265
  planning, 362–363
Sea Grant College Marine Advisory Service, 277, 289
Seaway Trail, New York, 263
Sectoral cooperation, 93–94, 97
Sectors, tourism, 5–9, 429
Selengut, Stanley, 387–389
Services, 41, 62–69
  and attractions, 61
  economic impact, 62

franchise, 63
  independent ownership of, 63
  nonprofit, 65
  planning, 67–69
  profits, 62
  quasi-government, 64–65
  sponsorship, 62
Shanghai Communique of 1972, 11
A Shared Experience, 294
Shenandoah National Park, 389
Shepard, Paul, 228, 230
Signs, 74
Simonds, M., 93
Simonelli, J., 71
Simonson, Lawrence, 276
Site analysis, 366–367
Site design, 347–352, 361, 438
  processes, 363–371
  functional relationships, 369
Site plans
  San Antonio River Walk, 378–387
  Ausable Forks, Adirondack Park, 422–424
  Blue Ridge Parkway, 389–393
  Franconia Notch, 393–397
  Great Lakes Crossroads Museum, 402–407
  Ironbridge Gorge Museum, 412–416
  Maho Bay Camps, 387–389
  Orange Valley Resort, 407–412
  Underground Atlanta, 401–402
  Victoria and Alfred Waterfront, 416–419
  Whiteman Park, 397–401
  Wilpena Station Resort, 419–422
Site scale, 25–27, 428
  planning-design conclusions, 371–373
Smardon, R., 92, 263
Smith, Adam, 65
Smith, Russell, 3
Smith, Stuart, 415
Smith, Valene, 37, 39
Smithsonian Institution, 71
Sobek Expeditions, Environmental Adventures, 98
Sorenson, J., 92
South Dakota, 49
Southern Kentucky Tourism Development Association, 276
Southwest Ontario Cultural Heritage Landscape Inventory, 270
Southwestern Heritage Preservation Commission, 317
Spain, 229
Spatial patterns, 118–120, 127

Spoleto Festival of Charleston, South
    Carolina, 50
Spotts, D.M., 37
St. Augustine, Florida, 271
St. Ignace, Michigan, 169
St. Maries, Idaho, 322–328
St. Lawrence River, 263
Stanley, D., 88
Statistical Abstract 1991, 393
Steiner, Frederick, 255, 256
Stern, Eliahu, 225
Stewart, George, 229
Stewart Island, Antarctica, 58
Stewart, W., 93
Stokowski, Patricia, 359
Stokvis, Jack, 354
Stubbs, Stephanie, 388
Successful Tourism Design, 352
Supply components, 57, 118
Supply side, 9, 17, 33, 39, 40, 41–43, 429
Sustainable Communities Project, 85
Sustainable development, 85–92
    defined, 85, 352–363, 431–432
Sustainable development statement, 90
Swan Valley Tourism Plan, 400
Sydney, 231
Synagraphic Computer Mapping Program
    (SYMAP), 172, 174, 176

Tahiti, 83, 285
Tamil-Gagil Island (Yap), 89
Tax abatement, 362
Taylor, Gordon, 39, 40, 81, 117
Tennessee Valley Authority, 390
Texas, 8, 81, 82, 229
    South Central, 171–180
Texas A&M University
    Department of Recreation, Park and
        Tourism Sciences, 171, 298, 307, 312,
        379
    College of Architecture, 180
Texas Agricultural Extension Service, 298,
    379
Texas Historical Commission, 81, 294
Texas traveler expenditures, 8, 44
Third World, 119,
Thompson, Arsene, 393
Thoreau, H.D., 83, 230
Thybo, Eva, 23
Tichnell, D. 84
Tighe, A.J., 50
Topography, 45–46
Touring circuits, 172
Tourism
    defined, 4–5, 29, 427

development, 90
external factors, 43–52
impacts, 18
low-impact, high-impact, 90–91, 441
potential, 121
product, 33
sectors, 5–10, 21
system, 33, 41–44
Tourism Action Committee, Alberta, 235,
    258
Tourism Development Training Guide,
    238–246
Tourism in Japan 1991, 215
Tourism Management, 34
Tourism Potential—Aided by Computer
    Cartography, 139, 181
Tourism Research for Non-Researchers, 36
Tourism Stream of the Globe '92
    Conference, 90
Tourist and Resort Extension Service,
    Michigan State University, 121, 161,
    274
Trancik, Roger, 193–199, 422–423
Transportation, 41, 69–70
    intermodal, 69, 70
    planning, 69–70
    scope, 69
Travel causes, 43
Travel markets, 33–39
    defined, 34
    Delphi method, 35
    surveys of, 34
*Travel, Tourism and Hospitality Research,
    A Handbook for Managers and
    Researchers,* 34
Trist, Eric, 148

U.S. Army Corps of Engineers, 289
U.S. Bureau of Outdoor Recreation, 65
U.S. community guide, 246–248
U.S. Department of Health and Human
    Services, Administration for Native
    Americans, 358
U.S. Department of Interior, 317
U.S. Economic Development
    Administration, 246
U.S. Federal Highway Administration,
    Department of Transportation, 262,
    362
U.S. Forest Service, 275, 290
U.S. National Park Service, 74, 92, 99,
    274, 276, 297, 316, 322, 387
U.S. National Tourism Policy Act of 1981,
    113, 151
U.S. Peace Corps, 290

U.S. Small Business Administration, 67
U.S. State Department, Citizens
    Emergency Center, 112
U.S. Travel and Tourism Administration,
    50, 238, 246
U.S. Travel Data Center, 35
U.S. Travel Outlook Forum, 34
U.S. Works Progress Administration, 345,
    378
Ueker, Raymond, 360
Underground Atlanta, 401–402
United Kingdom, 329
    planning in, 19
United Nations Educational, Scientific,
    and Cultural Organization
    (UNESCO), 412
United States, 8, 14, 34, 37, 43, 46, 50, 63,
    64, 228, 231, 263, 271, 275, 294, 345
University of California Research
    Expeditions Program (UREP), 93
University of Guam, 290
University of Guelph, 270
University of Idaho, 323
University of Kentucky, 276
University of Minnesota, Tourism Center,
    245
University of Missouri, 246
Unplanned development, 3
Upcountry South Carolina, 139–144, 186–
    193
Update Tourism & Commercial Recreation,
    275
Urban attractions, 61
Urban-rural integration, 429–430
USDA Cooperative Extension Service, 67,
    274, 275
*Using Tourism & Travel as a Community
    and Rural Revitalization Strategy,* 275
Uysal, Muzaffer, 35

Vacationscape: Designing Tourist Regions,
    378
Van Hyning, I., 92
Vancouver, British Columbia, 90
VanDoren, Carlton, 119
Var, Turgut, 312
Vegetative cover, 45, 46
Venezuela, 113
Victoria & Albert Museum, London, 58
Victoria & Alfred Waterfront, Cape Town,
    South Africa, 416–419
Virgin Islands, 263

Visitor
    capacities, 88
    impact, 432
    satisfactions, 11–13, 58, 62, 72, 74
    sequence, park, 357–358
    volume, 60
Visitors Guide, 1992, (Ironbridge Gorge),
    416

Wall, Geoffrey, 5, 119
Walt Disney World, 44, 80, 92
Warren, Winonah, 358
Water, 44–45
Waterton National Park (Canada), 91
Watt, Carson, 344
Weaver, Glenn, 246, 247
Weighting of resource factors, 172, 175,
    182
Wekiwa Springs State Park, 44
Wendt, C., 99
Western Australian Tourism Commission,
    36, 249, 346, 352, 354, 397
White, Judy 147
Whiteman Park, 397
Whiteman Park, Perth, Australia, 397–401
Whitman, S., 44
Wight, P., 91, 98, 238
Wildlife, 45, 46
Williams, P., 86, 87
Williams, M., 89
Williams, Michael, 420
Williamsburg, Virginia, 8, 58, 271
Wilpena Station, 89
Wilpena Station Resort, Australia, 419–
    422
Wilpena Station Resort Site Plan, 420
Wilson, A. Meriwether, 289
Wisconsin, 229
World Heritage Site, 412
World Tourism Conference, 12, 113
World Tourism Organization (WTO), 113
Worldwatch Institute, 82
Worms, Allan, 276

Xeriscape, 359–360

Yap, 89

Zeppel, Heather, 47
Ziffer, K., 97
Zimmerman, Eric, 230
Zoning, 361, 362

About the Author

Dr. Clare A. Gunn is professor emeritus, Department of Recreation, Park and Tourism Sciences, Texas A&M University. His teaching and research career has spanned four decades and five universities. A pioneer in tourism education, he has responded to invitations to present papers and perform consulting work throughout the United States, Canada, and over a dozen countries worldwide. His concepts, presented in lectures, books, and journal articles, have influenced policies and practices, particularly bridging the fields of design, planning, and tourism.

Throughout his career, Dr. Gunn's major contribution to the field has been innovative planning concepts, processes, and advocacy for balancing tourism development with resource protection. Long before the terms ecotourism and sustainable development became popular, he offered constructive solutions to issues regarding the establishment of new tourism development in ways that enhanced rather than threatened resource quality.

The author has received many honors and awards, including a special citation from Governor Mark White of Texas "for thirty-eight years of inspirational teaching," a special award from the American Society of Landscape Architects for his book *Vacationscape: Designing Tourist Regions,* and a special commendation by a joint resolution of the Senate and House of the State of Texas. He has been named Fellow of the American Society of Landscape Architects and a "Distinguished Member" of the national honor society of landscape architectural educators, Sigma Lambda Alpha.

Dr. Gunn was the first to receive a Ph.D. in Landscape Architecture from an accredited university program, the University of Michigan. He received a master's degree, Land and Water Conservation, and a bachelor's degree, Landscape Architecture, from Michigan State University. He developed the tourism program and all tourism courses at Texas A&M University.

459

His tourism career began with many years of experience in advising tourist business operators and publishing technical assistance bulletins on tourism design and planning. His research has identified the tourism functioning system and basic planning principles for tourism destination development. His concepts of regional planning are well known and applied throughout the world.